C0-AUK-002

ANTEBELLUM BLACK NEWSPAPERS

ANTEBELLUM BLACK NEWSPAPERS

Indices to New York *Freedom's Journal* (1827-1829),
The Rights of All (1829),
The Weekly Advocate (1837),
and
The Colored American (1837-1841)

Edited by
DONALD M. JACOBS

Assisted by
HEATH PALEY, SUSAN PARKER, and
DANA SILVERMAN

GP

GREENWOOD PRESS
Westport, Connecticut • London, England

Library of Congress Cataloging in Publication Data

Jacobs, Donald M
Antebellum Black newspapers.

1. Afro-American newspapers--New York (City)--Indexes. I. Title. II. Title: Freedom's journal (1827-1829), The Rights of all (1829), The Weekly advocate (1837), and The Colored American (1837-1841)
E185.5.J33 016.071'47'1 76-2119
ISBN 0-8371-8824-5

Library of Congress Catalog Card Number: 76-2119
ISBN: 0-8371-8824-5

Greenwood Press, a division of Williamhouse-Regency Inc.
51 Riverside Avenue, Westport, Connecticut 06880

Printed in the United States of America

To my father-in-law, William Barkin, whose courage and strength of will have been both stimulus and inspiration, and to Dorothy Porter in appreciation of her continuing encouragement

Contents

PREFACE	*ix*
INDEX KEY	*xi*
NEW YORK *FREEDOM'S JOURNAL*	*3*
THE RIGHTS OF ALL	*161*
THE WEEKLY ADVOCATE	*207*
THE COLORED AMERICAN	*229*

Preface

The original idea for this project came during 1963 when I began research on my doctoral dissertation which dealt with Boston's Black community prior to the Civil War. After poring over newspaper after newspaper, I came to the conclusion that a good index for even one of the newspapers could have saved valuable time and would have been an invaluable tool both for me and for any other scholars working in the field.

However, it was not until 1972 that I was able to begin a project of this type. And even then the project could not have become a reality if there had not been a group of graduate students willing and able to do the often tedious work that indexing involves.

As editor, I have tried to make this both a valuable and easy-to-use tool for research scholars working in the area of Black history. Every effort has been made to make sure that the descriptive material included in each entry is both clear and concise. In addition to the month, day, and page, the column where the article begins is also designated. Editorials and letters sent to the newspaper are clearly delineated, and newspaper advertisements have been indexed in order to provide another useful dimension.

The four newspapers that comprise this project, the New York *Freedom's Journal, The Rights of All, The Weekly Advocate,* and *The Colored American,* were chosen for a variety of reasons. All four were published in New York City between 1827 and 1841, all were among the first newspapers published by blacks in the United States, and most issues of these newspapers are readily available to researchers. In addition, *The Rights of All* is a journalistic continuation of the

New York *Freedom's Journal,* while *The Weekly Advocate* immediately preceded the New York *Colored American* and was replaced by it.

The author sincerely hopes that researchers will find this work of value. Every effort has been made to assure completeness and to make this index as easy to use as possible. Undoubtedly errors will appear. A work of this scope, involving the efforts of several different individuals, cannot possibly escape error-free, but at least one can hope that the number of errors has been kept to a reasonable minimum and that the usefulness of this index as a research tool will far outweigh any errors of omission or commission that may be found.

The author would like to take the time to thank the Council on Library Resources and Northeastern University for the help each provided in the final preparation of this index for publication. Thanks also to the Boston Public Library for making its facilities readily available to the students who worked on this project. Particular appreciation goes to Ms. Dorothy Porter whose work in the area of black bibliography and black historiography is well-known nationwide, and without whose kind and continuing encouragement and helpful suggestions this project might never have come to fruition. Thanks, too, to Mr. David Hollis and Ms. Harriet Rosser, two graduate students who worked on some of the briefer newspaper materials as well as some of the indexing of advertisements. I also owe an enormous debt of gratitude to the typist for this project, Ms. Martha Vadney, whose awareness of style, clarity, and form saved much time and effort during the project's latter stages.

Finally, special thanks to the three students who did the vast majority of the actual indexing work, and therefore made this all possible, Mr. Heath Paley, Ms. Susan Parker, and Ms. Dana Silverman.

Donald M. Jacobs
Associate Professor of History
Northeastern University
Boston, Massachusetts
January 1976

Index Key

No effort has been spared to make this index as easy to use as possible. Each of the four newspapers has been indexed separately. Topic headings are listed alphabetically, while material relating to each specific topic or subject is listed in chronological order according to the date it appeared in the newspaper. For newspapers that published during the course of more than one calendar year (e.g., New York *Freedom's Journal* and New York *Colored American*), the materials published under the various topic or subject headings are clearly listed by year.

Note the following example:

ALLEN, REVEREND BISHOP RICHARD

	1827
—Minister of the African Methodist Episcopal Church	Aug 17 p91 c4
—Condemns colonization	*Nov 2 p134 c3-4 let.
	1828
—Description of birthday party; work for blacks praised	Feb 22 p191 c3

ALLEN, REVEREND WILLIAM A.

	1828
—Soliciting funds for new church and school for blacks in Rochester, New York	May 9 p51 c3

Materials that are either letters or editorials are designated "let." or "ed.". Advertising material and certain notices for each newspaper are listed both in a separate section and integrated into the main body of the index. In many cases where typographical errors have been made or obvious misspellings have been given by the newspaper, both the error and the correction have been provided.
For example:

–Olanda Equiano should be Olaudah Equiano and is listed
EQUIANO, OLANDA (Olaudah)

–John Redman should be John Remond and is listed
REDMAN (REMOND), JOHN

*November 2, 1827; page 134; columns 3 and 4; letter

Wherever possible and wherever necessary, a geographical location has been provided as part of the subject heading in cases where the individual or organization listed is not located in New York City. Where locations have not been given, it can generally be assumed that New York City is the proper geographical locale. However, in some cases the newspaper did not provide such information.

ANTEBELLUM BLACK NEWSPAPERS

New York *Freedom's Journal*

The first newspaper published by blacks in the United States, the New York *Freedom's Journal* appeared weekly between March 16, 1827 and March 28, 1829. Co-edited by the Reverend Samuel Cornish, a Presbyterian minister, and John Russwurm, one of the first blacks to graduate from a college in the United States (Bowdoin, 1826), *Freedom's Journal* became a critically important forum for issues of major concern to the black community such as colonization, slavery, race unity, and self-elevation.

As the two editors made clear in the first issue, it was time for the black man to begin speaking out for himself: "We wish to plead our own cause. Too long have others spoken for us. Too long has the publick been deceived by misrepresentations." Only recently unshackled by the chains of slavery, blacks now had to begin to make their way amidst a hostile climate: "The civil rights of a people being of the greatest value, it shall ever be our duty to vindicate our brethren, when oppressed; and to lay the case before the publick. . . . Our vices and our degredation are ever arrayed against us, but our virtues are passed by unnoticed."

In an even-handed manner, aware both of the problems that blacks in America faced and the inability of some members of the race to rise to the difficult challenge of being black in white America, *Freedom's Journal*'s editors went about their weekly task in an effort to bring the nation's thousands of free blacks closer together. Even race leaders from outside New York such as Boston's David Walker were provided with a forum through which they could express their views.

Black unity was a major theme of much of the material that appeared in *Freedom's Journal,* but Samuel Cornish's resignation as co-editor of the paper only a few months after it had begun publication, apparently as a result of a disagreement with John Russwurm, demonstrated how difficult unity was to achieve. Soon the colonization issue began to divide the black community even more, as John Russwurm began to conclude that there was little hope for the black man in America. By the end of 1828 he had turned *Freedom's Journal* into a pro-colonization newspaper. Finally, his decision to leave the United States for Liberia led the paper to cease publication late the following March, ending a two-year effort to focus journalistically on the concerns of the nation's black community.

Freedom's Journal published regularly, failing to appear only on December 28, 1827; January 4, 1828; and November 28, 1828. The single issue that could not be located but apparently published was that of March 28, 1828.

NEW YORK FREEDOM'S JOURNAL

Published Weekly, March 16, 1827-March 28, 1829

A

ABERNATHY, MR.	
	1827
-Describes hair-dressing techniques	Apr 27 p28 c1
ABOLITION	
	1827
-Pledges support for abolition of slavery	Apr 6 p13 c2-4 Apr 13 p17 c2-4
-Twelve anti-slavery societies set up in Maryland, Virginia, Washington, D.C.	Apr 6 p15 c2 Apr 13 p17 c2-4
-Slavery to be abolished in New York July 4, 1827	Apr 20 p22 c2-3
-Explains the advantages and necessity of abolition	Apr 27 p25 c1-3 p30 c4
-Thanks those who helped passage of New York Abolition Law; Advises blacks to remain in agriculture after freedom	May 4 p31 c1
-Brazil and England sign treaty to end slave trade	May 11 p35 c3
-Praises the dedication of abolitionists	Jun 15 p55 c2-3 p57 c4 ed.
-Short history of abolitionist legislation in New York State	Jun 22 p58 c1 p66 c4
-States more money should be used for abolition and less for colonization	Jul 6 p67 c1 let.
-Admonishes abolitionists of Virginia for fearing state government	Jul 27 p79 c3

-Blacks create respectable, intelligent communities to attain abolition	Aug 31 p98 c3-4 let.
-Free states should force end of slavery in slave states	Sep 7 p101 c3
-Countries without slaves prosper more than those with slaves	Sep 14 p105 c1-2
-Appeals to people to work for abolition	Nov 30 p151 c1-2 ed.
-Plea to all abolition societies to work for abolition in Washington, D.C.	Dec 7 p154 c3
-Supreme Court of Missouri upholds Ordinance of 1787 forbidding slavery in Northwest Territory	Dec 14 p159 c1
	1828
-Appeal to people of New England to work for abolition	Aug 15 p163 c3
-All future children of slaves in the United States should be free	Oct 10 p230 c2
	1829
-Calls for abolition; otherwise revolution is probable	Jan 31 p344 c1-2
-See also Abolition (England); Abolition (New York State); Abolition (Pennsylvania); Abolition Society of Stark County, Ohio; American Convention for Promoting the Abolition of Slavery; Emancipation (General): Emancipation (New York State); Miner, Mr.; Slavery; Washington, D.C.	

ABOLITION (England)

	1827
-British abolitionist feels confident slavery will soon end in British colonies	Aug 10 p86 c1-2 let.
-Plea for women to organize for abolition movement	Aug 24 p93 c4
	1828
-Reverend Wilson suggests working for abolition by appealing to people's Christianity	Mar 7 p195 c1-4 p196 c1
-Reader asks for organization to collect money to buy slaves' freedom	Apr 11 p19 c2-3 let.

-Slavery will not cease until tariff protection for colonial planters stops; people should petition Parliament to end slavery — May 2 p41 c2-3
-Summarizes progress of British abolition movement — Aug 29 p180 c1-3
-Bill before Parliament to free all future children of slaves — Oct 10 p230 c2
-Character of British abolitionists defended — Nov 21 p275 c1-2
-Committee formed in London for gradual worldwide abolition — Dec 5 p282 c1-3
-See also African Institute; Anti-Slavery Society (England); Bathurst, Lord; Cane, Otway; Society for the Mitigation and Gradual Abolition of Slavery Throughout the British Dominion

ABOLITION (Pennsylvania)

<u>1828</u>

-Society elects officers and committees for 1828 — Jan 11 p166 c4

ABOLITION SOCIETY OF STARK COUNTY, OHIO

<u>1827</u>

-Outlines course abolition societies should follow and resolves to work for abolition in the United States and Washington, D.C. — Dec 7 p153 c1-4

<u>1828</u>

-Lists objectives and officers — Sep 19 p203 c2-3

<u>1829</u>

-Resolves to petition Congress about slavery in Washington, D.C., help American Colonization Society, and advise Blacks of Ohio to educate their children to hasten emancipation — Feb 7 p353 c1-3, p354 c1

-<u>Freedom's</u> <u>Journal</u> supports advice of Society to Free Blacks — Feb 7 p354 c3 ed.
-See also Dunbar, George; Gardner, William; Michever, Barach; Myers, John; Raynolds, William

THE ACADEMY
-See Gloucester, Stephen

ADAMS, JOHN	
	<u>1828</u>
-Remains and those of wife Abigail placed in First Parish Church, Quincy, Massachusetts	Apr 25 p36 c1
	<u>1829</u>
-Anecdote about his feeling inferior to George Washington	Jan 9 p321 c1-2
ADAMS, JOHN QUINCY	
	<u>1828</u>
-Describes journey from Providence to Quincy, Massachusetts	Aug 22 p173 c2
-Requires future daughter-in-law to free a slave before marrying his son	Aug 29 p178 c3 p179 c1 let.
ADVERTISEMENTS AND NOTICES	
-African Free School (New York)	Jan 11, '28 p168 c2
-African Mutual Instruction Society	Sep 14, '27 p108 c3
-Appo and Sammons (Tailors)	Apr 27-May 4, '27 pp 28, 32 c3 Oct 12, '27 p123 c4
-Augustus, Richard (Dinner Celebration)	Jun 22-Jun 29, '27 pp60, 64 c3
-Augustus, Scipio C. (Boarding House)	Aug 15, '28 p166 c3
-Baltesto, Joseph (Reward for Slave's Return)	Aug 15, '28 p166 c3
-Boyer, C. (Inn)	Jun 15, '27 p56 c2
-Collier, W. and W. (Black Newspaper, <u>African Observer</u>)	Oct 3, '28 p223 c1
-Cornish, Samuel (Wants Land for Presbyterian Church)	Mar 30-May 4, '27 pp 12, 16, 20, 24, 28, 32, c3
-Cornish, Samuel (Selling Land to Blacks Only)	Mar 30-May 4, '27 pp12, 16, 20, 24, 28, 32 c3
-Curtis, John (Concert by Freed Slave)	Feb 7, '29 p351 c3
-Draper, G. and R. (Tobacco Products)	Oct 5, '27 p120 c3
-Dubois, Henry (Reward for Runaway Apprentice)	Aug 31, '27 p100 c2
-Everett, George W. (Library Collection Agency)	Mar 30-May 4, '27 pp 12, 16, 20, 24, 28, 32 c3

-Gilbert, James (Clothing)	Nov 16, '27 p143 c4
-Gloucester, Jeremiah (Philadelphia School)	Nov 2, '27 p136 c3
-Gloucester, Stephen (Philadelphia School)	Sep 12, '28 p199 c1-Mar 28, '29 p411 c3
-Gold, Mr. (Instructor in English Grammar)	Nov 16, '27 p144 c3
-Goldsberry, Nicholas (Cleans and Dyes Clothes)	Nov 14, '28 p271 c1-Mar 21, '29 p403 c2
-Green, Sarah (Cures for Diseases)	Jun 11, '27 p48 c2
-Haines, Edward (Mead Garden)	May 2, '28 p47 c1-Sep 19, '28 p208 c3
-Hall, Henry P. (Sale of Hairdressing Shop)	Aug 31, '27 p100 c2
-Hamer and Smith (Cleaning Business)	Aug 3, '27 p84 c3
-Harrison, Lewis (Boarding House)	Jul 25, '28 p143 c1-Mar 28, '29 p412 c2
-Henry, Cornelius (House for Rent)	Dec 26, '28 p307 c1-Mar 28,'29 p411 c3
-Hinton, Frederick (Gentleman's Dressing Room -Philadelphia)	Oct 12, '27 p123 c4
-Hughes, Reverend B. F. (School Opens; Curriculum Advertised)	Mar 16, '27 p4 c3 Mar 23-May 4, '27 pp8, 12, 16, 20, 24, 28, 32 c3
-Jennings, Thomas L. (Wants Used Clothing)	Mar 30- May 4 '27 pp12, 16, 20, 24, 28, 32 c3
-Johnson, Eliza (Boarding House)	Jun 13, '28 p95 c1-Sep 19, '28 p208 c2
-Johnson, Richard (Boarding House)	Feb 29, '28 p196 c2
-Johnson, Sarah (Millinery Shop)	May 2, '28 p46 c3
-Johnson, William P. (Shoe Store)	Apr 4, '28 p11 c3-Mar 28, '29 p411 c3
-Jones, Gracy (Boarding House)	Apr 25, '28 p39 c3-Sep 5, '28 p191 c1
-Kelly, James K. (Newark, New Jersey- Wants Hairdresser)	Apr 25, '28 p40 c1-May 2, '28 p47 c2
-Law, James (Tailoring and Clothes Cleaning)	May 18, '27 p40 c3
-Lewis, Peter (Barber Shop for Blacks)	Sep 26, '28 p215 c1-Nov 7, '28 p263 c2

-Lively, William (Baltimore School)	Jul 11, '28 p127 c2-Aug 29, '28 p184 c2
-Marriage (Reference to Advertisements for wives in a British newspaper)	Aug 1, '28 p148 c1
-Mermier, B. (Restaurant)	Dec 14, '27 p159 c4
-Moleston, Solomon, and John Robinson (Tailor Shop)	May 18, '27 p40 c3
-Mortimer, Charles (Shoe Repair) (China and Glass Repair)	Mar 30-May 4, '27 pp12, 16, 20, 24, 28, 32, c3 Sep 21, '27 p112 c4
-Mutual Instruction Society (School for Black Adults Reopening)	Oct 3, '28 p218 c3
-New York <u>Freedom's</u> <u>Journal</u> (Printing Facilities)	Jan 25, '28 p176 c2
-Parker, William (Restaurant)	May 2, '28 p47 c1
-Peterson, Daniel (Inexpensive Clothing)	Mar 30-May 4, '27 pp12, 16, 20, 24, 28, 32, c3
-Pierson, Nicholas (Mead Garden for Blacks Only)	Jun 8, '27 p52 c2
-Protecting Society of the City and County of Philadelphia (Attacks Kidnapping of Free Blacks)	Apr 25, '28 p39 c2-3
-Quonn, M. (Cleaning Establishment)	May 9, '28 p55 c1
-Roberts, John (Oil for Sale)	Aug 24, '27 p96 c3
-Ruggles, David (Butter for Sale) (Grocery Store)	May 9-30, '28 pp 55, 59 (63), 71, 79 c2 Aug 22, '28 p174 c2 Sep 5, '28 p192 c2-Mar 21, '29 p403 c2
-Russwurm, John (Evening School for Blacks)	Nov 7, '28 p263 c1-Dec 5, '28 p287 c1
-St. Phillips Church	Sep 28, '27 p115 c4 Oct 5, 19 '27 pp119, 127 c4
-Seaman, David (Boarding House)	Sep 5, '28 p191 c1
-Shippard, Joseph (School for Free Blacks, Richmond, Virginia)	May 16, '28 p58 c1
-Short, Charles (Union Hotel)	Jul 13, '27 p72 c3
-Sickles, John Jr. (Drug Store)	Apr 20, 27 '27 pp24, 28, c3
-Smith, John (Cleaning and Tailoring)	Apr 20-May 4, '27 pp24, 28, 32 c3
-Suder, Adam (Cabinet and Coffin Maker)	Feb 29, '28 p195 c4

-Thompson, J. C. and Company (Tailoring, Cleaning, and Clothing)	Sep 26, '28 p215 c1- Mar 21, '29 p403 c2
-Thorp, Dr. (Medical Services)	Jul 20,'27 p76 c3
-Union Inn (Advertised by C. Boyer)	Jun 15, '27 p56 c2
-Vanliew, N. (Boot Polish)	Aug 8, '28 p159 c2- Mar 28, '29 p412 c3
-Walker, David (Cleaning and Selling Clothing)	Oct 31, '28 p255 c1- Mar 28, '29 p411 c3
-Wiles, F. (Boarding House)	Sep 14, '27 p108 c3
-Wood, Aaron (Adult Evening School for Blacks)	Sep 26, '28 p215 c1- Mar 28, '29 p411 c2
-Zabriska, Thomas (Reward for Return of Horse and Carriage)	Nov 9, '27 p140 c4

AFRICA

	1827
-Describes early Portuguese exploration and search for John Preston	Apr 6 p2 c2
-Relates unsuccessful jehad in Foota Terra	Apr 20 p21 c2-3
-Christian influence has stopped tribal wars in South Africa	May 4 p31 c2
-Describes lion hunt in South Africa	Jun 15 p53 c4 p54 c1-2
-Slave trade continuing despite British attempts to stop it	Jul 13 p71 c3
-States African nations capable of self-government	Jul 20 p73 c3
-Collection of Woloff proverbs (Senegal River Area)	Dec 7 p154 c1
-Describes caverns in South Africa	Dec 7 p156 c2
-Describes project to educate blacks from Africa in France	Dec 14 p159 c1-2
	1828
-Describes Ashanti village	Jun 20 p101 c1-2
-Describes geography around Niger River	Oct 10 p226 c1
-Frenchman explores Timbuctoo and surrounding areas	Dec 26 p305 c1-2
	1829
-Cradle of civilization, but declined after Barbarian invasions	Feb 7 p349 c1-3 p350 c1
-Describes physical beauty of African people	Feb 14 p375 c1-3

-Short history of Africa describing birth of Ciro in Africa	Feb 21 p369 c2-3 p370 c1 Feb 26 p373 c3 p374 c1-2
-Describes European's trip to Timbuctoo	Feb 26 p377 c2-3 p378 c1
-See also American Colonization Society; Egypt; Liberia; Rahahmon, Prince Abduhl; Sierra Leone	
AFRICAN ASSOCIATION FOR MUTUAL RELIEF (New York City)	
	1827
-Celebrates their 17th anniversary in Zion Church	Mar 30 p2 c4
-Will hold an extra meeting in mid-April	Apr 13 p19 c4
	1828
-Thomas Jennings praises its work	Apr 4 p12 c1-3
AFRICAN EDUCATION AND BENEVOLENT SOCIETY OF CHILICOTHE, OHIO	
	1827
-Louis Woodson, Chairman, stresses importance of education for blacks	Apr 6 p13 c4, p14 c1
AFRICAN FEMALE DORCAS ASSOCIATION	
	1828
-Society of black women of New York City to promote education of black children	Feb 1 p179 c1-2
-Meeting of Board of Managers, February 4th at 7:00 p.m.	Feb 1 p179 c4
-Elects officers and decides to hold weekly meetings	Feb 15 p187 c4
-Sewing classes will meet twice weekly to make clothes for students of African Free School	Mar 7 p197 c1
-To meet October 1 to admit new members and collect dues	Sep 26 p214 c1-2
-Meeting changed to October 6 because of poor weather	Oct 3 p218 c3
-Asks for clothing for black children	Nov 21 p278 c2-3 let
	1829
-Praises work and asks women in other cities to form similar groups	Jan 9 p319 c1-2 ed.

-Reports amount of clothing collected and receives praise	Feb 7 p356 c1
-See also Miller, William; Paul, Reverend Benjamin; Quinn, Mrs. Margaretta R.; Quinn, Reverend William; Regulus, Mrs. Henrietta D.; Rush, Reverend Christopher; Todd, Samuel; Williams, Reverend Peter; Women (Black)	

AFRICAN FREE METHODIST SOCIETY

	1827
-Meeting house to be consecrated on May 6th	May 4 p31 c4
-See also Quinn, Reverend William	

AFRICAN FREE SCHOOL (New York)

	1828
-Advertises	Jan 11 p168 c2
-Reports Samuel Cornish will be soliciting students and African Dorcas Association will be collecting clothes for school children	Mar 7 p197 c1
-Asks for contributions to mineral collection	May 23 p70 c1
-Reports good progress	Jun 13 p93 c2
-A reader praises the school	Jul 18 p130 c3 p131 c1 let.
-Building a new school house	Aug 22 p173 c3
-See also African Female Dorcas Association; Manumission Society of New York	

AFRICAN GRAND MASONIC LODGE (Boston, Massachusetts)

	1828
-John Hilton delivers speech tracing development of Boston lodge and asking members to continue working	Nov 7 p257 c1-3 p258 c1-2
-See also Hall, Prince; Sanderson, Thomas; Smith, Boston	

AFRICAN HARMONIC SOCIETY OF PHILADELPHIA

	1827
-Announces second sacred concert	Apr 6 p15 c4

AFRICAN IMPROVEMENT SOCIETY (New Haven, Connecticut)	
	1827
-Passes resolution to work for improvement of moral and intellectual condition of Blacks	Apr 20 p22 c3-4
-*Freedom's Journal* hopes society will work to expand black education	Aug 10 p86 c3-4 p87 c1 let.
-Society holds meeting to support *Freedom's Journal*	Aug 17 p91 c1-3
AFRICAN INSTITUTE (England)	
	1828
-1827 Annual Report traces development of slavery in Empire, describes inequality of free blacks and asks for abolition	Feb 29 p193 c1-4 p194 c1-2
-Annual Report calls for end of slavery and slave trade	Mar 14 p199 c1-3
AFRICAN INVESTIGATOR	
	1827
-Paper published in Tripoli	Dec 14 p159 c3
AFRICAN MANUFACTURER	
	1828
-New black newspaper to start publication October 10	Oct 3 p223 c1
AFRICAN METHODIST EPISCOPAL CHURCH (National)	
	1828
-Holds annual meeting in Philadelphia	Jun 6 p81 c2-3
AFRICAN METHODIST EPISCOPAL CHURCH (New York)	
	1827
-Will hold a camp meeting in Flushing	Aug 17 p91 c4
	1828
-To hold annual conference	Jun 6 p81 c3
-Joined by First Coloured Wesleyan Methodist Church of New York City	Jun 6 p82 c3

AFRICAN MISSION SCHOOL SOCIETY
(Hartford, Connecticut)

	1829
-Society praised	Feb 26 p375 c3
-Prints constitution and by-laws	Feb 26 p378 c1-3
-Describes school and its purposes	Mar 7 p386 c3 p387 c1 let.

AFRICAN MUTUAL INSTRUCTION
SOCIETY (New York City)

	1827
-Advertises re-opening of school for both sexes	Sep 14 p108 c3
-School praised	Nov 23 p147 c1-2 ed.

AFRICAN OBSERVER, THE

	1827
-Philadelphia paper to emphasize Africa, slavery, and improvement for blacks	Apr 6 p15 c2
-New York Freedom's Journal recommends paper	Apr 13 p19 c3
	1828
-American Convention for Promoting Abolition of Slavery buys five subscriptions	Feb 8 p181 c3
-Stops publication because of lack of funds	May 9 p51 c3

THE AFRICAN UNITED ECCLESIASTICAL
SOCIETY (New Haven, Connecticut)

	1827
-Asks for aid in religious life	May 4 p31 c4

AFRICAN WOOLMAN BENEVOLENT
SOCIETY (Brooklyn, New York)

	1827
-Present at 17th anniversary celebration of African Association for Mutual Relief	Mar 30 p2 c4
	1828
-Celebrated own anniversary on March 3	Mar 21 p207 c2

AGRICULTURE

	1827
-Advises New York blacks to stay in agriculture after freedom	Jun 22 p58 c3

-Stresses importance of agriculture and advises blacks to stay in it — Aug 31 p98 c2-3
-Method for improving trees — Sep 21 p112 c1
-Advises blacks to remain in farming and explains wealth possibilities — Nov 9 p139 c3
-Liberian farmer invents a new plough — Nov 9 p139 c4

1828

-Farmer in Ceylon uses elephants for ploughing — Jan 25 p175 c3
-Too much attention given to cotton growing and not enough to corn — May 30 p74 c3, p75 c1
-Sweet potatoes may be raised in Massachusetts — May 30 p76 c3
-Potatoes introduced in Greece — Jul 4 p118 c2
-Corn crops in North and South Carolina excellent — Oct 24 p245 c3

AINOS, SUSAN

1827

-Marries Micheal Douge — Apr 6 p15 c4

ALABAMA

1827

-Prohibits importation of slaves for sale or hire after August 1 — Apr 20 p23 c3
-Extends laws over Indian nations — Apr 27 p27 c3

1828

-Selma experiences slight earthquake — May 9 p50 c1

ALBINOS

1828

-Described — Aug 22 p172 c2

ALCOHOL

1827

-Explains cure for drunkenness — Mar 30 p9 c1-2
-Describes death resulting from alcoholism — May 4 p31 c1
-Describes effects of alcoholism in marriage of a young couple — May 25 p42 c4, p43 c1
-Defines a drunkard — Jun 1 p48 c2
-Relates anecdote of a man giving up drinking — Jun 8 p50 c1-2
-Describes the feelings of a wife of an alcoholic — Jun 29 p61 c3-4

-Describes effects of an alcoholic mother on families — Jun 29 p61 c4
-Prints imaginary will of an alcoholic — Jul 27 p78 c4

1828

-Describes strict laws of Sweden against intoxication — Apr 4 p14 c1
-Describes death of a young mother from alcoholism — Apr 4 p15 c1
-Describes two instances of death from alcohol — May 2 p42 c1
-Disadvantages of intoxication discussed — May 16 p58 c2
-Method to restore sobriety — Jun 20 p102 c3
-Explains effects on a family of alcoholic members — Aug 1 p147 c3
-Warns that excessive use of alcohol shortens life — Sep 26 p212 c3, p213 c1

-See also Beecher, Dr. (Lyman); Self-Improvement (Blacks); Temperance

ALLEN, REVEREND BISHOP RICHARD

1827

-Minister of African Methodist Episcopal Church — Aug 17 p91 c4
-Condemns colonization because blacks are not literate enough to rule — Nov 2 p134 c3-4 let.

1828

-Description of birthday party; work for blacks praised — Feb 22 p191 c3

ALLEN, REVEREND WILLIAM A.

1828

-Soliciting funds for new church and school for blacks in Rochester, New York — May 9 p51 c3

AMERICAN BOARD OF FOREIGN MISSIONS

1827

-Anniversary celebration in New York City — Oct 26 p131 c3

AMERICAN COLONIZATION SOCIETY

1827

-Asks Congress for aid — Mar 16 p3 c4
-Englishman states it is too slow moving — Apr 16 p1 c2
-States society's intention to liberate slaves — May 18 p38 c3

-States Society not interested in supporting slavery	Jun 8 p50 c2 let.
-Southern Masonic Lodges working with Society	Jun 29 p63 c4
-Criticizes motives of some members	Jul 6 p66 c2-3 let.
-Criticizes lack of planning	Jul 6 p66 c4 p67 c1 let.
-Defense of Society's aims	Aug 24 p94 c1-3 let.
-Work of Society has favorably changed views of many slave holders	Aug 24 p94 c2-3 let.
-A reader questions belief that blacks cannot attain equality in the United States	Aug 31 p98 c3-4 let.
-Reader defends Society and condemns <u>Freedom's Journal</u>'s criticism	Sep 7 p101 c4 p102 c1-2 let.
-Reader criticizes Society stating free blacks have every right to remain	Sep 7 p102 c2-3 let.
-Society advised that people will eventually give support	Sep 14 p106 c3-4
-<u>Freedom's Journal</u> will investigate motives of Society	Sep 14 p107 c2-3 ed.
-Judge (Bushard) Washington, Virginia Society president, deals in internal slave trade	Sep 14 p107 c3-4
-Defense of motives of Society and praise for members' characters	Sep 21 p109 c4 p110 c1-2
-Criticism of Reverend Miller's views on colonization	Sep 21 p110 c3-4
-Belief that blacks in Liberia are much happier than when they were in America	Sep 28 p114 c2-4
-Society seen as a tool of slave holders	Sep 28 p114 c4 p115 c1-2
-Aim of the Society is to perpetuate slavery	Sep 28 p115 c2-3
-Belief that Liberia and Sierra Leone will stop the slave trade	Oct 5 p117 c4 p118 c1-2
-People in the Society should work for equality	Oct 5 p118 c2-4
-View that the Society will help end slavery	Oct 12 p122 c3-4
-Influence of the Society on emancipation noted	Oct 19 p126 c2-4
-Work of the Society will greatly harm free blacks who remain	Oct 19 p126 c4 p127 c1

-Objections of abolitionists to the Society	Oct 26 p130 c2-3
-Belief that more blacks will emigrate when the Society can afford to transport greater numbers; for government help	Nov 2 p134 c2-3
-Condemns idea of leaving United States and going to Liberia	Nov 2 p134 c4
-Receives $100 from Grand Masonic Lodge of Vermont	Nov 2 p135 c4
-Free blacks enjoy equal rights and therefore do not need to colonize	Nov 9 p137 c4 p138 c1
-Motive of Society is to remove blacks before they are too powerful	Nov 9 p138 c1-3
-Criticizes views of John H. Kennedy on Liberia	Nov 9 p138 c1-3
-View that free blacks must remain to aid slaves	Nov 16 p141 c3-4 p142 c1 ed.
-John H. Kennedy asks readers to judge Society fairly	Nov 16 p142 c1-2
-Kennedy concludes that Liberia is the savior of United States blacks	Nov 23 p145 c4 p146 c1
-Slavery weakened by work of free blacks	Nov 30 p150 c2-4
-Society criticized for removing blacks most active in abolition	Dec 7 p153 c3
-View that Society's motive is to decrease the number of free blacks in the United States	Dec 7 p154 c1-2
-Emancipation possible if abolition societies work with American Colonization Society	Dec 21 p162 c3-4
	<u>1828</u>
-South Carolina Senate feels Congress cannot give money to the Society	Jan 11 p166 c1
-Free blacks should not colonize until all blacks are free	Jan 25 p175 c2-3
-Government involvement criticized	Feb 22 p191 c2-3
-View that the society is made up mainly of slaveholders	Feb 29 p194 c1-2

-Reveals racist actions of many members of the Society	Mar 7 p196 c4 p197 cl
-Senator Chambers asks Congress to aid the Society	Mar 7 p197 cl
-Senate Foreign Relations Committee feels colonization is too expensive	May 30 p74 c3
-Criticism of Society for not asking blacks their opinions on colonization	Jul 11 p123 cl-2 let.
-View that blacks are good enough to stay in the United States	Jul 18 p129 cl-3 p130 cl let.
-Resolves to support trade between Liberia and the United States	Oct 17 p238 c3
-Collected $1,479.10 during the summer of 1828	Oct 24 p246 c2
-Questions Society view that blacks could govern well in Liberia; for education of blacks in the United States	Dec 19 p297 cl-2
	<u>1829</u>
-Many slave owners will free slaves if Society will transport them to Liberia	Jan 2 p309 c2-3
-To transport 150 emigrants shortly	Jan 2 p311 cl
-Applicants for colonization must show proof of freedom and good character; next sailing January 20, 1829	Jan 9 p321 c3
-Describes Society's beginnings and early work	Jan 24 p334 cl
-Reader witnesses blacks leaving for Liberia	Feb 7 p352 cl-2 let.
-Abolition Society of Stark County, Ohio promises monetary aid	Feb 7 p353 cl
-Work of Society praised	Feb 14 p360 cl-2
-View that paper has been wrong about the Society's motives	Feb 21 p370 c2-3 ed.
-Describes 18th annual meeting	Mar 7 p384 cl-2
-See also Clay, Henry; Kennedy, John H.; Liberia; Russwurm, John	

AMERICAN CONVENTION FOR PROMOTING THE ABOLITION OF SLAVERY

	1827
-Twentieth biennial meeting in October in Philadelphia	Aug 24 p95 c4 Sep 7 p103 c4
-Outlines rules for representation	Aug 24 p95 c4
-Subscribes to <u>Freedom's Journal</u>	Dec 21 p163 c2
	1828
-Publishes minutes of 20th biennial meeting	Feb 1 p177 c3-4 p178 c1-4
-Elects officers, lists delegates, receives communications, passes series of resolutions, etc.	Feb 8 p181 c2-4 p182 c1
-Text of petition for aiding the education of blacks and suggested programs of abolition society	Feb 15 p185 c3-4 p186 c1
-Advises abolition societies to work for abolition in Washington, D. C., work for end to slave trade, etc.	Feb 22 p189 c4 p190 c1-2
-Sub-committee asks help in research on slavery versus free labor	Mar 21 p207 c3
-Calls for abolition of slavery in Washington, D.C. and asks help from public	Dec 19 p296 c1-3
-Work praised by <u>Freedom's Journal</u>	Dec 19 p296 c 3 ed.
-Holds annual meeting in November; passes resolutions	Dec 19 p297 c2-3 p298 c1-3
	1829
-Condemns slavery in Washington, D.C. and describes cruelties of domestic slave trade	Mar 7 p382 c2-3 p383 c1-2
-<u>Freedom's Journal</u> defends new position on colonization	Mar 7 p386 c1-3 ed.

AMERICAN HEMLOCK
-See Circuta Maculata

AMERICAN INSURANCE COMPANY

	1828
-Reports great profits	May 23 p68 c3

AMO, ANTHONY WILLIAMS (Guinea)

1827

-Eighteenth century professor of philosophy at the University of Wittemburg — May 18 p37 c4

1828

-Describes education and career — Nov 14 p265 c1-2

ANDERSON, REVEREND CHARLES (Newark, New Jersey)

1828 - 1829

-Agent for the Freedom's Journal — Nov 7 '28 p264 c3 - Mar 28, '29 p412 c3

ANDERSON, DR. JAMES

1827

-Author of Observations on Slavery argues West Indian slave labor costs three times that of free labor — Aug 24 p93 c1

ANDREWS, CHARLES C.

1827

-Teacher in New York African Free School — Nov 9 p138 c4 let.

ANIELLO, THOMAS
-See Masaniello

ANIMALS

1827

-Story of a gander who lived with horses — Aug 3 p81 c3-4
-Describes a cat raising rabbits — Aug 10 p88 c1-2
-Describes a cat and mouse living together — Aug 17 p92 c3
-Explains origin and behavior of the turkey — Oct 12 p121 c3-4
-Relates story of a Tiger raised by humans in India — Oct 26 p132 c2
-Describes a dog who was taught to steal — Nov 2 p133 c4 p134 c1
-Explains a method for stopping hydrophobia — Nov 9 p140 c2
-Describes the roar of a lion — Dec 7 p156 c1-2

1828

-Story of an ox who rescued a boy being attacked by a bull — Jan 18 p169 c4
-Describes the actions of a pig being slaughtered — May 9 p52 c2-3

-Explanation of the wisdom of elephants	May 23 p65 c3
-Anecdotes about cats	May 23 p66 c3 p67 c1
-Description of a boa constrictor	May 30 p73 c1-3
-Describes a 72 foot whale found off Cape Cod	May 30 p74 c3
-Praises the intelligence and loyalty of dogs	Jun 6 p85 c3 p86 c1
-Story of a cat that drowns a man	Aug 1 p150 c3 p151 c1
-Sheep seeks aid of a human in saving her lamb	Aug 8 p153 c3
-Anecdote about a loyal dog who saved his master	Sep 5 p188 c3
-Describes cattle and ostrich population of South America	Sep 12 p194 c1-2
-Condemns whaling	Oct 17 p236 c3
	<u>1829</u>
-Describes the movement of various animals	Jan 24 p336 c1-2
-Praises the wisdom of elephants	Feb 7 p354 c1-3
ANNICHIARICO, CIRO	
	<u>1827</u>
-Life story related	Dec 14 p157 c1-4
ANTHONY, HENRY B. M.	
	<u>1827</u>
-Died March 23, 1827 (Seven month old son of James W. Anthony)	Mar 30 p3 c4
ANTI-COLONIZATION	
-See American Colonization Society; Colonization	
ANTI-SLAVERY SOCIETIES	
-See Abolition	
ANTI-SLAVERY SOCIETY (England)	
	<u>1828</u>
-States slavery will not end as long as colonists have protective tariffs helping them	Jun 27 p105 c1-3
-Meets to discuss why the government has not abolished slavery; also resolves to work for abolition as soon as possible	Jul 4 p113 c1-3 p114 c1-2 Jul 11 p121 c1-3

ANTOINETTE, MARIE

	1827
-Described by Edmund Burke	Nov 23 p145 c3-4

APPO AND SAMMONS

	1827
-Advertise tailor shop in Philadelphia	Apr 27-May 4 pp28, 32 c3
-Moved to 64 Walnut Street	Oct 12 p123 c4

ARCHITECTURE

	1828
-Describes Arabian arches	Sep 26 p213 c1
	1829
-Describes physical layout of villages in Java	Feb 7 p352 c3
-See also Home Construction	

ART

	1828
-Description of ancient Etruscan figure	May 2 p44 c1-2
-An artist depicts humans in animal forms	Sep 5 p186 c3 p187 c1
-Describes oldest oil painting in England (Of Chaucer)	Dec 26 p304 c1
-See also Architecture	

ASBURY CONNEXION

	1827
-Will hold annual conference April 21 at Asbury Church	Apr 13 p19 c4

ASHLEY, GENERAL

	1827
-Describes his discovery of Great Salt Lake	Apr 27 p26 c4

ASHMAN, MR. (JEHUDI)
-See Ashmun, Mr. (Jehudi)

ASHMUN, MR. (JEHUDI)

	1828
-Founder of Liberia returns to the United States due to health	Aug 29 p182 c1
-Dies August 25; eulogy and description of funeral	Sep 12 p197 c2-3 p198 c1

ASLETT, ROBERT

	1828
-Stole money from Bank of England while deputy cashier	Sep 12 p196 c3 p197 c1

ASTRONOMY

1828

- -Describes invention of the telescope in 1599 — Sep 26 p212 c1
- -Comet visible from Boston — Nov 7 p258 c3

1829

- -Encke comet may collide with earth in 200 million years — Jan 31 p342 c3 p343 c1

ASYLUM FOR INDIGENT BOYS (Boston)

1828

- -Reports statistics of admission and placement after graduation — May 2 p42 c1

ATLEE, EDWIN P.

1827

- -Secretary of American Convention for Promoting Abolition of Slavery — Aug 24 p95 c4

1828

- -Secretary of Abolition Society of Pennsylvania — Jan 11 p166 c4
- -Secretary of 20th Biennial Meeting of American Convention for Abolition of Slavery — Jan 25 p177 c3

AUGUSTUS, RICHARD

1827

- -Advertises a dinner to be held on July 5 — Jun 22-29 pp60, 64 c3

1828

- -Appointed to committee to plan New York Abolition celebration — May 16 p61 c3

AUGUSTUS, SCIPIO C. (New Haven Connecticut)

1828

- -Advertises boarding house in New Haven — Aug 15 p166 c3

1829

- -Agent for the <u>Freedom's Journal</u> — Jan 2, '29 p316 c3 - Mar 28, '29 p412 c3

AUSTRALIA

1828

- -Describes dishonest colonists transported from England — Apr 18 p29 c2-3

AUTERIVE, MARGINY D.

	1828
-Demands money for cruel treatment of a slave while in government service	Jan 25 p174 c1-2
-Congress rules in favor of Auterive	Feb 8 p183 c3

B

BACHELORHOOD

	1827
-Imaginary memoirs of a bachelor	Nov 9 p137 c3
	1828
-Warns young men of match makers	May 16 p61 c1-2
-Describes ways of embarrassing women	Aug 1 p146 c1-2
-Praises the life of a sailor	Sep 12 p195 c2
-Young engaged man complains about fiance's extravagance	Sep 19 p203 c1-2 let.
	1829
-Compares flirts to modest men	Jan 2 p311 c2-3
-Advises young men to read	Jan 9 p318 c2-3
-Asks people to be kind to old bachelors	Feb 27 p367 c1-2
-See also Bachelor's Journal	

BACHELOR'S JOURNAL

	1828
-First issue published April 28	May 2 p42 c2
-Article praising publication's intent	May 9 p50 c2-3 let.
-Ceases publication	Oct 3 p222 c3

BACKHOUSE, WILLIAM

	1827
-One of the founders of New York Manumission Society	Oct 12 p122 c2

BAETESTO, JOSEPH (Boston)

	1828
-(Advertisement) $5 reward offered for the return of a mulatto runaway	Aug 15 p166 c3

BALLOONS

	1828
-Traces their development	Apr 4 p13 c2

BALTIMORE (Maryland)

	1827
-Institutes a curfew for blacks	Aug 3 p83 c2
	1828
-Debating a bill prohibiting blacks from driving cabs and drays	May 16 p60 c1-2
-Experiences severe thunder storm June 4	Jun 13 p90 c1
-Describes blacks in Baltimore	Jul 25 p143 c3 let.
-Describes limited rights of free blacks	Aug 15 p163 c1-2 let.
-Condemned for allowing slave trade	Oct 31 p254 c1-2 let.
-See also Lundy, Benjamin; Slave Trade	

BANAKER, BENJAMIN
-See Bannaker, Benjamin

BANE, PETER

	1827
-Committee member of the People of Color of New York	Apr 20 p23 c4

BANE, MRS. SARAH

	1828
-Elected treasurer of the African Female Dorcas Association	Feb 15 p187 c4

BANKS, GEORGE

	1828
-Receives compensation for time unjustly imprisoned	Feb 29 p195 c4

BANNAKER, BENJAMIN

	1827
-Account of black astronomer who published almanacs in 1794 and 1795 in Philadelphia	May 18 p38 c1

BAPTIST GENERAL TRACT SOCIETY

	1828
-Holds anniversary celebration in Philadelphia	Jan 18 p170 c2

BAPTIST, W. D. (Fredericksburgh, Virginia)

	1827 - 1829
-Agent for the Freedom's Journal	Jul 27, '27 p80 c4 Mar 28, '29 p412 c3

BARNUM, NANCY

	1827
-Marries Thomas VanTuyl	Apr 27 p26 c4

BARRINGTON (Rhode Island)

	1827
-No taxes in 1826	May 4 p31 c4

BARRINGTON, GEORGE

	1828
-High Constable of Paramatta, New South Wales in late 18th century	Nov 7 p260 c1

BARTON, ZEBULIN

	1827
-One of the founders of the New York Manumission Society	Oct 12 p122 c2

BASTARD SECILY

	1827
-See Circuta Maculata	Apr 27 p27 c2

BATHORY, ELIZABETH

	1827
-Describes murder of many young girls in the 17th century	Jun 22 p58 c1

BATHURST, LORD

	1827
-His liberal system of slave laws for West Indies rejected	Sep 7 p102 c4 p102 c1
	1828
-Slave laws defeated in Parliament	Apr 4 p14 c3 p15 c1
-His proposals explained	Sep 19 p204 c1-2

BEADLE, DR. (Manchester, England)

	1827
-Intends to swim from Liverpool to Runcoin	Aug 3 p83 c3

BEARD, GOVERNOR

	1827
-Issues Berbice Papers allowing equal legal treatment for whites and blacks	Mar 16 p3 c2
-See also Berbice Papers	

BEATTIE, DR.

	1827
-View that only half the present labor force would be needed with free labor	Aug 17 p89 c1-2

BEECHER, DR. (Lyman)

1828

-Lectures on intemperance — May 30 p74 c1-2

BELGARDE

1827

-Haitian leader planned overthrow of President Boyer — Aug 3 p83 c1-2

BELLS

1827

-Describes some of the largest bells in existence — Aug 10 p88 c1

BENEVOLENT SOCIETY FOR PEOPLE OF COLOUR (Alexandria, Virginia)

1827

-Proposes to work for end of slavery and slave trade — May 26 p41 c3-4 p42 c1

-States that free labor is cheaper and produces better results than slave labor — Jun 1 p45 c3-4 p46 c1-2

-Explains expense of owning slaves — Jun 8 p49 c1-3

-Promotes abolition and explains rapid advancement of free states — Jun 15 p53 c1-4

-Describes slavery's bad effects on children of slave-holders — Jun 22 p57 c1-2

-See also Florida

BERBICE PAPERS

1827

-Abolish certain distinctions between whites and free blacks — Mar 16 p3 c2-3

BERTRAND, MR. (Montreal, Canada)

1827

-Robbed of $1,231 in goods — Apr 6 p15 c2-3

BICKERSTITH, EDWARD

1827

-Writes letter for Church Missionary Society requesting black American missionaries — Mar 16 p2 c2-3

BIESTEL, ANDREW

1827

-Shot himself at home in Mt. Pleasant, Pennsylvania — May 4 p31 c3

BIRDS

1828

-Traces history of canaries in Europe — Aug 22 p173 c1

BLACKLOCK (Poet)

1828

-Biographical sketch — Dec 26 p306 c1-2

BLACKS (Albany, New York)

1827

-Meet March 27th to celebrate announced abolition of slavery in New York — Apr 20 p22 c2-3

BLACKS (Boston, Massachusetts)

1827

-Meeting at David Walker's house; resolution to support the Freedom's Journal — Mar 16 p3 c1-2

1828

-Meeting and vote of approval of the Freedom's Journal — Apr 25 p38 c1-2
-Hold dinner in honor of Prince Abduhl Rahahmon — Aug 29 p179 c3
-Describes dinner held for Prince Rahahmon — Sep 5 p186 c1-3
-Further detailed description of dinner for Prince Rahahmon — Oct 24 p243 c1-3
-See also African Grand Lodge of Boston; General Colored Association of Boston; Hall, Prince; Walker, David

BLACKS (Highland County, Ohio)

1827

-Petitions for the same rights as white citizens — Dec 14 p158 c3

BLACKS (New Haven, Connecticut)

1827

-Celebrate slavery's abolition in New York — Jul 13 p71 c3

BLACKS (New York, New York)

1827

-Will hold a meeting Monday, April 23, 1827 — Apr 20 p23 c4
-Meet April 23rd and resolve to celebrate abolition of slavery in New York — Apr 27 p26 c4 p27 c1
-Resolve not to hold procession to celebrate slavery's abolition in New York State — Jun 29 p63 c3
-Form the Jordan Missionary Society to preach the Bible to Blacks of New York — Dec 7 p154 c4

BLAGDEN, REVEREND

1828

-Feels education produces moral character — May 23 p66 c1-2

BLANCHET, ABBE
-See Stories

BLOOM, CATHERINE

1827

-Marries Mark Jordan — Apr 20 p23 c4

BLUE, MOSES

1827

-Appointed to Committee of People of Color of New York for celebration of New York Abolition — May 4 p30 c4

BOLIVAR, SIMON

1827

-Declares himself dictator of Colombia — May 4 p31 c3

BOOKS

1827

-Describes the many steps in publication — May 18 p40 c2-3

BOORMAN, JEREMIAH

1828

-Saves two boys from drowning — Jan 25 p175 c1

BORNEO

1827

-Description of a captured native — Oct 12 p121 c1-3

BOSTON (Massachusetts) -General

1827

-Statue of Washington arrives — May 4 p31 c2
-Description of Boston, her schools, and her black population — Nov 2 p135 c1-3 let.
-Praise of Boston and description of famous sites — Nov 9 p138 c4 p139 c1-3 let.

1828

-Reports number of churches of each denomination — Feb 22 p190 c4
-Work resumed on Bunker Hill monument — May 2 p42 c3
-Lists number of schools and students in Boston area — Nov 7 p258 c3
-See also Blacks (Boston)

BOSTON COLUMBIAN CENTINEL

	1827
-Criticizes New York Enquirer's description of ex-Queen of Haiti	May 11 p34 c1-2

BOWEN, JOHN AND COMPANY

	1827
-Partially burned	Mar 16 p3 c3
-See also Joseph, Francis	

BOWERS, JOHN

	1827
-President of society to raise money for a school in Philadelphia for coloured youth	May 11 p34 c2

BOWLER, WILLIAM B. (Port-au-Prince, Haiti)

	1828 - 1829
-Agent for the Freedom's Journal	Sep 19,'28 p208 c3-Mar 28,'29 p412 c3

BOWNE, THOMAS

	1827
-One of the founders of the New York Manumission Society	Oct 12 p122 c2

BOYER, C.

	1827
-Union Inn (Advertises)	Jun 15 p56 c2

BOYER, JEAN PIERRE (President of Haiti)

	1827
-Addresses country concerning plot to overthrow his government	Aug 3 p83 c2-3
-See also Belgarde	

BRADDOCK, THOMAS (Alexandria, Virginia, D.C.)

	1827 - 1829
-Agent for the Freedom's Journal	Aug 24, '27 p96 c4 Mar 28, '29 p412 c3

BROUGHAM, MR.

	1827
-Explains disadvantages of severe punishment of slaves	Aug 17 p89 c1-2

BROWN, DR.

	1827
-Killed by Randall Smith	Apr 27 p27 c3
-See also Smith, Randall	

BROWN, DAVID

1828

-Sentenced to prison for helping a slave escape — Aug 8 p155 c1

BROWN, ROBERT

1827

-One of the founders of the New York Manumission Society — Oct 12 p122 c2

BROWN, WILLIAM (London, England)
-See Paine, Thomas

BROWNELL, DR. JOSEPH

1828

-Traveling doctor — Oct 17 p235 c1-2

BURKE, EDMUND

1827

-States people work better when they are working for themselves and not as slaves — Aug 17 p89 c1-2
-Describes Marie Antoinette — Nov 23 p145 c3-4

1828

-Describes leaders in French Revolution's Reign of Terror — Aug 8 p157 c2

BURLIM, MATTHEW

1827

-Acquitted in murder trial — May 11 p35 c1

BURLING, EBENEZER S.

1827

-One of the founders of the New York Manumission Society — Oct 12 p122 c2

BURLING, THOMAS

1827

-One of the founders of the New York Manumission Society — Oct 12 p122 c2

BURIAL (Methods)

1827

-Describes simple way to bury people — Mar 30 p4 c1
-Man recounts being buried alive — Aug 17 p89 c2-4
-Description of Hindoo practices — Nov 23 p148 c2

BURR, MR.

1828

-Leaves $96,000 to missionaries and various colleges — May 2 p43 c3

BYRON, LORD

	1828
-Anecdote about his attraction for women	Apr 25 p36 c2
-Poem "A Woman's Tear"	Jun 6 p87 c1

C

CADIZ (Spain)

	1827
-Experiencing cold weather; causing deaths from pulmonary complaints	Mar 16 p3 c3

CANADA

	1827
-Many blacks settling in Northwest Canada and cultivating tobacco	Aug 3 p83 c1
-Legislature and Governor disagree over appointment of a Speaker of the House	Dec 7 p155 c2

CANE, OTWAY

	1828
-Plans to move that all black children in the West Indies be free after 1830	Aug 15 p166 c2

CAPITEIN, JAMES ELIZA JOHN

	1827
-Dutch slave became minister to Guinea	May 18 p37 c4

CAREY, MATTHEW (Philadelphia)

	1829
-Pledges $100 a year to the American Colonization Society in order to decrease the number of blacks in the United States	Jan 24 p335 c3

CARLISLE, ROBERT

	1828
-Slave dealer killed by slaves	Feb 22 p190 c4

CARTHAGE

	1827
-Describes ancient Egyptian colonization	Aug 31 p97 c4 p98 c1-2

CARTINAN, WILLIAM

1827

-One of the founders of the New York Manumission Society — Oct 12 p122 c2

CARTWRIGHT, MAJOR

1827

-Brings first Esquimaux woman to England in 1776 — Apr 27 p28 c3

CARY, LOTT

1829

-Leader of Liberia after death of Jehudi Ashmun — Feb 7 p352 c1

CESAR (North Carolina)

1827

-Popular black poet — May 18 p38 c1

CHAMBERS, MR.

1828

-Asks Senate to aid the American Colonization Society — Mar 7 p197 c1

CHARLES II (England)

1828

-Anecdote concerning his fooling scientists — May 30 p76 c1-2

CHARLES, JOHN

1827

-Died March 22 — Mar 30 p3 c4

CHARLESTON (South Carolina)

1827

-Experiences great rainfall — Aug 17 p91 c3

CHEENY, ANN W.

1827

-Recovers $600 from Samuel Mathews for breach of promise — Mar 16 p3 c4

CHEROKEE PHOENIX

1828

-Describes paper printed in both English and Cherokee — Apr 4 p15 c3

CHINA

1827

-Describes Chinese beauty — Mar 16 p4 c3
-Revolution in Tartary — May 11 p35 c3
-Describes process of sugar cane growing — Aug 24 p93 c2
-Describes Egyptian colonization of ancient China and cites similarities between the two civilizations — Aug 24 p94 c2-3

	1828
-Describes city of Canton	May 9 p53 c1
	1829
-Describes two beautiful women who escaped from China to Europe	Jan 24 p336 c1
CHRISTOPHE, HENRI (Haiti)	
	1827
-Rose from a slave to be King	May 18 p38 c2
CHRISTOPHER, MR.	
	1827
-Killed by Randall Smith	Apr 27 p27 c3
-See also Smith, Randall	
CHRYSTIE, JOHN	
	1828
-Being hunted for murder	Oct 24 p245 c1
-Arrested	Oct 31 p254 c3
CHURCH MISSIONARY SOCIETY OF LONDON	
	1827
-Requests black American missionaries	Mar 16 p2 c3-4
CIRCUTA MACULATA	
	1827
-Describes death of three children after eating Circuta Maculata	Apr 27 p27 c2
CIVIL RIGHTS	
	1828
-Lists voting qualifications of each state of the United States	Aug 22 p171 c1-2
-Relates incident of two blacks denied _habeus corpus_ in Maryland	Dec 12 p293 c1-2
-See also Racism	
CLAIRBORNE (Alabama)	
	1827
-Large wildcat attacks mother and child	Apr 27 p27 c2-3
CLAPPERTON, CAPTAIN	
	1827
-Arrives in Africa and proceeds to Timbuctoo	Mar 16 p3 c3
	1828
-Describes his death in Sockatoo in April	Jun 13 p93 c3

CLARBORNE, CYNTHIA

	1827
-Marries William Patterson	Mar 30 p3 c4

CLARK, WILLIAM

	1828
-Appointed Treasurer of the United States	Jun 13 p90 c1

CLARKSON SOCIETY

	1827
-Present at the 17th anniversary of the African Association for Mutual Relief	Mar 30 p2 c4

CLAXTON, NATHANIEL

	1828
-Moves to 25 Chapel Street (New York City)	May 23 p70 c3

CLAY, HENRY

	1827
-Criticized for believing slaves to be pieces of property	Dec 7 p153 c2
-States aim of American Colonization Society is to decrease the number of free blacks in the United States	Dec 7 p154 c2
	1829
-As Secretary of State, requests British government to return fugitive slaves in Canada	Jan 16 p325 c1-3 p326 c1

CLIMATE

-See Haiti; Lyons (France); Meteorology; New York (Weather); Wilkesborough (North Carolina)

CLINTON, CHARLES A.

	1828
-Appointed city clerk in New York	May 16 p60 c3

CLINTON, DeWITT

	1828
-Obituary	Feb 22 p191 c4
-Albany Boat Company to build boat in his memory; city contemplating a statue in his memory	Mar 7 p197 c2

-Praises his work and asks for financial aid for his family — Apr 4 p10 c2-3 p11 c1

-His property sold by the sheriff — Jun 6 p85 c1

CLIZBY, IRA

1828

-Appointed to the correspondence committee of the New York Manumission Society — May 9 p49 c1

CLOCKS

1828

-Traces their development — Nov 14 p269 c2-3

COCK, ELIJAH

1827

-One of the founders of the New York Manumission Society — Oct 12 p122 c2

COGSWELL, JAMES

1827

-One of the founders of the New York Manumission Society — Oct 12 p122 c2

COLDEN, CADWALLADER D.

1828

-President of the New York Manumission Society — Feb 1 p179 c2

COLLER, ANTHELME

1828

-Describes his career as a criminal — Oct 24 p244 c1-2

COLLIER, W. & W.

1828

-Advertises coming publication of a new black newspaper, the African Manufacturer — Oct 3 p223 c1

COLLINS, THOMAS
-See Smith, Captain John

COLONIZATION

1827

-Francis Wright feels blacks should be prepared for liberty — May 11 p34 c1
-Editors of Freedom's Journal speak against colonization — Jun 8 p50 c4 p51 c1-2

-Freed slaves settled in Pennsylvania instead of going to Africa — Jul 6 p67 c2-3

-View that colonization will not help maintain slavery	Jul 27 p77 c3-4 p78 c1
-A British abolitionist feels slave-holders are involved in colonization	Aug 10 p86 c1-2
-Reverend Richard Allen condemns colonization because Blacks are not educated enough to govern themselves	Nov 2 p134 c3-4 let.
	1828
-Money spent on colonization would be better spent on education	Feb 15 p187 c2-3 ed.
-Thomas Jennings condemns colonization since Blacks are Americans	Apr 4 p12 c1-3
	1829
-Kentuckian suggests slaves work for money to be used for passage to Africa	Feb 14 p361 c1
-*Freedom's Journal* openly supports colonization	Feb 14 p362 c1-2 ed.
-See also American Colonization Society; Clay, Henry; Liberia; Ohio Colonization Society; Russwurm, John; United States Congress; Wright, Frances	
"COLOURED INHABITANTS OF FREDERICKSBURGH, VIRGINIA"	
	1827
-Celebrate abolition of slavery in New York State on July 4th	Jul 13 p70 c4
COLUMBIA (Colombia)	
	1827
-Describes government, church, economy and education since independence	Jul 27 p78 c3
-Reports dissention between heads of state	Nov 16 p143 c3
	1828
-Experiences terrible earthquake, November 1827	Mar 14 p201 c3
-Declares war on Peru	Aug 22 p173 c3
-Describes conspiracy against government	Dec 12 p292 c3 p293 c1
-See Bolivar, Simon	

THE COLUMBUS ENQUIRER	
	1828
-Cherokee newspaper	May 9 p50 c2
COOPER, ALLEN	
	1827
-Assaulted by George W. Steele; trial described	Mar 30 p3 c2-3
CORDER, WILLIAM	
	1828
-Tried in England for incestuous marriage to daughter-in-law	Oct 17 p233 c1-3 p234 c1-3
CORNELL, ROBERT C.	
	1828
-Treasurer of the New York Manumission Society	Feb 1 p179 c2
CORNISH, REVEREND SAMUEL	
	1827-1829
-General Agent for the *Freedom's Journal*	Mar 16, '27 p4 c3- Mar 28, '29 p412 c3
	1827
-Describes objectives of the New York *Freedom's Journal*	Mar 16 p4 c4
-Wishes to buy two lots for a Presbyterian Church	Mar 30-May 4 pp12, 16, 20, 24, 28, 32 c3
-Offers 2000 acres in New York for sale to blacks only	Mar 30-May 4 pp12, 16, 20, 24, 28, 32 c3
-Resigns from *Freedom's Journal* to devote time to the ministry	Sep 14 p107 c2-3
-Receives letter describing Boston and its black population	Nov 2 p135 c1-3 let.
-Receives letter describing Boston and Salem, Massachusetts	Nov 9 p138 c4 p139 c1-3 let.
	1828
-Appointed general agent of Board of Trustees of African Free Schools in New York; *Freedom's Journal* pleased	Jan 11 p166 c3-4 p167 c2
-Advisor to African Female Dorcas Association	Mar 7 p197 c1

-Work for African Free School praised — Jun 13 p93 c2
-See also African Female Dorcas Association; African Free School of New York; New York Freedom's Journal (Goals)

CORR, REVEREND CHARLES

1827
-Obituary and eulogy — Dec 7 p155 c3-4

COUNCELL, EDWARD

1828
-Wins $5,000 in a lottery — Jun 6 p85 c2

COWES, JAMES (New Brunswick, New Jersey)

1827 -1829
-Agent for the Freedom's Journal — Mar 16, '27 p4 c3- Mar 28, '29 p412 c3

COWLEY, R. (Cooley) (Baltimore, Maryland)

1827- 1828
-Agent for the Freedom's Journal — Mar 16, '27 p4 c3- Feb 15, '28 p188 c4

COX, REVEREND ROBERT

1827
-Emancipates slaves upon his death — Apr 13 p18 c3

COX, REVEREND SAMUEL H.

1827
-Supports the Freedom's Journal — Mar 16 p4 c4; Mar 30 p4 c4

CRAFTS, WILLIAM

1827
-White who greatly helped blacks in Charleston, South Carolina — Jul 6 p65 c3-4

CRANEY, THOMAS

1828
-Obituary and eulogy — Jul 25 p139 c2-3

CRIME

1827
-Differentiates between causes of crimes committed by blacks and whites — Mar 30 p3 c2
-Describes the trial and execution of a criminal in England — Nov 30 p150 c1-2

	1828
-Describes execution of criminals in Burma	Jan 18 p171 c2
-Capital punishment merely repeats the original crime	May 2 p44 c3
-Statistics concerning inmates of a juvenile prison in New York City	May 30 p74 c2
-Story of an Englishman of the early 18th century who tricked highway robbers	Oct 17 p236 c2-3
-Describes trial of highway robbers in Troy, New York	Oct 24 p242 c3
-Condemns punishment and imprisonment for debtors	Oct 31 p250 c1-3 p251 c1 let.
	1829
-Describes murders in England	Feb 21 p266 c2-3
-Describes murder trial in Edinburgh, Scotland	Mar 7 p384 c3 p385 c1
CROMWELL, OLIVER	
	1827
-Anecdote about his guns	Apr 20 p24 c2
	1828
-Anedcote about high standard of his army	Apr 4 p14 c2
-Would have felt no compunction about killing King Charles I in battle	Aug 24 p172 c3
CUFFEE, CAPTAIN PAUL	
	1827
-Memoirs appearing in the Edinburgh Review, August 1811	Mar 16 p1 c3-4 Mar 23 p5 c1-2 Mar 30 p9 c1 Apr 6 p13 c1 Apr 13 p17 c1-2
-Early friend of the American colonization Society	Sep 12 p110 c1
CUGUANO, OTTOBAH	
	1827
-Former slave who wrote on slavery and the slave trade	May 18 p38 c1
	1828
-Describes capture and attainment of freedom	Nov 21 p276 c2-3
CUMMINGS, DAVID (Captain)	
	1827
-Dies from accident while repairing boat	May 4 p31 c1

CUNNINGHAM, SEYMOUR

1827

-Runaway slave apprehended in Boston; city's blacks then buy his freedom — May 25 p41 c1-2

CURTIS, JOHN

1829

-Freed slave musician to give a concert in New York City (Advertisement) — Feb 7 p351 c3

CURTIS, JOSEPH

1828

-Appointed to the correspondence committee of the New York Manumission Society — May 9 p48 c1

CUSICK, DAVID

1827

-Publishes a history of American Indians — Aug 3 p83 c2

CUSTOMS

1828

-Explains use of Yule Log in England — Nov 21 p277 c2

1829

-Satrical comment on many polite customs — Jan 31 p343 c1-2

CUTTING, LEONARD M.

1827

-One of the founders of the New York Manumission Society — Oct 12 p122 c2

D

d'ALMEYDRA, MANUEL PEDRO

1828

-Describes his life as a slave trader — Apr 25 p33 c1-3 p34 c1

DALEY, WILLIAM

1827

-Appointed Secretary of the African Education Benevolent Society of Chilicothe (Ohio) — Apr 6 p2 c1

DARROW, COLONEL GEORGE

1827

-Sentenced to five years in the Ohio penitentiary for counterfeiting — Apr 20 p24 c1-2

DASHALL, DICK

1828

-Searching for a wife — Oct 10 p226 c2-3 let.

DAUGHTERS OF ISREAL (New York City)

1828

-Celebrate their anniversary with a parade — Aug 15 p166 c1

DAURENCE, JOSEPH

1827

-One of the founders of the New York Manumission Society — Oct 12 p122 c2

DAVAUGH, JONATHAN

1827

-Found guilty of murdering Tobias Martin — May 4 p31 c4

DAVIES, PRESIDENT (Princeton University)

1827

-Description of preaching and anecdote of encounter with George III — Nov 30 p152 c2

DAVIS, CHARLES

1828

-Attempted suicide to prevent return to slavery — Oct 24 p245 c3

DAVIS, MARY

1827

-Describes kidnapping of her son in 1812 — Mar 16 p2 c3-4

DAY, MALHOUN

1828

-Appointed to committee to collect clothing for children of the African Free School — Mar 7 p197 c1

-Appointed to the correspondence committee of the New York Manumission Society — May 9 p49 c1

DE GRASS, GEORGE (Brooklyn and Flushing, New York)

1827 - 1829

-Agent for the Freedom's Journal — Dec 7, '27 p156 c4- Mar 28, '29 p412 c3

DEAFNESS	
	<u>1828</u>
-Describes societies for the deaf in the United States	Aug 29 p174 c1
DEARBORN, LYDIA (Boston, Massachusetts)	
	<u>1829</u>
-Corrects the crippled foot of a child	Jan 2 p311 c1-2
DEATH	
	<u>1827</u>
-Reports proportion of deaths of women to men	May 4 p31 c3
-Reports deaths in England	May 4 p31 c3
-Discusses inevitability of death	Jun 8 p50 c3-4
-Discusses skeletons	Nov 30 p150 c4 p151 c1
-Anonymous eulogy	Dec 7 p154 c2-3
	<u>1828</u>
-Statistics for deaths in New York City in 1827	Feb 15 p187 c4
-Description of man being revived after hanging	May 9 p53 c1-2
-Young girl describes feelings at death of her mother	Jun 20 p102 c1-2
	<u>1829</u>
-Explains why black is the mourning color	Jan 2 p314 c1-2
DEBATING	
	<u>1827</u>
-Explains advantages of a debating society	Sep 7 p102 c4 let.
DEBOYES, HENRY	
	<u>1828</u>
-Appointed to committee to plan 1828 celebration of New York abolition	May 16 p61 c3
DEMONSTRATIONS (Mob)	
	<u>1827</u>
-Feels demonstrations can only hurt the black cause	Jun 29 p63 c2-3 ed.
DEMPSEY, MR.	
	<u>1827</u>
-Sentenced to five years for murdering his wife	Apr 27 p26 c4

DENHAM, COLONEL

1828

-Appointed Lieutenant Governor of Sierra Leone — Feb 22 p191 c1
-Dies and is eulogized — Oct 10 p230 c1

DENNIS, REVEREND (Massachusetts)

1828

-Stresses the importance of knowledge — Aug 8 p153 c1-2

DERHAM, JAMES (Dirkum)

1827

-Former slave who was the best doctor in New Orleans in the early 18th century — May 18 p38 c1

1828

-Freed slave who became an excellent doctor in New Orleans — Nov 14 p265 c3

DEWAR, JAMES

1828

-Sold a free black woman into slavery — Sep 5 p189 c1-3 p190 c1

DICKINSON, DOCTOR (Barbadoes)

1827

-Feels slave labor is more expensive than free labor — Aug 24 p93 c1

DICKINSON, R. (Thomas Dickson) (Liverpool, England)

1828 - 1829

-Agent for the Freedom's Journal — Jul 25, '28 p144 c3- Mar 28, '29 p412 c3

DIRKUM, JAMES
-See Derham, James

DISEASE

1827

-Discourse on inevitability of illness — Oct 5 p118 c4

1828

-Cause of seasickness explained — Aug 15 p164 c2-3
-Outbreak of small pox in New Jersey — Aug 22 p174 c2

DIXON, DOCTOR

1827

-Arrives in Africa and proceeds to Timbuctoo — Mar 16 p3 c3

DOUGE, MICHAEL

-Marries Susan Ainos — 1827 — Apr 6 p15 c4

DRAPER, G. & R.

-Tobacco products for sale to blacks only through Samuel Cornish (Advertisement) — 1827 — Oct 5 p120 c3

DRAYTON, REVEREND HENRY
-See First Coloured Wesleyan Methodist Church of New York City

DUBOIS, HENRY
-Offers reward for return of runaway apprentice — 1827 — Aug 31 p100 c2

DUELING

-Describes practice of dueling and frequency in the United States — 1827 — May 25 p42 c1-2; Jun 1 p45 c1-2

-Made illegal in the United States — 1828 — Feb 1 p179 c4

DUNDAR, GEORGE

-President of Abolition Society of Stark County, Ohio explains Society's views on slavery — 1827 — Dec 7 p153 c1-4

-Listed as President of Abolition Society of Stark County, Ohio — 1828 — Sep 19 p208 c3

DUTCHER, SAMUEL, JR.

-Delivers Albany speech on New York emancipation and education of blacks — 1827 — Jul 20 p74 c2-3

DUTTON, REVEREND

-Shop burns down — 1827 — Apr 6 p3 c2

E

EDDY, THOMAS

	1827
-Supports Freedom's Journal	Mar 16-30, pp4, 8, 12, c4
-Obituary	Sep 21 p111 c4

EDUCATION (Blacks)

	1827
-New York Common Schools report enrollment and expenditures for 1826	Mar 16 p1 c4 p2 c1
-Stresses the importance of education to improve the Black's position	Mar 30 p10 c3-4 Apr 6 p14 c3-4
-Describes selfishness of the uneducated and the role of Sabbath schools in education	Apr 13 p18 c2-3
-Describes harm done by an ignorant teacher	Apr 20 p24 c1
-Shows advantage of education through two anecdotes	Apr 27 p28 c2
-Stresses importance of education at an early age	May 11 p34 c2
-Blacks in Philadelphia form a society to raise money for a school	May 11 p34 c2
-Stresses necessity of education and worth of African Free Schools	May 18 p38 c4 p39 c1-2
-People of Color of Belmont County, Ohio open a school	May 25 p43 c4
-Gives advantages of African Free Schools and lists those in existence	Jun 1 p47 c1-3
-States education will eventually remove prejudice	Jun 8 p50 c2-3
-Stresses importance of education in uniting all African peoples	Jun 15 p55 c1-2
-Public education established in Haiti by the republican government	Jun 29 p62 c2-4
-Adults should teach children morality by example	Jul 13 p70 c1
-Samuel Dutcher, Jr., explains limitless opportunities for blacks if educated.	Jul 20 p74 c1-3

-View that education will stop prejudice of whites; favors formation of literary associations	Jul 27 p78 c4 let.
-Reader states education is the most important thing for blacks	Aug 3 p82 c3-4 let.
-Reader stresses importance of education for females	Aug 10 p86 c2-3 let.
-Development of public libraries will be very important to blacks	Oct 5 p119 c1-3
-Music school at St. Phillip's Church in New York City advertised	Oct 19 p127 c4
-Stresses importance of education and urges attendance at evening and Sabbath schools	Nov 23 p147 c1-2 ed.
-Expresses hope new year will bring education to more blacks	Dec 21 p162 c2-3
-New York Manumission Society divides city into districts and plans house-to-house campaign for African Free Schools	Dec 21 p163 c1-2
-School for blacks 2-5 years old planned for New York City	Dec 21 p163 c2
	<u>1828</u>
-South Carolina prohibits blacks being educated	Jan 11 p166 c1
-Effort to solicit black families to enlarge enrollment in African Free Schools of New York	Jan 11 p166 c4
-Outlines advantages of attending Sabbath Schools	Jan 18 p170 c1
-Nursery school planned for blacks in Philadelphia	Feb 1 p179 c2-3
-Describes nursery schools in England	Feb 8 p182 c1-2
-Summer school for blacks in Portsmouth, New Hampshire paid for by the town	Feb 8 p183 c2
-American Convention for Promoting Abolition of Slavery asks country to help in education of blacks	Feb 15 p185 c3-4
-Agent for <u>Freedom's Journal</u> solicits aid from whites for black education	Feb 15 p187 c1-2 let.
-View that the best education for blacks comes through school with whites	Feb 15 p187 c2-3 ed.

-Describes a life of ignorance and advises education — Mar 14 p200 c2-4
-Thomas Jennings advises blacks to learn a trade to raise their position — Apr 4 p12 c1-3
-Reverend Peter Williams stresses importance of schools for blacks — Jun 13 p92 c1-3 p93 c1
-Asks more blacks to educate their children — Sep 12 p194 c3

1829

-Hopes slaves in West Indies will be allowed an education — Jan 31 p341 c3 p342 c1
-African Infant School of New York City moves location — Mar 7 p382 c1
-See also African Free School of New York City; Asylum for Indigent Boys; Infant School Society of Philadelphia; Manumission Society of New York; Nursery Schools; School Society of Philadelphia

EDUCATION (General)

1827

-Any class of people can become educated — Jul 6 p66 c1
-Lists advantages of using newspapers in schools — Jul 6 p66 c1-2
-Best time to study is at night — Jul 13 p70 c1
-Outlines educational system of Columbia (Colombia) — Jul 27 p78 c3
-Attack on military academies — Aug 31 p97 c3-4
-Describes educational system in Hungary — Oct 19 p128 c2
-Teaching seen as the most important profession in the world — Nov 2 p136 c2

1828

-Stresses advantages of knowing a trade — Apr 11 p18 c3
-Reverend Mr. Blagden states that education produces moral character — May 23 p66 c1-2
-Reverend Peter Williams advises starting Christian education early — Jun 6 p84 c1-3
-Reverend Mr. Dennis stresses the importance of knowledge — Aug 8 p153 c1-2
-Two hundred infant schools in England started in the past year — Aug 8 p155 c3

-Lists number of schools and students in the Boston area	Nov 7 p258 c3
-Vermont school teacher describes meals at homes of students	Nov 21 p275 cl-2
-Education civilizes man and makes him appreciate life	Nov 21 p276 cl-2
-Man cannot rise above animal level without education	Dec 19 p294 c4 p295 cl
	1829
-Number of students in New England colleges given	Jan 9 p322 c2

EGYPT

	1827
-Discusses Egyptian culture and relation of Black race to Egyptians	Apr 6 p3 cl-2
-Discusses physical closeness of ancient Egyptians and Ethiopians	Apr 13 p18 c4 p19 cl
-Professor Scyffarth of Leipzig translates hieroglyphics concerning dynasties, Jewish slavery, and contact with Mexico	May 18 p40 c2
-Explains Hebrew slavery in ancient Egypt	Jun 29 p61 cl-3
-States that Egypt was the center of ancient culture	Jul 6 p65 cl-2 Jul 13 p69 cl-2
-Traces the origins of African people to Egypt	Aug 17 p90 c2-4
-Describes Egyptian colonization of China and cites similarities between the two civilizations	Aug 24 p94 c3-4
-Traces Egyptian emigrations to Greece, Carthage, and Sidonia	Aug 31 p97 c4 p98 cl-2
-Retained greatness because of importance of agriculture	Aug 31 p98 c2-3
-States Egyptians were black	Dec 12 p290 c2
	1829
-Seen as birthplace of civilization	Feb 7 p349 cl-3
-See also Carthage; Ethiopia; Greece; Sidonia	

ELIZABETH I (England)

1827

-Expresses admiration of her abilities — Aug 17 p92 c2

1828

-Describes her belief in superstition — Jan 18 p170 c1-2

EMANCIPATION (General)

1827

-Methods of emancipation discussed — Apr 13 p17 c2-4

-See also Abolition; American Colonization Society; Colonization

EMANCIPATION (New York)

1827

-Emancipation celebrations planned for July 4th and 5th — Jun 22 p58 c3

-Advises blacks to stay in agriculture — Jun 22 p58 c3

-Asks blacks to thank God for abolition and act dignified — Jun 29 p62 c4, p63 c1

-Reader feels there should only be one celebration for abolition — Jun 29 p43 c1-2 let.

-People of Colour of Otsege County will hold celebration in Cooperstown, New York — Jun 29 p63 c4

-Describes celebration in New York City — Jul 6 p67 c1

-Governor Daniel D. Tompkins sets date for abolition — Jul 13 p70 c2

-Reader praises abolition celebration — Jul 13 p70 c3-4 let.

-Colored Inhabitants of Fredericksburgh, Virginia celebrate New York abolition — Jul 13 p70 c4

-Parade to celebrate abolition planned — Jul 13 p71 c1

-Blacks of Albany hold parade to celebrate abolition — Jul 13 p71 c3

-Describes celebration in Cooperstown, New York — Jul 13 p71 c3

-Speech delivered in Albany on emancipation — Jul 13 p71 c3

-Friendship Society of Baltimore celebrates abolition — Jul 20 p74 c4

-People in Rochester, New York celebrate emancipation — Jul 20 p75 c4

-Reverend Nathaniel Paul in Albany delivers speech praising men who worked for New York Abolition — Aug 10 p85 c3

-Reader defends speech given in Connecticut on celebration of New York Emancipation — Sep 7 p101 c4 let.
-William Hamilton delivers speech at African Zion Church celebration — Oct 12 p122 c1-2

1828

-Celebration planned for July 5 in New York City — May 9 p54 c2
-Committee appointed to run July 5 celebration — May 16 p61 c3
-Announces celebration of 2nd anniversary of abolition — Jul 4 p115 c3
-Describes New York City celebration of 2nd anniversary of abolition — Jul 11 p122 c2-3
-Describes emancipation celebration held in Chatham, New York — Jul 18 p131 c3
-Condemns celebration in Brooklyn — Jul 18 p134 c1-2 ed.
-Blacks in Rochester hold no celebration due to lack of funds — Jul 25 p138 c2
-People of Brooklyn deny bad conduct at celebration — Aug 1 p147 c1; p148 c3 let.
-Restates criticism of Brooklyn celebration — Aug 1 p150 c3 ed.

EMBREE, LAURENCE

1827

-One of the founders of the New York Manumission Society — Oct 12 p122 c2

EMMET, MR.

1827

-Obituary and eulogy for New York lawyer — Nov 23 p147 c2

ENTERTAINMENT

1827

-A concert of sacred music to be held on October 2 at St. Phillip's Church, New York City — Sep 28 p115 c4
-Sacred music concert date changed — Oct 5 p119 c4
-Praise for concert at St. Phillip's — Oct 12 p123 c2 let.

1829

-Dancing defined as undesirable — Jan 9 p318 c3
-John Curtis, freed slave, to give instrumental concert in New York City — Feb 7 p351 c3

EPISCOPAL CHURCH

1827

-Lists number of clergy as of 1827 — Apr 27 p27 c2

EQUIANO, ALANDO (Olaudah)

1827

-African slave who acquired freedom, wrote memoirs, and attacked slave trade and slavery — May 18 p38 c1

-See also Vasa, Gustavus (Vassa)

ERSKINE, GEORGE

1828

-Collecting money to buy children out of slavery — Jun 13 p94 c3

ETHIOPIA

1827

-Explains high culture of Ethiopians — Jul 13 p69 c1-2

1828

-Traces black origins to ancient Ethiopians and describes Ethiopia's advanced culture — Dec 5 p285 c2-3 p286 c1-2

-See also Egypt; Greek Mythology

EUROPEAN NEWS

1827

-Prince Hatzfield of Prussia dies in Austria — Mar 30 p3 c4

-Lists estimated wheat consumption of England — Mar 30 p4 c1-2

-Recounts attempt on Charles I's life during Civil War — Mar 30 p4 c2

-Relates courtship of two serving people in England — Mar 30 p4 c2

-England receives 3,000,000 Pounds from Spain for losses during Wars of South American independence — Apr 6 p15 c3

-Caracas experiences February earthquake — Apr 6 p15 c3

-Lord Liverpool becomes very ill on voyage from Boston — Apr 6 p15 c3-4

-Portuguese rebels defeated by British — Apr 6 p15 c4

-Describes a divorce law in India — Apr 20 p24 c2

-British conquer and loot part of India — Apr 20 p24 c2

-Reports 1825 population of Rome	Apr 20 p24 c3
-Describes hairdressing in South America	Apr 20 p24 c3
-Indians upset about Russian advance into Persia	Apr 27 p27 c3
-Guardin of France dead at age 60	Apr 27 p27 c3
-Portuguese troop mutinying	Apr 27 p27 c3
-Terrible storm in Canary Islands	Apr 27 p27 c3
-German Prince plans to marry widow of King of Haiti	Apr 27 p27 c3
-Describes building of tunnel under the Thames	May 4 p31 c2
-English mechanic has built a model of Solomon's temple	May 4 p31 c3
-English sugar tariffs to be raised	May 4 p31 c3
-Anecdote about Spanish-Portuguese rivalry	May 4 p32 c2
-George Canning becomes Premier of England	May 11 p35 c2
-Small pox in Sweden and Bavaria	May 11 p35 c3
-England sends money to needy Beethoven	May 11 p35 c3
-England unhappy about Peal's resignation	May 18 p39 c3
-Weavers leaving England for the United States for better wages	May 18 p39 c3
-Lists new cabinet in England	Jun 8 p51 c2
-Tunnel under Thames bursts	Jul 6 p67 c1-2
	1828
-New government formed in England under Duke of Wellington	Mar 21 p206 c4
-Committee set up in England's Parliment to investigate Common Law	Apr 18 p31 c2-3
-Spectators fall in water when newly launched boat hits dock in England	May 2 p43 c2-3
-Woman in England convicted of child murder with no specific evidence	May 23 p69 c1
-Describes coronation procedure of an English King	May 30 p76 c2-3
	1829
-King of Sweden gives speech on budget	Jan 31 p342 c2-3

EVERETT, GEORGE W.

	1827
-Advertises collection agency for libraries	Mar 30-May 4 pp12, 16, 20, 24, 28, 32 c3

EYRE, SIR SIMON

	1828
-Short description of his career as a shoemaker	May 23 p65 c3

F

FAMILY LIFE

	1827
-Advises how to raise children to make them happy	Apr 20 p21 c4
-Advises strong parental control and consistency of actions	Aug 3 p81 c3
-Advises parents to get children to school on time	Nov 30 p157 c1
	1828
-Advises parents not to allow children to gamble	Jan 18 p171 c3
-Reverend Peter Williams advises parents to start religious education early and set a good example	Jun 6 p85 c1-3
-Reverend Peter Williams advises against physical punishment and stresses importance of religious education	Jun 13 p92 c1-3 p93 c1
-Incident about a mother who left her two year old alone and his getting into trouble	Nov 21 p274 c1 p275 c3
-Describes feeling that mothers have for their children	Dec 12 p291 c2
	1829
-Important to impress values in early childhood	Jan 9 p320 c2-3
-Children should be dressed plainly and made to work	Jan 9 p321 c1
-Describes duties of children	Feb 26 p376 c2-3

FASHION

	1828
-Explains foolishness of great expenditure on fashion	May 30 p75 c1-2 ed.
-Reports first use of silk stockings	May 30 p77 c2
-Wide mouths on women are fashionable in Turkey	Jul 25 p138 c3
-Describes female fashion of the 16th century	Jul 25 p141 c2
-Describes making of leghorn hats	Jul 25 p141 c2-3
	1829
-Criticizes people who follow fashion instead of common sense	Jan 9 p320 c3 p321 c1
-Describes uniform of a German university student	Jan 24 p334 c2-3

FERNANDO PO

	1828
-Describes work on island to prepare for arrival of colony from Sierra Leone	Jun 13 p91 c1-2

FINLEY, REVEREND ROBERT

	1827
-Founder of American Colonization Society	Sep 21 p110 c1

FIRES

	1827
-At corner of Grand and Wooster streets in New York City	Apr 6 p15 c3
-At Reformed Dutch Church of Patterson, New Jersey	Apr 6 p15 c3
	1828
-Description of a fire in New York City	Feb 22 p191 c3-4
-Reports fire in a stable between the Bowery and Elizabeth Street; also a fire on Bayard Street, New York City	May 30 p78 c1-2
-Description of a fire in ancient Rome where a black slave chose to die rather than live in slavery	Jun 6 p82 c1-2

FIRST COLOURED WESLEYAN METHODIST CHURCH OF NEW YORK

1828

-Recognizes Reverend Henry Drayton as superintendent and joins African Methodist Episcopal Church of New York City — Jun 6 p82 c3

FIRST COLOURED WESLEYAN METHODIST CHURCH OF TROY, NEW YORK

1828

-Organizes and adopts rules of Methodist Episcopal Church — Jul 25 p139 c3; Aug 29 p170 c3

FISHER, SAMUEL

1827

-Relates story concerning the ghost of a friend's husband — Jun 29 p62 c2

FLORIDA

1827

-Benevolent Society for People of Colour, Alexandria, Virginia, hopes Florida will be a free state — Jun 15 p53 c1-4
-Reports lawlessness in Tallahassee — Dec 7 p155 c1

FONTAINE, JAMES (Virginia)

1827

-Murdered by his slaves — Jun 29 p63 c4

FOREIGN MISSIONARY SOCIETY OF NEW YORK AND BROOKLYN

1828

-Holds first annual meeting — Jan 18 p170 c2

FRANCIS, MRS. MARGARET A.

1828

-Elected president of the African Female Dorcas Association — Feb 15 p187 c4

1829

-Holds weekly meetings of Dorcas Association in her house — Feb 7 p355 c1

FRANKLIN, BENJAMIN

1827

-Cited as an example for youth to follow — Oct 26 p132 c2; Dec 21 p164 c2

	1829
-Good sense seen as his outstanding characteristic	Jan 16 p327 c1
FRANKLIN, SAMUEL	
	1827
-One of the founders of the New York Manumission Society	Oct 12 p122 c2
FRANCISCO, PETER	
	1829
-Described as one of the strongest men in the country	Feb 21 p366 c3 p367 c1
FRATELLI DE LA MISERICORDIA (Brotherhood of Mercy) (Pisa, Italy)	
	1827
-Describes work of this order	May 4 p29 c4 p30 c1 May 11 p33 c4 p34 c1
FRIENDSHIP SOCIETY OF BALTIMORE, MARYLAND	
	1827
-Celebrates New York emancipation	Jul 20 p74 c4
FROST, COLONEL WILLIAM	
	1827
-Discovers knife inside a dead hog	Apr 20 p23 c3
-Great amount of snow in Quebec	Apr 27 p27 c4
-Describes justice in Islam	Apr 27 p28 c2
FUEL SAVING FUND	
	1827
-Society formed to help poor during winter	May 25 p43 c1-2
FULLER, THOMAS	
	1827
-Black resident of Washington, D.C. a good mathematician	May 18 p38 c1
	1828
-Describes mathematical abilities	Nov 14 p265 c3 p266 c1

G

GALLATIN, ALBERT

1829

-Refuses to turn over fugitive slaves in Canada — Jan 16 p325 c1-3 p326 c1

-Paper praises Mr. Gallatin's and British government's decision on fugitive slaves — Jan 16 p330 c1-2 ed.

GALLAUDET, REVEREND
-See Rahahmon, Prince Abduhl

GAMBLING

1828

-Traces origins of lotteries — Sep 26 p212 c1-2
-Explains history of playing cards — Nov 21 p277 c1
-See also Horse Racing

GARDINER, W. R. (Port-au-Prince, Haiti)

1827 - 1828

-Agent for the Freedom's Journal — Mar 23, '27 p8 c4-Sep 12, '28 p200 c3

GARDNER, JOHN

1827

-Marries Anne Smithens — Apr6 p15 c4

GARDNER, WILLIAM

1828

-Corresponding Secretary of the Abolition Society of Stark County, Ohio — Sep 19 p203 c3

GARRIGUES, EDWARD B.

1828

-Secretary of Abolition Society of Pennsylvania — Jan 11 p166 c4

GATES, ALFRED

1827

-Loses two children and his house in a fire — Mar 16 p3 c4

GENERAL COLOURED ASSOCIATION OF BOSTON

1828

-Addressed by David Walker on black solidarity — Dec 19 p295 c1-3 p296 c1

GENIUS OF UNIVERSAL EMANCIPATION

1828

-Praises paper and urges support for it — Mar 21 p207 c2-3 ed.
-See also Lundy, Benjamin

GEOFFREY, L'ISLET

1828

-Black French map maker who explored Madagascar — Nov 14 p265 c2-3

GEOLOGY

1828

-Describes effects of earthquakes — Jul 11 p125 c1
-Describes coal deposits in England — Aug 15 p164 c3

GEORGE III (England)

1828

-Prohibited clergy from praising him — May 30 p77 c2-3

GEORGE, REVEREND SAMUEL (Waterloo, Upper Canada)

1828 - 1829

-Agent for the Freedom's Journal — May 30, '28 p80 c3- Mar 28, '29 p412 c3

GILBERT, JAMES

1827

-Clothes dressing establishment (Advertisement) — Nov 16 p143 c4

GILBERT, THOMAS

1828

-Appointed to committee to plan New York Abolition celebration — May 16 p61 c3

GILL, REVEREND GEORGE M.

1827

-Superintendent of schools in Liberia — Oct 12 p122 c3

GLASKO, ISAAC C. (Glasgow) (Norwich, Connecticut)

1827 - 1829

-Agent for the Freedom's Journal — Aug 3, '27 p84 c4- Mar 28, '29 p412 c3

GLOUCESTER, JEREMIAH (Philadelphia)

	1827
-To deliver speech on education to raise money for school in Philadelphia	May 11 p34 c2
-Advertises school in Philadelphia	Nov 2 p136 c3
	1828
-Dies	Jan 11 p167 c4
-Poem praising Gloucester and mourning his death	Jan 25 p176 c1
-Copies of portriats of him to be sold by his family	Mar 14 p201 c2-3

GLOUCESTER, JOHN (Philadelphia)

	1827
-Secretary of Philadelphia Society raising money for a school	May 11 p34 c2
	1828
-Copies of portrait of him to be sold by family	Mar 14 p201 c2-3

GLOUCESTER, STEPHEN (Philadelphia)

	1828
-His school ("The Academy") praised	Oct 10 p226 c1-2 ed.
	1828 - 1829
-"The Academy" and night school advertised	Sep 12, '28 p199 c1- Mar 28, '29 p411 c3

GOFORTH, WILLIAM

	1827
-One of the founders of the New York Manumission Society	Oct 12 p122 c2

GOLD, MR.

	1827
-Advertises instruction in English grammar	Nov 16 p144 c3

GOLDSBERRY, NICHOLAS

	1828 - 1829
-Cleaning and dying (Advertisement)	Nov 14, '28 p271 c1- Mar 21, '29 p403 c2

GOODMAN, BRADLEY

	1828
-Appointed to committee to plan the celebration of New York abolition	May 16 p61 c3

GOOMS, NATHAN

1828

-Free black who turns in runaway slaves — Nov 14 p267 c2

GRANT, DOCTOR

1827

-Operates on a blind man and restores his sight — Mar 16 p2 c4 p3 c1

GRANT TUDOR E. (Utica, New York)

1828 - 1829

-Agent for the Freedom's Journal — Jul 11, '28 p128 c3- Mar 28, '29 p412 c3

GRANVILLE, J.

1827

-Receives medal from Haiti for defense of a United States newspaper editor — Nov 2 p135 c3

GREECE

1827

-Describes ancient Egyptian colonization — Aug 31 p97 c4 p98 c1-2

1829

-Describes slavery in ancient Greece — Jan 24 p333 c1-2
-Barbaraus state until Egyptian colonization — Feb 7 p349 c1-2
-Dr. John D. Russ criticizes morals of Greek people — Feb 7 p350 c2-3 p351 c1 let.

GREEK MYTHOLOGY

1827

-Shows respect for Ethiopian wisdom and knowledge — Jul 20 p73 c1

GREEK WAR FOR INDEPENDENCE

1827

-New York City blacks hold a ball to aid struggle for Greek independence — Mar 30 p3 c1
-Freedom's Journal denounces aid for Greek independence — Mar 30 p3 c1
-Fund in Boston reaches $11,000 — May 4 p31 c3
-Fortress at Athens well supplied — May 11 p35 c3
-Doctor Thomas (Philadelphia Barber) donates one days' proceeds to the cause — May 25 p43 c2
-Greeks defeat Turks at Piraeus — Jul 27 p79 c3

-British sending naval aid	Jul 27 p79 c3-4
-Greeks suffer great defeat at Asomato	Aug 10 p87 c3
-European powers decide to unite to save Greece	Aug 17 p91 c3
-Russian Consul General appointed	Dec 14 p159 c2
-European powers defeat Egyptian fleet	Dec 21 p163 c3
	1828
-Compares ancient Greek battle to defeat of Turks	Jan 18 p171 c2
-Ladies' Serving Circle of Boston contributes $60	Feb 1 p179 c4
-Description of negotiations between Turkish government and European powers	Feb 29 p195 c1-2
-Arguments in British Parliment over the war	Mar 21 p206 c4 p207 c1-2
-Greek Committee of New York City soliciting all city churches for money	Mar 21 p207 c4
-People of Utica, New York organize to help Greece	Apr 11 p21 c2
-Describes proposed battle	Apr 18 p31 c2
-Ladies of New London, Connecticut send 1700 pieces of clothing	Apr 25 p37 c2
-$220.22 collected in Lenox, New York	May 2 p42 c2
-Brookfield, Missouri collects $200	May 2 p43 c1
-Woman of Providence, Rhode Island makes clothes for Greeks	May 23 p68 c2
-Cargo worth $50,000 sent to Greeks	Jun 6 p85 c1
-States time should be spent freeing blacks as well as Greeks	Dec 12 p290 c2-3 p291 c1 ed.
	1829
-Greeks defeating Turks in many battles	Jan 16 p326 c1-3

GREEN, CHARLES

	1827
-Describes trip in a balloon	Aug 10 p87 c3

GREEN, JAMES

	1827
-Drowns in Savannah, Georgia	Apr 13 p19 c4

GREEN, SARAH	
	1827
-Advertises curing of diseases	Jun 11 p48 c2
GREEN MOUNTAIN FOREST REQUIEM, THE	
	1829
-Paper to be published about religion, morality, agriculture and memory of dead	Jan 24 p338 c1
GREENOUGH, MR. H. (Boston, Massachusetts)	
	1828
-Sculptor commissioned to make busts of John Adams, John Quincy Adams, and John Marshall	May 2 p43 c2
GREETINGS	
	1827
-Explains methods of greeting in different countries	Jun 15 p54 c3-4
GRICE, HEZEKIAH (Baltimore, Maryland)	
	1827 - 1829
-Agent for the Freedom's Journal	Aug 3, '27 p84 c4- Mar 28, '29 p412 c3
GUNPOWDER	
	1828
-Traces invention and explains composition	Sep 26 p213 c1
GUSTAVSON, COUNT (Sweden)	
	1828
-Describes his poverty and respect felt for him	Aug 8 p155 c1
GWYNN, NELL	
	1827
-Gives biographical sketch	May 11 p36 c2-3

H

HACKETT, CHARLES (Baltimore, Maryland)	
	1827
-Agent for the Freedom's Journal	Mar 16, '27 p4 c3- Jul 27, '27 p80 c4

HAINES, EDWARD	
	1828
-Advertises mead garden	May 2 p47 cl- Sep 19 p208 c3
HAIR-DRESSING	
	1828
-Describes unsuccessful attempt to dye hair	May 16 p58 c2
-Explains use of wigs	Jun 27 p109 c3
-See also Abernathy, Mr.	
HAITI	
	1827
-Awaits advice from France concerning tariffs	Mar 16 p3 c2
-Revolution described as a symbol to Blacks	Apr 6 p2 c4
-Describes discovery and early history of Haiti	Apr 20 p22 cl-2
-Describes treatment of slaves before revolution	Apr 27 p26 c3
-Describes beginnings of the revolution	May 4 p30 c2-3
-Reports union doing well	May 4 p31 cl
-Describes revolts in 1792 and 1793 and Napoleon's measures in 1802	Jun 15 p54 c4 p55 cl
-Describes republican government set up after Independence won	Jun 29 p62 c2-4
-Public education established	Jun 29 p62 c2-4
-Haiti seen as example of Black capacities	Jul 13 p69 cl-2
-Plot discovered to overthrow President Jean Pierre Boyer	Aug 3 p83 c2-3
-Representative sent to England and France to negotiate commercial treaties	Sep 21 p111 cl
-Description of geography, climate and trade	Oct 12 p122 c4 p123 cl-2
-Benjamin Lundy to transport freed slaves from America	Dec 21 p162 c3
	1828
-Story about fight for independence	Jan 18 p170 c3-4 p171 cl Jan 25 p174 c3-4 Feb 8 p182 c2-4 Feb 15 p186 c3-4

-Reports small, unsuccessful revolt	Apr 11 p21 c1
-Eighteen people tried for conspiracy against government	Jun 13 p91 c1
-Americans try to use counterfeit money	Jun 27 p106 c2-3
-Experiences political and economic problems	Jul 11 p123 c3
-Government decides to ease taxes and promote foreign trade	Aug 8 p155 c2-3
-Foreigners must register with government upon arrival	Oct 31 p254 c2
-Reports effects on economy of American use of counterfeit money	Nov 14 p267 c3
-Experiencing peaceful, happy period	Dec 12 p291 c1-2 ed.
-Detailed description of barbarous practices of French while in control of the island	Dec 12 p293 c2-3 p294 c1-2
	1829
-Favorable country for American Blacks to emigrate to	Jan 16 p329 c1-2
-Describes reception of two American abolitionists	Feb 14 p360 c3
-See also Belgarde; Boyer, Jean Pierre; Hamilton, Jeremiah; L'ouverture, Toussaint	

HALE, MATTHEW

	1828
-Registrar of Manumission Society of New York	Feb 1 p179 c2

HALE, SARAH J.

	1828
-To publish two ladies' magazines in Boston	Jan 18 p171 c4

HALE, THOMAS

	1828
-Secretary of the Manumission Society of New York	Feb 1 p179 c2
-Appointed to correspondence committee of the New York Manumission Society	May 9 p49 c1

HALL, HENRY P.

	1827
-Advertises sale of hair-dressing shop	Aug 31 p100 c2

HALL, PRINCE

	1828
-Founder of the African Grand Masonic Lodge of Boston	Nov 7 p257 c1
-Praised for work in the Grand Masonic Lodge of Boston	Nov 7 p257 c3

HAMER AND SMITH

	1827
-Cleaning business (Advertisement)	Aug 3 p84 c3

HAMILTON, ALEXANDER

	1827
-One of the founders of the New York Manumission Society	Oct 12 p122 c2
	1828
-Description of tomb	Jan 25 c175 c1

HAMILTON, JEREMIAH

	1828
-Accused of passing counter-feit money in Haiti	Jun 27 p106 c2-3
-Admits passing counterfeit money	Jun 27 p106 c3 p107 c1 let.
-Captain of boat conveying money describes Hamiton's involvement	Jun 27 p110 c1
-Condemns a Black for cheating the Haitian government	Jul 4 p115 c1 ed.
-Severely criticized	Aug 29 p178 c1-2 let.
-Haitian citizen praises <u>Freedom's Journal</u> for exposing Hamilton and gives details of what he did in Haiti	Nov 14 p267 c2-3 let.

HAMILTON, WILLIAM

	1827
-Committee member of People of Colour of New York	Apr 20 p23 c4
-Named chairman of People of Colour of New York	Apr 27 p26 c4
-Delivers speech celebrating New York emancipation in African Zion Church	Oct 12 p122 c1-2

HAMLIN, JOHN

	1827
-Murdered by slaves	Apr 6 p15 c2
-Murderers tried and sentenced to death	Apr 6 p15 c3

HANFORD, MRS.

	1827
-Sentenced to prison for killing her son	Apr 27 p27 c3

HANNIBAL

	1827
-Black who was Lieutenant-General under Peter the Great	May 18 p37 c4
	1828
-Describes career of Hannibal under Peter the Great	Nov 14 p265 c1

HANWAY, JAMES

	1827
-Anecdote about his thin physique	Apr 20 p24 c2

HARDENBURG, SAMUEL

	1827
-Marshall of parade to celebrate New York Abolition	Jul 13 p71 c1
	1828
-Appointed Grand Marshall of New York Abolition Celebration	May 16 p61 c3

HARRISON, LEWIS

	1828 - 1829
-Boarding house (Advertisement)	Jul 25, '28 p143 c1-Mar 28, '29 p412 c2

HARTE, REVEREND WILLIAM (Barbadoes)

	1827
-Criticized by Black parishioners for racism in sermon and communion	Dec 14 p158 c3

HARTFORD (Connecticut)

	1827
-Agent of paper describes city and condition of Blacks there	Aug 31 p99 c1-3

HATCH, ISAAC

	1828
-Appointed to a committee to collect clothing for children of the African Free School	Mar 7 p197 c1

HAWYER, HENRY

	1827
-Imprisoned for burning house of Stephan Rathbone	Mar 16 p3 c4
-See also Rathbone, Stephan	

HEALTH

	1827
-Describes cure of a hypochondriac	Apr 13 p20 c2
-Notes a doctor who blamed illness on poor cooking	Apr 13 p20 c2
-Gives cure for toothaches	May 4 p32 c2
-Gives cure for consumption (Tuberculosis)	Jun 8 p52 c2
-Gives cure for hydrophobia	Jul 6 p68 c2
-Explains cause of most diseases	Aug 10 p88 c2
-Recipe for relief of rheumatism	Aug 31 p100 c2
-Cure for ring worm	Aug 31 p100 c2
-Remedy for toothaches	Sep 21 p112 c2
-Remedy for poor eye-sight	Nov 2 p136 c2
-Statistics on type of people who become insane	Nov 23 p147 c3
	1828
-Cure for burns	Jan 11 p167 c3
-Description of the pain of a toothache	Feb 15 p186 c2-3
-Cure for ring worm	Feb 22 p191 c2
-Cure for toothache	May 9 p52 c2
-Explains conditions that warrant eye glasses	Jul 18 p132 c2
-Remedy for illness from drinking cold water	Aug 1 p147 c2
-Remedy for whooping cough	Oct 24 p246 c3
-Advises how to avoid catching colds	Nov 7 p260 c3
-Explains first use of eye glasses	Nov 21 p277 c3
	1829
-Cure for foot blisters	Jan 24 p337 c2
-Cure for seasickness	Jan 31 p343 c3
-Cure for rheumatism	Feb 7 p350 c2
-Cure for headaches	Feb 21 p368 c2-3

HEBER, BISHOP

	1827
-Excerpt from Sermon in 1823 on life	Jul 6 p65 c4 p66 c1
-See also India; Poetry	

HEBRREW TALES

	1827
-Extracts from stories	Mar 30 p2 c2

HENISON, WILLIAM (North Carolina)

	1827
-Sentenced to death for minor theft	May 18 p38 c3

HENRY III (England)

	1828
-First English King to coin gold	Nov 14 p269 c3

HENRY VI (England)

	1828
-Exposes an imposter who had supposedly experienced a miracle	Oct 31 p253 c2-3

HENRY VIII (England)

	1827
-Describes reasons for his many marriages	May 18 p40 c2
-Issues a proclamation in 1457 on women's behavior	Jun 29 p64 c2
	1829
-Story of how he tricked an abbott	Jan 16 p327 c2

HENRY, CORNELIUS

	1828 - 1829
-Renting a new two-story house (Advertisement)	Dec 26, '28 p307 c1- Mar 28, '29 p411 c3

HENSHAW, SETH (New Salem, North Carolina)

	1828 - 1829
-Agent for the Freedom's Journal	Jan 11, '28 p168 c4- Mar 28, '29 p412 c3

HERODOTUS

	1827
-States that Blacks are physically superior to Whites	Jul 20 p73 c1

HICKS, GEORGE

	1828
-Falsely accused of betraying an escaped slave in Washington, D. C.	Jun 27 p110 c3

HILTON, JOHN	
	1828
-Delivers speech to African Grand Masonic Lodge of Boston (June, 1828)	Nov 7 p257 c1-3 p258 c1-3
-See also African Grand Masonic Lodge of Boston	
HINTON, FREDERICK	
	1827
-Advertises a Gentleman's Dressing Room in Philadelphia	Oct 12 p123 c4
HISTORY	
	1827
-Describes downfall of great ancient civilizations	Apr 20 p23 c1-3
-Very brief sketch of Fall of Rome	Sep 21 p112 c2
HODGSON, ADAM	
	1827
-Writes a letter to Jean Baptiste explaining that free labor is cheaper than slave labor	Aug 10 p85 c1-2 Aug 17 p89 c1-2 Aug 24 p93 c1-3 Aug 31 p97 c1-2
-Compares South American slavery to feudalism and examines system of paying slaves	Sep 7 p101 c1-2 Sep 14 p105 c1-2
HOGAN, EWING	
	1827
-Wanted for murder of John Wills	Apr 27 p26 c3-4
HOLLAND	
	1827
-Describes Dutch punishment for idlesness	Apr 6 p1 c1-2
HOLLAND, FREDERICK (Brooklyn, New York)	
	1827 - 1829
-Agent for the Freedom's Journal	Dec 14, '27 p160 c4- Mar 28, '29 p412 c3

HOME CONSTRUCTION

1827

-Relays James Miller of Glasgow's method of building a cottage — Mar 30 p4 c2

HOPKINS, POLLY

1828

-Complains about husband's drinking and other bad habits — Sep 12 p195 cl let.

HORSE RACING

1828

-Explains origin — Aug 8 p158 cl-2

HORTON, GEORGE M.

1828

-Recounts his education as a slave — Aug 8 p153 c2-3
-Poem, "On the Evening and Morning" — Aug 15 p166 c2
-People plan to buy his freedom — Aug 29 p179 c2-3
-Poem, "On the Poetic Music" — Aug 29 p182 c2-3
-Poem"Gratitude" — Sep 5 p190 c2
-Paper asks for money to buy his freedom — Sep 12 p194 c3 p195 cl ed.

-Praises David Walker for contributing and asks for aid of others — Oct 3 p218 c3

HOTTENTOTS
-See London Missionary Society

HOUSE FOR JUVENILE OFFENDERS (Boston, Massachusetts)

1829

-Gives statistics of enrollment and changes name to Juvenile Institute — Jan 31 p346 c2

HOWARD, MR.

1828

-Attempts prison reform in England — Oct 31 p253 cl-2

HOWARD, PETER (New Orleans, Louisiana)

1828 - 1829

-Agent for the Freedom's Journal — Jul 4, '28 p120 c3- Mar 28, '29 p412 c3

HOWLAND, SARAH

1827

-Being tried for murder in Newport, Rhode Island — Apr 27 p26 c4

HOYT, REVEREND O. P.
-See Slavery

HUGH MAXWELL, THE

1827

-Ship provides service between Albany and New York — Mar 16 p3 c4

HUGHES, REVEREND B. F. (Newark, New Jersey)

1827

-Advertises opening of school — Mar 16 p4 c3
-Advertises curriculum — Mar 23-May 4 pp8, 12, 16, 20, 24, 28, 32 c3

-To address Boyer Lodge to celebrate St. John's Day — Jun 22 p58 c3
-Speaks to Boyer Lodge concerning conduct of Masons — Jul 20 p75 cl
-Speech to Boyer Lodge praised — Jul 20 p75 cl ed.
Jul 27 p79 cl ed.

1827 - 1828

-Agent for the Freedom's Journal — Mar 16, '27 p4 c3-
Oct 31, '28 p256 c3

HUME, DAVID

1827

-Sees slave labor as much more expensive than free labor — Aug 17 p89 cl-2

I

IFFLAND, DR. VON

1827

-Tells of treating a dog in Quebec — Apr 6 pl6 c2

INDIA

1828

-Bishop Heber describes Indian people — May 16 p62 c3
p63 cl-2

INDIANS (American)

1827

- -Describes an Indian tracking a thief — Apr 27 p28 c2
- -Kankakees in great need — May 4 p31 c3
- -Describes a Cherokee village — Jul 13 p71 c2
- -Three Indians executed in Georgia for killing Whites — Jul 27 p79 c2
- -Indian, David Cusick, publishes history of Indians — Aug 3 p83 c2
- -Describes treatment of a witch — Nov 23 p147 c2

1828

- -Cherokees develop written language — Feb 8 p183 c3-4
- -Chief of a tribe in Nova Scotia petitions the government to stop sale of liquor to Indians — Mar 21 p207 c4
- -Osages and Pawnees at war — Apr 4 p13 c2
- -Choctaws establish school for their children — Aug 1 p151 c1-2
- -Condemns Whites for killing too many Indians and describes admirable qualities of Indian culture — Nov 7 p260 c1-2
- -Reports meeting between President Adams and Chief of Winnebagos concerning possibility of peace — Dec 19 p297 c1-2

1829

- -Describes marriage ceremony of Canadian Indians — Jan 9 p321 c3 p322 c1
- -Winnebagos ready to live peacefully — Jan 16 p326 c3
- -Two Winnebagos tried for killing White settlers — Jan 16 p333 c2-3
- -Relates death of last member of Squirrel tribe — Jan 24 p337 c1-2
- -Osage nation at war with settlers — Jan 31 p342 c2
- -Describes ordination of an Indian to Baptist ministry — Jan 31 p346 c1-2
- -See also Cherokee Phoenix; Columbus Enquirer

INDUSTRIALIZATION

1827

- -First cotton factory in Virginia established — Aug 10 p87 c1

-Three-wheeled, horeseless carriage developed in Dublin	Sep 7 p103 c2
-Describes use of a gasoline engine on a boat	Sep 7 p104 c2
-James Radcliffe applies steam engine to canal boats	Sep 21 p111 c1
	1828
-Describes new engine and proposed trial run	Apr 4 p15 c3
-Improved method of copper plate printing invented	Apr 25 p39 c2
-Lists British laws prohibiting use of faulty dyes in clothing industry	Sep 26 p212 c2-3

INFANT SCHOOL SOCIETY (Philadelphia, Pennsylvania)

	1828
-Infant school for Blacks opening with 40 students	May 9 p51 c3
-School praised	Jul 11 p122 c1-2 let.

INSECTS

	1827
-Gives recipe for an insecticide	Jun 15 p56 c2
-Describes way to keep insects away	Sep 7 p104 c2
	1828
-Circulatory systems discovered in insects	May 16 p63 c3
-Reports giant spiders in Brazil	May 30 p77 c3
-Describes insect fights	Jun 20 p102 c1
-Gives insecticide for moths	Aug 8 p159 c1

INTEMPERANCE
-See Alcohol; Beecher, Dr. (Lyman); Temperance

IRELAND

	1827
-Forming a society under Lord Farnham for reformation	Mar 16 p3 c2
-Describes Irish Egg trade	Mar 16 p4 c2-3
	1828
-Little emigration in 1827 because of good crops	Sep 19 p205 c3
-Catholics demanding emancipation	Nov 21 p274 c2-3

J

JACKSON, ANDREW

1829

- -Burned in effigy at Hartford, Connecticut — Feb 7 p354 c1
- -Gave soldier who had lost both arms in battle, $100 — Mar 7 p382 c2

JAMAICA

1827

- -Gives statistics on slaves brought to island — Aug 17 p90 c1

1828

- -Rejects liberal slave laws of Lord Bathurst — Sep 19 p204 c1-2
- -Has not obeyed Parliament in appointing a Protector of Slaves to guarantee good treatment — Dec 12 p289 c1-3 p290 c1

1829

- -Reports trouble with Black population — Jan 2 p310 c2-3
- -Reports persecution of missionaries — Mar 7 p381 c1-3 p382 c1
- -See also Bathurst, Lord

JAMES I (England)

1828

- -Anecdote about the Spanish ambassador and a professor of sign language — May 2 p45 c2-3
- -Three of his dogs fight a lion — Oct 17 p237 c1-2

JAY, JOHN

1827

- -One of the founders of the New York Manumission Society — Oct 12 p122 c2

JAY, PETER A.

1828

- -Second Vice-President of the New York Manumission Society — Feb 1 p179 c2

JAY, REVEREND WILLIAM

1829

- -Short discourse on the pleasures of a home — Feb 7 p352 c2-3

JEFFERSON, THOMAS

1827

-Excerpt of 1814 letter showing lack of hope for end of slavery in present generation — Apr 20 p21 c1
-Foresees struggle over slavery — Sep 7 p101 c3

JENNINGS, THOMAS L.

1827

-Wishes to buy used clothing (Advertisement) — Mar 30-May 4 pp12, 16, 20, 24, 28, 32 c3
-Committee member of People of Colour of New York — Apr 20 p23 c4
-Named Secretary of People of Colour of New York — Apr 27 p26 c4
-Named to committee for celebration of slavery's abolition in New York — May 4 p30 c4

1828

-Speaks on education and opposition to colonization — Apr 4 p12 c1-3

JOHN II (Sweden)

1828

-Describes his assassination — May 9 p52 c3

JOHNSON, ARCHIBALD

1827

-Tried for helping a slave to escape — May 18 p39 c2

JOHNSON, ELEANOR J.
-See Johnson, Richard B.

JOHNSON, ELIZA

1828

-Boarding house (Advertisement) — Jun 13 p95 c1-Sep 19 p208 c2

JOHNSON, JEFFREY

1828

-Appointed to committee to plan celebration of slavery's abolition in New York — May 16 p61 c3

JOHNSON, RICHARD

1828

-Boarding house (Advertisement) — Feb 29 p196 c2

JOHNSON, RICHARD B.

	1827
-Death of nine year old daughter, Eleanor, in Philadelphia	Apr 13 p19 c4

JOHNSON, SAMUEL

	1828
-Views on importance of perseverance	Apr 4 p11 c1

JOHNSON, SARAH

	1828
-Millenary shop (Advertisement)	May 2 p46 c3

JOHNSON, WILLIAM P.

	1828
-Appointed to committee to plan celebration of slavery's abolition in New York	May 16 p61 c3
	1828 - 1829
-Advertises shoe store	Apr 4, '28 p11 c3- Mar 28, '29 p411 c3

JOKES

	1827
-Polish joke	Mar 30 p4 c2
	1828
-Two jokes	Mar 14 p202 c1
-Anecdote about a Parisian in Amsterdam	Aug 15 p165 c2-3

JONES, GRACY

	1828
-Boarding house (Advertisement)	Apr 25 p39 c3- Sep 5 p191 c1

JONES, JOSEPH

	1827
-Chosen Vice-President of the Jordan Missionary Society	Dec 7 p154 c4

JONES, WILLIAM

	1828
-Appointed to committee to plan celebration of slavery's abolition in New York	May 16 p61 c3

JORDAN, MARK J.

	1827
-Marries Catherine Bloom	Apr 20 p23 c4

JORDAN MISSIONARY SOCIETY

1827

-Formed to spread Bible among New York Blacks — Dec 7 p154 c4

JOSEPH, FRANCIS

1827

-Dies fighting fire at John Bowen and Company — Mar 16 p3 c3

JUDKINS, JOEL

1827

-Commits suicide — Mar 16 p3 c4

JUSTICE (General)

1828

-Short explanation on virtue of justice — May 16 p61 c1

-Example of a man wrongly accused of murder in Pennsylvania — Oct 10 p227 c2-3

JUVENILE GAZETTE (Providence, Rhode Island)

1828

-Smallest paper in the world — May 9 p50 c1

K

KELLY, JAMES K. (Newark, New Jersey)

1828

-Desires a hair dresser for one year (Advertisement) — Apr 25 p40 c1; May 2 p47 c2

KEEFE, JOHN

1827

-One of the founders of the New York Manumission Society — Oct 12 p122 c2

KEEN, MR. M (Vermont)

1829

-Condemns slave trade in Washington, D.C. — Jan 2 p309 c1-2

KENNEDY, JOHN H. (Philadelphia, Pennsylvania)

1827

-Writes a series of articles favorable to the American Colonization Society — Sep 14 p106 c3-4; Sep 21 p109 c4, p110 c1-2

Sep 28 p114 c2-4
Oct 5 p117 c4
p118 c1-2
Oct 12 p122 c3-4
Oct 19 p126 c2-4
Oct 26 p130 c2-3
Nov 2 p134 c2-3
Nov 16 p142 c1-2
Nov 23 p145 c4
p146 c1

-Views on Liberia and colonization criticized — Nov 9 p138 c1-3 ed.
-See also American Colonization Society

KIDNAPPING

1827

-Kidnapping termed a felony punishable by imprisonment — Apr 20 p23 c3-4
-People kidnapped from Philadelphia for slavery — Jul 6 p67 c4
-Describes penalty in ancient Israel for kidnapping for slavery — Jul 20 p73 c4, p74 c1
-Two free Black girls kidnapped in Charleston, South Carolina — Aug 31 p99 c4

1828

-Two Black boys kidnapped from Philadelphia returned — Jan 18 p171 c1-2
-Description of death of one of the Philadelphia boys — Feb 15 p186 c1-2
-Two Black boys kidnapped in 1825 returned to Philadelphia — May 23 p68 c3
-Mayor of Philadelphia offers a reward for kidnappers of Blacks — Jul 25 p141 c3
-Formation of a Protective Society against kidnapping suggested in New York City — Dec 5 p283 c2-3
-See also Dewar, James; O'Connor, Andrew; Pisco, Eliza; Protecting Society for the City and County of Philadelphia; Smith, Captain John

KNAPP, SAMUEL L.
-See Masons

L

LADY ADAMS, THE

1827

-Ship burned on whaling expedition (1823) Mar 16 p3 c3

LAIGHT STREET CHURCH

1828

-Resolves to restore honor to Sunday May 23 p68 c2

LAING, MAJOR

1828

-Conducted extensive explorations in interior of Africa May 16 p61 c3

LATHROHP, J. W.

1827

-Recording Secretary of Abolition Society of Stark County, Ohio Dec 7 p153 c1-4

LAURENCE, JOHN

1827

-One of the founders of the New York Manumission Society Oct 12 p122 c2

LAW, JAMES

1827

-Tailor and cleaning shop (Advertisement) May 18 p40 c3

LAWRENCE, CAPTAIN JAMES

1828

-Description of his tomb and praise of his courage in battle Jan 25 p175 c1

LAWRENCE, PETER

1827

-Dies Mar 16 p4 c3

LEAD POISONING

1827

-Three men die from drinking beer conveyed in lead pipes Aug 10 p87 c1

LEE, HENRY

1827

-Secretary of the Jordan Missionary Society Dec 7 p154 c4

LEE, JAMES

1828

-Receives pastorship of new Methodist Episcopal Church in New York City — Jan 25 p174 c2-3

LEE, PHILLIP

1829

-Slave in Virginia for whom money is being collected to buy the freedom of his wife and children — Jan 31 p341 c1-3

LEE, PROFESSOR

1829

-Praises Professor Lee's intellect and knowledge of nine languages — Jan 2 p310 c1-2 let.

LEVECK, CHARLES H.

1827

-Recording Secretary of the Bush Education Society of Philadelphia — Sep 28 p115 c4

LEWIS, ENOCH

1827

-Begins publishing The African Observer — Apr 6 p15 c2
-See also The African Observer

LEWIS, PETER

1828

-Barber shop for Blacks (Advertisement) — Sep 26 p215 c1-
Nov 7 p263 c2

LEWISTOWN, PENNSYLVANIA

1827

-Experiences terrible wind storm — Apr 20 p23 c3

LIBERIA

1827

-Praised for success — Aug 24 p94 c2 let.
-Members of American Colonization Society report on the culture present in Liberia — Sep 28 p114 c1
-Excerpt from American Colonization Society's report on progress of Liberia — Oct 12 p122 c3-4
-Liberians building ships to transport Blacks from America — Nov 2 p134 c2-3

-Farmer of Liberia invents a new plough — Nov 9 p139 c4

1828

-Relates report of happiness of Liberians — Jan 25 p175 c2-3
-Praises rapid advancement of Liberians — Jan 25 p175 c2-3
-Suitability of climate of Liberia questioned — Feb 29 p194 c2-3
-Reports fatalities on a voyage bringing colonists from America — May 16 p60 c1

-Reports progress of colony and describes colonists — Jun 20 p100 c1-3
-Suitability of colony questioned — Jul 18 p129 c1-3 let.
-Products of Liberia displayed in Washington office of Colonization Society — Aug 29 p179 c1 let.
-Founder, Mr. Ashmun, returns to states due to poor health — Aug 29 p182 c1
-Reports progress of settlement and construction of a new town, Millsburg — Nov 7 p261 c2

1829

-Short description of the colony — Feb 21 p367 c2-3
-See also American Colonization Society; Ashmun, Mr. (Jehudi); Cary, Lott; Randall, Dr. Richard

LIBERTY

1827

-Short discourse on freedom — Nov 9 p140 c2
-"The Captive" by Stearne; laments captivity and loss of liberty — Nov 23 p145 c4
-Describes role of press in retaining liberty for society — Dec 21 p162 c4 p163 c1

1829

-Describes man's desire for liberty — Feb 21 p370 c1-2
-See also Civil Rights

LIVELY, WILLIAM

1828

-School in Baltimore (Advertisement) — Jul 11 p127 c2-Aug 29 p184 c2

LOCKWOOD, STEPHEN

1827

-Badly burned in explosion of the ship Oliver Ellsworth — Mar 30 p3 c3

LONDON AFRICAN ASSOCIATION

1827

-Excerpts from 21st report regarding slave trade; condemns United States for internal slave trade — Sep 14 p105 c3-4 p106 c1

LONDON MISSIONARY SOCIETY

1828

-Work of Society has revealed capabilities of Hottentots — Jun 13 p93 c2

LOPEZ, MR.

1827

-Fire burns his grocery store — Mar 30 p3 c3

LOUIS XI (France)

1827

-Anecdote about an encounter with a priest — Jun 22 p60 c2

L'OUVERTURE, TOUSSAINT

1827

-Describes life of T. L'ouverture — May 4 p30 c1-2; May 11 p33 c1-2

-Describes battle with French troops and arrest — May 18 p37 c1-3

-Short description of his character — May 18 p38 c1-2

-See also Haiti

LOVERIDGE, PRINCE

1827

-Delivers speech at 17th anniversary of the African Association for Mutual Relief — Mar 30 p2 c4

LUBOMIRSAKA, PRINCESS

1827

-Shoots a bear to save her own life — Apr 27 p28 c1

LUNDY, BENJAMIN

1827

-Editor of the Genius of Universal Emancipation assaulted by a slave dealer — Apr 27 p27 c2

-Receives news from Haiti — May 4 p31 c2

-To transport emancipated slaves to Haiti — Dec 21 p162 c3

	1828
-Makes 1,600 mile anti-slavery trip on foot through New England and up-state New York	Oct 24 p243 c1
	1829
-His work for abolition praised	Feb 21 p368 c1-2 ed.
-See also Genius of Universal Emancipation; Woodfolk, Mr. (Slave Dealer)	
LYONS (France)	
	1827
-Records -13 degrees on February 24	Mar 16 p3 c3

M

MADISON, MRS. BETSEY	
	1827
-Dies	Mar 16 p4 c3
MAGNY, GENERAL	
	1827
-Resigns from governorship of Haiti	Mar 16 p3 c2
MALIBRAN, E.	
	1828
-Tried in New York for involvement in the slave trade	May 30 p77 c3
MANN, THOMAS	
	1827
-Appointed to committee to arrange celebration of abolition anniversary in Cooperstown, New York	Jun 29 p63 c4
MANUMISSION SOCIETY OF NEW YORK	
	1827
-Founders: William Backhouse, Zebulon Barstow, Thomas Bowne, Robert Brown, Ebenezer S. Burling, Thomas Burling, Elijah Cock, James Cogswell, Leonard M. Cutting, Joseph Daurence, Laurence Embree, Samuel Franklin,	

William Goforth, Alexander Hamilton, John Jay, John Keefe, John Laurence, John Murray, William Shotwell, Melancton Smith, Colonel Robert Thorp, Matthew Vicker, Peter Yates	Oct 12 p122 c2
-Given credit for quickening emancipation in New York	Oct 12 p122 c2
-Work of Society praised	Nov 9 p137 c4 p138 c1
-Praises work of its school	Nov 16 p141 c3
-Hold meeting to discuss progress of African Free Schools in New York	Dec 21 p163 c1-2
	1828
-Joint meeting with trustees of African Free Schools to enlarge enrollment	Jan 11 p166 c3-4
-Holds meeting to plan Society for Black women in New York	Jan 25 p175 c4
-Elects officers for 1828	Feb 1 p179 c2
-Appoints committee to write to abolitionists throughout the country urging support for emancipation in Washington, D. C.	May 2 p46 c2-3
-Asks people of Baltimore to aid in working for abolition in Washington, D.C.	May 9 p49 c1 let.
-Petitions Congress to abolish slavery in Washington, D.C. and asks New York Legislature for support	May 9 p49 c1-3 p50 c1
-Society praised for operating African Free School	Jul 18 p130 c3 p131 c1 let.
-Work in Black education praised	Sep 12 p194 c3
-Holds meeting	Oct 17 p235 c1
-See also African Female Dorcas Association; African Free School	

MANUMISSION SOCIETY OF NORTH CAROLINA

	1828
-Will meet in September	Aug 22 p173 c2

MANUMISSION SOCIETY OF STARK COUNTY, OHIO
-See Abolition Society of Stark County, Ohio

MARANDER, JOHN

	1827
-Appointed to committee of People of Colour of New York for celebration of abolition of slavery	May 4 p30 c4

MARRIAGE

	1827
-North Carolina court allows husbands physically to punish wives	May 11 p35 c2
-Anecdote about a reluctant bridegroom	Jun 22 p58 c2
-Persian anecdote about taming a wife	Jul 20 p74 c2
-Description of a happy marriage	Aug 24 p94 c4 p95 c1
-Young girl complains about fortune-hunting suitors	Sep 7 p102 c3-4
-Explains marriage customs of different countries	Sep 21 p109 c1-3 Sep 28 p113 c1-3 Oct 5 p117 c1-3
-Description of courting customs in the Alps	Oct 19 p125 c3-4 p126 c1
-Anecdote about a man who deserted his wife for seventeen years	Oct 26 p130 c1-2
-Portland, Maine doctor advises girls not to marry until age 24 or 25	Nov 23 p147 c2
	1828
-Attributes marital unhappiness to marriages based on physical attraction	Jan 11 p166 c2-3
-Describes marriage of bride and groom of 60 and 66 years	May 2 p44 c1
-Explains history of the wedding ring	May 23 p69 c3
-Explains image of the perfect wife	Jun 20 p97 c2-3 p98 c1
-Anecdote about marital problems	Jul 4 p115 c2
-Warns against marrying for money	Aug 1 p146 c2
-Lists methods to detect married couples	Aug 1 p146 c3
-Lists advertisements for wives appearing in a British paper	Aug 1 p148 c1

-Advises marriage for love, not money — Aug 22 p172 c1-2 let.
-Husband complains about wife's gossiping — Sep 5 p187 c1-2 let.
-Wife complains about husband's drinking and other bad habits — Sep 12 p195 c1 let.
-Husband sells wife at an auction — Sep 19 p205 c1-2
-Describes marriage as the only thing females think about from the age of fifteen — Sep 26 p210 c1-2

1829

-Outlines duties to occupy time of wives — Jan 9 p317 c3, p318 c1
-Describes duties of wives — Feb 21 p367 c2
-Describes duties of husbands — Feb 21 p367 c3, p368 c1

MARTIN, TOBIAS

1827

-Murdered by Jonathan Davaugh — May 4 p31 c4

MARYLAND

1827

-Repeals law authorizing immediate sale out-of-state of Blacks convicted of petty crimes — Apr 6 p15 c2

1828

-Condemned for allowing slavery and the slave trade — Oct 31 p254 c1-2
-See also Weems, Mr.

MASANIELLO (Thomas Aniello)

1827

-Describes revolt led against Austrians in 1647 — May 4 p29 c2-4, May 11 p33 c2-4

MASONS

1827

-Southern lodges working with the American Colonization Society — Jun 29 p63 c4
-Boyer Lodge of New York City holds St. John's Day celebration — Jul 13 p70 c4
-Grand Lodge of Vermont contributes $100 to American Colonization Society — Nov 2 p135 c4

-Describes Black lodge in Boston — Nov 9 p139 c1 let.
-Franklin Lodge at Danville, Kentucky resolves that the domestic slave trade is wrong — Nov 30 p151 c3

1828

-Baptist Society of LeRoy, New York requests that Baptist masons leave the order — Feb 22 p190 c4
-Samuel L. Knapp to publish book correcting misconceptions about masonry — Nov 7 p262 c1
-See also Hall, Prince; Hilton, John; Sanderson, Thomas; Smith, Boston

MASSACHUSETTS SOCIETY FOR SUPPRESSING INTEMPERANCE
-See Sprague, Charles

MATANZAS

1827

-No Blacks allowed to land without permission of governor — Apr 6 p15 c2

McDOUGAL, ALEXANDER

1827

-One of the founders of the New York Manumission Society — Oct 12 p122 c2

M'ELHENY, THOMAS

1827

-Acquitted in murder trial — May 11 p35 c1

MERMIER, B.

1827

-Restaurant (Advertisement) — Dec 14 p159 c4

METALLURGY

1828

-Describes process of gilding and making gold plate — Aug 8 p157 c2

METEOROLOGY

1829

-Rainfall for Pennsylvania (1827 and 1828) — Jan 9 p319 c1

METHODIST EPISCOPAL CHURCH

1828

-Establishes new church in New York under pastorship of James Lee — Jan 25 p174 c2-3

MEXICO

1829

-Condemns unorganized revolt against the government — Jan 31 p342 c1-2

MICHEVER, BARACH

1828

-Corresponding Secretary of the Abolition Society of Stark County, Ohio — Sep 19 p203 c3

MILLEDGVILLE, GEORGIA (Corporation of)

1827

-Taxes each Black who intends to work $25 — Apr 6 p15 c3

MILLER, CAPTAIN

1827

-Drowns in sea accident off Connecticut — May 4 p31 c1

MILLER, JAMES

1828

-Appointed to committee to plan celebration of slavery's abolition in New York — May 16 p61 c3

MILLER, BISHOP SAMUEL

1827

-Offers prayer at 17th anniversary of African Association for Mutual Relief — Mar 30 p2 c4

-Will superintend annual conference of Asbury Connexion — Apr 13 p19 c4

-Criticized for views on colonization — Sep 21 p110 c3-4 ed.

-Cancels subscription because of disappointment with <u>Freedom's Journal</u> — Sep 21 p110 c4 let.

-Preaches against <u>Freedom's Journal</u> — Oct 26 p131 c1-2

MILLER, WILLIAM

1827

-Appointed to committee of People of Colour of New York for celebrating New York's abolition — May 4 p30 c4

1828

-Advisor to the African Female Dorcas Association — Feb 1 p179 c1-2

-Helps lead religious services on the 2nd anniversary of New York abolition — Jul 11 p122 c3
-See also African Female Dorcas Association

MINER, MR. (Maryland)

1829

-Moves that committee for Washington, D.C. investigate slavery and slave trade there — Jan 16 p328 c2-3
-Paper praises motion — Jan 16 p330 c1-2 ed.
-Motion passed — Jan 16 p330 c2

MISSIONARIES

1827

-Have stopped tribal warfare in South Africa — May 4 p31 c2
-Criticized for ignoring slavery in their own country — Sep 14 p106 c4 p107 c1-2

1828

-Society in Philadelphia to distribute Bibles in South America — Mar 21 p207 c4

1829

-Persecuted in Jamaica — Mar 7 p381 c1-3 p382 c1

-See also Foreign Missionary Society of New York and Brooklyn; London Missionary Society

MITCHELL, JOHN (New York City)

1827

-Delivers speech after parade celebrating slavery's abolition in New York — Jul 13 p71 c1

MITCHELL, DOCTOR SAMUEL

1828

-Contributor to the mineral collection of the African Free School of New York — May 23 p70 c1

MOLESTON, SOLOMON, AND JOHN ROBINSON

1827

-Tailor shop (Advertisement) — May 18 p40 c3

MOLIERE

1828

-Tested his plays on friends before their completion — May 16 p61 c2

MORAL REFORM

	1827
-Advises against procrastination	May 11 p36 c2
-Describes way to lead a happy life	May 18 p40 c2
-Stresses importance of honesty	May 25 p44 c2
-States how children should treat parents	Jun 22 p58 c2-3
-Advises not to kill animals unnecessarily	Jul 13 p70 c2
-Warns that bad conduct will hurt the whole Black race	Jul 13 p71 c1-2
-Stresses the self-satisfaction of living a good life	Jul 20 p75 c1-2
-Advises people to mind their own business	Aug 3 p81 c2-3
-Describes the death of a man who swore too much	Aug 3 p82 c2
-Outlines proper food, drink and clothing	Aug 3 p82 c2
-Advises youth to follow the ten commandments to avoid crimes	Aug 10 p85 c4
-Warns not to give unkind advice to friends	Aug 24 p96 c1
-Advises against procrastination	Sep 21 p110 c2-3
-Advises care so as not to hurt anyone's reputation	Sep 28 p116 c2
-Stresses the importance of being magnanimous	Oct 26 p130 c4 p131 c1
-Says happiness is a result of benevolence	Dec 14 p158 c2-3
	1828
-Describes proper morality	Apr 4 p15 c2
-Describes way to speak and act in order to be liked by others	May 16 p63 c3
-Relates economic loss suffered by a family because of carelessness	May 30 p77 c2
-Condemns people who slander others	Jun 20 p98 c1-2
-Admonishes people who look in windows	Jun 20 p98 c3
-Warns against vanity and conceit	Jun 27 p107 c1-2
-Warns against being too proud	Jun 27 p109 c3
-Explains that happiness is attained through giving	Jul 25 p139 c1-2
-Describes evils of lotteries	Aug 1 p148 c3 p149 c1

-Advises one to pay debts and return borrowed items on time	Aug 8 p154 c1
-Describes modesty	Aug 22 p171 c2-3
-Criticizes men who are foppish	Sep 5 p188 c1-2
-Anecdote about guilt feelings after stealing	Nov 21 p275 c3
-Warns families to be economical	Dec 26 p303 c1-2
	1829
-Black vagabonds seen as harmful to the Black situation	Jan 9 p319 c1-2
-Outlines proper conduct for public streets	Jan 16 p327 c2-3
-Warns against laziness of heirs to fortunes	Jan 16 p329 c3
-Advises modesty	Jan 31 p344 c2-3
-Describes proper dress	Feb 14 p358 c2-3
-Condemns slander	Feb 14 p360 c2
-Describes ways to build character	Feb 21 p368 c3 p369 c1
-Advises using careful judgment before making decisions	Feb 28 p374 c3
MORAVIANS	
	1827
-Describes selection of a marriage partner	Mar 16 p4 c2
-Describes a house for spinsters and bachelors	Apr 6 p16 c2
	1829
-Describes a Moravian funeral	Jan 2 p311 c2
MORGAN, MR.	
	1827
-State offers a reward for his discovery	Mar 30 p11 c2
MORNING CHRONICLE, THE (New York)	
	1827
-Published by Baldwin, Roberts, Brooks and Lawson	Mar 16 p3 c4
MORTIMER, CHARLES	
	1827
-Shoe repair shop (Advertisement)	Mar 30-May 4, pp12, 16, 20, 24, 28, 32 c3
-Repair shop for china and glass (Advertisement)	Sep 21 p112 c4

MORTON, GEORGE C.

1828

-Domestic slave trader transporting slaves from Baltimore to New Orleans — Nov 7 p259 c2

MOTT, RICHARD JR.

1828

-Assistant Secretary of the New York Manumission Society — Feb 1 p179 c2

MOZART

1828

-Description of Mozart's career — May 23 p65 c1-3

MULLEN, JOHN

1827

-Killed in accident with a windmill — May 4 p31 c2

MURPHY, JOHN C.

1828

-To preach a sermon to aid Abduhl Rahahmon — Dec 12 p295 c1

MURRAY, JOHN

1827

-One of the founders of the New York Manumission Society — Oct 12 p122 c2

MUSIC

1827

-Praise of music's powers — Oct 26 p130 c3-4

1828

-Improved method of making string instruments developed — Apr 11 p21 c3

-Praises concert at St. Elizabeth's Church in New York City — Dec 26 p306 c3 p307 c1 let.

MUSKRAT ROOT
-See Circuta Maculata

MUTUAL INSTRUCTION SOCIETY

1828

-Reopens a school for Black adults — Oct 3 p218 c3

MUTUAL AID SOCIETIES (General)

1827

-Praises work of socieites for mutual relief — Mar 30 p2 c4

-See also African Association for Mutual Relief; Brooklyn Woolman Society; Clarkson Society;

Loveridge, Prince; Miller, Bishop Samuel; Rush, Reverend; Union Society; Wilberforce Society; Williams, Robert

MYERS, JOHN

1828

-Vice-President of the Abolition Society of Stark County, Ohio — Sep 19 p203 c3

N

NAMES

1828

-Lists nicknames of famous people — May 30 p77 c1-2

NAPOLEON I

1827

-Describes Napoleon's frugality — Jun 22 p60 c2

1828

-Anecdote about one of Napoleon's generals in Italy — Jul 4 p116 c3
-Excerpt from speech to guards when going to Elba — Jul 18 p132 c2-3
-Short biographical sketches of Napoleon's family — Sep 12 p196 c1-2
-Anecdote about Napoleon's son's desire to join army — Oct 10 p228 c2

1829

-Describes education of Napoleon's son — Feb 14 p359 c1
-See also Haiti

NATURE

1827

-Discourse on beauty of nature — Oct 19 p126 c1-2

NEEDHAM, DAVID

1827

-Murdered by Mr. Parker near Lynn, Massachusetts — Apr 20 p23 c4

NEWBOLD, GEORGE

1828

-First Vice-President of the New York Manumission Society — Feb 1 p179 c2

NEW HARMONY GAZETTE (Indiana)

1827

-Describes contents of March 7 issue — Apr 20 p23 c3

NEW HAVEN (Connecticut)

1827

-Blacks form society for improvement — Apr 27 p27 c1

-City sponsors two schools three months a year for Black children — Aug 10 p86 c3-4 p87 c1

-See also Blacks (New Haven)

NEW YORK (Weather)

1827

-Terrible wind storms damage western part of state — Apr 27 p26 c3

-Experiences late snow storms — May 4 p31 c2

NEW YORK AFRICAN FREE SCHOOL

1827

-Thanks Freedom's Journal for issues of paper and reports contents of library — Nov 9 p138 c4 let.

NEW YORK ASYLUM FOR THE DEAF AND DUMB

1827

-Summarizes enrollment and expenditures (1826) — Mar 16 p2 c1

NEW YORK AUXILIARY BIBLE AND COMMON PRAYER SOCIETY

1827

-Donates two copies of Megarey's Octavo Edition of Book of Common Prayer to St. Phillip's Church — Apr 27 p26 c4

NEW YORK ENQUIRER

1827

-Racist views criticized — Aug 17 p90 c1-2 let.

-Writing of editor, Major Noah, criticized as racist — Aug 24 p95 c1-3 ed.

NEW YORK FREEDOM'S JOURNAL (Agents)

1827 - 1829

-Charles Anderson, Scipio C. Augustus, W. D. Baptist, William B. Bowler, Thomas Braddock, *James Cowes, R. Cowley (Cooley), George De Grasse, R. Dickinson (Thomas Dickson), W. R. Gardiner, Reverend Samuel George, Isaac C. Glasko (Glasgow), Tudor E. Grant, Hezekiah Grice, Charles Hackett, Seth Henshaw, Frederick Holland, Peter Howard, Reverend B. F. Hughes, *Reverend Nathaniel Paul, *Reverend Thomas Paul, Joseph Pell, *John W. Prout, *John Remond (Raymond), William Rich, Isaac Rodgers, Reuben Ruby, Leonard Scott, Joseph Shepherd, Lewis Sheridan, *Stephen Smith, John C. Stanley, Austin Steward, Calvin Stockbridge, Isaac Talbot, Samuel Thomas, J. B. Vashon, Reverend R. Vaughan, *David Walker, *Francis Webb, Reverend W. P. Williams (Paul P. Williams), *George C. Willis, R.P.G. Wright, *Theodore Wright — *Mar 16, '27 p4 c4-Mar 28, '29 p412 c3

*Agent for all issues. (See index under surname for length of terms of other agents)

NEW YORK FREEDOM'S JOURNAL (General)

1827

-Office moved to 152 Church Street — May 4 p30 c4
-Reader praises paper — Jul 13 p70 c3 let.

1828

-Advertises printing facilities — Jan 25 p176 c2
-American Convention for the Abolition of Slavery buys five subscriptions — Feb 8 p181 c3
-Praised for exposing both sides of issues — Feb 22 p191 c2-3 let.
-Publishes index to Volume I (Mar 16, 1827-Mar 21, 1828) — Mar 21 p208 c2-4

-Office moved to 149 Church Street	May 2 p46 cl
-Intends to publish names of delinquent subscribers	May 23 p70 cl
-Appeals to readers to pay for subscriptions	Jul 11 p124 c3
-Praised for fight against slavery	Oct 31 p254 cl-2 let.
-Defends paper and asks opponents to publish their own	Dec 5 p283 c2 ed.

NEW YORK FREEDOM'S JOURNAL (Goals)

	1827
-To further the cause of Black people through education, economic development, improved civil rights, literary development, greater knowledge of Africa and destruction of slavery	Mar 16 pl cl-3 p4 c4 ed.
-Report the news	Mar 16 p4 c4
-Correct misconceptions about Black people	Mar 30 p3 c2-3
-Defend Black peoples' causes	Mar 30 p4 c4 ed. Apr 6 pl6 c4 ed.
-Reader criticizes objectives of Freedom's Journal	Sep 7 pl01 c4 pl02 cl-2 let.
-Editor defends the goals of Freedom's Journal	Sep 7 pl03 cl ed.
-Goals praised	Oct 26 pl31 cl-2
-Praised by the Society for the Mitigation and Gradual Abolition of Slavery Throughout the British Dominion	Nov 9 pl38 c3 let.
	1828
-Reader encourages efforts of Freedom's Journal	Feb 8 pl82 c4 pl83 cl let.
-Objective is to be a defense against slander and an editorial tool for Blacks	Apr 25 p37 c3 ed. May 2 p48 cl ed. May 9 p56 c2-3 ed.

NEW YORK MANUMISSION SOCIETY
-See Manumission Society of New York

NEW YORK OBSERVER

1827

-Publishes testimonials to the New York Freedom's Journal — Mar 30 p4 c4

NEWSPAPERS (General)

1828

-Criticizes unorganized format of newspapers — Oct 10 p228 c1

1829

-Condemns people who steal papers — Jan 2 p310 c3
-Satirizes people who don't pay for their subscriptions — Jan 2 p312 c2-3
-Hopes newspapers use high standards since they are used for educational purposes — Jan 16 p329 c2
-Ridicules people who dislike everything they read in newspapers — Jan 24 p336 c3 p337 c1
-Describes necessary qualities of an editor — Feb 26 p377 c1-2

NEWTON, SIR ISAAC

1828

-Realizes he was only the beginning of many great discoveries in science — May 16 p61 c2
-Biographical sketch — Dec 26 p306 c2-3

NEXSEN, E. JR.

1827

-Accepts office of Treasurer of Jordan Missionary Society and praises aims of Society — Dec 7 p154 c4 p155 c1

NIAGARA (New York)

1827

-Blacks outnumber Whites, four-to-one — Aug 3 p83 c4
-Recounts a vessel's trip over the falls — Sep 21 p111 c1

NIAMBANNA (King of Sierra Leone)

1827

-Educated in England — May 18 p38 c1

NICHOLS, REVEREND DOCTOR

1828

-Appointed President of Harvard — Jan 25 p175 c3

NOAH, MAJOR

1827

-Editor of the New York <u>Enquirer</u> publishes anti-Black materials — Aug 24 p95 c1-3

NORTH CAROLINA

-See Manumission Society of North Carolina; Wilkesborough

NOYELLE, PETER de

1828

-Operated on for jaw tumor — May 2 p42 c3

NUTRITION

1827

-Lists nutritional value of bread, meat and vegetables — Sep 7 p104 c1

O

<u>OBSERVATIONS ON SLAVERY</u>

-See Anderson, Dr. James

OBSERVER (<u>Freedom's Journal</u> Column)

1827

-Young girl asks advice on choosing a husband — Sep 7 p102 c3-4

-Short man asks advice to make women like him — Sep 14 p107 c2

-Criticizes women who talk too much — Oct 5 p118 c4 p119 c1

-Praise for concert held at St. Phillip's Church — Oct 12 p123 c2

-Stresses the importance of modesty in women — Oct 26 p130 c4

-Objects to the American Colonization Society — Nov 2 p134 c4

-Reader objects to men who stare at women in church — Nov 2 p134 c4 p135 c1 let.

-Young man complains about female company — Nov 9 p138 c3 let.

-Elderly man complains about drafts in church — Nov 9 p138 c4 let.

-Young engaged girl asks advice on her marriage — Nov 16 p142 c2 let.

-Asked to visit Philadelphia — Nov 16 p142 c2 let.

-Male reader refutes charge of staring at women in church — Nov 16 p142 c3 let.

O'CONNOR, ANDREW

1828

-Suspected of kidnapping Black children for slavery — Aug 8 p155 c3

OHIO COLONIZATION SOCIETY

1829

-Finds Blacks of Ohio would rather stay in Ohio than leave for Africa — Jan 31 p344 c3 p345 c1

ORMSBEE, REVEREND JOHN

1828

-Reports popularity of religion in Broome, New York — Jan 18 p170 c3

ORPHANAGES
-See Orphan Asylum Society; Shelter for Coloured Orphans

ORPHAN ASYLUM SOCIETY

1827

-Calls for 159 children — May 4 p31 c2
-$537.33 collected at St. Patrick's Cathedral — Sep 7 p103 c3

OSON, JACOB

1828

-Describes ordination and plans to be a minister in Liberia — Mar 14 p200 c4
-Dies and is eulogized — Oct 3 p219 c2-3

P

PAINE, THOMAS

1827

-Relates an anecdote about Paine's religious beliefs — Mar 30 p10 c3-4
-Bodily remains in home of William Brown of London — Jun 15 p56 c2

PAPACY

1827

-Statistics concerning the number of Popes and their nationalities — Oct 26 p132 c1

PAPER

1828

-Traces the development of writing material — Aug 29 p181 c2-3

-Produced from straw and grass — Oct 24 p246 c1

1829

-Paper table clothes invented in Paris — Jan 24 p335 c1

PARK, THOMAS (Mungo)

1828

-Describes his death while exploring in Africa — Jul 4 p117 c1-2

PARKER, WILLIAM

1828

-Restaurant with oysters as a specialty (Advertisement) — May 2 p47 c1

PARLIAMENT (England)

1828

-Origin traced to Roman times — Nov 21 p276 c3

1829

-Discussing what to do with fugitive slaves in Canada — Jan 24 p333 c1

PARROTT, RUSSELL (Philadelphia)

1827

-Strong attack upon colonization — Jul 27 p77 c3-4 p78 c1

PATRIOTISM

1828

-Notes anecdotes concerning patriotism — Mar 21 p206 c2-3

PATTERSON, CAPTAIN JOSEPH

1827

-Fell overboard from sloop _Lad Tompkins_ and drowned — Mar 16 p3 c4

PATTERSON, WILLIAM

1827

-Marries Cynthia Clarborne — Mar 30 p3 c4

PAUL, REVEREND BENJAMIN

1827

-Delivers speech in Albany at abolition celebration — Aug 10 p85 c3

1828

-Advisor to African Female Dorcas Association — Feb 1 p179 c1-2

-See also African Female Dorcas Association

PAUL, REVEREND NATHANIEL (Albany, New York)

1827 - 1829

-Agent for the Freedom's Journal — Mar 16, '27 p4 c3- Mar 28, '29 p412 c3

PAUL REVEREND THOMAS (Boston, Massachusetts)

1827 - 1829

-Agent for the Freedom's Journal — Mar 16, '27 p4 c3- Mar 28, '29 p412 c3

PELL, JOSEPH (Hudson, New York)

1828 - 1829

-Agent for the Freedom's Journal — May 23, '28 p72 c3- Mar 28, '29 p412 c3

PENNSYLVANIA

1828

-Criticism of 1813 bill before state legislature prohibiting immigration of Blacks into Pennsylvania — Feb 22 p190 c2-3 let. Feb 29 p194 c3-4 p195 c1 let.

-Criticizes 1813 bill requiring Free Blacks visiting Pennsylvania to be registered — Mar 7 p196 c2-4 let.

-Further pleas not to pass 1813 law — Mar 14 p200 c2 let.

-Criticizes 1813 bill which allows Free Blacks to be sold if not registered — Mar 21 p205 c4 p 206 c1 let.

PENNSYLVANIA GAZETTE

1828

-Criticized for sarcastic description of Blacks — Mar 14 p201 c1-2 ed.

PEOPLE OF COLOUR OF NEW YORK (Association)
-See Bane, Peter; Blue, Moses

PEPPER, PETER

1827

-Relates love life — May 4 p30 c3

PEROUSE, LA

1827

-Describes ship's voyage and disappearance — May 25 p42 c2-3 Jun 11 p45 c2-3

PERSIA

	1827
-Harem stictly guarded	May 25 p44 c1
-Description of violence of Persian society	Dec 14 p158 c1-2
	1828
-List of Persian proverbs	Feb 15 p187 c1

PETERSON, DANIEL

	1827
-Store for inexpensive clothing (Advertisement)	Mar 30-May 4 pp12, 16, 20, 24, 28, 32, c3

PHILADELPHIA (Pennsylvania)

	1827
-Spent $2,220,000 for poor relief in twenty years	Aug 10 p87 c4
-Society started to buy products of freemen only	Sep 14 p107 c4
	1828
-Describes position of Blacks in Philadelphia	Jul 11 p122 c1-2
-Citizen complains about number of Blacks in the city	Jul 18 p130 c1-3
-Blacks answer complaint	Jul 25 p140 c1-2

PHILADELPHIA MUSEUM

	1827
-Exhibiting a chameleon	May 4 p31 c2

PHILADELPHIA AND NEW YORK UNION STAGE LINE

	1827
-Young mulatto run over by coach	Apr 6 p15 c2
-Accident victim dies	Apr 13 p19 c3

PHYSICS

	1828
-Short discussion of atoms	Apr 11 p19 c1

PIERCE, WILLIAM

	1827
-Dies in Charlestown, Massachusetts marine hospital	Apr 13 p19 c4

PIERSON, NICHOLAS

	1827
-Mead garden for Blacks only	Jun 8 p52 c2

PIGEON BERRY

	1827
-Poisons a Rochester family	Mar 16 p3 c4

PIGGOT, REVEREND MR.

	1827
-Roof of house destroyed by windstorm	Apr 20 p23 c3

PIRACY

	1827
-Massachusetts ship taken by pirates and crew killed	Jun 22 p59 c1-2
-Describes career of a French pirate named Tardy	Jun 29 p61 c4 p62 c1-2
-Tardy executed for murder	Aug 10 p87 c2
	1828
-Description of piracy by Turks	Jan 11 p166 c1-2 let.

PISA, ITALY

	1827
-Describes leaning tower	May 18 p40 c1

PISCO, ELIZA (Baltimore, Maryland)

	1828
-Black free eleven years feared kidnapped	Aug 15 p166 c3

PITCAIRN'S ISLAND

	1828
-Explains founding by mutinous members of <u>H.M.S. Bounty</u> (1789) and describes colony at present	Nov 21 p278 c1-2

PLATO

	1827
-Short excerpt on truth	Jun 1 p48 c1
	1828
-Views on truth	Jan 18 p171 c3

PODOTSKY, COUNT

	1828
-Servant gives life to save Count's (1776)	May 30 p73 c3

POETRY

	1827
-"The African Chief" by Eryant	Mar 16 p4 c1

-"The Flower of Friendship" by Ella	Mar 30 p4 cl
-"Greece"	Mar 30 p4 cl
-"Sea Shore Stanzas" by Barry Cornwall	Mar 30 p4 cl
-"The Bible" by the author of "Leisure Hours at Sea"	Apr 6 p16 cl
-"There was a Time I Never Sighed" from The Crystal Hunter	Apr 6 p16 cl
-"Emblems" by the Reverend Henry Stebbing	Apr 13 p20 cl
-"Questions and Answers" by J. Montgomery	Apr 13 p20 cl
-"The African Lament for Mungo Park" by P.M.J.	Apr 20 p24 cl
-"The Dead Trumpeter"	Apr 27 p28 cl
-"Human Life"	Apr 27 p28 cl
-"The Song of the Janissary"	May 4 p32 cl
-"Moving Day"	May 4 p32 cl
-"The Pilgrims Tale"	May 11 p36 cl
-"Warnings"	May 11 p36 cl
-"The Swedish Stranger"	May 18 p40 cl
-"Retrospection"	May 18 p40 cl
-"Sympathy"	May 25 p44 cl
-"Sonnet" by Vincenzio da Filicaja	May 25 p44 cl
-"Men" by Bishop King	May 25 p44 cl
-"The Old Man"	Jun 1 p48 cl
-"Domestic Blues" from Rouge et Noir	Jun 1 p48 cl
-"The Black Beauty" from Solomon's Songs	Jun 8 p52 cl
-"The Sorrows of Angola"	Jun 8 p52 cl
-"Stanzas"	Jun 8 p52 cl
-"Masonic Procession" by "Milford Bard", from Masonic Mirror	Jun 15 p56 cl
-"Behave Yourself Before Folk"	Jun 15 p56 cl
-Poem from The Ladies' Album	Jun 22 p60 cl
-Stanzas from R. H. Wilde	Jun 22 p60 cl
-"The Nomes of England" by Joanna Baillie	Jun 29 p64 cl
-"Kindred Hearts"	Jun 29 p64 cl
-"The Bride's Farewell"	Jul 6 p68 cl
-"Thoughts of Sadness"	Jul 6 p68 cl
-"The Gypsy Girl's Phrophecy" by William Gilmore Simms, Jr.	Jul 13 p72 cl
-"The Young Indian's Song"	Jul 13 p72 cl
-Discusses the excellence of contemporary African poetry	Jul 20 p73 c2
-"Hymn for St. Stephen's Day" by Bishop Heber	Jul 20 p76 cl
-"Stanzas" by T. Hood	Jul 20 p76 cl
-"The Honest Man"	Jul 20 p76 cl

-"A Retrospective Review" by T. Hood	Jul 27 p80 c1
-Short verse on marriage	Jul 27 p80 c1
-"Lines in Sympathy"	Aug 3 p84 c1
-"Friends"	Aug 3 p84 c1
-"The Gray Hair"	Aug 10 p88 c1
-"Di Tanti Palpiti"	Aug 10 p88 c1
-Poem describing the slave trade	Aug 17 p89 c4 p90 c1
-"Yorkshire" by Hubert Knowles	Aug 17 p92 c1
-Lines by G. Tucker	Aug 17 p92 c1
-"Pity For Poor Africans"	Aug 24 p93 c4 p94 c1
-"Resignation" by James Grocott, Jr.	Aug 24 p96 c1
	Aug 31 p100 c1
-"Slavery"	Sep 7 p101 c3-4
-"Freedom"	Sep 7 p104 c1
-"Greek Song"	Sep 7 p104 c1
-"Africa"	Sep 14 p108 c1
-"Questions and Answers"	Sep 14 p108 c1
-"The Maniac - A Ballad"	Sep 21 p112 c1
-Verses	Sep 21 p112 c1
-"Burial Felicity"	Sep 28 p116 c1
-"Is It So?"	Sep 28 p116 c1
-Poem about death	Oct 5 p120 c1
-A hymn by Bishop Heber	Oct 5 p120 c1
-"To Greece"	Oct 12 p124 c1
-"To A Beautiful Jewish Girl of Athena"	Oct 12 p124 c1
-Stanza	Oct 19 p128 c1
-"My Country" by Rodgers	Oct 19 p128 c1
-"On Hearing of the Death of a Young Friend"	Oct 26 p132 c1
-A hymn	Oct 26 p132 c1
-"Weep, Emeline, Weep"	Nov 2 p136 c1
-"The Negro Boy"	Nov 2 p136 c1
-"Hymn to Humanity by Phyllis Wheatley	Nov 9 p140 c1
-"Hymn to the Morning" - Phyllis Wheatley	Nov 9 p140 c1
-"The Dream - A Fragment"	Nov 16 p144 c1
-"To Caroline" by George Canning (Prime Minister of England)	Nov 23 p148 c1
-"Here We Three Meet Again" by George Canning	Nov 23 p148 c1
-Stanza	Nov 30 p152 c1
-"Lines on a Deceased Friend"	Nov 30 p152 c1
-"Impromptu"	Nov 30 p152 c1
-"Adieu, To Thee"	Dec 7 p156 c1
-"On Viewing the Lifeless Remains of a Very Dear Friend"	Dec 7 p156 c1
-"Song of Emigration"	Dec 14 p160 c1
-"Via Crucis, Via Lucis"	Dec 14 p160 c1

-"The Penitent Profligate"	Dec 21 p164 c1
-"Christmas Address"	Dec 21 p164 c1
-"Hymn for the Infant School"	Dec 21 p164 c1-2
	1828
-"The Carrier"	Jan 11 p168 c1
-"The Gondola Glides" by T. K. Hervey	Jan 11 p168 c1-2
-"Reflections on the Past Year"	Jan 18 p172 c1
-"To the Bride"	Jan 18 p172 c1
-"Lines on the Death of Jeremiah Gloucester"	Jan 25 p176 c1
-Lines on remaining unmarried	Jan 25 p176 c1
-"Lines to a Sister, on the Death of Her Infant"	Feb 1 p180 c1
-Verses	Feb 1 p180 c1
-Verses	Feb 8 p184 c1
-A song	Feb 8 p184 c1
-"A Dirge" by the Reverend G. Croly	Feb 8 p184 c1-2
-"Slave" by James Montgomery	Feb 15 p188 c1
-"A Song" by Mrs. Dugald Stewart	Feb 15 p188 c1-2
-Two short untitled poems	Feb 22 p192 c1
-"Punning" by T. Hood	Feb 29 p194 c1
-"Sympathy"	Mar 7 p198 c1
-"The Old Man's Comfort" by R. Southey	Mar 7 p198 c1
-"Enigma"	Mar 7 p198 c1
-"To S. L. F."	Mar 14 p202 c1
-"The Tears of a Slave"	Mar 14 p202 c1
-"To Rosa"	Mar 21 p208 c1
-Verses about a May Queen	Mar 21 p208 c1
-Poem concerning cattiness of women	Apr 4 p10 c1
-Song about lovers	Apr 4 p11 c3
-"Ingratitude"	Apr 11 p23 c1
-"The Slattern"	Apr 11 p23 c1
-"Serenade"	Apr 11 p23 c1
-"Spring"	Apr 18 p27 c1
-"The Magic Mirror"	Apr 18 p27 c1-2
-"An Evening Walk in Bengal" by Bishop Heber	Apr 18 p27 c2-3
-"Hebrew Melody" from The London Keepsake for 1828	Apr 25 p39 c2
-"To the Moon"	May 2 p47 c1
-"On Finding a Violet the First of the Season"	May 9 p54 c3
-"To F"	May 9 p54 c3
	May 16 p58 c3
-"Is This The Time To Be Gloom and Sad?"	May 16 p58 c3
-Two short poems	May 23 p70 c2
-A song by T. H. Bailey	May 23 p70 c2-3
-"To Miss Caroline E."	May 30 p78 c3
-"The Charm of Fiction"	May 30 p78 c3

-"Life"	May 30 p78 c3
-"The Brobdignag Bonnets for Blue" from the London Mirror (March 1828)	Jun 6 p86 c3
-"A Women's Tear" by Lord Byron	Jun 6 p87 c1
-"The Lay of Poor Louise" from Sir Walter Scott's The Fair Maid of Perth	Jun 13 p94 c3
-A short poem about youth	Jun 20 p102 c3
-"On the Death of a Young Friend"	Jun 27 p111 c1
-"The African Slave"	Jun 27 p111 c1
-"The Son of Mungo Park"	Jul 4 p117 c2
-"The Crucifixion"	Jul 4 p119 c1
-"The Knight's Farewell"	Jul 18 p135 c1
-"Slavery" by George Horton	Jul 18 p135 c1
-"The Charm of Beauty"	Jul 25 p143 c1
-"Hopes"	Aug 1 p151 c2
-"The Vanity of Beauty"	Aug 8 p158 c2
-"To My Sister" by Edward Everett	Aug 8 p158 c3
-"On the Evening and Morning" by George M. Horton	Aug 15 p166 c2
-"Resolutions"	Aug 22 p174 c3
-"On the Poetic Music" by George M. Horton	Aug 29 p182 c2-3
-Poem by William Pitt Palmer on Slavery	Aug 29 p182 c2-3
-"Recollections of My Childhood"	Sep 5 p190 c2
-"Sonnet To The Housatonic"	Sep 5 p190 c2
-"Gratitude" by George M. Horton	Sep 5 p190 c2-3
-"Take Particular Notice" by Jane Hobart	Sep 5 p190 c3
-"The Sailor" by Cunningham	Sep 12 p195 c1
-"The Slave Ship"	Sep 12 p198 c3
-"On the Sabbath"	Sep 19 p206 c3
-"The Departed"	Sep 19 p207 c1
-Elegiac Song (Air) "Absence"	Sep 26 p214 c2-3
-"Autumn"	Sep 26 p214 c3
-"Serena Sleeps"	Oct 3 p222 c3
-Song (Air) "Bonnie Doon"	Oct 3 p227 c3 p228 c1
-"What is Truth"	Oct 10 p231 c1
-"Zara's Ear-rings" from Lockhart's Spanish Ballads	Oct 17 p239 c1
-"Abduhl Rahahmon"	Oct 24 p247 c1
-"On the Death of a Young Man"	Oct 31 p255 c1
-"To Adeline"	Nov 7 p262 c2
-"The Place of Rest" by Mary Anne Browne	Nov 7 p262 c2-3
-"The Captive African Chief" by Amos Blanchard	Nov 7 p262 c3 p263 c1 Nov 14 p270 c1-3

-"The Slave's Soliloquey"	Nov 21 p278 c3 p279 c1
-"On a Tree Blighted by the Wind"	Dec 5 p286 c3
-Poem by John Mason Good	Dec 12 p294 c3
-"Forget Me Not" by F. G. Hallock	Dec 19 p299 c3
	<u>1829</u>
-"A Vision"	Jan 2 p314 c3 p315 c1
-"Death of Ashmun"	Jan 9 p322 c3
-"Things Like That"	Jan 24 p336 c3
-"The Feast of Life"	Jan 24 p338 c3
-"Signs"	Jan 24 p338 c3
-"Frost at Midnight" by Samuel Taylor Coleridge	Jan 31 p346 c3
-"Epigram" by Coleridge	Feb 7 p354 c3
-"Sighs" by Mrs. Henry Rolls	Feb 14 p363 c1
-"To A Girl Thirteen Years of Age"	Feb 21 p371 c1
-See also Horton, George	
POKE WEED	
-See Pigeon Berry	
POLAND	
	<u>1827</u>
-Describes Polish salt mines	Oct 26 p132 c1
<u>THE POLITICAL PRIMER, OR A HAND-BOOK FOR THE JACKSONITES</u>	
	<u>1828</u>
-Support for a pro-John Quincy Adams paper soon to be published	Apr 25 p36 c3
PORTUGAL	
	<u>1827</u>
-Experiencing trouble with Spain and England	Mar 16 p3 c2-3
PORTER, CATHERINE	
	<u>1827</u>
-Marries Jacob Sharp	Apr 13 p19 c4
POVERTY	
	<u>1827</u>
-Corrects misconceptions about Black poverty	Mar 30 p3 c2
-See also Fuel Saving Fund	
PREJUDICE	
-See Racism	
PRESTER JOHN	
-See Africa	

PRESTON, JOHN

1828

-Vice President of the Pennsylvania Abolition Society — Jan 11 p166 c4

PRICE, DOCTOR RICHARD

1828

-Starts insurance plan in 1775 to liquidate England's National Debt — Oct 31 p252 c3

PRINTING

1828

-Anecdote about a man who operated a portable printing press — Aug 29 p170 c1-2

PRISON REFORM
-See Howard, Mr.

PRITCHARD, THOMAS

1828

-Obituary — Jul 11 p126 c3

PROTECTING SOCIETY OF THE CITY AND COUNTY OF PHILADELPHIA

1828

-Advertises efforts to stop kidnapping of Free Blacks — Apr 25 p39 c2-3

PROUT, JOHN W. (Washington, D.C.)

1827 - 1829

-Agent for the Freedom's Journal — Mar 16, '27 p4 c3- Mar 28, '29 p412 c3

PROVERBS

1827

-Sixteen listed — Dec 21 p164 c2

1828

-Arabic proverbs — Nov 14 p269 c1

PRUSSIA
-See European News

PURNEL, JOHN (Philadelphia)

1827

-Black arrested in Boston for selling Free Black children into slavery — Jun 8 p51 c3
-Tried and sentenced to 42 years for alleged kidnappings — Jun 22 p59 c1

PURVIS, WILLIAM

1828

-Obituary and praise of character — Apr 11 p19 c1

Q

QUAKERS
-See Society of Friends

QUINN, MRS. MARGARETTA R.

1827

-Elected Secretary of the African Female Dorcas Association — Feb 15 p187 c4

QUINN, REVEREND WILLIAM

1827

-To deliver sermon at the consecration of the African Free Methodist Society — May 4 p31 c4

1828

-Advisor to the African Female Dorcas Association — Feb 1 p179 c1-2
-See also African Female Dorcas Association

QUON, M. (Quonn)

1828

-Cleaning business (Advertisement) — May 9 p55 c1

R

RACISM

1827

-Describes racism in employment — Apr 13 p19 c1-3
-Describes racism in employment — Apr 27 p27 c1
-Denies belief that Blacks are intellectually inferior — May 18 p37 c3-4 p38 c1-2
-Describes education of Blacks in public schools — Jun 1 p47 c1-3

-Describes arrests of innocent Blacks for crimes comitted by White pirate, Tardy	Jun 29 p61 c4 p62 c1-2 Jul 6 p65 c3-4
-Stresses discrepancy between the Declaration of Independence and treatment of Blacks	Jun 29 p62 c4
-Explains why the American Colonization Society wants to send Blacks to Africa	Jul 6 p66 c3-4 let.
-Asserts that Blacks are equal to Whites	Jul 13 p69 c1-2
-Cites ancient history to show equality of Blacks	Jul 20 p73 c1-3
-Invites Whites to prove their superiority	Jul 27 p79 c1
-Steam ship <u>Hudson</u> will not provide accommodations for Blacks	Aug 3 p82 c3-4 let.
-Slave in Alabama burned to death with no trial for killing a White	Aug 3 p82 c4 p83 c1
-Discourse on the unhappiness of being Black in a prejudiced world	Aug 10 p86 c2
-Slave states have unfair representation in Congress because slaves are counted in the population figures	Aug 10 p87 c2
-View that West Indies' Blacks suffer great oppression	Aug 10 p87 c2
-Condemns racist writing of Major Noah of New York <u>Enquirer</u>; feels Jews should not be racist since they are also oppressed	Aug 24 p95 c1-3
-Agent of paper describes racism in Hartford, Connecticut	Aug 31 p99 c1-3
-Reader criticizes <u>Freedom's Journal</u>'s exposure of racism by Whites	Sep 7 p101 c4 p102 c1-2 let.
-Explains White justification of slavery	Sep 28 p115 c2
-Washington, D.C. enacts a law requiring proof of freedom of Blacks	Nov 16 p142 c3-4 ed.
-Criticizes Christians who do not work for abolition	Nov 23 p146 c1-3
-Minister of Barbadoes criticized for racist sermon and racist method of offering communion	Dec 14 p158 c3

-Expresses hope that the new year will bring an end to racism and slavery	Dec 21 p162 c2-3
	<u>1828</u>
-South Carolina prohibits education and employment of Blacks	Jan 11 p166 c1
-Explains oppression of Free Blacks in the West Indies	Feb 29 p193 c1-4 p194 c1-2
-Reveals racist actions of many members of the American Colonization Society	Mar 7 p196 c4 p197 c1
-Denounces theory that one race is different from another	Apr 18 p26 c1-2
-View that coloration of races results from climate, not biological differences	May 9 p51 c1-2
-Black in Charleston, South Carolina who changed his color to White	May 9 p52 c1
-Agent of paper complains of racism in travel accommodations	Jun 27 p107 c2-3
-Describes unequal legal status of Free Blacks in the United States	Jul 25 p138 c1-2
-A Black condemns the use of the word "Negro"	Aug 29 p178 c2 let.
-Traces British prejudice against Jews	Sep 5 p188 c2
-Reader complains about Whites who don't want Blacks to walk on the same streets with them	Sep 12 p197 c1
-Different racial coloration can result from dietetic and cultural differences	Sep 19 p201 c2-3 p203 c1
-Lists the number of slaves in a South Carolina district that are unrepresented because they cannot vote	Sep 26 p211 c1-2
-Black man and woman publically whipped in Bergen, New Jersey for larceny	Sep 26 p213 c3 p214 c1
-A reader feels Blacks are happier as slaves than free	Nov 14 p268 c1 let.
	<u>1829</u>
-Describes Blacks as superior because of their physical beauty	Feb 14 p357 c1-3

-See also American Colonization Society; Civil Rights; New York Enquirer; Pennsylvania; Randolph, Mr.; Richmond Savings Institution; United States Congress

RADCLIFFE, JAMES

1827

-Applies steam power to canal boats — Sep 21 p111 c1

RAHAHMON, PRINCE ABDUHL

1828

-African Prince who attained freedom after 48 years of slavery — May 16 p57 c1-2
-Thanks those who helped him; plans to bring the Bible to his homeland — Jun 27 p109 c1-2 let.
-Arrives in New York City — Aug 1 p150 c3
-Character and intellect praised — Aug 29 p179 c1-2 let.
-People of Colour of Boston hold dinner in his honor — Aug 29 p179 c3
-Receives $50 in Providence, Rhode Island to aid in buying his children — Oct 3 p219 c3
-Committee of five appointed in New York to raise $8,500 to free his children — Oct 24 p245 c3
-Poem "Abduhl Rahahmon" — Oct 24 p247 c1
-Describes the city of Timbuctoo and the area between it and the coast — Oct 31 p252 c1-2
-Reverend Gallaudet is writing a pamphlet on Rahahmon — Nov 7 p262 c1
-Seeking money in New York City to buy his enslaved children — Dec 12 p291 c2
-John C. Murphy to preach sermon soliciting money for Rahahmon — Dec 19 p295 c1
-$25 collected at sermon by Mr. Murphy — Dec 19 p296 c3
-See also Blacks (Boston); Murphy, John C.; Poetry; Sierra Leone

RALEIGH, SIR WALTER

1828

-Ideas on flattery — Aug 8 p157 c2

RANDALL, DOCTOR RICHARD

1828

-Appointed Governor of Liberia by the American Colonization Society — Sep 26 p211 c2

RANDOLPH, MR.

1828

-States slaves should be treated as property and are happier than freemen — Jan 25 p174 c1-2

RATHBONE, STEPHEN

1827

-Loses two children when his house burns down — Mar 16 p3 c4

RAWLE, WILLIAM

1828

-President of the Pennsylvania Abolition Society — Jan 11 p166 c4
-Chairman of the 20th Biennial Meeting of the American Convention for the Abolition of Slavery — Jan 25 p177 c3

RAYMOND, JOHN (Salem, Massachusetts)
-See Remond, John

RAYNER, DAVID

1827

-Dies fighting a fire at John Bowen and Company — Mar 16 p3 c3

RAYNOLDS, WILLIAM

1828

-Recording Secretary of the Abolition Society of Stark County, Ohio — Sep 19 p203 c3

READING ROOM SOCIETY (Philadelphia, Pennsylvania)

1828

-William Whipper to give address praising Society — Jun 6 p82 c3
-Whipper's address published — Jun 20 p98 c1
-Outlines Society's goal to raise the intellectual level of Blacks — Dec 26 p301 c1-3 p304 c3

RECIPES

1827

-Recipe for potato pudding — Nov 2 p136 c2

1828

-Recipe for peach pie — Sep 12 p195 c3

RECORDER AND TELEGRAPH

1827

-Editors plan a weekly paper for children — May 4 p31 c3

REDWING, THE

1827

-British ship brings news from Africa — Mar 16 p3 c3

REGULUS, MRS. HENRIETTA D.

1828

-Elected assistant secretary of the African Female Dorcas Association — Feb 15 p187 c4

RELIGION (General)

1827

-Excerpt from a sermon by Dr. Spring on the worth of the Bible — Jun 22 p57 c2-3
-Describes almost monastic life of a minister — Nov 16 p141 c1-3

1828

-Discusses the ability to think clearly in an empty church — Jan 25 p174 c4 p175 c1

-Slavery defined as contradictory to Christianity — Mar 7 p195 c1-4 p196 c1

-Reports the number of churches of each denomination in New York City — May 2 p42 c2
-Admires lively preaching — May 2 p44 c2-3
-Priests of Baden petition for the abolition of celibacy — Aug 22 p171 c3
-Describes the first burning of heretics — Aug 22 p173 c1
-Condemns a southern minister for searching for runaway slaves — Oct 31 p251 c2 ed.
-Christian church condemned for not taking an active role against slavery — Oct 31 p254 c1-2 let.
-A man claiming to be Christ appears in Washington, D.C. — Dec 26 p303 c2-3

RELIGION (Islam)

1828

-Excerpt from a Muslim sermon about God — Sep 19 p204 c2-3 p205 c1

REMOND, JOHN (Salem, Massachusetts)

	1827 - 1829
-Agent for the *Freedom's Journal*	Mar 16, '27 p4 c3- Mar 28, '29 p412 c3

RICH, WILLIAM (Troy, New York)

	1828 - 1829
-Agent for the *Freedom's Journal*	May 23, '28 p72 c3- Mar 28, '29 p412 c3

RICHMOND SAVINGS INSTITUTION

	1827
-Will not take deposits from Blacks	Apr 13 p19 c3-4

RIDDLES

	1827
-Riddle written by George Canning (Prime Minister of England)	Nov 23 p148 c2
	1829
-Puzzle	Jan 31 p345 c3

RIDOUT, PETER

	1827
-Free Black of Baltimore dies while at work	Aug 17 p91 c3

RIOTS

	1828
-Riot occurs at a black camp meeting near Gloucester, New Jersey	Aug 29 p181 c1

ROBERTS, JOHN

	1827
-Oil for sale (Advertisement)	Aug 24 p96 c3

ROBERTSON, JOHN

	1827
-Appointed to Committee of People of Colour of New York for abolition celebration	May 4 p30 c4

ROBINSON, B.

	1828
-Store in Philadelphia robbed	Apr 25 p37 c1

ROCHESTER (New York)

	1827
-Oldest native resident is seventeen; of 8,000 population, no adults living there	Apr 20 p23 c3

	1828
-Blacks building a church and school	May 9 p51 c2-3
-Building of church and school completed	Oct 3 p218 c2
RODGERS, ISAAC (New London, Connecticut)	
	1827
-Agent for the *Freedom's Journal*	Mar 16, '27 p4 c3-Jul 27, '27 p76 c4
ROUSSEAU, JEAN JACQUES	
	1827
-Views on everyday conversation	Dec 21 p164 c2
RUBY, REUBEN (Portland, Maine)	
	1827 - 1828
-Agent for the *Freedom's Journal*	Mar 16, '27 p4 c3-Apr 11, '28 p24 c3
RUGGLES, DAVID	
	1828
-Advertises fresh butter for sale	May 9-30 pp55, 59 (63) 71, 79 c2
-Advertises grocery store	Aug 22 p174 c2 Sep 5, '28 p192 c2-Mar 21, '29 p403 c2
RUSH, REVEREND CHRISTOPHER	
	1827
-Denounces tobacco industry	Mar 30 p2 c3
-Offers prayer at 17th anniversary of the African Association for Mutual Relief	Mar 30 p2 c4
	1828
-Advisor to the African Female Dorcas Association	Feb 1 p179 c1-2
-Helps read religious service on the 2nd anniversary of New York abolition	Jul 11 p122 c3
-See also African Female Dorcas Association; Tobacco	
RUSH EDUCATION SOCIETY (Philadelphia, Pennsylvania)	
	1827
-Will hold the second quarterly meeting at the Second African Presbyterian Church	Sep 28 p115 c4 Oct 5 p119 c4

RUSS, DOCTOR JOHN D.

	1829
-Criticizes morals of Greeks	Feb 7 p350 c2-3 p351 cl let.

RUSSIA

	1827
-View that when slave and free labor are in competition free labor is more productive	Aug 24 p93 c3
	1828
-Anecdote about a French soldier in Russia during the Napoleonic Wars	Feb 22 p191 cl-2
-Diamond in Tsar's sceptre is one of the most expensive in the world	Apr 25 p37 cl
-Describes the rule and assassination of Paul I	Jun 6 p80 cl-3 Jun 13 p89 cl-3 Jun 20 p97 cl-2
-Declares war on Turkey	Jun 20 p99 cl
-Defeating Turks	Aug 29 p178 c2-3
-Describes the burning of Moscow during the Napoleonic Wars	Sep 5 p185 cl-3 p186 cl Sep 12 p193 cl-3 Sep 19 p201 cl-3
-Immense cannon in the Kremlin	Oct 24 p242 c2-3
-Hopes that Nicholas I will retain place in Europe	Nov 7 p260 c2-3
-Reports the number of Russians over 100 years old in 1825	Nov 21 p274 c3

RUSSWURM, JOHN B.

	1827
-Describes goals of the <u>Freedom's Journal</u>	Mar 16 p4 c4 ed.
	1828
-Sees paper a defense against racial slander and an editorial tool for Blacks	Apr 25 p37 c3 ed. May 2 p48 cl ed. May 9 p56 cl ed.
-Desires thirty farmers to work in Haiti	May 23 p70 c3
-Announces opening of evening school for Blacks (Advertisement)	Nov 7 p263 cl- Dec 5 p287 cl
	1829
-Feels American Colonization Society is laying a good Foundation in Liberia	Feb 14 p360 cl ed.

-States Freedom's Journal's change in position on colonization; sees it as the best program for blacks; earlier opposing views mistaken	Feb 14 p362 c2-3 ed.
-Wishes passengers bound for Liberia good luck	Feb 14 p362 c3 p363 c1
-Praises Colonization Society; mistaken in condemning it before	Feb 21 p370 c2-3 ed.
-Defends change in position and supports colonization; but sees hardships in Liberia	Mar 7 p386 c1-3
-Admires those who now advocate colonization; sees colonization speeding emancipation; colonization the best alternative for American Blacks	Mar 14 p394 c1-3 ed.
-Announces resignation from Freedom's Journal; cites paper's accomplishments: Dissemination of useful knowledge; defense of the Black community; emphasizing the need for education; recent emphasis on need for Liberian migration	Mar 28 p410 c1-3 ed.
-See also American Colonization Society; Colonization	

S

SAINT PHILLIP'S CHURCH

	1827
-Collects money for New York Auxiliary Bible and Common Prayer Book Society	Apr 27 p26 c4
-Advertises concert of sacred music	Sep 28 p115 c4
-Concert date changed	Oct 5 p119 c4
-Concert of sacred music praised	Oct 12 p123 c2 let.
-Music school advertised	Oct 19 p127 c4
-Desires a new pew	Nov 9 p139 c4
-See also New York Auxiliary Bible and Common Prayer Society; "Observer" (Freedom's Journal column)	

SAINT THOMAS EPISCOPAL CHURCH (Philadelphia, Pennsylvania)

1828

-Purchases a new organ — Apr 18 p26 c2-3 let.

SALEM, MASSACHUSETTS

1827

-Description of Salem and her Black population — Nov 9 p139 c3-4 let.

1828

-Free Blacks erecting a church — Mar 14 p201 c3

-Celebrates 200th anniversary — Oct 3 p221 c3

SANCHO, IGNATUIS

1827

-Spanish slave who became a literary scholar in England — May 18 p38 c1

SANDERSON, THOMAS

1828

-One of the founders of the African Grand Lodge of Masons (Boston, Massachusetts) — Nov 7 p257 c1

SAXE WEIMAR, DUKE OF

1829

-Witnesses the horrible treatment of a female slave in New Orleans — Jan 9 p317 c1-3

SCHOOL SOCIETY OF PHILADELPHIA

1827

-Blacks form a society to collect money for schools — May 11 p34 c2

-Society has collected $800 — Jun 29 p63 c4

SCOTLAND

1828

-Relates story of a noble regaining his lost estate — Sep 19 p201 c3 p202 c1-2

SCOTT, HENRY

1827

-Appointed to the committee of People of Colour of New York to celebrate slavery's abolition — May 4 p30 c4

SCOTT, LEONARD (Trenton, New Jersey)

1827 - 1829

-Agent for the Freedom's Journal — Jun 15, '27 p56 c4- Mar 28, '29 p412 c3

SCOTT, SIR WALTER

	1828
-Poem "The Lay of Poor Louise" (from The Fair Maid of Perth)	Jun 13 p94 c3

SCUDDER, LOT

	1827
-Describes his insanity	Dec 14 p158 c4 p159 c1

SEA SERPENTS

	1827
-Ship reports seeing a sea serpent	Jun 8 p49 c4 p50 c1
-Description of a sea monster seen off Nantucket Sound	Oct 19 p127 c3
-Appears off coast of Norway	Nov 16 p143 c3
	1828
-Describes mermaid supposedly seen off coast of Wales	Oct 3 p220 c1

SEAMAN, DAVID

	1828
-Boarding house in New York City (Advertisement)	Sep 5 p191 c1

SEAMAN, WILLET

	1828
-Appointed to the correspondence committee of the New York Manumission Society	May 2 p49 c1

SECOND AFRICAN PRESBYTERIAN CHURCH (Philadelphia)

	1828
-Will open for worship	May 2 p46 c3

SEDGEWICK, ALBERT

	1827
-Commits suicide	Apr 27 p27 c3

SELF-IMPROVEMENT (Blacks)

	1827
-Describes how one should spend spare time	Apr 13 p17 c4
-Describes what kind of friends to keep in order to lead a good life	Apr 20 p22 c2
-Describes the foolishness of conceit	Apr 20 p22 c4 p23 c1
-Explains that discreet conduct will help improve one's position	Apr 20 p23 c2

-Advises people to face each problem as it arises	Apr 27 p25 c3-4
-Advises one not to pretend to be what one is not	Apr 27 p26 c2
-Describes men such as Benjamin Franklin who raised themselves to high positions	May 25 p42 c3-4
-Describes the foolishness of wishing for the impossible	Jun 1 p46 c3-4
-Praises societies of Blacks and urges society for temperance	Jun 1 p46 c4 p47 c1
-New York Freedom's Journal supports the idea of a society for temperance	Jun 1 p47 c1
-Urges people to live better, more moral lives	Jun 15 p55 c3 ed.
-Cites people who have been successful because of independent thinking	Jul 20 p74 c3-4
-Austin Steward delivers a speech on how Blacks can elevate themselves	Jul 27 p78 c1-3
-View that Blacks will not rise economically if they don't stay in agriculture	Aug 31 p98 c2-3
-Explains advantages for Blacks in expressing themselves through a debating society	Sep 7 p102 c4 let.
-View that the good life will be gained through the use of the Bible	Nov 23 p145 c4 p146 c1
	1828
-Brief description of the best time for thinking	Mar 7 p197 c4
-Explains how everyone can be successful through hard work	Oct 31 p249 c1-3 p250 c1
	1829
-Hopes the new year will bring better conditions	Jan 2 p314 c3 ed.
-See also Conduct; Education; Moral Reform; Reading Room Society for Mental Improvement (Philadelphia, Pennsylvania)	

SELYVEN, JAMES

1828

-To be executed for robbing a store — May 16 p60 c2-3

SEPARATISM

1827

-Argument for states for Blacks only — Jul 27 p77 c1-2

-Idea of a Black state condemned — Dec 7 p153 c3-4

1828

-Joseph Watson of Ohio suggests that Blacks live in separate communities — Dec 5 p283 c1-2 let.

1829

-Lewis Woodson, an Ohio Black, supports the idea of separate Black communities — Jan 31 p345 c1 let.

SEXTUS IV, POPE

-See Wessell, John

SEXTUS V, POPE

1827

-Gives short biography and describes his rise to the Papacy — Apr 20 p21 c3-4; Apr 27 p26 c1-2

SHAKERS

1828

-Describes sect called Shakers — Oct 17 p236 c1-2

1829

-Describes Shakers in Harvard, Massachusetts — Jan 29 p334 c2

SHAKESPEARE, WILLIAM

1828

-Traces ancestry — Apr 18 p29 c3

SHARP, JACOB

1827

-Marries Catherine Potter — Apr 13 p19 c4

SHELTER FOR COLOURED ORPHANS

1828

-Describes this Society started by Quaker women — Mar 14 p199 c4, p200 c1-2; Mar 21 p205 c3-4

SHEPHERD, JOSEPH (Shepard) (Richmond, Virginia)

- Agent for the Freedom's Journal — 1828 - 1829: Feb 29, '28 p194 c4-Mar 28, '29 p412 c3

SHERIDAN, LEWIS (Elizabethtown, North Carolina)

- Agent for the Freedom's Journal — 1828 - 1829: Jan 11, '28 p168 c4-Mar 28, '29 p412 c3

SHERMAN, ROGER

- Describes his career — 1828: Jul 25 p142 c1

SHIELDS, JOHN (New Haven, Connecticut)

- Agent for the Freedom's Journal — 1827 - 1828: Jul 27, '27 p80 c4-Dec 26, '28 p308 c3

SHIPPARD, JOSEPH

- School for Free Blacks in Richmond, Virginia (Advertisement) — 1828: May 16 p58 c1

SHIPS

1827

- Dutch ships Wassener and Waterloo sink off Holland coast — Mar 16 p3 c2
- British ship Redwing brings news from Africa — Mar 16 p3 c3
- Describes explosion on the Oliver Ellsworth — Mar 30 p11 c3
- Describes explosion on the Montreal — Apr 27 p26 c3

1828

- Describes the burning and sinking of The Sun — Sep 12 p197 c1-2
- Crew of Oeno massacred in the Pacific — Oct 10 p226 c3 p227 c1-2

SHORT, CHARLES

- Union Hotel (Advertisement) — 1827: Jul 13 p72 c3

SHOTWELL, WILLIAM

1827

-One of the founders of the New York Manumission Society — Oct 12 p122 c2

SICKLES, JOHN JR.

1827

-Drug store (Advertisement) — Apr 20, 27 pp24, 28 c3

SIDONIA

1827

-Describes ancient Egyptian colonization — Aug 31 p97 c4 p98 c1-2

SIERRA LEONE

1827

-Being inspected for colonization — Mar 16 p3 c4
-British capture a Brazilian slave ship — May 25 p43 c3

1828

-England plans to transport settlers to a better climate — Jan 11 p167 c2-3
-Colonel Denham appointed Lieutenant-Governor of the colony — Feb 22 p191 c1
-Described as terrible climate for Europeans — Oct 31 p252 c1
-Abduhl Rahahmon describes Timbuctoo and surrounding areas — Oct 31 252 c1-2

1829

-Describes settlement's beginning (1787) — Jan 24 p333 c3 p334 c1
-Condemns climate that causes disease and death — Jan 24 p338 c2
-Story of an English trader who marries and abandons a woman of Sierra Leone — Feb 14 p357 c3 p358 c1-2

-See also Fernando Po; Niambanna; Slave Trade

SILLIMAN'S JOURNAL

1827

-Describes a floating island in a lake (Newburyport, Massachusetts) — Apr 6 p15 c3

SIPKINS, THOMAS

1827

- Appointed to the Committee of People of Color of New York for the celebration of slavery's abolition — May 4 p30 c4

SLAVE BELINDA

1827

- Petitioned Massachusetts legislature for her freedom in 1782 — May 18 p38 c1

SLAVE REVOLTS

1827

- Reports a revolt of 300 slaves in Georgia — Jun 22 p58 c4

1828

- Riot of slaves of Rio De Janeiro, Brazil — Oct 10 p230 c1

SLAVE TRADE

1827

- Still carried on in Cuba — Jul 27 p79 c3
- Virginia is the center of the internal slave trade — Aug 10 p86 c1
- Poem describing the slave trade — Aug 17 p89 c4 p 90 c1
- Dialogue describing the slave trade — Aug 17 p89 c4 p90 c1
- Excerpts from the Twenty-First Report of the London African Association on the cruelties of the slave trade — Sep 14 p105 c3-4 p106 c1
- Actions of Liberia and Sierra Leone will help stop the slave trade — Oct 5 p117 c4 p118 c1-2
- Brazil agrees to stop the slave trade in three years — Dec 7 p155 c1

1828

- American Convention for Promoting the Abolition of Slavery urges an end to the domestic slave trade — Feb 15 p185 c4 p186 c1
- Reverend Wilson condemns the slave trade as an unchristian act — Mar 7 p195 c1-4 p196 c1

-Describes the first trial for involvement in the slave trade	Mar 14 p199 c1
-Explains the uselessness of stopping the slave trade if slavery still exists	Mar 14 p199 c1-3
-Discusses the Brazilian slave trade	Apr 11 p20 c1
-E. Malibian tried in New York City for involvement in the slave trade	May 30 p77 c3
-Describes a trader who killed 136 slaves during the middle passage	Jul 11 p125 c2-3
-States that slavery will not end until the slave trade completely ceases	Aug 29 p180 c1-3
-Describes the effects on a captured African Prince of being sold into slavery	Sep 12 p194 c2-3
-Poem, "The Slave Ship"	Sep 12 p198 c3
-Describes the cruel treatment of slaves being marched to a sale	Sep 26 p211 c1
-Calls for the immediate end to the domestic slave trade	Oct 17 p233 c3 p235 c1 ed.
-Describes the slave trade in Baltimore, Maryland	Oct 31 p254 c1-2 let.
-Describes the terrible conditions on a slave ship going from Baltimore to New Orleans	Nov 7 p259 c2
-Poem "The Captured African Chief" by Amos Blanchard	Nov 7 p262 c3 p263 c1 Nov 14 p270 c1-3
-Reader describes the cruelty of the slave trade in separating families	Nov 14 p268 c1-3 let.
-Describes slaves being sold off in the south	Dec 12 p292 c2
-Story of slave ship owners who tell authorities that one of their captives is a prince who owns all the other Blacks on board	Dec 26 p303 c3
	<u>1829</u>
-British capture a slave ship bound for Havana, Cuba	Jan 2 p310 c2
-Norfolk slave dealers plan to sell 10,000 slaves in New Orleans	Jan 16 p329 c3

-Explains the origin of the slave trade	Jan 24 p333 c2-3 p334 c1
-Describes the manner in which slaves are advertised in Rio de Janiero	Jan 31 p345 c2-3
-See also Lee, Phillip; Washington, D.C.; Young, Thomas	
SLAVERY (Ancient)	
	<u>1829</u>
-Describes Greek slavery	Jan 24 p333 c1-2
-See also Slavery (Hebrew)	
SLAVERY (British)	
	<u>1827</u>
-Female slave suing the crown for her freedom	Aug 24 p95 c3
-Reports the cost of a slave in the West Indies	Sep 28 p114 c1-2
-Lists punishments set by slave laws	Oct 5 p119 c3
-"Letters on the necessity of a prompt extinction of British Colonial Slavery" available	Oct 12 p123 c2-3
-Description of whips used	Oct 26 p131 c2
-Relates the story of a slave who gained his freedom	Nov 30 p149 c3-4 p150 c1
-Description of Somerset Case which ruled any slave free once brought into England	Nov 30 p150 c1
-Gives the number of slaves in the West Indies in 1818 and 1824	Dec 7 p154 c3
	<u>1828</u>
-Decision in the Somerset Case overruled	Jan 11 p167 c1-2
-Traces the development of slavery in the West Indies	Feb 29 p193 c1-4 p194 c1-2
-Reverend Wilson condemns slavery from a Christian point of view	Mar 7 p195 c1-4 p196 c1
-African Institution states that slavery and the slave trade must end	Mar 14 p199 c1
-Describes the terrible treatment of slaves in South Africa and the unlikelihood of an end to the system	Apr 4 p9 c1-3

-Liberal slave laws of Lord Bathurst defeated	Apr 4 p14 c3 p15 c1
-Describes the emotional problems of a slave married to a freeman	Apr 11 p17 c1-3
-Describes the evil character of slave holders resulting from slavery	Apr 18 p25 c1-3
-Blames the system of slavery for cruelties, not the individual people involved	Apr 25 p33 c1-3 p34 c1
-View that people opposed to slavery will advocate it after a short exposure to the system	May 2 p41 c1-2
-Explains results of the law making children the same status as the mother	Aug 1 p147 c1-2
-Slave owners ignoring Parliament's resolution to ready slaves for freedom	Nov 21 p274 c1-3 p275 c1-2
-Duke of Wellington states Parliament cannot force colonists to treat their slaves better	Dec 5 p281 c1-3 p282 c1
-Abolitionists feel colonies must obey Parliament	Dec 12 p289 c1-3 p290 c1
-Describes slavery in Bermuda as mild	Dec 26 p302 c1-3
-Describes slavery in the East Indies	Dec 26 p302 c3 p303 c1
	1829
-Hopes slaves will be allowed an education	Jan 31 p341 c3 p342 c1
-See also Abolition (England); Anti-Slavery Society (England); Slave Trade; Society for the Mitigation and Gradual Abolition of Slavery Throughout the British Dominion; West Indies	

SLAVERY (Hebrew)

	1827
-Explains Hebrew slavery in Egypt	Jun 29 p61 c1-3 Jul 6 p65 c1-2
-Relates the history of Hebrew slavery and compares it with modern slavery	Jul 13 p69 c3-4 p70 c1

-Describes the slaves of ancient Hebrews	Jul 20 p73 c3-4 p74 cl Jul 27 p77 c2-3 Aug 3 p81 cl
-Explains the difference between Hebrew and modern slavery	Aug 3 p81 cl-2

SLAVERY (Spanish)

	1827
-Describes slavery in Cuba	Nov 30 p149 cl-3
	1828
-Seen almost non-existent in Mexico	Sep 26 p211 cl
-Outlines liberal laws regarding a slave's ability to purchase his freedom	Nov 14 p266 cl-3 p267 cl
	1829
-Describes the introduction of slavery into the Spanish colonies	Feb 14 p359 c3

SLAVERY (United States)

	1827
-Describes the sale of a slave	Mar 16 p4 cl-2
-Describes slavery and how slaves should be treated	Mar 30 pl cl-4
-Englishman describes slavery	Apr 6 pl c2-4
-Gives reasons for White reluctance to end slavery	Apr 20 p21 cl-2
-Describes atrocious treatment of Africans everywhere	Apr 27 p26 c3
-Argues that slavery is defined in the Bible	May 4 p29 cl-2
-New York Evening Post describes slaves as content and happy	May 11 p34 c3-4
-Refutes theory that slaves are happy	May 11 p34 c3-4 p35 cl
-Essay "Othello" dennounces slavery	May 18 p38 cl
-Reverend O. P. Hoyt warns of revolt of Blacks if slavery continues	May 18 p38 c2-3
-Compares modern slavery to Hebrew slavery in Egypt	Jun 29 p61 cl-3
-Stresses discrepancy between the Declaration of Independence and slavery	Jun 29 p62 c4

-Expresses possiblity of slave revolt	Jun 29 p62 c4 p63 cl
-Describes dogs used to find runaway slaves	Jul 6 p67 c3
-States relation of ancient slavery to modern slavery	Jul 13 p69 c3-4 p70 cl
-Explains laws of certain slave states regarding Blacks	Jul 27 p77 c4
-Explains difference between ancient Hebrew and modern slavery	Aug 3 p81 c2
-Describes fatal punishments used by slave holders	Aug 3 p82 cl
-Adam Hodgson explains why free labor is cheaper than slave labor	Aug 10 p85 cl-2
-Cites views of philosophers and historians	Aug 17 p89 cl-2 Aug 24 p93 cl-3 Aug 31 p97 cl-2
-Hodgson compares South American slavery with feudalism	Sep 7 pl01 cl-2 Sep 14 pl05 cl-2
-Describes abuses of British slavery	Aug 24 p93 cl-2
-Poem "Pity For Poor Africans"	Aug 24 p93 c4 p94 cl
-Describes punishment for harboring fugitive slaves	Aug 31 p99 c3
-Poem "Slavery"; criticizes Congress for allowing slavery's extension	Sep 7 pl01 c3-4
-A reader attacks methods used by slave owners	Sep 28 pl14 c4 pl15 cl-2
-Gives White justification for slavery	Sep 28 pl15 c2
-Outlines reasons slaveholders will never give up slaves	Oct 12 pl22 c3-4
-Condemns slaves and free Blacks who use slave-produced goods	Oct 19 pl27 c2-3 ed.
-View that slave owners are not Christian	Nov 23 pl46 cl-3
-View that slaves are treated best under the Spanish	Nov 30 pl49 cl-3
-Slaveholders greatly fear educating Blacks	Nov 30 pl50 c2
-Criticizes lack of rights of American slaves	Nov 30 pl51 cl-2 ed.
-View that slaveholders are foolish not to fear revolt	Nov 30 pl51 c2-3 let.

-Explains why free labor is cheaper than slave	Dec 7 p153 c3
-Describes case of a female runaway slave	Dec 21 p163 c2-3
	1828
-House Way and Means Committee feels slaves are human beings	Jan 25 p174 c1-2
-Judicial view that slaves travelling with masters to a free state can decide whether or not to return	Jan 25 p174 c2
-Slavery's origin traced to the Biblical story of Ham	Mar 7 p196 c1-2
-Theory of slavery originating from the Bible argued	Mar 7 p196 c1-2
-Condemns people who buy products made by slaves	Mar 14 p199 c3-4
-Poem "The Tears of a Slave"	Mar 14 p202 c1
-Condemns sale of a free Black into slavery in Washington, D.C.	Apr 25 p36 c1
-Story of an African Prince and slave who attained his freedom and returned to Africa	May 16 p57 c1-2
-Describes time as a comfort for the cruelties of slavery	May 16 p63 c2
-Poem "The African Slave"	Jun 27 p111 c1
-Poem "Slavery" by George Horton	Jul 18 p135 c1
-Describes the cruel treatment of a slave girl in New Orleans	Sep 12 p194 c2
-New York court case concerning the status of slaves when in free states	Oct 3 p222 c1
-Describes the poor treatment of elderly slaves	Oct 10 p228 c1-2
-Condemns a southern minister searching for a runaway slave in New York City	Oct 31 p251 c2 ed.
-Advises runaway slaves to leave New York City to avoid apprehension	Oct 31 p251 c2
-Runaway slaves caught in Norfolk, Virginia	Oct 31 p251 c3
-Condemns Blacks who betray runaways	Nov 7 p259 c1-2 ed.
-Further warning against Blacks who turn in runaways	Nov 14 p267 c2
-Europeans seen as hypocrites for having slaves yet speaking of the equality of man	Nov 21 p276 c2
-Poem "The Slave's Soliloquy"	Nov 21 p278 c3 p279 c1

-Further warnings to runaways — Dec 5 p283 c2-3
-Describes conditions of slaves in Brazil — Dec 12 p292 c3

1829

-Canada refuses to return American runaway slaves — Jan 9 p321 c2
-British Parliament discusses what to do with American fugitive slaves in Canada — Jan 23 p333 c1
-Slavery compared to the devil — Jan 23 p336 c3
-See also Abolition; Burke, Edmund; Clay, Henry; Gallatin, Albert; Hodgson, Adam; Hume, David; Racism; Saxe Weimar, Duke of; Smith, Adam

SLOCUM, PETER M.

1828

-Discovers improved technique in making string instruments — Apr 11 p21 c3

SMALLEY, JOHN

1828

-Work for Blacks through the New York Manumission Society praised — Sep 19 p203 c2 let.

SMITH, ADAM

1827

-Free labor is cheaper than slave labor — Aug 10 p85 c1

SMITH, BOSTON

1828

-One of the founders of the African Grand Lodge of Masons (Boston, Massachusetts) — Nov 7 p257 c1

SMITH, ELIZABETH

1827

-Notes her engagement and marriage — Apr 6 p16 c2

SMITH, CAPTAIN JOHN (Alias Thomas Collins)

1828

-Arrested for kidnapping Black children — Oct 24 p246 c1
-Sentenced to twenty-one years for kidnapping — Nov 7 p258 c3

SMITH, JOHN

1827

-Cleaning and tailor business (Advertisement) — Apr 20-May 4 pp24, 28, 32, c3

SMITH, JOHN (Maine)

1827

-Sentenced to prison for attempted rape — Apr 27 p27 c3

SMITH, JOHN (Slave Dealer)

1827

-Describes attempted prison escape — Mar 30 p3 c3

SMITH, MELANCTON

1827

-One of the founders of the New York Manumission Society — Oct 12 p122 c2

SMITH, MOSES

1828

-Free Black who turns in runaway slaves — Nov 14 p267 c2

SMITH, RANDALL

1827

-Sentenced to seven years for killing Dr. Brown — Apr 27 p27 c3

SMITH, STEPHEN (Columbia, Pennsylvania)

1827 - 1829

-Agent for the Freedom's Journal — Mar 16, '27 p4 c3-Mar 28, '29 p412 c3

SMITHENS, ANNE

1827

-Marries John Gardner — Apr 6 p15 c4

SNAKES

1827

-Describes a snake stalking prey — Aug 3 p82 c1-2

1828

-Describes method of catching snakes in Asia — Oct 10 p228 c3

SNOW, PRINCE JR. (Coroner)

1827

-Inquires into the death of an infant girl — Mar 16 p3 c4

SOCIALISM
-See Utopian Socialism

SOCRATES

1827

-Anecdote about Socrates' views on friendship — Nov 9 p140 c1

SOCIETY FOR THE MITIGATION AND GRADUAL ABOLITION OF SLAVERY THROUGHOUT THE BRITISH DOMINIONS

1827

-Praises intentions of the _Freedom's Journal_ and asks to exchange publications — Nov 9 p138 c3 let.

SOCIETY OF FRIENDS (Quakers)

1827

-Worst enemies of slavery and probably the best supporters of colonization — Sep 21 p110 c1

1828

-Women start society for Black orphans — Mar 14 p199 c4 p200 c1-2

-Society divides over philosophy — Jun 13 p90 c1

SOLOMON

1828

-Views on fools — Apr 11 p22 c1
-Instance of wisdom — May 30 p76 c1

SOLOMON, BEN

1827

-Arabic scholar of the 18th century who was received in the English Court — May 18 p37 c4

SOMERSET

1827

-British slave who gained freedom while in England — Nov 30 p150 c1

SOMERSET CASE
-See Stowell, Lord

SOUTH AMERICA

1828

-Describes Brazilian blockade of Buenos Aires — Jun 13 p91 c3
-See also Bolivar, Simon; Columbia (Colombia); Slave Trade; Slavery (Spanish)

SOUTH CAROLINA

1827

-Describes harsh penal code — Jul 13 p71 c3

1828

-Allows private stockholders in State Bank; prohibits education and employment of Blacks; advises Congress not to give money to the American Colonization Society — Jan 11 p166 c1
-Criticized for laws concerning Black education — Jan 18 p169 c4
-Free Blacks have the right to hold property — Jan 25 p175 c3
-Charleston Grand Jury asks end to prohibition against Blacks migrating for employment — Jun 6 p81 c1
-Describes food market in Charleston — Dec 12 p291 c2

SPRAGUE, CHARLES

1827

-Delivers a speech on alcoholic husbands and wives to the Massachusetts Society for Suppressing Intemperance — Jun 29 p61 c3-4

SPRING, REVEREND DOCTOR
-See Religion

SQUIRRELS

1827

-Describes squirrels planting acorns — Apr 13 p20 c2

STANLEY, JOHN C. (Newbern, North Carolina)

1828 - 1829

-Agent for the Freedom's Journal — Jan 11, '28 p168 c4- Mar 28, '29 p412 c3

STEEL

1827

-Lists chemical composition of steel — Sep 7 p104 c1

STEELE, GEORGE W.

1827

-Assaulted Allen Cooper; imprisoned and fined — Mar 30 p3 c2-3

STEPHENS, JANE

	1827
-Announces desertion of her husband, James, who denies being married to her	Oct 12 p123 c4 Nov 30 p151 c4 Dec 7 p155 c4

STEPHENS, WILLIAM J.

	1828
-His death explained	Aug 8 p153 c3

STEPHENSON, MR. (Scotland)

	1828
-Describes his funeral arrangements	Mar 21 p206 c1-2

STEWARD, AUSTIN (Rochester, New York)

	1827
-Delivers a speech in Rochester on emancipation in New York	Jul 20 p75 c4
-Extract from Spain on emancipation; advises Blacks how to live	Jul 27 p78 c1-3
	1827 - 1829
-Agent for the <u>Freedom's Journal</u>	Jun 15, '27 p56 c4- Mar 28, '29 p412 c3

STOCKBRIDGE, CALVIN (North Yarmouth, Maine)

	1827 - 1829
-Agent for the <u>Freedom's Journal</u>	Apr 13, '27 p20 c4- Mar 28, '29 p412 c3

STONE, WILLIAM

	1828
-Appoints a committee to collect clothing for children of the African Free School	Mar 7 p197 c1
-Serves on the Correspondence Committee of the New York Manumission Society	May 9 p49 c1

STORCH, A.K. (Russian Economist)

	1827
-View that people are more productive when free than when enslaved	Aug 10 p85 c1-2

STORIES

	<u>1827</u>
-"The Dean of Badajoz-A Tale" by the Abbe Blarchet	Apr 6 p1 c1-2 Apr 13 p17 c4 p18 c1-2
-"The Ice Shop"	Jun 1 p46 c2-3 Jun 8 p49 c2-3
-"The Haunted House" by L. E. Lorimer	Sep 21 p109 c3-4
-"Ellen" by Washington Irving	Oct 5 p117 c3-4
-"The Marvelous Doctor" by Ettrick Sheppard	Oct 19 p125 c1
-"The Spanish Professor"	Oct 19 p125 c1-3 Oct 26 p129 c1-4 p130 c1
-"Emily Milbourne" by Humphrey Ravelin	Nov 2 p133 c1-4
-"The Bashful Man"	Nov 9 p137 c1-3
-"Seduction"	Nov 23 p145 c1-3 p146 c3-4
-"The Stout Gentleman" by Washington Irving	Dec 21 p161 c1-4 p162 c1
	<u>1828</u>
-"Ver-Vert" or "The Parrot of the Nuns"	Jan 11 p165 c1-4 Jan 18 p169 c1-3 p 170 c3-4
-"Nights in the Guard House" from <u>The Military Sketch Book</u> or "The Story of Maria DeCarmo"	Jan 25 p173 c1-4 Feb 1 p177 c1-2 Feb 8 p181 c1-2 Feb 15 p185 c1-3 Feb 22 p189 c1-4
-"Teresa-A Haytien Tale"	Jan 18 p170 c3-4 p171 c1 Jan 25 p174 c3-4 Feb 8 p182 c2-4 Feb 15 p186 c3-4
-"Charles Seville"	Apr 11 p18 c1-3 May 23 p69 c2-3
-"The House of Weeping" from the <u>German of Reichter</u>	Apr 11 p20 c1-3 p21 c1 Apr 18 p28 c1-3 p29 c1
-"Mr. Duffle's Adventure" from <u>Blackwood's Magazine</u>	Apr 11 p22 c1-3
-"A Story of the Olden Time in Italy"	Apr 18 p30 c1-3 p31 c1-2
-"The Disinterment"	Apr 25 p34 c1-3 p35 c1-3

-"An Odd Scene"	May 2 p45 cl-2
-"Recollections of Tommy Tompkins"	May 30 p75 c2-3 Jun 6 p81 cl-2
-"Madame Christophe"	Jun 27 p106 cl-2 Jul 4 p116 cl-3 Jul 11 p124 cl-3
-Story about a fighter in the American Revolution	Jun 27 p108 cl-3 p109 cl
-"Vanderdickin's Message Home" from <u>Blackwood's</u> Magazine	Jul 25 p137 cl-3 p138 cl Aug 1 p145 cl-3 p146 cl
-"The Commercial Gentleman"	Aug 8 p156 cl-2
-"A Life of Trials"	Aug 8 p156 c2-3 p157 cl
-"The Sleep Walker"	Aug 15 p161 cl-3 p162 cl-3
-"Moss-Side"	Aug 22 p169 cl-3 p170 cl Aug 29 p177 cl-3 p178 cl
-"A False Alarm" from <u>The Eastern Galaxy</u>	Sep 26 p209 cl-2
-"The Brewery of Egg Shells"	Sep 26 p209 c2-3 p210 cl-2
-"The Family Party" from <u>Sayings and Doings</u>	Oct 3 p217 cl-3 p218 cl Oct 10 p225 cl-3 p226 cl
-"Dr. Holley's Dying Scene" by Mrs. Holley	Oct 3 p220 cl-2
-"Dr. Pair's Vanity"	Oct 3 p220 c2-3
-"Cockney in Paris"	Oct 24 p241 cl-3 p242 cl-2
STOWELL, LORD	
	<u>1828</u>
-Act of over-ruling Somerset decision criticized	Jan 11 p167 cl-2
-See also Somerset Case	
STRANG, JESSE	
	<u>1827</u>
-Confesses murder of Mr. Whipple	Jun 22 p58 c3-4
STRONG, JONATHAN	
	<u>1827</u>
-British slave who escaped and retained his freedom	Nov 30 p149 c3-4 p150 cl

STROUD, GEORGE M.

1828

-Writing a book, A Sketch of the Laws which Relates to Slavery in the Several States of the United States of America — Feb 1 p178 c3

SUDER, ADAM

1828

-Builds cabinets and coffins (Advertisement) — Feb 29 p195 c4

SUICIDES

1827

-New Hampshire man hangs himself — Apr 6 p15 c3

1828

-Statistics of suicides in Paris from 1794 to 1824 — Dec 12 p290 c1-2
-See also Sedgwick, Albert

SUPERSTITIONS

1827

-Anecdote about sailors' superstitions — Jul 6 p68 c2

1828

-Describes belief in ghosts of some famous people — Sep 12 p196 c2-3
-Description of a witch in Baltimore — Oct 3 p220 c3 p221 c1
-Story of a Scotch prophetess — Oct 17 p237 c1

1829

-Reports suspected witchcraft in Portsmouth, New Hampshire — Feb 14 p359 c1
-Describes superstitions of sailors — Feb 14 p360 c1

SWEARINGEN, GEORGE VAN

1829

-Arrested for murdering his wife — Jan 9 p318 c1-2

SWIFT, JONATHAN

1827

-Anecdote about his preaching about pity — Aug 17 p92 c2
-Ridicules a wife's unceasing praise of her husband — Dec 21 p164 c2

1828

-Anecdote concerning an encounter with poor people — Oct 17 p237 c1
-Accidently preaches a funeral sermon on Easter — Oct 17 p237 c3 p238 c1

SWITZERLAND

1828

-Abolishes capital punishment — May 23 p68 c1

T

TALBOT, ISAAC (Portland, Maine)

1828 - 1829

-Agent for the <u>Freedom's Journal</u> — Apr 18, '28 p32 c3- Mar 28, '29 p412 c3

TALLEYRAND, PRINCE

1827

-Attacked by Manbreiul — Mar 16 p3 c2

TARDY (Pirate)
-See Piracy; Racism

TEMPERANCE

1827

-B. F. Hughes addresses Boyer (Masonic) Lodge on temperance — Jul 20 p75 c1
-Advises Blacks to keep out of grog shops — Jul 20 p75 c2
-Austin Steward advises freed Blacks of New York not to drink alcohol — Jul 27 p78 c1-3
-Massachusetts Society for Suppression of Intemperance resolves to stop use of alcohol among the young — Nov 16 p143 c1

1828

-Sulphuric acid in alcohol cures intemperance — Feb 15 p187 c3
-American Society for the Promotion of Temperance has $14,000 in funds — Feb 22 p190 c4
-Dr. Beecher discloses evils of alcohol and urges the halt of its usage — May 30 p74 c1-2
-See also Alcohol; Beecher, Dr. (Lyman); Self-Improvement (Blacks); Sprague, Charles

TENNESSEE

	1827
-Reports meteorite shower	Jun 22 p58 c4
-"Cotton" factory operated by slaves	Nov 9 p139 c3

TEXAS

	1827
-Revolt occurs because of law prohibiting importation of slaves	Apr 20 p22 c3

THALES (Ancient Greece)

	1827
-Relates conversation with a sophist	Jun 8 p52 c2

THOMAS, HENRY

	1827
-Appointed to committee in Cooperstown, New York to arrange celebration of slavery's abolition in New York	Jun 29 p63 c4

THOMAS, SAMUEL (Liverpool, England)

	1827 - 1829
-Agent for the Freedom's Journal	Nov 30, '27 p152 c4- Mar 28, '29 p412 c3

THOMPSON, REVEREND ABRAHAM

	1827
-His life eulogized	Mar 16 p2 c1

THOMPSON, J.C. AND COMPANY

	1828
-Clothing, tailoring and cleaning (Advertisement)	Sep 26, '28 p215 c1- Mar 21, '29 p403 c2

THOMPSON, RACHEL
-See Thompson, Thomas (New York, New York)

THOMPSON, THOMAS (Newark, New Jersey)

	1827
-Dies	Apr 20 p23 c4

THOMPSON, THOMAS (New York, New York)

	1827
-Two year old daughter, Rachel, dies	Apr 20 p23 c4

THORP, DR.

	1827
-Medical services (Advertisement)	Jul 20 p76 c3

THORP, COLONEL ROBERT

	1827
-One of the founders of the New York Manumission Society	Oct 12 p122 c2

TOBACCO

	1827
-Reverend Dr. Rush explains the bad effects of tobacco	Mar 30 p2 c3

TODD, SAMUEL

	1827
-Elder of the African Methodist Episcopal Church of New York	Aug 17 p91 c4
	1828
-Advisor to the African Female Dorcas Association	Feb 1 p179 c1-2
-See also African Female Dorcas Association	

TOMPKINS, DANIEL D.

	1827
-New York Governor asks the state legislature for the abolition of slavery as of July 4, 1827	Jul 13 p70 c2

TRADE

	1827
-England exports more to South America than to the United States	Mar 30 p4 c3

TROTH, HENRY

	1828
-Secretary of the Pennsylvania Abolition Society	Jan 11 p166 c4

TUCKER, BENJAMIN

	1828
-Vice-President of the Pennsylvania Abolition Society	Jan 11 p166 c4

TURKISH ARMY

	1827
-Recruiting Asians	Mar 16 p3 c3
	1828
-Describes its use of the sabre	Aug 22 p171 c2
-Sultan plans strong resistance against the Russians	Nov 7 p258 c2

U

UNION INN

	1827
-C. Boyer (Advertisement)	Jun 15 p56 c2

UNLEY, JOHN

	1827
-Daughter Phebe Jane dies	Apr 6 p15 c4

UNLEY, PHEBE JANE
-See Unley, John

UNION SOCIETY

	1827
-Appeared at the 17th anniversary of the African Association for Mutual Relief	Mar 30 p2 c4

UNITED STATES CONGRESS

	1827
-American Colonization Society asks for aid	Mar 16 p3 c4
-Criticized for not supporting the American Colonization Society and for perpetuating slavery	Sep 21 p110 c1
-Criticized for racism in Washington, D.C.	Nov 16 p142 c3-4 ed.
-Twentieth Congress convenes	Dec 14 p159 c1
	1828
-Advised by South Carolina not to give aid to the American Colonization Society	Jan 11 p166 c1
-House Ways and Means Committee states slaves are people, not property	Jan 25 p174 c1-2
-Senator Chambers asks the Senate to aid the American Colonization Society	Mar 7 p197 c1
-New York Manumission Society petitions an end to slavery in Washington, D.C.	May 9 p49 c1-3 p50 c1
-1,062 Washington, D.C. residents petition Congress for the abolition of slavery	May 9 p50 c3
-Senate Foreign Relations Committee feels colonization is too expensive	May 30 p74 c3

1829

-Statistics of representation from free and slaves states — Jan 2 p309 c2
-Representative Miner of Maryland favors investigation of slavery and the slave trade in Washington, D.C. — Jan 16 p328 c2-3
-Representative Miner's motion passed — Jan 16 p330 c2

-Abolition Society of Stark County, Ohio petitions for an end to slavery in Washington, D.C. — Feb 7 p353 cl
-House Committee states that slavery will stay in Washington, D.C. — Feb 21 p365 cl-3 p366 cl

-Discusses chance of abolition in Washington passing through Congress — Feb 21 p370 cl
-Reprints bill before Congress to stop slavery in Washington, D.C. — Feb 26 p373 cl-3
-Discusses abolition of slavery in Washington, D.C. — Feb 26 p374 cl-2 ed.

UTOPIAN SOCIALISM

1828

-Description of a cooperative Owenite Community in Pennsylvania — Dec 5 p284 cl-3

V

VANLIEW, N.

1828 - 1829

-Boot polish for shining boots and shoes (Advertisement) — Aug 8, '28 p159 c2- Mar 28, '29 p412 c3

VAN TUYL, THOMAS

1827

-Marries Nancy Barnum — Apr 27 p26 c4

VASA, GUSTAVUS (Vassa)
-See Equiano Olandah (Olaudah)

VASHON, JOHN B. (Carlisle, Pennsylvania)

-Agent for the Freedom's Journal — 1828 - 1829: Feb 1, '28 p180 c4-Mar 28, '29 p412 c3

VASTER, BARON DE

-Describes superiority and beauty of blacks — 1829: Feb 14 p357 c1-3

VAUGHAN, REVEREND R. (Richmond, Virginia)

-Agent for the Freedom's Journal — 1827 - 1828: Nov 2, '27 p136 c4-Feb 22, '28 p192(162) c4

VICKER, MATTHEW

-One of the founders of the New York Manumission Society — 1827: Oct 12 p122 c2

VIRGINIA
-See Slave Trade; Slavery

VIRGINIA HOUSE OF DELEGATES

-Removes slavery as punishment for a crime — 1827: Mar 16 p3 c4

VOICE FROM THE TIDE WATER COUNTRY, A

-Pro-Jackson paper to be published — 1827: Apr 25 p36 c3

W

WALKER, DAVID (Boston)

-Holds meeting of the People of Colour of the city of Boston in his house — 1827: Mar 16 p3 c1-2

-Speaks in support of Freedom's Journal at a meeting of Boston Coloured — 1828: Apr 25 p38 c1-2

-Praised for contributing money to buy the freedom of George Horton — Oct 3 p218 c3

-Advertises clothing store (new and used) and cleaning business in Boston — Oct 31,'28 p255 c1-Mar 28, '29 p411 c3

-Calls for Blacks of the United States to unite to improve their position — Dec 19 p295 c1-3 p296 c1

1827 - 1829

-Listed as agent for the Freedom's Journal — Mar 16, '27 p4 c3-Mar 28, '29 p412 c3

-See also General Coloured Association of Boston

WALLIS, MRS. BETSEY

1827

-Offers $100 for the return of her son, John — May 4 p31 c4

WAR OF 1812

1828

-Recounts sea battle between two privately owned ships — Aug 8 p154 c2-3 p155 c1

-Describes impressment of sailors — Oct 17 p237 c3

WARD, COLONEL (Virginia)

1827

-Frees 150 slaves upon his death and leaves them land — May 4 p31 c4

WARWICK (Rhode Island)

1827

-Coal mine discovered — May 4 p31 c3

WASHINGTON, D.C.

1827

-Freedom's Journal criticizes law requiring proof of freedom of Blacks — Nov 16 p142 c3-4 ed.

-Abolition Society of Stark County, Ohio resolves to fight for abolition in Washington, D.C. — Dec 7 p153 c4

-Plea to all Abolition Societies to work for abolition in Washington, D.C. — Dec 7 p154 c3

	1828
-Citizens petition Congress for a halt to the slave trade in Washington, D.C.	Feb 1 p178 c3-4
-Freedom's Journal supports petition of citizens concerning the slave trade	Feb 1 p179 c3 ed.
-Law passed protecting freed slaves from being sold into slavery	Feb 8 p183 c2
-Experiences slight earthquake	Mar 21 p207 c4
-Condemns the sale of a free Black into slavery in Washington, D.C.	Apr 25 p36 c1
-Criticized for the continuance of the domestic slave trade	May 2 p46 c1-2
-New York Manumission Society asking abolitionists throughout the country for help in Washington, D.C.	May 2 p46 c2-3
-1,062 residents petition Congress for abolition	May 9 p51 c3
-Agent of paper describes points of interest between New York City and Washington, D.C.	Jun 27 p107 c2-3 let.
-Describes city and many famous buildings	Aug 15 p163 c2-3 ed.
-Describes Free Blacks and slave trade in Washington, D.C.	Aug 29 p178 c3 p179 c1-2 let.
-People in Boston meet to work for abolition in Washington, D.C.	Aug 29 p181 c2
-Abolitionists throughout country petitioning Congress about Washington, D.C.	Nov 7 p259 c2-3
-Condemns government for allowing slavery and the slave trade in the seat of liberty, Washington, D.C.	Nov 7 p259 c3
-Reader condemns the slave trade in Washington, D.C.	Nov 14 p268 c1-3 let.
-American Convention for Promoting the Abolition of Slavery calls for abolition in Washington, D.C.	Dec 19 p296 c1-3
-Petitions being collected throughout the country to end slavery in Washington	Dec 26 p303 c3

1829

-Mr. M. Keen of Vermont condemns the slave trade in Washington, D.C. — Jan 2 p309 c1-2
-Condemns a reader who wants slavery to continue in Washington, D.C. — Jan 31 p345 c3
-Describes support for the movement for abolition in Washington, D.C. — Feb 14 p362 c1
-Condemns Congress's slowness in stopping slavery in Washington, D.C. — Feb 26 p375 c2-3 ed.
-See also United States Congress; Winer, Mr.

WASHINGTON, JUDGE BUSHROD

1827

-President of Virginia Colonization Society deals in the internal slave trade — Sep 14 p107 c3-4

1828

-Rules slaves traveling in free states with their masters can decide whether or not to return — Jan 25 p174 c2

1829

-Chairs the 12th annual meeting of the American Colonization Society — Mar 7 p384 c1-2

WASSENER, THE (Dutch Ship)

1827

-Sinks off the Holland coast — Mar 16 p3 c2

WATERLOO, THE (Dutch Ship)

1827

-Sinks off the Holland coast — Mar 16 p3 c2

WATERS, HAYDEN

1827

-To deliver a speech at the Cooperstown celebration of New York abolition — Jun 29 p63 c4

WATSON, JOSEPH
-See Separatism

WATSON, ROBERT

1827

-Murdered at his home in Montreal — Apr 20 p23 c4

WEBB, FRANCIS (Philadelphia, Pennsylvania)	
	1827 - 1829
-Agent for the Freedom's Journal	Mar 16, '27 p4 c3- Mar 28, '29 p412 c3
WEDDINGS	
	1827
-Gloucester girl sells her teeth to buy wedding clothes	Apr 6 p2 c3
WEEMS, MR.	
	1828
-Maryland Congressman explains the origin of slavery as being from God	Mar 7 p196 c1-2
WELLS, JOHN	
	1827
-Murdered by Ewing Hogan	Apr 27 p26 c3-4
WESLEY, REVEREND S.	
	1827
-Relates anecdote about Wesley and a clerk	Apr 6 p16 c1-2
WESSELL, JOHN	
	1827
-Anecdote about his encounter with Pope Sextus IV	Aug 17 p92 c1
WEST, HENRY	
	1827
-Chosen President of the Jordan Missionary Society	Dec 7 p154 c4
WEST INDIES	
	1827
-Jamaica and Barbadoes divided into two dioceses	Mar 30 p3 c4
-Describes thoughtfulness of West Indians	Apr 13 p20 c1
-New York Evening Post describes West Indian slavery as good	May 11 p34 c3-4
-Refutes theory that slavery is not cruel	May 11 p34 c3-4 p 35 c1
-Free Blacks control most of the land, but suffer great legal oppression	Aug 10 p87 c2
-Describes judicial procedure, prisons and treatment of slaves in Santa Domingo	Sep 14 p106 c1-3
-Experiences great gales	Sep 21 p111 c2

-Black population statistics (1825) — 1829 Feb 26 p379 c1
-See also Anderson, Dr. James; Slave Trade; Slavery (British)

WHEATLY, PHILLIS (Boston, Massachusetts) (Phyllis Wheatley)

1827
-Slave girl who wrote poetry and achieved freedom — May 18 p38 c1
-Her poetry on slavery praised — Nov 2 p135 c2
-Two poems, "Hymn to Humanity" and "Hymn to the Morning" appear — Nov 9 p140 c1

WHIPPLE, ELSIE D.

1827
-Tried for being an accessory to the murder of her husband — Aug 10 p87 c1

WHIPPLE, MR.

1827
-Murdered by Jesse Strang — Jun 22 p58 c3-4

WHIPPER, WILLIAM
-See Reading Room Society for Mental Improvement (Philadelphia, Pennsylvania)

WILBERFORCE SOCIETY

1827
-Appeared at the 17th anniversary of the African Association for Mutual Relief — Mar 30 p2 c4

WILBERFORCE, WILLIAM (England)

1828
-Speaks on abolition at meeting of the Anti-Slavery Society of Great Britian — Jul 4 p113 c1-3, p 114 c1

WILES, F.

1827
-Boarding house (Advertisement) — Sep 14 p108 c3

WILKESBOROUGH, NORTH CAROLINA

1827
-Wilkesborough experiences earthquake in May — Jun 15 p55 c3

WILLIAMS, FRANCIS

1827
-Jamaican educated in England who wrote in Latin — May 18 p37 c4

WILLIAMS, JOHN

	1827
-Tried in New York for being a runaway slave	Oct 12 p123 c3
-Returned to his master	Oct 26 p131 c2

WILLIAMS, JOHN

	1828
-Relates experience of being buried alive in Burnswick Theater in London	May 9 p53 c2-3 p54 c1-2 May 16 p57 c3 p58 c1

WILLIAMS, LEVEN

	1828
-Appointed to committee to plan New York abolition anniversary celebration	May 16 p61 c3

WILLIAMS, REVEREND PETER

	1828
-Advisor to the African Female Dorcas Association	Feb 1 p179 c1-2
-Delivers a sermon on the importance of an early Christian education	Jun 6 p84 c1-3
-Advises against the physical punishment of children and stresses the importance of schools	Jun 13 p92 c1-3 p93 c1

-See also African Female Dorcas Association; Education (Blacks)

WILLIAMS, RICHARD

	1828
-Superintends camp meeting in Flushing, New York	Sep 12 p199 c1

WILLIAMS, ROBERT

	1827
-Delivers speech at the 17th anniversary of the African Association for Mutual Relief	Mar 30 p2 c4

WILLIAMS. REVEREND W. P.(Paul P. Williams) (Flushing, New York)

	1827 - 1829
-Agent for the Freedom's Journal	Jun 15, '27 p56 c4- Mar 28, '29 p412 c3

WILLIS, GEORGE C. (Providence, Rhode Island)

	1827 - 1829
-Agent for the *Freedom's Journal*	Mar 16, '27 p4 c3- Mar 28, '29 p412 c3

WILSON, REVEREND D.

	1828
-Condemns British Slavery from a Christian viewpoint	Mar 7 p195 c1-4 p196 c1

WOLFENBUTTEL, PRINCESS CHARLOTTE CHRISTINA SOPHIE DE (Russia)

	1827
-Biographical sketch	Dec 14 p157 c4 p158 c1

WOMEN (Black)

	1828
-Black women of New York form the African Female Dorcas Association	Feb 1 p179 c1-2
-See also African Female Dorcas Association	

WOMEN (General)

	1827
-Praises womanhood	Apr 13 p20 c2
-Describes advantages in employing women	Apr 13 p20 c2
-Advises women not to lose their tempers	Apr 20 p24 c2
-Describes results of gossiping and cattiness	May 11 p34 c2-3
-View that the law imprisoning females for debts should be abolished	May 11 p35 c2
-Anecdote about perfectionists	Jun 15 p54 c2-3
-Expresses admiration for intelligent, sensible women	Jun 15 p56 c2
-Criticizes women who talk too much	Jun 22 p57 c2-3
-Lists duties of a wife	Jun 22 p60 c1
-Praises the compassion of women	Jul 27 p79 c1
-Describes proper conduct for church	Aug 17 p90 c4 p91 c1
-Story about the problems of a single woman	Sep 28 p113 c3-4 p114 c1
-Criticism of women who talk too much	Oct 5 p118 c4 p119 c1

Entry	Date / Page / Column
-Stresses the importance of modesty in women	Oct 26 p130 c4
-Excerpt from an imaginary spinster's diary	Nov 2 p133 c1
	<u>1828</u>
-Complains of women's cattiness	Apr 4 p10 c1 let.
-Describes health benefits of women's kisses	Apr 4 p14 c2
-Praises the virtue of women	Apr 11 p18 c3
-Discusses difficulties in courting a silly woman	Apr 11 p19 c1
-Describes a beautiful woman	Apr 11 p19 c1
-Satirical dialogue ridiculing avaricious women	Jul 18 p131 c1-2
-Advises women to act dignified in public	Jul 18 p132 c1
-Explains male reverence of beautiful women	Jul 18 p133 c1
-Articles about love included since politics could not interest ladies	Aug 1 p150 c1
-Elenna Clothilda Angelina complains about her fiance	Oct 3 p219 c1-2 let.
	<u>1829</u>
-Frenchman describes Turkish women	Jan 9 p320 c1-2
-Describes female who climbed a high mountain that only men had attempted	Feb 14 p336 c3
-See also African Female Dorcas Association; Daughters of Israel; Marriage; Women (Black); Women's Rights	

WOMEN'S RIGHTS

Entry	Date / Page / Column
	<u>1827</u>
-Reader stresses the importance of education for females	Aug 10 p86 c2-3
	<u>1828</u>
-Describes position of women in medieval and early modern eras	Aug 8 p154 c1-2
-Georgia to pass laws defining wives' rights when husbands desert	Dec 12 p291 c3

WOOD, AARON

Entry	Date / Page / Column
	<u>1828 - 1829</u>
-Adult evening school for Blacks (Advertisement)	Sep 26, '28 p215 c1- Mar 28, '29 p411 c2

WOODFOLK, MR. (Slave Dealer)

1827

-Tried and fined $1 for beating Benjamin Lundy — Apr 27 p27 c2
-See also Lundy, Benjamin

WOODSON LOUIS (Lewis)
-See African Education and Benevolent Society of Chilicothe, Ohio; Separatism

WRIGHT, FRANCES

1827

-Establishes asylum for slaves in Nashoba, Tennessee — May 11 p34 c1

1828

-Describes her asylum for slaves in Tennessee — Jun 6 p81 c3 p82 c1

1829

-Her program condemned by the <u>Baltimore Emerald</u> — Jan 16 p328 c1-2

WRIGHT, R. P. G. (Schenectady, New York)

1827 - 1829

-Agent for the <u>Freedom's Journal</u> — Jul 27, '27 p80 c4- Mar 28, '29 p412 c3

WRIGHT, THEODORE (Princeton, New Jersey)

1827 - 1829

-Agent for the <u>Freedom's Journal</u> — Mar 16, '27 p4 c3- Mar 28, '29 p412 c3

Y

YALE COLLEGE

1827

-Description of building and contents of library — Aug 17 p91 c2

YATES, PETER

1827

-One of the founders of the New York Manumission Society — Oct 12 p122 c2

YOUNG, THOMAS

	1828
-First person to be tried for involvement in the slave trade (Found innocent)	Mar 14 p199 c1

Z

ZABRISKA, THOMAS

	1827
-Offers reward for return of stolen horse and carriage (Advertisement)	Nov 9 p140 c4

The Rights of All

After the New York *Freedom's Journal* ceased publication late in March, 1829, the Reverend Samuel Cornish, who had served with John Russwurm for six months as co-editor of that newspaper, decided to try to pick up where the *Freedom's Journal* had left off. Cornish initially planned to publish *The Rights of All* as a weekly, but probably due to the expense decided instead temporarily to publish the paper as a monthly. However, during its brief existence *The Rights of All* appeared only six times, once each month from May 29 to October 9, 1829, going out of business after the publication of the October issue.

Many have expressed the view that Samuel Cornish severed his connection with John Russwurm and the New York *Freedom's Journal* over the colonization issue, but this does not appear to have been the major reason for Cornish's resignation in September, 1827. While he did strongly oppose African colonization by American Blacks, the actual reason for Cornish's resignation has not yet come to light. It should be pointed out that John Russwurm did not begin to show a noticeable shift in favor of colonization until late in the *Freedom's Journal*'s second year of publication, some time after Cornish's departure.

Important, too, is the fact that in the first issue of *The Rights of All* (May 29, 1829, p2, cl-3), Cornish explains that his earlier resignation from the *Freedom's Journal* cannot really be "supported by abundant and satisfactory reasons". Yet in the same editorial, he takes a strong position against colonization and what he describes as John Russwurm's "sudden change" in favor of the colonization scheme.

The Rights of All addresses itself to the colonization issue as much as any other during its brief tenure, and much space is also given to the plight of many of Cincinnati's blacks who, as a result of a serious race riot in that city, were forced to leave Ohio and move to

Canada. While slavery is not often discussed, especially valuable are the frequent references to the activities of black groups not only in New York City but also in Connecticut.

While, due to its brief life, not nearly as successful as the *Freedom's Journal* in depicting the Free Black community in the North, *The Rights of All* nonetheless provides an important continuing chapter in the story of the Black experience in the United States prior to the Civil War.

RIGHTS OF ALL

Published Monthly, May 29-October 9, 1829

A

ABDUCTION	
-See Kidnapping	
ABOLITION	
-See Emancipation	
ABOLITION SOCIETIES	
-Christians urged to join	Sep 18 p34 c1 ed.
-Attacked by Francis Scott Key	Oct 9 p42 c3 ed.
-Praised for bringing emancipation in many states	Oct 9 p42 c3 ed.
ADVERTISEMENTS AND NOTICES	
-Augustus, Scipio C. (Boarding House)	May 29 p8 c3
-Baltimore Union Seminary	Sep 18 p39 c3
-Bane, Peter (Boarding House)	May 29-Sep 18 pp7, 15, 23, 31, 39 c3 Oct 9 p48 c2
-Gilbert, James (Tailor)	May 29-Sep 18 pp8, 16, 24, 32, 40 c1
-Green, Sarah (Indian Doctress)	Jun 12 p15 c1 Jul 17-Sep 18 pp23, 31, 40, c3 Oct 9 p48 c2
-Hanes, Edward (Living Accommodations)	Jun 12 p11 c3 Jul 17 p23 c2 Aug 7 p31 c3 Sep 18 p40 c1
-Harrison, Lewis (Boarding House)	May 29 p7 c3 Jun 12 p16 c2 Jul 17 p23 c3 Aug 7 p32 c2 Sep 18 p40 c2 Oct 9 p48 c1
-Johnson, Mrs. Sarah (Sewing)	May 28 p8 c2 Jun 12-Aug 7 pp16, 24, 32 c1 Sep 18-Oct 9 pp40. 48 c2

-Johnson, W.P. (Boarding House)	May 29 p7 c3 Jun 12 p15 c3 Jul 17 p23 c2 Aug 7 p31 c3 Sep 18 p40 c2 Oct 9 p48 c1
-Johnson, William P. (Footwear)	May 29-Aug 7 pp8, 16, 24, 32 c3 Sep 18 p40 c3 Oct 9 p48 c1
-Mortimer, Charles (Footwear)	May 29-Sep 18 pp8, 16, 24,32, 40, c1
-Ruggles, David (Coffee Shop) (Grocery Store)	Jul 17-Aug7 pp23, 31 c2 Sep 18-Oct 9 pp39, 47 c3
-Sage, Alpha (No Liquor Sales)	Jul 17 p23 c1
-Seaman, David (Boarding House)	May 29-Sep 18 pp8, 16, 24, 32, 40 c1
-Simpson, S. (Hair and Wigs)	Sep 18-Oct 9 pp39, 48 c2
-Thompson, R. Jr. (Boarding House)	Jul 17 p23 c3 Aug 7-Sep 18 pp31, 40 c1
-Thomson, J.C. (Clothes Cleaning)	May 29-Aug 7 pp8, 16, 24, 32 c3 Oct 9 p48 c2
-Walker, David (Clothing)	May 29 p8 c3 Jun 12-Aug 7 pp16, 24, 32 c2 Sep 18-Oct 9 pp39, 47 c3
-Wiles, Frances (Boarding House)	May 29-Sept 18 pp7, 16, 24, 32, 39 c3 Oct 9 p48 c1
AFRICA	
-Civilization labeled barbaric by recent missions	Aug 7 p27 c1 ed.
AFRICAN CONGREGATIONAL CHURCH (New Haven)	
-Founded	Sep 18 p35 c3
AFRICAN FEMALE DORCAS ASSOCIATION	
-To receive benefits from exhibition by New York Philomathean Society	Jun 12 p15 c3
AFRICAN FREE SCHOOL	
-Advertises education for colored children	May 29 p8 c2 Jun 12 p16 c2 Jul 17 p24 c2 Aug 7 p32 c2

Sep 18 p40 c2
Oct 9 p48 c3
-School's history soon to be published by Charles C. Andrews Aug 7 p29 c1
-Praised by Capt. Bassel Hall Sep 18 p34 c3 ed.
-Praised by British and Foreign School Society's travelling agent Sep 18 p35 c1 ed.

AFRICAN IMPROVEMENT SOCIETY (New Haven, Connecticut)
-Praised for founding school and church Sep 18 p39 c1 ed.

AFRICAN MISSION SCHOOL (Hartford, Connecticut)
-Attempts to civilize and christianize Africa praised Aug 7 p29 c2 ed.
-Advised to have blacks select own candidates for admission Aug 7 p29 c3 ed.

AGAS (and Ulemas)
-Among Russian prisoners after Silistria battle Jun 12 p14 c2

AGRICULTURAL LIFE
-Recommended to blacks as most suitable to their situation and interest May 29 p2 c3 ed.
-Blacks adapting to agriculture stressed by Charles C. Andrews Aug 7 p29 c3 ed.

AGRICULTURE
-See Agricultural Life; Andrews, Charles C.; Farmers

AKERLY, DR. S.
-Named to Greek School Committee May 29 p3 c2

ALBANY, THE (Steamboat)
-Departs from New York City, July 3 Jul 17 p18 c3 ed.

ALLEN, ALEXANDER
-Charged with forgery Jun 12 p14 c3
-Commits further crimes after acquittal on grounds of insanity Jul 17 p23 c1

ALLEN, DR.
-Mansion in Hyde Park described Aug 7 p30 c2

ALLEN, SARAH
-Marries Stephen N. Rogers Jun 12 p15 c2

AMERICAN COLONIZATION SOCIETY
-Criticizes <u>Rights of All</u> for opposing its programs — Sep 18 p36 cl ed.
-Speech given by the Reverend Gallaudet at Society's meetings — Oct 9 p43 c3 ed.
-Presents doctrines to New York citizenry — Oct 9 p43 c3 ed.
-See also Colonization; Liberia; Stockton, Captain

<u>AMERICAN MONTHLY MAGAZINE</u>
-Publishes May issue — May 29 p7 c2

AMERICAN SUNDAY SCHOOLS UNION
-Appoints the Reverend Robert Baird as general agent, replacing the Reverend Boyd — Jul 17 p23 cl

ANDERSON, REVEREND CHARLES (Newark, New Jersey)
-Listed as agent for <u>The Rights of All</u> — May 29-Oct 9 pp8, 16, 24, 32, 40, 48 c3

ANDRES, CHARLOTTE F.
-Marries J. Augustus Felix — Jun 12 p15 c2

ANDREWS, CHARLES C.
-Soon to publish a history of the New York African Free School — Aug 7 p29 cl
-Emphasizes need for education and agricultural life for blacks — Aug 7 p29 c3 ed.

AUGUSTA COUNTY (Virginia)
-Citizenry petition state convention delegates to consider emancipation — Aug 7 p25 cl let.

AUGUSTUS, SCIPIO C. (New Haven, Connecticut) (Advertisement)
-Listed as agent for <u>The Rights of All</u> — May 29-Oct 9 pp8, 16, 24, 32, 40, 48 c3
-Advertises opening of boarding house — May 29 p8 c3

AYRES, ROBERT B.
-Appointed to Philadelphia vigilance committee to obtain subscriptions for <u>The Rights of All</u> — Oct 9 p43 c2 ed.

B

BABYLON	
-Described as one of the ancient world's important cities	Oct 9 p46 c3
BAIRD, REVEREND ROBERT (New Jersey)	
-Appointed general agent for the American Sunday Schools Union	Jul 17 p23 c1
BALBECK	
-Described as one of the ancient world's important cities	Oct 9 p47 c1
BALDWIN, ENOS	
-Dies	May 29 p7 c3
BALTIMORE UNION SEMINARY (Notice)	
-School opens	Aug 7 p31 c3
-School advertises	Sep 18 p39 c3 Oct 9 p48 c1
BANE, PETER (Advertisement)	
-Advertises reopening of his boarding house	May 29-Sep 18 pp7, 15, 23, 31, 39 c3 Oct 9 p48 c2
BAPTIST, W.D. (Fredericksburgh, Virginia)	
-Listed as agent for <u>The Rights of All</u>	May 29-Oct 9 pp8, 16, 24, 32, 40, 48 c3
BARBADOES	
-To petition President to export food supplies from United States and other foreign ports	Jul 17 p23 c1
BARRADAS, GENERAL (Spain)	
-Defeats Mexicans at battle of Tampico	Oct 9 p47 c1
BARROW, THOMAS J.	
-Appointed treasurer of the Young Men's Society for the Promotion of Temperance	Jul 17 p17 c3
BEECHER, REVEREND LYMAN	
-Addresses the New York City Temperance Society	May 29 p1 c3

BENCH OF MAGISTRATES (British Honduras)
-Elected by both colored and whites to administer laws Jun 12 p9 c3

BENJAMIN FRANKLIN, THE (Steamboat)
-Arrives in New York from Providence) Aug 7 p31 c1

BERGH, C. AND CO.
-Launches the ship Erie May 29 p7 c2

BIRD, JAMES
-Appointed to Philadelphia vigilance committee to obtain subscriptions for The Rights of All Oct 9 p43 c2 ed.

BIRDS
-Discusses nesting habits of nicobar swallow May 29 p7 c2

BISSET, GEORGE
-Editor of the LaFourche (La.) Gazette drowns Aug 7 p30 c3

BLEECKER, JAMES
-Sells house and lot at 49 Wall Street to Joel Post Aug 7 p30 c3

BLISS, MR.
-Distributes May issue of American Monthly Magazine May 29 p7 c2

BOWLER, WILLIAM B. (Port-au-Prince, Haiti)
-Listed as agent for The Rights of All May 29-Oct 9 pp8, 16, 24, 32, 40, 48 c3

BOWLS, CLARICY
-Marries James Van Clief Sep 18 p39 c2

BOWSER, THOMAS
-Marries Margaret Peterson Jun 12 p15 c2

BOYD, REVEREND
-Resigns as general agent of the American Sunday Schools Union Jul 17 p23 c1

BRIDGES, CAPTAIN
-Reports defeat of Don Miguel's attack on island of Terciera Oct 9 p47 c2

BRITISH HONDURAS
-Maintains society with equal privileges for colored and whites Jun 12 p1 c3
-Seats in legislative assembly based on property holdings Jun 12 p1 c3
-See also Bench of Magistrates; Buxton, Fowell; Codd, Major General; Councils of the Settlement; Legislative Assembly; Maccauley, Zacariah; Wright, Mr.; Young, Dr.

BRODDOCK, THOMAS (Alexandria, D.C.)
-Listed as agent for The Rights of All May 29-Oct 9 pp8, 16, 24, 32, 40, 48 c3

BROOKS, MR.
-Store on South Street partly destroyed by fire Jul 17 p23 c1

BROUGHAM, HENRY
-Praised for his encouragement of education Jun 12 p9 c1 ed.

BROWER, MRS.
-Opens infant school in Savannah May 29 p6 c3

BROWN, ELISHA B.
-Appointed to Philadelphia vigilance committee to obtain subscriptions for The Rights of All Oct 9 p43 c2 ed.

BROWN, J. C.
-Heads board to collect money to aid Cincinnati free blacks emigrating to Upper Canada Aug 7 p26 c3 ed.

BROWN, JAMES
-Returns to United States after being replaced as envoy to France May 29 p7 c1

BUCHANNAN, JAMES
-His employee charged with forgery Jun 12 p14 c3

BUREN, REVEREND M.
-Appointed Corresponding Secretary to Greek School Committee May 29 p3 c2

BURROWS, S.
-Selected to receive public
donations to aid Cincinnati
free blacks planning migration
to Upper Canada — Aug 7 p26 c3 ed.

BUXTON, FOWELL
-Supports race equality in
British Honduras — Jun 12 p9 c3

C

CANADA
-Climate and soil praised — Aug 7 p29 c1
-See also Cincinnati Free
Blacks; Colonization; Forte,
Elijah; Indians

CANNON, PATTY
-Dies after being indicted for
multiple murders — May 29 p4 c2

CARRET, OSBORN
-Marries Mary Simons — Jun 12 p15 c2

CARROL, JOHN
-Marries Ann Ray — May 29 p7 c3

CASSEY, JOSEPH
-Appointed to Philadelphia
vigilance committee to obtain
subscriptions for <u>The Rights
of All</u> — Oct 9 p43 c2 ed.

CASTLE OF VONITZA
-See Turks

CATHOLIC QUESTION
-Anecdote depicting fears of
popery — May 29 p7 c1

CHANCELLOR OF NEW JERSEY
-Grants injunction to restrain
Paterson bank officers from
exercising corporate privileges — Jul 17 p22 c3

CHILD, LEWIS
-Dies — May 29 p7 c3

CHRISTIAN TROOPS IN EUROPE
-Occupy border of Wallachia — June 12 p14 c3

CHRISTIANS
-Urged to join abolition societies Sep 18 p34 cl ed.

CHURCH MISSIONARY SOCIETY OF ENGLAND
-Annual report containing converted native's narrative revealing barbaric African civilization Aug 7 p27 cl

CHURCHES
-Should apply same effort to abolish slavery as correction of other abuses Jun 12 p10 cl ed.

CHURCHES (Black)
-See African Congregational Church (New Haven); African Improvement Society (New Haven); Day, Reverend; Merwin, Reverend; Pineo, Reverend; Wright, Reverend T. S.

CHURCHES (Boston)
-Collection in Boston churches for Augusta fire victims May 29 p6 c3

CINCINNATI
-Population increase from 16,000 to 25,000 since 1825 Aug 7 p31 cl
-High increase in property values Aug 7 p31 cl

CINCINNATI (Free Blacks)
-Canadian governor offers three districts for settlement by Cincinnati blacks Aug 7 p26 c2 ed.
-Free Blacks migrate to Upper Canada rather than post bonds required by Cincinnati Corporation Aug 7 p26 c3
-Attacked by mob after refusing to leave city Sep 18 p38 c2 ed.
-See also Cincinnati Corporation; Colonization; Ohio; Ohio Supreme Court

CINCINNATI CORPORATION
-Passes legislation requiring free blacks to give bonds to secure residences Aug 7 p26 c2 ed.
-Gives blacks thirty days to comply with law Aug 7 p28 cl-3 ed.

CITIES OF THE ANCIENT WORLD
-See Babylon; Balbeck; Ephesus; Jerusalem; Ninevah; Palmyra; Persepolis

CITY GOVERNMENT CONVENTION (New York)
-Efforts soon to amend city charter — May 29 p6 c2
-Samuel Cornish urging protection of colored citizens denied licenses as carmen and porters — Jul 17 p22 c2 ed.

CIVIL RIGHTS
-Petition by Jews to Parliament requesting extension — Jun 12 p11 c2 ed.

CODD, MAJOR GENERAL
-Appointed by the crown to administer government in British Honduras — Jun 12 p9 c3

COLONIZATION
-Fails to ameliorate condition of colored in the United States — May 29 p2 c2 ed.
-Plan for western lands proposed — May 29 p6 c1
-Plan for purchase and settlement of land in New York recommended — Jun 12 p11 c1 ed.
-Objections of Samuel Cornish to Colonization — Jul 17 p21 c1 ed.
-Critized by Prince Abdul Rehammon — Jul 17 p22 c1 ed.
-Liberia seen suitable for missionaries but not for general population — Jul 17 p22 c1 ed.
-Canada migration preferable to loss of rights in United States — Aug 7 p26 c2 ed.
-Cincinnati blacks encouraged to migrate to Canada but warned against Africa and the American Colonization Society — Aug 7 p28 c1 ed.
-Policy favoring total black emigration disputed by the Reverend Paul — Sep 18 p33 c1
-See also American Colonization Society; Liberia; Rehammon, Prince Abdul; Stone, Colonel

COMEYN, JAMES
-Kidnapped in Philadelphia and later freed — May 29 p6 c3
-See also Heron, James; Vincent, James

COMMONS COUNCIL (New York City)
-Authorizes election of delegates for convention on city government — May 29 p6 c2

CONDOIT, JOHN
-Removed as Assistant Collector (Jersey City) — May 29 p6 c3

CONSTANTINOPLE
-Recaptured by Russians — Oct 9 p47 c3

COOPER, MR. (James Fenimore)
-Novelist dangerously ill at Marseilles last March — Jul 17 p23 c1

CORNISH, JAMES
-Appointed secretary for Philadelphia meeting of colored to increase support for The Rights of All — Oct 9 p43 c2 ed.

CORNISH, REVEREND SAMUEL E. (Editor of The Rights of All)
-Describes the newspaper's purposes — May 29 p2 c1 ed.
-Participates in meeting concerning the emancipation of Phillip Lee's family — Jun 12 p13 c1
-Leaves New York City to avoid July 4 celebration — Jul 17 p18 c1; Jul 17 p19 c1-2 ed.

COUNCILS OF THE SETTLEMENT (British Honduras)
-Allows freedom of debate between colored and whites — Jun 12 p1 c3

COUNTRY SCHOOL
-Pleasures of schoolmaster described — Oct 9 p45 c3 let.

COWES, JAMES C. (New Brunswick, New Jersey)
-Listed as agent for The Rights of All — May 29-Oct 9 pp8, 16, 24, 32, 40, 48 c3

COX, REVEREND
-Thanked for efforts in emancipation of family of Phillip Lee — Jun 12 p13 c1

CRIME
-See Desertion; Forgery; Grand Jury; Inebriation; Intemperance; Kidnapping; Murder; Penal Laws; Riots

CRONSTADT
-Occupied by Hungarian regiments — Jun 12 p14 c2

D

DAVIS, MR.
-Store on South Street partly destroyed by fire — Jul 17 p23 c1

DAY, REVEREND
-Gives charge at opening of African Congregational Church in New Haven — Sep 18 p35 c3

DEBTS
-Collection discussed at Boston meeting — May 29 p6 c3

DESERTION
-Two sailors of ship *La Ville de Marseilles* sent to galleys for desertion — May 29 p7 c1

DICKINSON, MAHLON
-Overseer for Joseph Stiles murdered by two slaves — Aug 7 p31 c1

DICKINSON, R. (Liverpool, England)
-Listed as agent for *The Rights of All* — May 29-Oct 9 pp8, 16, 24, 32, 40, 48 c3

DICKSON, JOHN
-Marries Sally Sherman — Jun 12 p15 c2

DUDLEY, LORD GUILFORD
-Executed with his wife, Lady Jane Grey, in 1554 — Aug 7 p27 c3

DUGAN, WILLIAM
-Stabbed to death by accountant Thomas Slaven — June 12 p14 c3

DUPIN
-Removed to Marseilles prison after assassination of Calemard de Lafayette — Jun 12 p14 c2

E

EARTHQUAKES
- -Characteristics listed May 29 p5 c2
- -Causes described Jun 12 p12 c1

ECONOMY
- -Cost of living rising in the United States Jun 12 p13 c2

EDUCATION (Blacks)
- -See African Free School; African Improvement Society (New Haven); African Mission School (Hartford); Andrews, Charles C.; Brower, Mrs.; Education (General); Field, Richard; Free Blacks (Education); Manumission Society of New York; Mitchell, Dr. Samuel; Schools; Titts, Peter

EDUCATION (General)
- -Greeks aided while colored ignored May 29 p3 c2
- -Invaluable in leveling class barriers Jun 12 p9 c1-3
- -Establishment of seminary of learning proposed Jul 17 p18 c1 ed.
- -Essential for happiness and respectability of blacks Aug 7 p29 c3 ed.
- -Means of expunging prejudice Sep 18 p33 c2 ed.
- -National system instituted in Haiti by King Henry Sep 18 p33 c3
- -See also Baltimore Union Seminary; Greece; Haiti; Brougham, Henry; Lancastrian System of Instruction

ELECTIVE FRANCHISE
- -Failure of qualified blacks to register criticized Oct 9 p42 c2 ed.

ELLIOT, REVEREND ANDREW
- -Dies May 29 p7 c3

EMANCIPATION
- -Plan proposed May 29 p6 c1 ed.
- -Necessary to maintain economic and political prosperity in Virginia Aug 7 p25 c1
- - Twelve slaves freed by Joseph L. Smith Sep 18 p35 c2 ed.
- -Plan to be proposed at Virginia convention Oct 9 p45 c2 ed.

-See also Fleming, John B.; Lee, Phillip; Smith, Joseph L.; Virginia Convention

EMIGRATION
-Natural remedy for over-population — Oct 9 p44 c2 ed.

ENGLISH, EDWARD
-Dies — May 29 p7 c3

EPHESUS
-Described as one of the most important cities of the ancient world — Oct 9 p47 c1

EQUALITY (British Honduras)
-Colored and white populations seem to have equal privileges — Jun 12 p9 c3
-See also Bench of Magistrates; Councils of the Settlement; Legislative Assembly

ERIE (Merchant Ship)
-Launched for voyages between New York and Havre — May 29 p7 c2
-James French serving as ship's Captain — May 29 p7 c2

EUROPEAN ATTITUDES
-Atmosphere more congenial to greatness of soul and righteousness than that of North America — Oct 9 p43 c3

EVERETT, MR.
-Honored at public dinner at Lexington, Kentucky — Jul 17 p23 c1

EXPLOSION
-In powder magazine of steam frigate Fulton — Jun 12 p12 c3
-33 killed, 22 injured in Fulton explosion — Jun 12 p12 c3

EXTRAVAGANCE
-Criticized — Jun 12 p13 c2
-Rage for traveling and public amusements criticized — Oct 9 p41 c2 ed.

F

FARMERS
- -Criticized for sending sons to cities May 29 p2 c3 ed.
- -See also Agricultural Life

FELIX, J. AUGUSTUS
- -Marries Charlotte F. Andres Jun 12 p15 c2

FIELD, RICHARD
- -Member of Board of Trustees of the African Free School May 29 p8 c2

FIREMEN
- -Several injured during fire at 28 South Street Jul 17 p23 c1

FIRES
- -Globe factory of Syracuse and adjoining Van Buren Tannery destroyed May 29 p6 c2
- -15-20 buildings burn down in Cincinnati May 29 p6 c3
- -Victims of Augusta fire aided by Boston churches May 29 p6 c3
- - Buildings at corner of Fulton and Cliff Streets damaged Jul 17 p22 c3
- -Upper part of store on 28 South Street destroyed Jul 17 p23 c1

FIRST BAPTIST CHURCH
- -Raises funds by sale of pews Jul 17 p23 c1

FLEMING, JOHN B.
- -Praised for help in emancipation of Phillip Lee's family Jun 12 p13 c1

FOOD SUPPLIES
- -Requested by Barbadoes inhabitants from United States Jul 17 p23 c1 let.

FORGERY
- -Committed by John Gantt May 29 p6 c3
- -Charges brought against Alexander Allen Jun 12 p14 c3

FORTE, ELIJAH
- -Secretary of board to ascertain prospects of Cincinnati free blacks migrating to Upper Canada Aug 7 p26 c3 ed.

FORTEN, JAMES
-Appointed to Philadelphia vigilance committee to obtain subscriptions to The Rights of All — Oct 9 p43 c2 ed.

FRANCE
-Concludes treaty of commerce with Haiti — Oct 9 p44 c1 ed.

FREE BLACKS (Amusement)
-Practice of attending trivial trials and following soldiers through streets criticized — Oct 9 p46 c2 ed.

FREE BLACKS (Cincinnati)
-See Canadian Governor; Cincinnati (Free Blacks); Cincinnati Corporation; Forte, Elijah; Ohio; Ohio Supreme Court

FREE BLACKS (Education)
-Urged to aid in development of educational institutions — Sep 18 p34 c2 let.

FRENCH, JAMES
-Commander of the ship Erie — May 29 p7 c2

FROST, DANIEL JR.
-Addresses the New York City Temperance Society — May 29 p1 c3

FULTON,THE
-Ship destroyed by explosion — Jun 12 p12 c3

G

GALLATIN, ALBERT
-Appointed chairman of Greek School Committee — May 29 p3 c2

GALLAUDET, REVEREND
-Speaks at meeting of American Colonization Society — Oct 9 p42 c3 ed.

GANO, DANIEL
-Selected to receive donations to help Cincinnati free blacks migrate to Upper Canada — Aug 7 p26 c3 ed.

GANTT, JOHN
-Convicted of forgery — May 29 p6 c3

GARDINER, PETER
-Appointed to Philadelphia vigilance committee to obtain subscriptions to The Rights of All — Oct 9 p43 c2 ed.

GARRISON, WILLIAM LLOYD
-Service on the Genius of Universal Emancipation praised — Oct 9 p44 c1 ed.

GAY, CALVIN
-Dies — May 29 p7 c3

GENIUS OF UNIVERSAL EMANCIPATION
-Established by Benjamin Lundy — May 29 p1 c2
-Praised and support requested — Oct 9 p44 c1 ed.
-See also Garrison, William Lloyd

GEOLOGY
-Changes in earth's surface believed to result from changes in climate — Aug 7 p27 c2

GEORGE, REVEREND SAMUEL (Waterloo, Upper Canada)
-Listed as agent for The Rights of All — May 29-Oct 9 pp8, 16, 24, 32, 40, 48 c3

GILBERT, JAMES (Advertisement)
-Advertises tailoring work — May 29-Sep 18 pp8, 16, 24, 32, 40 c1

GILLS, JAMES
-Brought to trial as Morgan conspirator — May 29 p7 c2

GLASKO, ISAAC C. (Norwich, Connecticut)
-Listed as agent for The Rights of All — May 29-Oct 9 pp8, 16, 24, 32, 40, 48 c3

GLOBE FACTORY (Syracuse, New York)
-Destroyed by fire — May 29 p6 c2

GORDON, WILLIAM S.
-Appointed to Philadelphia vigilance committee to obtain subscriptions to The Rights of All — Oct 9 p43 c2 ed.

GRAHAM, JAMES L.
-Appointed to rank of Colonel — May 29 p6 c2

GRANT, TUDOR E. (Utica, New York)
-Listed as agent for The Rights of All — May 29-Oct 9 pp8, 16, 24, 32, 40, 48 c3

GREECE
-Expels Turks from Livadia and captures Castle of Vonitza — May 29 p3 c3
-Education aided by New York Greek School Committee — May 29 p3 c2 let.
-See also Greek School Committee

GREEK SCHOOL COMMITTEE
-Formed to promote education in Greece — May 29 p3 c2
-Richard T. Hanes, E. Lord, Seth P. Staples, and Dr. S. Akerly named to the committee — May 29 p3 c2
-Arthur Tappan appointed Treasurer, Knowles Taylor appointed Recording Secretary, and the Reverend M. Burr appointed Corresponding Secretary to the committee — May 29 p3 c2

GREEN, SARAH (Advertisement)
-Advertises medical skills as an Indian Doctress — Jun 12 p15 c1; Jul 17 p23 c3; Aug 7 p31 c3; Sep 18 p40 c3; Oct 9 p48 c2

GREEN, THOMAS (Baltimore, Maryland)
-Listed as agent for The Rights of All — May 29-Oct 9 pp8, 16, 24, 32, 40, 48 c3

GREENWOOD, MRS. SARAH
-Dies — May 29 p7 c3

GREY, LADY JANE
-Executed in 1554 after ascending the English throne — Aug 7 p27 c3

GRIFFIN, MR.
-Arrested and imprisoned for robbing jewelry store — Jul 17 p23 c1

GURLEY, REVEREND
-Praised for help in emancipation of Phillip Lee's family — Jun 12 p13 c2

H

HAITI
- -National system of education instituted by King Henry — Sep 18 p33 c3
- -System of government supported by inhabitants — Oct 9 p43 c3
- -Progress unparalleled by any modern nation — Oct 9 p44 c1 ed.
- -Concludes trade treaty with France — Oct 9 p44 c1 ed.
- -Island's natural beauty and fertility of land noted — Oct 9 p46 c1 ed.

HALL, CAPTAIN BASSEL
- -Praised for his tribute to the New York African Free Schools — Sep 18 p34 c3 ed.

HAMILTON, MR.
- -Sworn in as District Attorney — May 29 p3 c3

HAMPTON, JANE
- -Marries Abraham Thomas — Aug 7 p31 c2

HANES, EDWARD (Advertisement)
- -Praised for accommodations — Jun 12 p11 c3
- -Advertises accommodations — Jul 17 p23 c2; Aug 7 p31 c3; Sep 18 p40 c1

HANES, RICHARD T.
- -Named to Greek School Committee — May 29 p3 c2

HARDY, WILLIAM H.
- -Building storing hardware and woodenware destroyed by fire — Jul 17 p22 c3

HARMAN, LEONARD
- -Appointed to Philadelphia vigilance committee to obtain subscriptions to *The Rights of All* — Oct 9 p43 c2 ed.

HARRISON, LEWIS (Advertisement)
- -Advertises opening of boarding house — May 29 p7 c3; Jun 12 p16 c2; Jul 17 p23 c3; Aug 7 p32 c2; Sep 18 p40 c2; Oct 9 p48 c1

HART, JOHN L.
-Appointed to Philadelphia vigilance committee to obtain subscriptions to <u>The Rights of All</u> — Oct 9 p43 c2 ed.

HARVEY, MATTHEW
-Nominated for Governor of New Hampshire by Jackson Democrat Party — Jul 17 p23 c1

HAZZARD, ELI
-Marries Grace Mitchell — Jun 12 p15 c2

HENDERSON, GEORGE
-Marries Eliza Stevens — May 29 p7 c3

HERON, JAMES
-Committed to prison for kidnapping James Comyn — May 29 p6 c3

HEWITT, REVEREND
-Attends meeting of New York City Temperance Society — May 29 p1 c3

HILL, CALEB
-Appointed to Philadelphia vigilance committee to obtain subscriptions to <u>The Rights of All</u> — Oct 9 p43 c2 ed.

HINTON, ELIZA AND FREDERICK (Trenton, New Jersey)
-Mourn daughter's death — Aug 7 p31 c2

HINTON, F. H.
-Appointed to Philadelphia vigilance committee to obtain subscriptions to <u>The Rights of All</u> — Oct 9 p43 c2 ed.

HOLLAND, FREDERICK (Buffalo, New York)
-Listed as agent for <u>The Rights of All</u> — May 29-Oct 9 pp8, 16, 24, 32, 40, 48 c3

HOPSON, JUSTICE
-Commits Five Points rioters for trial — Jun 12 p14 c3

HOSACK, DR.
-Hyde Park grounds described — Aug 7 p30 c2

HOUSTON, GOVERNOR (Tennessee)
-Departs for Arkansas Territory after resigning office — May 29 p6 c3

HOWARD, JOHN
-Account of his career and death in 1790 after studying prison conditions — Aug 7 p27 c3

HOWARD, PETER (New Orleans, Louisiana)
-Listed as agent for <u>The Rights of All</u> — May 29-Oct 9 pp8, 16, 24, 32, 40, 48 c3

HUDSON RIVER LINE
-Proprietors purchase use of wharf for one year — Aug 7 p31 c1

HUNGARIANS
-Regiments quartered in Cronstadt to prevent incursion of foreigners — Jun 12 p14 c2

HUNTER, WILLIAM
-Appointed clerk and translator in the State Department — May 29 p6 c2

HYDE PARK
-Landscape praised — Aug 7 p30 c2

HYDROGEN GAS
-Discovered in Catskill Creek; seen as lighting aid — Aug 7 p30 c3

I

INDIANS (Upper Canada)
-Petition Parliament to prevent intrusion of whites — Jun 12 p11 c2

INEBRIATION
-Probable cause of Greenwich riot — Jun 12 p14 c3
-See also Intemperance; New York City Temperance Society; Temperance

INTEMPERANCE
-Two-thirds of all crimes seen related to intemperance by New York City Temperance Society — May 29 p1 c3

J

JACKSON PARTY
-Nominates Matthew Harvey for Governor of New Hampshire — Jul 17 p23 c1

JAMES, CYRUS
-Admits participating in multiple murders — May 29 p4 c2

JAY, JOHN
-Eulogized after his death — May 29 p4 c1

JENNINGS, THOMAS
-Urges colored population to support The Rights of All — Aug 7 p26 c3 let.
Aug 7 p27 c1

JERUSALEM
-Described as one of the most important cities of the ancient world — Oct 9 p47 c1

JEWS
-Petition Parliament for extension of civil rights — Jun 12 p11 c2 ed.

JINKINS, CAPTAIN
-Captain of the Albany — Jul 17 p18 c3 ed.

JOCELYN, REVEREND SIMEON S.
-New Haven minister ordained as evangelist — Sep 18 p35 c3

-Praised for devotion to cause of colored population	Sep 18 p39 c1 ed.
JOHNSON, EBNEZER F.	
-Indicted for murder	May 29 p4 c3
JOHNSON, JARRED	
-Marries Rosannah Sefas	Aug 7 p31 c2
JOHNSON, JOSEPH	
-indicted for murder	May 29 p4 c2
JOHNSON, MRS. SARAH (Advertisement)	
-Advertises sewing	May 29 p8 c2 Jun 12 p16 c1 Jul 11 p24 c1 Aug 7 p32 c1 Sep 18 p40 c2 Oct 9 p48 c2
JOHNSON, W. P. (Advertisement)	
-Advertises reopening of boarding house	May 29 p7 c3 Jun 12 p15 c3 Jul 17 p23 c2 Aug 7 p31 c3 Sep 18 p40 c2 Oct 9 p48 c1
JOHNSON, WILLIAM P. (Advertisement)	
-Advertises footwear	May 29-Aug 7 pp8, 16, 24, 32 c2 Sep 18 p40 c3 Oct 9 p48 c1
JONES, CHIEF JUSTICE	
-Praises the career of the late John Jay	May 29 p4 c1
JULY 4TH	
-Manner of celebration criticized by Samuel Cornish	Jul 17 p18 c3 ed. Jul 17 p19 c1-2
JULY 6TH CELEBRATION (Abolition by England of Domestic Slavery)	
-Criticized by Samuel Cornish	Jul 17 p18 c3 ed.
-Criticized as riotous and disgraceful by colored man	Jul 17 p19 c2-3 let.
-Held in creditable manner this year	Jul 17 p19 c3

K

KAHL, F.
-Appointed U. S. Consul for Kingdom of Wirtemburg Jul 17 p23 c1

KEY, FRANCIS SCOTT
-Criticized for attacking abolition societies Oct 9 p42 c3 ed.

KING GEORGE IV (England)
-Celebrates birthday Jun 12 p14 c1

KING HENRY
-Institutes national system of education in Haiti Sep 18 p33 c3

L

LA FUENTE, GENERAL (Peru)
-Becomes President after coup d'etat Oct 9 p47 c2

LAFAYETTE, M. CALEMARD DE
-Assassinated by Dupin Jun 12 p14 c2

LAMBORDE
-Return with reinforcements awaited by Mexican troops Oct 9 p43 c3

LANCASTRIAN SYSTEM OF INSTRUCTION
-Described by Charles Andrews in his history of the African Free School Aug 7 p29 c1

LA VILLE DE MARSEILLES
-Ship deserted by two sailors May 29 p7 c1

LEE, PHILLIP (Washington, D.C.)
-Family emancipated Jun 12 p13 c1
-See also Cornish, Reverend Samuel E.; Cox, Dr.; Gurley, Reverend; Nicholas, W. S.; Paul, Reverend B.; Wright, Reverend T. S.

LEE, REVEREND
-Performs religious services at July 6th observance Jul 17 p19 c3

LEGISLATIVE ASSEMBLY (British Honduras)
-Elected by colored and whites who meet property qualification Jun 12 p1 c3

LEVECK, CHARLES (Philadelphia, Pennsylvania)
-Listed as agent for The Rights of All — Aug 7-Oct 9 pp32, 40, 48 c3

LIBERIA
-Fails to reduce colored population of the United States — Jun 12 p10 c2 ed.
-Supported as missionary colony and home for emancipated slaves; opposed as asylum for free blacks — Sep 18 p34 c3 ed.
-See also American Colonization Society; Colonization; Rehammon, Prince Abdul; Russwurm, John B.

LIBERTY
-See Emancipation

LICENSES
-Denied colored carmen and porters of New York — Jul 17 p22 c2 ed.

LIGHTNING
-Causes and results described — Jul 17 p20 c1
-Kills twelve head of cattle owned by Dr. John Magill — Jul 17 p23 c1

LIMA (Peru)
-Citizens rejoice at change of government — Oct 9 p47 c2

LIVADIA
-Returns to Greek control after expulsion of Turks — May 29 p3 c3

LIVELY, WILLIAM M. (Advertisement)
-Advertises opening of Baltimore Union Seminary — Aug 7 p31 c3

LOCKE, JOHN
-Quoted as urging a variety of knowledge — Jul 17 p20 c1

LORD, E.
-Becomes member of the Greek School Committee — May 29 p3 c2

LOUDOUN COUNTY (Virginia)
-Reduces crime and illness by temperance — May 29 p6 c3

LOUISIANA LEGION
-Reviewed on Publick Square — May 29 p6 c2 let.

LUNDY, BENJAMIN
-Member of Society of Friends and praised as anti-slavery reformer — May 29 p1 c1
-Praised for his work and support asked for his newspaper, The Genius of Universal Emancipation — Oct 9 p44 c1 ed.

M

MACCAULEY, ZACARIA
-Pleased over racial equality in British Honduras — Jun 12 p1 c3 let.

M'ILVAINE, REVEREND
-Addresses meeting of New York City Temperance Society — May 29 p1 c3

MAGILL, DR. JOHN D.
-Twelve head of his cattle killed by lightning — Jul 17 p23 c1

MALTHUS, THOMAS R.
-His views on overpopulation disputed — Oct 9 p44 c2 ed.

MANUMISSION SOCIETY OF NEW YORK
-Established African Free School — May 29 p8 c2
-Successful work described by Charles Andrews — Aug 7 p29 c1
-See also African Free School

MAXWELL, HUGH
-Participates in meeting of New York City Temperance Society — May 29 p1 c3

MERWIN, REVEREND
-Delivers sermon at opening of African Congregational Church — Sep 18 p35 c3

MEXICO
-Tampico captured by Spain — Oct 9 p43 c3

MIGUEL, DON (Portugal)
-Expedition defeated at Terciera — Oct 9 p47 c2
-Seizes two American vessels and imprisons crew — Oct 9 p47 c3

MILLER, REVEREND
-Performs religious services for July 6th observance — Jul 17 p19 c3

MILLER, CYRUS B.	
-Appointed to Philadelphia vigilance committee to obtain subscriptions to <u>The Rights of All</u>	Oct 9 p43 c2 ed.
MILLER, GEORGE	
-Appointed to Philadelphia vigilance committee to obtain subscriptions to <u>The Rights of All</u>	Oct 9 p43 c2 ed.
MISSIONARY WORK	
-Praised as best method to civilize and christianize Africa	Aug 7 p29 c2 ed.
MITCHELL, GRACE	
-Marries Eli Hazzard	Jun 12 p15 c2
MITCHELL, DR. SAMUEL	
-Dialogue with black child contained in Andrews' history of the African Free School	Aug 7 p29 c1
MONTGOMERY, MARY	
-Marries Henry Sabre	Jun 12 p15 c2
MORALITY TALE	
-Story of man rewarded for filial affection	Jul 17 p22 c3
MOREL, JUNIUS C.	
-Appointed to Philadelphia vigilance committee to obtain subscriptions to <u>The Rights of All</u>	Oct 9 p43 c2 ed.
MORGAN CONSPIRACY	
-See James Gills	
MORTIMER, CHARLES (Advertisement)	
-Advertises manufacture and repair of footwear	May 29-Sep 18 pp8, 16, 24, 32,40 c1
MORTON, JOHN	
-Dies	May 29 p7 c3
MURDERS	
-Related to intoxication by the New York City Temperance Society	May 29 p1 c3
-Multiple murders in Sussex County, Delaware	May 29 p2 c4
-M. Calemard de Lafayette assassinated by Dupin in Paris	Jun 12 p14 c2

-Foul play suspected in death of Irishman — Jun 12 p14 c3
-William Dugan stabbed to death by Thomas Slaven — Jun 12 p14 c3
-Mahlon Dickinson murdered by two slaves — Aug 7 p30 c3
-See also Grand Jury; New York City Temperance Society

N

NEVILLE, MONGAN
-Selected to receive donations to aid Cincinnati free blacks migrate to Upper Canada — Aug 7 p26 c3 ed.

NEW ENGLAND
-Boundary claims against Nova Scotia supported by 1755 French map — Jul 17 p23 c1

NEWTON, CAPTAIN
-*Fulton* commander leaves minutes before explosion — Jun 12 p12 c3

NEW YORK CITY TEMPERANCE SOCIETY
-Holds public meeting concerning relationship of crime to intoxication; hears addresses by Reverend Beecher and Reverend Frost — May 29 p1 c3
-See also Inebriation; Intemperance; Temperance

NEW YORK FREEDOM'S JOURNAL
-Criticized for views favorable to colonization — May 29 p2 c2 ed.

NEW YORK OBSERVER
-Criticized for asserting *The Rights of All* published only to counter *Freedom's Journal* support for colonization — Jun 12 p10 c1 ed.

NEW YORK PHILOMATHEAN SOCIETY
-To give exhibition to benefit African Female Dorcas Association — Jun 12 p15 c3

NICHOLAS, W. S.
-Appointed secretary of meeting concerning emancipation of Phillip Lee's family — Jun 12 p13 c1

NINEVAH
-Described as one of the most important cities of the ancient world oct 9 p47 cl

NOAH, MAJOR
-Contrasts atmosphere for blacks in America with England's Oct 9 p43 c3

NOVA SCOTIA
-Boundary claims against United States disputed by 1755 French map Jul 17 p23 cl

O

O'CONNELL, MR.
-Disapproves of northern congressmen who aquiesce to slavery Oct 9 p41 cl-2 ed.

OGDEN, COLONEL AARON
-Appointed assistant tax collector (Jersey City, New Jersey) May 29 p6 c3

OHIO
-State authorities criticized for their treatment of Cincinnati blacks Aug 7 p26 c2 ed.

OHIO SUPREME COURT
-Criticized for upholding decision requiring free blacks of Cincinnati to post bond or leave the city Aug 7 p26 c2 ed.
-Criticized for upholding act expelling free blacks from Cincinnati Sep 18 p36 cl ed.

P

PALMYRA
-Described as one of the most important cities of the ancient world Oct 9 p47 cl

PARLIAMENT (England)
-Petitioned by Jews for extension of civil rights Jun 12 pll c2 ed.

PASCHAL, BENJAMIN, JR.
-Chairs meeting of Philadelphia blacks for increasing support for The Rights of All — Oct 9 p43 c2 ed.

PATERSON BANK
-Restrained from exercising corporate privileges in New Jersey — Jul 17 p22 c3

PAUL, REVEREND BENJAMIN
-Chairs meeting regarding emancipation of family of Phillip Lee — Jun 12 p13 c1
-Receives letter from Prince Abdul Rehammon criticizing colonization in Liberia — Jul 17 p22 c1 ed.

PAUL, REVEREND NATHANIEL (Albany, New York)
-Listed as agent for The Rights of All — May 29-Oct 9 pp8, 16, 24, 32, 40, 48 c3
-Praised as one of the most enlightened black ministers — Aug 7 p30 c1 ed.
-Delivers address on color prejudice at Troy, New York — Sep 18 p33 c1-2

PELL, JOSEPH (Hudson, New York)
-Listed as agent for The Rights of All — May 29-Oct 9 pp8, 16, 24, 32, 40, 48 c3

PENNINGTON, AARON S.
-Appointed receiver for the creditors of the Paterson Bank — Jul 17 p22 c3

PERSEPOLIS
-Described as one of the most important cities of the ancient world — Oct 9 p47 c1

PETERSON, JONATHAN
-Reads laws at July 6th celebration — Jul 17 p19 c3

PETERSON, MARGARET
-Marries Thomas Bowser — Jun 12 p15 c2

PHILADELPHIA (Blacks)
-Measures taken by Philadelphia colored praised as a model for improvement — Oct 9 p43 c1 ed.
-See also Vigilance Committee

PIERCE, VICE-GENERAL
-Declines candidacy for re-election in New Hampshire Jul 17 p23 c1

PINEO, REVEREND
-Presides over opening of African Congregational Church in New Haven, Connecticut Sep 18 p35 c3

PITTSBURGH
-Rapid growth noted Jul 17 p22 c3

PIZARRO
-Flees to Chile after change of government in Peru Oct 9 p47 c2

PLATT, LIEUTENANT
-Son wounded in Fulton explosion Jun 12 p13 c1

PLUMB, SARAH
-Marries Haribal Westbroock Aug 7 p31 c2

POETRY
-Tranquility of evening described Jun 12 p15 c2
-God seen as omnipresent guide Jul 17 p23 c2
-Eulogy on the death of a little girl Aug 7 p31 c2

POLITICAL SYSTEMS
-See British Honduras

POPULATION
-Expansion can be controlled by emigration Oct 9 p44 c2 ed.

POST, JOEL
-Purchases house and lot on Wall Street from James Bleecker Aug 7 p30 c3

PRESBYTERIAN CHURCH
-Criticized for neglect of education of colored ministry May 29 p3 c2

THE PRESS
-Northern editors criticized for failing to comment on illegality of Ohio Supreme Court decision regarding expulsion of Cincinnati blacks Aug 7 p26 c2 ed.
-Several Virginia papers urge adoption of Virginia convention emancipation proposals Oct 9 p45 c2 ed.

PROUT, J. W. (Washington, D. C.)
-Listed as agent for The Rights of All — May 29-Oct 9 pp8, 16, 24, 32, 40, 48 c3

PUSHON, WILLIAM
-Selected to receive public donations to aid Cincinnati free blacks' migration to Upper Canada — Aug 7 p26 c3 ed.

Q

QUAKERS
-See Society of Friends

R

RAY, ANN
-Marries John Carrol — May 29 p7 c3

REDMAN, JOHN (Salem, Massachusetts) (Remond)
-Listed as agent for The Rights of All — May 29-Oct 9 pp8, 16, 24, 32, 40, 48 c3

REED, MR.
-Jewelry recovered from year-old robbery — Jul 17 p23 c1

REHAMMON, PRINCE ABDUL
-Letter to Reverend B. Paul criticizing colonization to Liberia — Jul 17 p22 c1 ed.

RELIGION
-Discussion of necessity to fear the Lord before knowledge can be worthwhile — Jul 17 p20 c3
-See also Catholic question; Churches; Presbyterian Church

RICH, WILLIAM (Troy, New York)
-Listed as agent for The Rights of All — May 29-Oct 9 pp8, 16, 24, 32, 40, 48 c3

THE RIGHTS OF ALL
-Objectives described by editor, the Reverend Samuel Cornish — May 29 p2 c1 ed.
-Originally to be weekly publication — May 29 p2 c2-3; Jun 12 p15 c2-3

-Temporarily resigned to it being a monthly publication — Jul 17 p22 c1

-Samuel Cornish asks subscribers to make payments — Aug 7 p26 c1

-Stockholders urge support for paper as only means of communication among blacks and between blacks and whites — Aug 7 p26 c3 ed.

-Vigilance committee formed in Philadelphia to increase support — Oct 9 p43 c2 ed.

-AGENTS: Reverend Charles Anderson; Scipio Augustus; W. D. Baptist; William Bowler; Thomas Broddock; James C. Cowes; R. Dickinson; Reverend Samuel George; Isaac C. Glasko; Tudor E. Grant; Thomas Green; Frederick Holland; Peter Howard — May 29-Oct 9 pp8, 16, 24, 32, 40, 48 c3

Charles Leveck — Aug7-Oct 9 pp32, 40, 48 c3

Reverend Nathaniel Paul; Joseph Pell, J. W. Prout; John Redman; William Rich; Leonard Scott; Lewis Sheridan; Stephen Smith; John C. Stanley; Austin Steward; C. Stockbridge; Isaac Talbot; Samuel Thomas; William Thomas; James B. Vashon; David Walker — May 29-Oct 9 pp8, 16, 24, 32, 40, 48 c3

Francis Webb — May 29-Jul 17 pp8, 16, 24, c3

William C. West — Oct 9 p42 c2

Reverend W. P. Williams; George C. Willis; R.P.G. Wright — May 29-Oct 9 pp8, 16, 24, 32, 40 48 c3

RIOTS

-Results in several injuries at Five Points; caused by inebriation at Greenwich — Jun 12 p14 c3

RIVES, WILLIAM C.

-Appointed envoy to France — May 29 p7 c1

ROBINSON, WILLIAM

-Appointed to Philadelphia vigilance committee to obtain subscriptions to The Rights of All — Oct 9 p43 c2 ed.

ROE, MRS. SARAH

-Dies — May 29 p7 c3

ROGERS, STEPHEN N.
-Marries Sarah Allen Jun 12 p15 c2

RUGGLES, DAVID (Advertisement)
-Delivers oration at July 6th observance Jul 17 p19 c3
-Advertises coffee shop and grocery store Jul 17 p23 c2
Aug 7 p31 c2
Sep 18 p39 c3
Oct 9 p47 c3
-Praised for refusing to sell spiritous liquors Oct 9 p43 c3 ed.

RUSSELL, CAPTAIN
-Reports Portuguese Don Miguel's seizure of two American ships Oct 9 p47 c3

RUSSIANS
-Gain victory over Turks at Silistria Jun 12 p14 c2
-Capture Constantinople from Turks Oct 9 p47 c3

RUSSWURM, JOHN B.
-Advised by Prince Abdul Rehammom not to come to Liberia Jul 17 p22 c1 let.

RYERSON, REVEREND (Upper Canada)
-Presents Indian petition to Parliament to prevent intrusion of whites Jun 12 p11 c2-3

S

SABRE, HENRY
-Marries Mary Montgomery Jun 12 p15 c2

SAGE, ALPHA (Advertisement)
-Advertises he will sell no more ardent spirits Jul 17 p23 c1

SANTA ANNA
-Defeated by Spaniards at Tampico Oct 9 p47 c1

SCHOOLS
-Infant school opens in Savannah May 29 p6 c3
-African Free School educates colored children May 29 p8 c2
-See also Education

SCOTT, LEONARD (Trenton, New Jersey)
-Listed as agent for The Rights of All — May 29-Oct 9 pp8, 16, 24, 32, 40, 48 c3

SEAMAN, DAVID (Advertisement)
-Advertises boarding house — May 29-Sep 18 pp8, 16, 24, 32, 40, cl

SEFAS, ROSANNAH
-Marries Jarred Johnson — Aug 7 p31 c2

SEWELL, SCIPIO
-Appointed to Philadelphia vigilance committee to obtain subscriptions for The Rights of All — Oct 9 p43 c2 ed.

SHERIDAN, LEWIS (Elizabethtown, North Carolina)
-Listed as agent for The Rights of All — May 29- Oc9 pp8, 16, 24, 32, 40, 48, c3

SHORTS, CHARLES
-Appointed to Philadelphia vigilance committee to obtain subscriptions for The Rights of All — Oct 9 p43 c2 ed.

SIMONS, MARY
-Marries Osborn Carret — Jun 12 p15 c2

SIMPSON, S. (Advertisement)
-Advertises ornamental hair and wigs — Sep 18 p39 c2; Oct 9 p48 c2

SISCO, MARY ANN
-Marries Anthony Waters — Jun 12 p15 c2

SLAVEN, THOMAS
-Fugitive after murdering William Dugan — Jun 12 p14 c3

SLAVE EXECUTIONS
-Two slaves executed for murder of overseer, Mahlon Dickinson — Aug 7 p31 cl

SLAVE LABOR
-Seen less productive than that of freemen in Virginia — Aug 7 p25 cl

SLAVE TRADE
-Wilberforce acclaimed for first advocating end to slave trade — May 29 p1 c1

SLAVERY
-Seen as evil which must end due to economic effects — Aug 7 p26 c1 ed.
-Criticized as conflicting with Declaration of Independence — Sep 18 p38 c1 ed.
-See also Virginia

SMITH, JOSEPH LEONARD (Maryland)
-Praised for freeing twelve slaves — Sep 18 p35 c2 ed.

SMITH, STEPHEN (Columbia, Pennsylvania)
-Listed as Agent for The Rights of All — May 29-Oct 9 pp8, 16, 24, 32, 40, 48 c3

SOCIETY OF FRIENDS(Quakers)
-Includes Benjamin Lundy as a member — May 29 p1 c1

SPAIN
-Struck by destructive earthquake — May 29 p5 c2
-Governor Van Ness of Vermont appointed Minister to Spain — May 29 p6 c2
-Captures Tampico from Mexico — Oct 9 p43 c3

SPANISH EMIGRANTS
-2000 in New Orleans due to law expelling them from Mexico — Aug 7 p30 c3

STANLEY, JOHN C. (Newbern, North Carolina)
-Listed as agent for The Rights of All — May 29-Oct 9 pp8, 16, 24, 32, 40, 48 c3

STAPLES, SETH P.
-Becomes member of Greek School Committee — May 29 p3 c2

STEAMBOATS
-Swan makes Philadelphia - New York trip in 9 hours 27 minutes — May 29 p7 c2

STEVENS, ELIZA
-Marries George Henderson — May 29 p7 c3

STEVENSON, ANDREW
-Unable to officiate at West Point exams — May 29 p7 c2

STEWARD, AUSTIN (Rochester, New York)
-Listed as agent for The Rights of All — May 29-Oct 9 pp8, 16, 24, 32, 40, 48 c3

STILES, JOSEPH
-His two slaves executed for murder of overseer, Mahlon Dickinson — Aug 7 p31 c1

STOCKBRIDGE, C. (North Yarmouth, Maine)
-Listed as agent for The Rights of All — May 29-Oct 9 pp8, 16, 24, 32, 40, 48 c3

STOCKTON, CAPTAIN
-Seen as honest, but misled, supporter of American Colonization Society — Oct 9 p42 c3 ed.

STONE, COLONEL
-Criticized for support of colonization — Sept 18 p34 c3 ed.

SULLIVAN, J.
-Selected to receive public donations to aid Cincinnati free blacks migrate to Upper Canada — Aug 7 p26 c3 ed.

SUSSEX COUNTY (Delaware)
-Grand jury indicts three for murder — May 29 p6 c3

SWAN
-Steamboat makes fast Philadelphia to New York trip — May 29 p7 c2

T

TALBOT, ISAAC (Portland, Maine)
-Listed as agent for The Rights of All — May 29-Oct 9 pp8, 16, 24, 32, 40, 48 c3

TALLMADGE, JAMES
-Proposes resolutions commemorating life of John Jay — May 29 p4 c1

TAMPICO
-Captured by Spaniards Oct 9 p43 c3

TAPPAN, ARTHUR
-Appointed Treasurer of Greek School Committee May 29 p3 c2

TAYLOR, KNOWLES
-Appointed Recording Secretary of Greek School Committee May 29 p3 c2

TEMPERANCE
-New York City Temperance Society holds public meeting May 29 pl c3
-Seen deterrent to crime and illness May 29 p6 c3
-Young Men's Society for Promotion of Temperance formed Jul 17 pl cl
-Samuel Cornish views temperance as necessity for colored advancement Jul 17 pl c3 ed.
-See also Inebriation; Intemperance; New York City Temperance Society; Young Men's Society for the Promotion of Temperance

THOMAS, ABRAHAM
-Marries Jane Hampton Aug 7 p31 c2

THOMAS, SAMUEL (Liverpool, England)
-Listed as agent for <u>The Rights of All</u> May 29-Oct 9 pp8, 16, 24, 32, 40, 48 c3

THOMAS, WILLIAM (Brooklyn, New York)
-Listed as agent for <u>The Rights of All</u> May 29-Oct 9 pp8, 16, 24, 32, 40, 48 c3

THOMPSON, EDWARD
-Marries Margaret Williams Sep 18 p39 c2

THOMPSON, JOHN P.
-Appointed to Philadelphia vigilance committee to obtain subscriptions for <u>The Rights of All</u> Oct 9 p43 c2 ed.

THOMPSON, R. JR. (Advertisement)
-Advertises boarding house Jul 17 p23 c3
Aug 7 p31 cl
Sep 18 p40 cl

THOMSON, J. C. (Advertisement)
-Advertises cleaning establishment — May 29-Aug 7 pp8, 16, 24, 32, c3; Oct 9 p48 c2

THROOP, GOVERNOR
-Appoints James Graham Colonel — May 29 p6 c2

TITTS, PETER S.
-Serves on African Free School Board of Trustees — May 29 p8 c2

TOBASCO, MRS. ANN
-Dies — May 29 p7 c3

TOLBOT, JESSE
-Appointed Corresponding Secretary of Young Men's Society for Promotion of Temperance — Jul 17 p17 c3

TOLLS
-Collection peak reached in Albany — May 29 p6 c3

TORREY, PROFESSOR JOHN
-Appointed President of Young Men's Society for Promotion of Temperance — Jul 17 p1 c3

TRANSPORTATION
-See steamboats

TRUMAN, GOVERNOR (Bermuda)
-Arrives from Providence on the Benjamin Franklin — Aug 7 p31 c1

TURKS
-Expelled from Livadia — May 29 p3 c3
-Defeated by Russians at Silistria — Jun 12 p14 c2
-Lose Constantinople to Russians — Oct 9 p47 c4

U

ULEMAS (and Agas)
-Among Russian prisoners after Silistria battle — Jun 12 p14 c2

UNION
-Threatened by states' infringement of rights of federal government by Ohio Supreme Court — Aug 7 p26 c2 ed.

UNITED STATES
-Superior court and Supreme Court adjourn out of respect to John Jay — May 29 p4 c1
-One-third revenue collected from foreign commerce and one-sixth from post office department paid in New York City — Aug 7 p31 c1

V

VAN ARSDALE, ELIAS
-Appointed receiver for creditors of Paterson bank — Jul 17 p22 c3

VAN BUREN, MR.
-Syracuse tannery destroyed by fire — May 29 p6 c3

VAN CLIEF, JAMES
-Marries Claricy Bowls — Sep 18 p39 c2

VAN KOUTEN, JOHN
-Dies — May 29 p7 c3

VAN NESS, GOVERNOR (Vermont)
-Appointed Minister to Spain — May 29 p6 c2

VAN WYCK, S.
-Building damaged by fire — Jul 17 p22 c3

VASHON, JAMES B. (Pittsburgh, Pennsylvania)
-Listed as agent for The Rights of All — May 29-Oct 9 pp8, 16, 24, 32, 40, 48 c3

VAUGHT, ELIZABETH
-Dies — Aug 7 p31 c2

VIGILANCE COMMITTEE (Philadelphia)
-Named to serve: Robert Ayres; James Bird; Elisha Brown; Joseph Cassey; James Forten; Peter Gardiner; William Gordon; Leonard Harman; John Hart; Caleb Hill; F. H. Hinton; Cyrus Miller; George Miller; Junius Morel; William Robinson; Scipio Sewell; Charles Shorts; John Thompson; William Whipper — Oct 9 p43 c2 ed.

VINCENT, JAMES
-Imprisoned for kidnapping May 29 p6 c3

VIRGINIA
-Declining morally and politically due to slavery Aug 7 p25 c1 let.
-Constitutional convention to be held in Richmond asked by Augusta County inhabitants to consider slave emancipation provision Aug 7 p25 c1
-Provision for abolition of slavery to be presented at constitutional convention Oct 9 p45 c2 ed.

W

WALKER, DAVID (Boston) (Advertisement)
-Advertises sale and cleaning of clothing May 29 p8 c3
Jun 12 p16 c2
Jul 17 p24 c2
Aug 7 p32 c2
Sep 18 p39 c3
Oct 9 p47 c3
-Listed as agent for The Rights of All May 29-Oct 9 pp8, 16, 24, 32, 40, 48 c3

WALLACHIA
-Border occupied by Christian troops Jun 12 p14 c2

WASHINGTON, D. C.
-Grand Jury finds true bill against Dr. Tobias Watkins May 29 p6 c2

WATERS, ANTHONY
-Marries Mary Ann Sisco Jun 12 p15 c2

WATKINS, DR. TOBIAS
-True bill found against him by Washington grand jury May 29 p6 c2

WATSON, MR.
-Philadelphia Mayor offers reward for accused Delaware murderer May 29 p4 c2

WATTS, DR. JOHN
-Directs public meeting of New York City Temperance Society May 29 p1 c3

WEBB, FRANCIS (Philadelphia, Pennsylvania)
-Listed as agent for The Rights of All — May 29-Jul 17 pp8, 16, 24 c3

WENDOVER, P. H.
-Part of house destroyed in Greenwich riot — Jun 12 p14 c3

WEST, WILLIAM C. (Philadelphia, Pennsylvania)
-Appointed agent for The Rights of All — Oct 9 p42 c2

WEST POINT EXAMINATIONS
-To be held in June — May 29 p7 c2
-Result in fair investigation — Jun 12 p15 c1

WESTBROOCK, HARIBAL
-Marries Sarah Plumb — Aug 7 p31 c2

WHIPPER, WILLIAM
-Appointed to Philadelphia Vigilance committee to obtain subscriptions to The Rights of All — Oct 9 p43 c2 ed.

WHITEFIELD, GEORGE
-Dies — Jun 12 p15 c2

WHITING, WILLIAM
-Appointed Recording Secretary of Young Men's Society for the Promotion of Temperance — Jul 17 p1 c3

WHITNEY, JOHN
-Brought to trial as Morgan conspirator — May 29 p7 c2

WHITTLE, WILLIAM
-Imprisoned until fine paid for Greenwich riot — Jun 12 p14 c3

WICKLIFFE, C. A.
-Louisville congressman to run again — May 29 p7 c2

WILBERFORCE, WILLIAM
-Praised for opposition to slave trade — May 29 p1 c1

WILES, FRANCES (Advertisement)
-Advertises boarding house — May 29 p7 c3
Jun 12 p16 c3
Jul 17 p24 c3
Aug 7 p32 c3

Sep 18 p39 c3
Oct 9 p48 c1

WILKINSON, JAMES
-Building damaged by fire — Jul 17 p22 c3

WILLIAMS, MARGARET
-Marries Edward Thompson — Sep 18 p39 c2

WILLIAMS, P.
-Urges colored to support The Rights of All — Aug 7 p26 c3 let.
Aug 7 p27 c1

WILLIAMS, REVEREND W. P. (Flushing, New York)
-Listed as agent for The Rights of All — May 29-Oct 9 pp8, 16, 24, 32, 40, 48 c3

WILLIS, GEORGE C. (Providence, Rhode Island)
-Listed as agent for The Rights of All — May 29-Oct 9 pp8, 16, 24, 32, 40, 48 c3

WINTERTON, WILLIAM
-Appointed First Vice-President of Young Men's Society for Promotion of Temperance — Jul 17 p1 c3

WORTH, JOHN S.
-Appointed Second Vice-President of Young Men's Society for Promotion of Temperance — Jul 17 p1 c3

WRIGHT, MR.
-Criticizes colored for seeking exclusive power — Jun 12 p1 c3

WRIGHT, R.P.G. (Schenectady, New York)
-Listed as agent for The Rights of All — May 29-Oct 9 pp8, 16, 24, 32, 40, 48 c3

WRIGHT, REVEREND THEODORE S.
-Praises Reverend Cox for aiding in emancipation of Phillip Lee's family — Jun 12 p13 c1
-Addresses members of new African Congregational Church in New Haven — Sep 18 p35 c3

Y

YOUNG, DR.
-Involved in debate over attempted white regulation of colored representation in British Honduras assembly Jun 12 pl c3

YOUNG MEN'S SOCIETY FOR THE PROMOTION OF TEMPERANCE
-Formed as auxiliary to New York City Temperance Society Jul 17 pl7 cl
-Officers: Professor John Torrey appointed President; William Winterton appointed 1st Vice-President; John Worth appointed 2nd Vice-President; Thomas Barrow appointed Treasurer; William Whiting appointed Recording Secretary; Jesse Tolbot appointed Corresponding Secretary Jul 17 pl c3
-See also Temperance

YPSILANTI, PRINCE DEMETRIUS
-Army expels Turks from Livadia May 29 p3 c3

The Weekly Advocate

The Reverend Samuel Cornish's goal of once again editing a weekly newspaper that would serve as a forum for the black point of view came to fruition in late February 1837 when he took over the reins of *The Weekly Advocate,* a black newspaper that had just begun publishing the month before under the propietorship of Philip A. Bell. Bell would later leave NewYork and further his journalistic reputation on the west coast where he would edit the *Pacific Appeal* and then later publish the *Elevator.* Bell was active in the anti-slavery movement in New York and took part in various community efforts to demonstrate black opposition to slavery.

At the outset, Bell noted that the goal of *The Weekly Advocate* was to provide the black readership with a newspaper that was clearly "*their paper,* in every sense of the word . . . devoted particularly to our own interests -- conducted by ourselves, devoted to our moral, mental and political improvement," as the *Advocate* stated in its first issue (January 7, 1837). It would oppose slavery and support immediate emancipation, attack colonization, and favor temperance, universal suffrage, and universal education.

After publishing nine issues during January and February, 1837, when Samuel Cornish joined forces with Bell, the name of the newspaper was changed to *The Colored American* beginning with the issue of March 4, 1837, signalling the birth of the longest-running black newspaper in the United States up to that time.

THE WEEKLY ADVOCATE

Published Weekly, January 7-February 25, 1837

(Nine Issues)

A

ABOLITION	
-Praised as proper subject for meeting houses	Jan 28 p2 c3 ed.
ADAMS, JOHN QUINCY	
-Presents petition in House of Representatives against recognition of Texas independence	Feb 4 p4 c2
ADELPHIC UNION (Library Association, Boston, Massachusetts)	
-Literary and scientific society formed by colored people of Boston	Feb 25 p2 c4
ADVERTISEMENTS AND NOTICES	
-Carter, John (Grocer)	Jan 14-28 p3 c4 Feb 11 p2 c4 Feb 18-25 p4 c4
-Directory for People of Color (New York City)	Jan 14 p2 c1 Jan 28-Feb 4 p3 c3 Feb 18-25 p3 c4
-Gayle, Anthony (Boarding House)	Jan 21 p3 c4 Feb 4 p1 c4 Feb 11 p2 c4 Feb 18-25 p4 c4
-Green, James (Dry Goods)	Jan 14-21 p3 c4 Feb 4 p1 c4 Feb 11-18 p3 c3
-Hicks Society (Monthly Meeting)	Feb 4 p3 c4
-Johnson, W.P. (Leather Goods)	Jan 14 p3 c4 Jan 21 p4 c4 Jan 28 p3 c4 Feb 4 p1 c4 Feb 11 p2 c4 Feb 18-25 p3 c4

-Michaels, Mrs. D. (Boarding House for Blacks)	Jan 14-28 p3 c4 Feb 4 p1 c4 Feb 11 p2 c4 Feb 18-25 p4 c4
-Michaels, Joseph (Odd Goods Bought and Sold)	Jan 14-21 p3 c4 Feb 4 p1, 2 c4 Feb 11 p2 c4 Feb 18-25 p4 c4
-Michaels, Joseph (Tutoring Service	Jan 28-Feb 4 p3 c4 Feb 18-25 p3 c4
-Michaels, Joseph (Segars)	Feb 18-25 p3 c4
-Nelson, Liberty H. (Grocer)	Jan 14-Feb 4 p3 c4 Feb 11 p2 c4 Feb 18-25 p4 c4
-Philomathean Society (Monthly Meeting)	Feb 4 p3 c4
-Sears, Robert (_Chart of the World_)	Jan 7 p3 c4 Jan 21 p3 c4 Feb 4 p3 c3 Feb 11 p2 c4 Feb 18-25 p4 c4
-Thompson, William (Crime "Theft"; Case of Mistaken Identity)	Jan 28-Feb 4 p3 c4
-Union Society (Monthly Meeting)	Jan 28 p3 c4
-Union Society (Extra Meeting)	Feb 4 p3 c4
-United Female Assistant Benefit Society (Exhibit)	Feb 18 p3 c4
-_Weekly Advocate_ (Agents Wanted)	Jan 14-Feb 4 p3 c4 Feb 18-25 p3 c4
-_Weekly Advocate_ (Advertisements Solicited)	Jan 28 p3 c2
-Wilson, William (Shoemaker)	Jan 14-Feb 4 p3 c4 Feb 18-25 p3 c4
-Young, John (Missing Person)	Feb 4 p3 c4

AMERICAN ANTI-SLAVERY SOCIETY

-Praised by black ministers of New York for appointment of agents to aid colored education and temperance	Feb 18 p2 c3 let.

ANCIENT HISTORY

-Phoenician Contributions	Feb 18 p4 c3

ATHEISM

-See Religion

AVARICE

-Criticized as a serious vice	Feb 11 p2 c3

B

BANKS, ROBERT (Buffalo, New York)	
-Appointed agent for <u>The Weekly Advocate</u>	Jan 7 p3 c4
-Delivers speech before colored Female Dorcas Society on the importance of female influence	Feb 11 p2 c1 let.
-Sends $5 to <u>The Weekly Advocate</u>	Feb 25 p3 c3
BARNEY, REVEREND ISAAC	
-Praises American Anti-Slavery Society for appointing agents to aid colored education and temperance	Feb 18 p2 c3-4
-Notes the situation of the nation's colored	Feb 18 p3 c1-2 let.
BELL, PHILIP A.	
-Proprietor of <u>The Weekly Advocate</u>	Jan 7 p1 c1
-Appointed secretary for meeting of colored petitioning New York legislature to grant jury trial for accused fugitive slaves	Feb 22 p1 c1 Feb 25 p3 c3
BEMAN, REVEREND A. G.	
-Secretary of Connecticut Temperance Society of Colored People; attends meeting to form total abstinence society	Jan 28 p1 c4
THE BIBLE	
-Praise for the world's most important book	Jan 21 p3 c3
-See also Religion	
BLACKS	
-See Cleveland (Blacks); Colored (Females); Colored (General); Directory for Colored People; Free People of Color	
BOWERS, JOHN C. (Philadelphia, Pennsylvania)	
-Appointed agent for <u>The Weekly Advocate</u>	Jan 7 p3 c4
-Praises <u>The Weekly Advocate</u>'s support of immediate emancipation for bondsmen	Feb 25 p3 c1-2 let.

BREWER, WILLIAM (Wilkes Barre, Pennsylvania)
-Appointed agent for The Weekly Advocate — Jan 7 p3 c4

BRITISH AND FOREIGN BIBLE SOCIETY
-Distributed 100,000 bibles to liberated slaves in the West Indies in the past year — Feb 25 p4 c3

BURNS, MRS. AMELIA
-Dies — Jan 21 p3 c3

BUTLER, JOHN (Brooklyn, New York)
-Marries Mary Ennalls — Jan 14 p3 c4

C

CALHOUN, JOHN C.
-Offers resolution concerning British seizures of slaves on United States' vessels forced into port by weather — Feb 4 p4 c2

CARPENTER, T. (New Rochelle, New York)
-Sends $1 to The Weekly Advocate — Feb 25 p3 c3

CARTER, JOHN (Advertisement)
-Grocer — Jan 14-28 p3 c4; Feb 11 p2 c4; Feb 18-25 p4 c4

CELIBACY
-Criticized as contrary to the order of nature and of God — Feb 18 p4 c3

CHAMBER OF COMMERCE (New York)
-Petitions Senate requesting employment of national vessels as relief force during inclement seasons — Feb 4 p4 c2

CHINA
-Description — Feb 11 p2 c3

CLARK, EDWARD V.
-Appointed secretary for meeting of colored petitioning state legislature to grant jury trial to arrested fugitive slaves — Feb 22 p1 c1; Feb 25 p3 c3

CLARK, M. M.
-Appointed secretary of meeting of Cleveland blacks petitioning state legislature protesting oppressive legislation — Feb 18 p2 c2-3 let.

CLAY, HENRY
-Criticized for condemnation of free people of color — Feb 25 p4 c1 ed.

CLEVELAND (Blacks)
-Hold meeting to protest oppressive Ohio laws — Feb 25 p2 c2-3 let.
-See also Clark, M. M.; Malvin, John

COLONIZATION
See Human Rights

COLORED FEMALE DORCAS SOCIETY (Buffalo, New York)
-Addressed by Robert Banks on the importance of female influence — Feb 11 p2 c1-3 let.; Feb 18 p4 c1-3 let.

COLORED (Females)
-Urged to use influence for the good of the race — Jan 7 p1 c4 ed.

COLORED (General)
-Condemned by editor of the <u>New York Transcript</u> — Jan 21 p2 c1 ed.
-Struggle against disadvantages cited; character praised — Jan 21 p2 c2-3 ed.
-Larger proportion than whites poor and ignorant because recently slaves or descended from slaves — Feb 11 p1 c4 ed.
-New York blacks hold meeting to petition state legislature concerning rights of blacks (slavery; trial by jury for fugitive slaves; equal voting rights) — Feb 22 p1 c1 (Special Extra Edition)
-National statistics and situation noted by New York ministers — Feb 18 p2 c3-4 let.; Feb 18 p3 c1-2 let.
-Cleveland blacks hold meeting to protest oppressive Ohio laws — Feb 25 p2 c2 let.
-Warned about slave agents and kidnappers in northern cities — Feb 25 p2 c3

CONOVER, SAMUEL (New York City)
-Named agent for The Weekly Advocate Feb 4 p2 c2

CORNISH, REVEREND SAMUEL E.
-Praises American Anti-Slavery Society's appointment of agents to aid colored education and temperance; notes the situation of the nation's colored Feb 18 p2 c3-4
Feb 18 p3 c1-2 let.

-Appointed head of The Weekly Advocate's editorial department Feb 25 p3 c2-3

CORNISH, WILLIAM A.
-Praises American Anti-Slavery Society's appointment of agents to aid colored education and temperance Feb 18 p2 c3-4
-Notes the situation of the nation's colored Feb 18 p3 c1-2 let.

CRAIG, MR. (Michigan)
-Takes seat in House of Representatives after Michigan admitted as state Feb 4 p4 c2

CROSS, MARTIN (Catskill, New York)
-Appointed agent for The Weekly Advocate Jan 7 p3 c4

D

DAVIS, HENRY
-Chairs meeting of colored requesting jury trial for fugitive slaves, equal voting rights, and repeal of laws authorizing holding of person as slave in New York Feb 22 p1 c1
Feb 25 p3 c3

DEATH
-Described as leveller of all mankind Feb 11 p2 c3

DEBTORS
-Advised to meet obligations Jan 7 p3 c1 ed.

DEISM
-Criticized as religion without faith — Feb 25 p2 c4 ed.

DIRECTORY FOR PEOPLE OF COLOR (Advertisement)
-New York City Directory — Jan 14 p2 c1; Jan 28 p3 c3; Feb 4 p3 c3; Feb 18-25 p3 c4

DISTRICT OF COLUMBIA
-Petition presented in House of Representatives by Mr. Haley against abolition of slavery in District of Columbia — Feb 4 p4 c2

DOWNING, GEORGE
-Delivers address, "Possibility of Great Changes", at meeting of Phoenixonian Literary Society — Feb 18 p3 c2 ed.

DUNLOP, MRS. N.
-Death of her mother, Letetia Wintus, reported — Jan 21 p3 c3

E

EDUCATION
-Its promotion by American Anti-Slavery Society praised by New York City colored ministers — Feb 18 p2 c3
-Importance of reading stressed — Feb 11 p2 c3
-Knowledge is power, especially religious knowledge — Feb 18 p1 c3-4; Feb 18 p2 c1-2 ed.

ELLIS, T. (Newark, New Jersey)
-Sends $1 to <u>The Weekly Advocate</u> — Feb 25 p3 c3

EMANCIPATION
-See Immediate Emanicpation

ENNALLS, MARY
-Marries John Butler — Jan 14 p3 c4

ETOE, REVEREND TIMOTHY
-Praises American Anti-Slavery Society appointment of agents to aid colored education and temperance — Feb 18 p2 c3

-Notes the situation of the nation's colored — Feb 18 p3 c1-2 let.

F

FIELDS, JAMES (New York City)
-Listed as agent for <u>The Weekly Advocate</u> — Feb 25 p1 c1

FOSTER, HENRY
-Vice-President of the New York State Temperance Society of Colored People; attends meeting to form total abstinence society — Jan 28 p1 c4

FRANCHISE
-Petition sent to Troy, New York Legislature requesting equal voting privileges — Feb 22 p1 c1

FRANKLIN, BENJAMIN
-Biographical data — Jan 28 p1 c2; Feb 4 p1 c2

FREE PEOPLE OF COLOR
-Called "free" in name only — Jan 14 p2 c2 ed.
-Reasons given for poverty, ignorance, and crime -- recent slavery — Feb 11 p1 c4 ed.
-Virtues cited in response to condemnation by Henry Clay — Feb 25 p4 c1-3 ed.

FUGITIVE SLAVES
-Account of two Louisiana slaves in Utica, New York — Feb 25 p2 c3-4

G

GARNETT, Mr.
-Recites poem entitled "Alonzo" at meeting of Phoenixonian Literary Society — Feb 18 p3 c2 ed.

GAYLE, ANTHONY (Advertisement)
-Boarding House — Jan 21 p3 c4; Feb 4 p1 c4 -Feb 25 p4 c4

GRANGER, MR.
-Presents petition of 1200 merchants and citizens calling for a National Bank — Feb 4 p4 c2

GREAT BRITAIN
-Seizes slaves from United States' ships forced into her ports by weather — Feb 4 p4 c2

GREEN, JAMES (Advertisement)
-Dry Goods Store — Jan 14-21 p3 c4
Feb 4 p1 c4
Feb 11 p2 c3
Feb 18 p3 c3

GRIFFIN, WILLIAM P. (Albany, New York)
-Appointed agent for The Weekly Advocate — Jan 7 p3 c4

H

HALEY, MR. (Connecticut)
-Presents petition against the abolition of slavery in the District of Columbia — Feb 4 p4 c2

HALLOCK, T. AND S. (Chester, New York)
-Send $2 to The Weekly Advocate — Feb 25 p3 c3

HAMILTON, WILLIAM
-Dies; eulogized by the New York Philomathean Society — Jan 7 p3 c3

HICKS SOCIETY (Notice)
-Monthly meeting — Feb 4 p3 c4

HUMAN RIGHTS
-View that colonization has had a fair trial and failed — Feb 25 p4 c3

I

IMMEDIATE EMANCIPATION
-Inalienable right of every slave — Jan 21 p2 c4 ed

-Criticized by the New York Sun — Jan 28 p2 c3 ed.
-Praised by John C. Bowers — Feb 25 p3 c1 let

INTEMPERANCE
-Evils described — Jan 28 p3 c1 ed.
-Liquor manufacturers and vendors criticized — Feb 25 p2 c2 ed.

J

JENNINGS, WILLIAM S. (Boston, Massachusetts)
-Appointed agent for The Weekly Advocate — Jan 7 p3 c4
-Urges support for The Weekly Advocate — Feb 18 p2 c2-3 let.
-Sends $20 to The Weekly Advocate — Feb 25 p3 c3

JINNINGS, W. S.
-See William S. Jennings

JOHNSON, RICHARD (New Bedford, Massachusetts)
-Appointed agent for The Weekly Advocate — Jan 7 p3 c4

JOHNSON, W. P. (Advertisement)
-Leather Goods — Jan 14 p3 c4
Jan 21 p4 c4
Jan 28 p3 c4
Feb 4 p1 c4
Feb 11 p2 c4
Feb 18-25 p3 c4

K

KIDNAPPING
-Of colored; described by David Ruggles — Jan 14 p2 c4 let.

KING, MR. (Alabama)
-Elected president, protem, of the United States Senate — Feb 4 p4 c2

L

LANDLORDS
-Criticized for evicting poor and laboring classes — Jan 28 p2 c3 ed.

LYON, L. (Michigan)
-Takes seat as Senator after Michigan admitted as state — Feb 4 p4 c2

M

MAIL
-5,000 letters delivered daily in New York City — Feb 11 p2 c3

MALVIN, JOHN
-Chairs meeting of Cleveland blacks to petition Ohio legislature protesting oppressive laws — Feb 25 p2 c2-3 let.

MERCHANTS
-Their success depends on their enterprise — Jan 7 p3 c2 ed.
-New York merchants petition for a national bank — Feb 4 p4 c2

MICHAELS, MRS. D. (Advertisement)
-Boarding House for blacks — Jan 14-28 p3 c4; Feb 4 pl c4; Feb 11 p2 c4; Feb 18-25 p4 c4

MICHAELS, JOSEPH (Advertisement)
-Odd goods bought and sold — Jan 14-21 p3 c4; Feb 4 pl c4; Feb 11 p2 c4; Feb 18 p4 c4; Feb 25 p4 c4
-Segars (Cigars) — Feb 18-25 p3 c4
-Tutoring service — Jan 28 p3 c4; Feb 4 p3 c4; Feb 18-25 p3 c4

MICHIGAN
-Admitted as state and Congressional Representatives seated — Feb 4 p4 c2
-See also Craig, Mr.; Lyon, L.; Norvell, John

MINISTERS	
-Criticized for opposing use of meeting houses for abolition meetings	Jan 28 p2 c3 ed.
-New York City ministers praising American Anti-Slavery Society for appointing agents to aid colored in education and temperance	Feb 18 p2 c3 let.
MITER, JOHN J.	
-Appointed agent by American Anti-Slavery Society	Feb 18 p2 c3 let.
MOORE, GEORGE W. (New Haven, Connecticut)	
-Appointed agent for _The Weekly Advocate_	Jan 7 p3 c4
-Sends $3 to _Weekly Advocate_	Feb 25 p3 c3
MORAL COURAGE	
-Praised as important quality	Feb 4 p2 c3 ed.

N

NATIONAL BANK	
-Requested by petition of 1200 merchants and citizens of New York	Feb 4 p4 c2
-See also Merchants	
NELSON, LIBERTY H. (Advertisement)	
-Grocer	Jan 14-Feb 4 p3 c4 Feb 11 p2 c4 Feb 18-25 p4 c4
-Listed as agent for _The Weekly Advocate_	Feb 25 pl cl
NEW YORK COLORED AMERICAN	
-See _The Weekly Advocate_	
NEW YORK EVANGELIST	
-Offers best wishes to _The Weekly Advocate_	Feb 4 p3 cl-2 ed.
NEW YORK LEGISLATURE	
-Petitioned by blacks to repeal laws authorizing the holding of a person as a slave in New York, to grant trial by jury to colored arrested as fugitive slaves; and to give colored equal voting rights	Feb 22 pl cl Feb 25 p3 c3

NEW YORK PHOENIX SOCIETY
-Praised for usefulness Jan 14 p3 c2 ed.

NEW YORK SUN
-Criticized for opposing immediate abolition Jan 28 p2 c3-4 ed.

NEW YORK TRANSCRIPT
-Editor criticized for condemnation of colored people Jan 21 p2 c1 ed.

NORVELL, JOHN (Michigan)
-Fakes seat as Senator after Michigan admitted as state Feb 4 p4 c2

P

PARENTS
-Advised on how to raise children Feb 25 p1 c2 ed.

PAYNE, WILLIAM (Newburgh, New York)
-Appointed agent for The Weekly Advocate Jan 7 p3 c4

PECK, JOHN (Carlisle, Pennsylvania)
-Appointed agent for The Weekly Advocate Jan 7 p3 c4

PENNY DAILY PRESS
-Critized as gross slanderers and moral contaminators Jan 21 p3 c1 ed.
-Criticized for evil influence Jan 28 p2 c4 ed.

PERSEVERANCE
-Considered necessary for success Jan 28 p3 c2 ed.

PETITION, RIGHT OF
-Threatened by Congress tabling abolition petitions Jan 21 p2 c3 ed.

PHILOMATHEAN SOCIETY
-Eulogizes death of William Hamilton Jan 7 p3 c3
-Monthly meeting (Notice) Feb 4 p3 c4

PHILOSOPHY (Desultory Reflections)
-On the past and its value Feb 28 p1 c1-3

PHOENIXONIAN LITERARY SOCIETY
(New York City)
-Performance praised as a "Mental Feast" Feb 18 p3 c2-3 ed.
-See also Downing, George; Garnett, Mr.; Reason, Charles; Reason, P.; Sidney, Thomas S.; Zuill, J. T.

POETRY
-Eulogy to the slave mother Jan 7 p3 cl
-Describes the coming of the new year Jan 7 p4 cl
-Slavery condemned Jan 14 p4 cl
-Description of snow storm Jan 21 p4 cl
-Views all men as neighbors Feb 11 p2 cl
-Exalts Heaven Feb 18 p4 cl
-Depicts churchyard scene Feb 25 p4 cl

POOR, THE
-Blacks urged to help those less fortunate Jan 7 p2 c3 ed.

Q

QUAKERS (Society of Friends)
-See Trial by Jury

R

RAYMOND, REVEREND JOHN T.
-Praises American Anti-Slavery Society's appointment of agents to aid colored education and temperance Feb 18 p2 c3-4 let.
-Notes the situation of the nation's colored Feb 18 p3 cl-2

READING
-See Education

REASON, CHARLES
-Delivers prize essay "Influence of the Press" at meeting of Phoenixonian Literary Society Feb 18 p3 c2 ed.

REASON, P.
-States objective of semi-annual meeting of the Phoenixonian Literary Society — Feb 18 p3 c2 ed.

RED SEA, THE
-Description — Jan 7 p3 c3 let.

RELIGION
-Observance of the Sabbath urged — Jan 7 p2 c4 ed.; Jan 28 p2 c1-2 ed.
-Study of the Bible seen essential — Jan 21 p2 c3 ed.
-Infidel doctrines criticized; atheism attacked — Feb 4 p2 c1-2 ed.
-Religious knowledge most important for the reform of mankind — Feb 25 p1 c3 ed.
-View of different religious beliefs — Feb 25 p2 c4; Feb 25 p3 c1 ed.
-See also Education

REMOND, CHARLES (Providence, Rhode Island)
-Appointed agent for _The Weekly Advocate_ — Jan 7 p3 c4

RICH, WILLIAM (Troy, New York)
-Appointed agent for _The Weekly Advocate_ — Jan 7 p3 c4

RUGGLES, DAVID
-Warns free blacks of kidnapping threat — Jan 14 p2 c4 let.

RUSH, REVEREND CHRISTOPHER
-Praises American Anti-Slavery Society for appointing agents to aid colored education and temperance — Feb 18 p2 c3-4
-Notes the situation of the nation's colored — Feb 18 p3 c1-2 let.

S

SABBATH
-See Religion

SEARS, ROBERT
-Commences printing and publishing of _The Weekly Advocate_ — Jan 7 p1 c1

SEARS, ROBERT (Advertisement)
-Advertises his Chart of the World — Jan 7 p3 c4; Jan 21 p3 c4; Feb 4 p3 c3; Feb 11 p2 c4; Feb 18-25 p4 c4

SEARS, ROBERT (Chart of the World)
-Description of the United States — Jan 7 p4 c2; Jan 14 p1 c1; Jan 21 p1 c1
-Descriptions of nations of the world — Jan 28 p4 c1-4; Feb 4 p4 c1-4

SHAD, ABRAHAM D. (Chester, Pennsylvania)
-Appointed agent for The Weekly Advocate — Jan 7 p3 c4

SHIELDS, P. (New York City)
-Listed as agent for The Weekly Advocate — Feb 25 p1 c1

SIDNEY, THOMAS S.
-Recites Garnett poem "Alonzo" at Phoenixonian Literary Society meeting — Feb 18 p3 c3

SIMMONS, REVEREND JAMES
-Praises American Anti-Slavery Society's appointment of agents to aid colored education and temperance — Feb 18 p2 c3-4
-Notes the situation of the nation's colored — Feb 18 p3 c1-2 let.

SLAVE TRADE (Washington, D. C.)
-Slave trade in Washington, D.C. condemned — Jan 14 p2 c3 ed.

SLAVERY
-Physical and moral effects described — Jan 21 p2 c4 ed.
-Recognition of Texas' independence opposed by Young Men's Anti-Slavery Society — Feb 4 p4 c2

SMITH, GERRITT
-Donates $10 to The Weekly Advocate — Feb 25 p3 c3

STATE TEMPERANCE SOCIETY OF COLORED PEOPLE (Connecticut)
- -Met in New Haven (Nov 9, 1836) and resolved to form a total abstinence society — Jan 28 p1 c4

SWEARING
- -Strongly criticized — Feb 25 p1 c2-3

T

TEMPERANCE
- -Connecticut meeting resolves to form a total abstinence society — Jan 28 p1 c4
- -Promotion by American Anti-Slavery Society praised by New York City colored ministers — Feb 18 p2 c3 let.
- -Attack against drinking — Feb 25 p2 c2
- -See also Intemperance; State Temperance Society of Colored People (Connecticut)

TEXAS
- -Recognition of independence by United States opposed by Philadelphia Young Men's Anti-Slavery Society — Feb 4 p4 c2

THEATRE
- -Evil influence criticized — Jan 7 p2 c4 let.
- -Criticized as a vice — Feb 4 p2 c4
- -Young men warned against its destructive influence — Feb 11 p1 c3 ed.

THOMPSON, WILLIAM (Notice)
- -Crime (theft); case of mistaken identity — Jan 28 p3 c4; Feb 4 p3 c4

TRIAL BY JURY
- -Requested for colored by Society of Friends — Feb 22 p1 c1
- -Requested by colored in petition to New York legislature — Feb 22 p1 c1

TROY, NEW YORK LEGISLATURE
- -Petitioned by blacks for equal voting privileges — Feb 22 p1 c1

U

UNION SOCIETY (Notice)
-Monthly meeting Jan 28 p3 c4
-Extra meeting Feb 4 p3 c4

UNITED FEMALE ASSISTANT BENEFIT SOCIETY (Notice)
-Exhibit Feb 18 p3 c4

UNITED STATES
-Geographical, historical, and statistical account Jan 7 p2 c3

V

VASHON, JOHN B. (Pittsburgh, Pennsylvania)
-Appointed agent for The Weekly Advocate Jan 7 p3 c4

VICE-PRESIDENT MARTIN VAN BUREN
-Resigns seat as president of Senate before inauguration as President Feb 4 p3 c2

W

WARD, SAMUEL R. (Newark, New Jersey)
-Appointed agent for The Weekly Advocate Jan 7 p3 c4

WATTLES, AUGUSTUS
-Appointed agent by American Anti-Slavery Society Feb 18 p2 c3 let.

WEEKLY ADVOCATE, THE
-Commences publication and sets goals: moral improvement and amelioration of the colored race Jan 7 p1 c1 ed.
-Agents: Banks, Robert; Bowers, John C.; Brewer, William; Conover, Samuel; Cross, Martin; Fields, James; Griffin, William P.; Jennings, William S.;

Johnson, Richard; Moore, George W.; Nelson, Liberty H.; Payne, William; Peck, John; Remond, Charles; Rich, William; Shad, Abraham D.; Shields, P.; Vashon, John B.; Ward, Samuel R.; Whipper, William	Jan 7 p3 c4-Feb 25 pl cl
-Editor pledges unity of purpose to aid his people; cites popular reactions to his paper	Jan 28 pl c4 ed.
-Asks for colored support; price of paper to remain unchanged	Jan 28 p2 c4 Feb 18 pl c4 ed. Feb 18 p2 cl
-Letters solicited	Feb 4 p3 c3 Feb 18 p3 c3
-Notice to Agents	Feb 18-25 pl cl
-Reverend Samuel Cornish appointed head of editorial department; name changed to _Colored American_	Feb 25 p3 c2
WEEKLY ADVOCATE, _THE_ (Notice)	
-Agents wanted	Jan 14-Feb 4 p3 c4 Feb 18-25 p3 c4
-Advertisements solicited	Jan 28 p3 c2
-Hopes for exchanges with other newspapers	Feb 18 pl cl Feb 25 p3 c4
WHIPPER, WILLIAM (Columbia, Pennsylvania)	
-Appointed agent for _The Weekly Advocate_	Jan 7 p3 c4
WILLSON, HIRAM	
-Appointed agent by the American Anti-Slavery Society	Feb 18 p2 c3 let.
WILSON, WILLIAM (Advertisement)	
-Shoemaker	Jan 14-28 p3 c4 Feb 4 p3 c4 Feb 18-25 p3 c4
WINTUS, MRS. LETETIA	
-Dies	Jan 21 p3 c4
-See also Mrs. N. Dunlop	

WRIGHT, MR.
-Presents memorial in Senate from New York Chamber of Commerce requesting employment of national vessels for relief during inclement weather Jan 21 p3 c3

WRIGHT, REVEREND THEODORE S.
-Praises American Anti-Slavery Society's appointment of agents to aid colored education and temperance Feb 18 p2 c3-4
-Notes the situation of the nation's colored Feb 18 p3 c1-2 let.

Y

YATES, WILLIAM
-Appointed agent by American Anti-Slavery Society Feb 18 p2 c3 let.

YOUNG, JOHN (Advertisement)
-Missing person Feb 4 p3 c4

YOUNG MEN'S ANTI-SLAVERY SOCIETY (Philadelphia)
-Petition Congress against recognition of Texas' independence Feb 4 p4 c2

Z

ZUILL, J. T.
-Address partially delivered before the Phoenixonian Society Feb 18 p3 c3

The Colored American

The New York *Colored American* published for more than four-and-one-half years, between March, 1837 and December, 1841, under the leadership of Philip Bell, The Reverend Samuel Cornish, and The Reverend Charles B. Ray. An earlier victim of discrimination, Ray had been forced to leave Wesleyan College in 1832 due to the University administration's concern over the negative reaction of southern students and alumni to Ray's admission. An indefatigable general agent for the *Colored American,* Ray traveled all across the North to build up support for the paper. By 1840 he had replaced Cornish as editor and had taken over many of Philip Bell's duties as proprietor. His descriptions of his travels in the paper's behalf offer an excellent picture of life in the North.

Concerned over slavery's effects upon Blacks, the difficult and seemingly deteriorating situation faced by the nation's free Blacks, and the need to provide Blacks with the opportunity to speak out in their own behalf, the *Colored American* was determined to succeed in its effort to "open a channel of communication for the interchange of thought" among northern Blacks. This goal the paper was largely able to fulfill.

Among the topics receiving full coverage were colonization, the West Indies as a possible haven for Blacks, The *Amistad* case, the burgeoning convention movement, and the struggle for an unrestricted franchise in New York. Particularly striking are the references to literally scores of Black organizations and societies, particularly in the Northeast, formed to help improve the race situation politically, economically, and socially. These groups attest to the fact that while racial unity was often elusive nationally, the concern for the well-being of one's brethren remained strong within the Black community. This is clearly seen throughout the period this important newspaper published.

The New York *Colored American* published more sporadically than *Freedom's Journal.* Issues that were not available for this index included those of February 24, 1838; April 26, 1838; March 23-May 24, 1839; November 30, 1839-February 29, 1840; October 23, 1841; November 6, 1841; November 27, 1841; December 11-18, 1841.

THE COLORED AMERICAN

Published Weekly, March 4, 1837-December 25, 1841

A

ABOLITION (England)

	1837
-Questions about slavery raised by British Abolitionists	Apr 1 p2 c4 let.
-Person connected with slavery criticized	Apr 8 p1 c2
-Apprenticeship section of emancipation bill criticized	Apr 8 p1 c2
-Apprenticeship conditions explained	Jun 3 p1 c1
-Proposal that British Christians convey anti-slavery sentiments to slave-owners in the United States	Nov 11 p4 c1
	1838
-Movement in Parliament to complete abolition in the West Indies	Feb 17 p4 c1
-Apprenticeship system should be abolished along with slavery	Mar 3 p3 c2
-Petition presented in Parliament against apprenticeship system in West Indies	Mar 22 p3 c3
-Description of anti-slavery meeting	Apr 19 p3 c2
-Bill to amend apprenticeship act read in Parliament	Apr 19 p3 c3
-Women present petition to Queen for end to all slavery in colonies	May 3 p3 c2
-England determined to put an end to international slave trade	Jul 7 p3 c3

-England praised for West Indian policy	Jul 21 p3 c1
-Religious feeling guided Parliament toward emancipation	Jul 28 p3 c1
-England continues to oppose slavery among her neighbors	Sep 15 p3 c2
-America must learn from England's example of emancipation	Oct 13 p1 c3
	1839
-Blacks free to settle in Britain without fear of racism	Sep 14 p2 c3
	1840
-World anti-slavery convention to be held in London	Apr 4 p2 c4
-American Anti-Slavery Society appoints delegates to London anti-slavery convention	May 30 p3 c1
-Thomas Fowell Buxton's book on Africa described; does not call for colonization	Jun 13 p3 c1
-Charles Remond addresses anti-slavery meeting in Perth, England	Dec 5 p1 c4
-See also British and Foreign Anti-Slavery Society	

ABOLITION (Egypt)

	1839
-Pasha announces immediate abolition of slavery	Jun 1 p2 c2 let.

ABOLITION (France)

	1839
-French governor investigates state of Blacks in British West Indies concerning possible abolition there	Aug 3 p2 c5
	1840
-De Tocqueville advocates emancipation in French West Indies	Mar 14 p3 c2
-Churches established in West Indies to help prepare for emancipation	Mar 28 p3 c3
-King Louis Phillipe expresses abhorrence of slavery; supports abolition	Jul 25 p1 c3
	1841
-Slavery soon to end in French Colonies	May 29 p2 c3

ABOLITION (United States)

	1837
-Stresses moral responsibility of free blacks toward slaves	Mar 4 p2 c3 ed.
-Foresees changed attitude toward anti-slavery cause due to growing religious fervor	Mar 4 p2 c4 ed.
-Praises Anti-Slavery Society and attacks Colonization Society	Mar 4 p2 c4 ed.
-Relates emancipation's struggle against racial prejudice	Mar 4 p3 c1 ed.
-Preamble to the Constitution of the Geneva, New York Anti-Slavery Society (1836)	Mar 4 p3 c1
-Defines abolition	Mar 4 p3 c4
-Gambling attacked as evil that slows emancipation effort	Mar 11 p1 c2
-Notes speeches at 1821 New York Constitutional Convention that opposed continuance of slavery	Mar 11 p2 c2
-Martin Van Buren presents views on abolition in inaugural address	Mar 11 p2 c3
-Van Buren criticized for views on abolition and slavery	Mar 11 p2 c3
-Stresses strength of reform movements	Mar 11 p2 c3
-Eminent abolitionists sign petition recommending _New York Colored American_	Mar 11 p3 c2
-Free Blacks of New York petition state legislature for repeal of slave laws	Mar 11 p3 c2
-Terrible changes for the United States if abolition does not take place	Mar 25 p2 c2
-Abolition cause most important	Mar 25 p3 c2
-Notes color prejudice among white abolitionists in Maine	Mar 25 p4 c2
-Dartmouth College has abolition society of 88 members	Apr 22 p3 c1
-Abolitionists create a conscience about slavery and racism	May 6 p2 c2
-Abolition around the world described	Jun 3 p1 c1
-_Colored American_ opposes slave insurrections; favors changing slaveowners' minds	Jun 17 p1 c1 ed.
-_Colored American_ calls for prayers for slaveholders	Jun 24 p2 c1 ed.

-Society of Friends (New York) calls on people to help end slavery — Jul 15 p4 c1
-New England abolition schism censured for loss of peaceful spirit — Oct 7 p3 c2 ed.
-Education of free blacks urged as abolitionist tactic — Oct 28 p1 c2
-Successes of liberated West Indies blacks cited as proof of positive influence of freedom — Nov 4 p1 c3
-Funds requested to further cause of anti-slavery — Nov 4 p3 c3
-Need to purify United States government from curse of slavery — Nov 4 p3 c4
-True religion seen as the only means of emancipation and enfranchisement — Dec 16 p2 c2

1838

-View that Elijah Lovejoy's death should unify and enlarge the anti-slavery movement (Gerrit Smith) — Jan 13 p1 c4 let.
-Lovejoy's paper, the Alton Observer, will be published in Cincinnati until it can resume publication in Illinois — Jan 13 p3 c4
-Vermont takes precedence as an abolitionist state — Mar 15 p4 c1 let.
-Isaac Knapp (Boston) prepares a history of the controversy respecting slavery involving the Anti-Slavery Societies — Mar 29 p1 c3
-View that slavery can be overcome through the efforts of free blacks — Apr 12 p3 c3
-An equivocal position on slavery criticized — Apr 19 p3 c2 ed.
-Massachusetts passes anti-slavery resolutions — May 3 p2 c4
-Massachusetts declared thoroughly "abolitionized" — May 3 p2 c4 ed.
-Dr. Sleigh criticized as destructive to the Union — Jun 16 p2 c4
-Benefits of immediatism versus gradualism discussed — Jun 23 p1 c1
-Speech criticizing law barring schools for blacks printed — Jul 7 p1 c1
-View that the abolition cause is in God's hands — Jul 14 p2 c1
-Abolition is being discussed everywhere — Jul 28 p2 c1 let.

-Anti-abolitionists counselled to take their arguments to the West Indies	Aug 11 p2 c2
-Examples cited of students becoming abolitionists	Aug 18 p2 c4 let.
-July 4th ceremony in Troy, Michigan pleads for an end to slavery	Aug 18 p3 c1
-During year ending May 1838, the American Anti-Slavery Society took in $32,534.63; the American Bible Society-$29,790.74	Aug 25 p2 c4
-Abolition must be achieved before conditions for Free Blacks can really improve; abolitionists must end slavery; only free blacks can improve themselves	Sep 1 p2 c4 ed.
-Christians are awakening to their anti-slavery duty	Oct 6 p2 c1 ed.
-Account of local abolition meetings in Elmira, New York	Oct 13 p2 c1 let.
-Abolition seen making distinct progress	Oct 27 p2 c3
-Cause of abolition moving ahead	Nov 3 p3 c2 ed.
-Abolition does not incite slaves to rebellion	Nov 17 p4 c1
-Education of blacks seen as the key to emancipation	Dec 1 p2 c1 let.
-Political action not seen as the answer to the slavery problem	Dec 22 p3 c3
-<u>Colored American</u> claims 100,000 involved in Anti-Slavery Societies	Dec 29 p2 c1
	<u>1839</u>
-City-wide abolition meeting in New York; proceedings discussed	Feb 9 p2 c2 ed.
-New York Abolition Convention evaluated	Mar 9 p2 c1 ed.
-Movement gaining strength in Maryland	Jun 15 p3 c2 let.
-Anti-slavery societies help the welfare of Free Blacks	Jun 22 p1 c1
-Kentuckian praises abolition efforts	Jul 20 p2 c2 let.
-Abolition movement in Pennsylvania said to be the equal of those elsewhere	Aug 3 p3 c1
-Abolition seen to have a good effect on blacks	Aug 17 p2 c5 let.

-Frenchman praises the abolition movement in the United States	Aug 24 p2 c4 let.
-Formation of anti-slavery political party discouraged	Aug 31 p3 c1 ed.
-Blacks cannot trust whites to head the abolition movement	Oct 5 p2 c2
-Physical force is not the answer; truth and righteousness are the only way	Oct 12 p2 c1
-Abolition cannot be advanced by political intrigue	Oct 19 p3 c2 ed.
-Freeing the slaves will not be enough; moral changes are also necessary	Nov 2 p2 c1
-Abolition movement is neither dying nor destructive	Nov 9 p1 c1
-Speech of George Thompson	Nov 9 p1 c5
-Immediate emancipation is the best method	Nov 16 p3 c1
	<u>1840</u>
-State of the abolition movement noted; schisms cited	Mar 21 p2 c2
-Movement seen stagnating; losing its appeal	Mar 28 p2 c1
-World anti-slavery convention to be held in England (June 1840); it will be difficult for Americans to go	Apr 18 p2 c3
-Some prominant blacks in the South oppose abolition movements	Apr 25 p2 c2
-Speech of ex-slave holder quoted	May 2 p1 c1
-<u>Colored</u> <u>American</u> endorses black conventions	May 2 p3 c1
-Summary of Dr. Brisbane's speech to the Female Anti-Slavery Society of Cincinnati	May 2 p3 c1
-Baptist Anti-Slavery Convention appeals to slaveholders	Jun 20 p1 c1
-Letter of support from Jamaica read at American Anti-slavery Society convention	Jun 20 p3 c1
-Women not received as delegates at London convention	Aug 8 p2 c3
-Outlook for anti-slavery cause not optimistic in Congress	Dec 26 p2 c4 let.
	<u>1841</u>
-Two hundred citizens of Washington, D.C. sign abolitionist memorial	Jan 2 p3 c1 let.
-Text of abolitionist memorial to Congress	Jan 9 p2 c2

-Abolitionists seen to favor liquor	Mar 20 p4 c3 let.
-Abolition seen not dying away	May 8 p2 c2
-Abolitionists accused of underrating talents of blacks	May 22 pl c4 let.
-Colored American disagrees with letter criticizing abolitionists	May 22 p2 c4
-Abolition seen as having an affect on the South; the end of slavery seen	May 29 p2 cl
-View that anyone is entitled to speak against slavery	Jun 12 pl cl
-Reform has not been destroyed in the churches	Jul 10 pl c3 let.
-"Ultraism" explained and justified	Aug 21 pl c2
-See also Abolition (United States) (Political Action versus Moral Suasion); Emancipation	

ABOLITION (United States) (Political Action versus Moral Suasion)

	1838
-The "Political Association" formed by New York blacks	Jun 16 p2 c3
-View that abolitionists should vote for the best man, irrespective of party	Nov 17 p3 cl ed.
	1839
-Political, not moral effort, necessary	Jun 1 p3 c3
-Both parties accused of sell-out to slaveholders	Jul 13 pl c5
-Political action discussed	Jul 27 p2 cl Aug 17 p3 cl Aug 24 p3 cl
-Political action praised	Aug 17 p3 c3 let.
-Formation of anti-slavery political party discouraged	Aug 31 p3 cl
-Abolitionist cause would be injured by political party	Sep 7 p3 cl
-Samuel Cornish says political action will corrupt abolition movement	Oct 5 p3 cl
-Difference between legislative action and political intrigue clarified	Oct 19 p3 c2
-Voters urged to favor anti-slavery ballot	Oct 19 p4 cl let.
-New York Colored American praised for calling Convention	Nov 2 p2 c3,5 let.

-View that convention should convince friends of errors	Nov 2 p2 c5
-View that only qualified candidates should be supported	Nov 2 p3 cl let.
-Address of committee on political action	Nov 2 p3 c2
-Some stop delivery of Colored American because of its stand	Nov 2 p3 c5
-Paper supports voting for abolitionists	Nov 9 p2 c2
-Opposition to political abolition is not the Colored American's stand	Nov 9 p2 c2
-Criticism of political action	Nov 9 p3 cl let.
-Criticism of Samuel Cornish	Nov 9 p3 cl let.
-Paper explains stand favoring political abolition	Nov 16 p2 cl ed.
-View that moral abolition will defeat racism	Nov 16 p2 cl
	1840
-Idea that moral action must be primary	Mar 14 p2 cl let.
-Colored American supports political abolition, but questions an independent ticket	Apr 18 p2 c4
-Convention nominates Gerrit Smith for Governor of New York on the Liberty Party Ticket	Aug 22 p2 c4
-Many abolitionists plan to vote a straight party ticket in the presidential election	Aug 29 p2 c3
-Candidates of both major parties seen favorable to slavery	Sep 12 pl c2
-Abolition of slavery can be brought before the people as a political question	Sep 26 pl c4
-Should have more discussion of candidates in the Colored American	Oct 3 p2 cl let.
-Colored American says to vote the Liberty Party ticket for all offices	Oct 3 p2 c2
-Support requested for Liberty Party ticket	Oct 10 pl cl
-Moral suasion urged as a means of elevating blacks	Oct 31 p2 cl
-Enfranchised blacks urged to vote in the presidential election	Oct 31 p2 c4

-Colored men have no duty to vote the Abolition ticket; a third party would injure the abolitionist cause — Oct 31 p3 c1 let.
-Straight anti-slavery ticket urged — Oct 31 p3 c1
-Votes for the men rather than the parties urged — Oct 31 p3 c2 let.
-Adherance to party tickets viewed as ineffectual — Oct 31 p3 c3
-Denial that abolition principles are unconstitutional — Nov 14 p2 c1

1841

-James G. Birney again nominated for President — May 22 p2 c3
-Convention that nominated Birney described — May 29 p1 c2

ABOLITION
-See also American and Foreign Anti-Slavery Society; Anti-Slavery (Art); Anti-Slavery Magazine; Anti-Slavery (poetry); Anti-Slavery Society; Baptist Anti-Slavery Convention; British American Journal of Liberty; Colored Citizens of New Bedford, Massachusetts; Colored Young Men of New York City; Concert of Prayer; Convention Movement; Geneva, New York Colored Anti-Slave Society; London Anti-Slavery Convention; Massachusetts Abolition Society; Methodist Anti-Slavery Society; New Hampshire Congregational and Presbyterian Society for the Abolition of Slavery; New York Anti-Slavery Society; Ohio Anti-Slavery Society; Philadelphia City and County Anti-Slavery Society; Political Association; Virginia Convention for Abolition of Slavery; Wayne County Anti-Slavery Society

ABOLITION DISCUSSION (Notice)

1840

-At Vocal Hall — Dec 12 p3 c3

ABOLITIONISTS (Black)

	1837
-Should stay in the United States and help improve conditions here	Jul 15 p2 c1
-New England black abolitionists censured for lack of forbearance	Oct 7 p3 c2 ed.
-Extremism of Boston abolitionists denounced	Oct 14 p3 c2
	1838
-View that black abolitionists are doing Christ's work	May 3 p2 c1 ed.
	1839
-Make modest demands	Jun 1 p2 c1 ed.

ABOLITIONISTS (General)

	1838
-Seen as the true friends of the South	May 3 p4 c2
-Aiding in destruction of racism	Jun 2 p2 c3 ed.
-Now seen time to saturate public with anti-slavery literature	Jun 9 p3 c3 ed.
-Seen achieving results by their activities	Jun 23 p1 c4
-Must support the American Anti-Slavery Society	Jul 28 p2 c1 let.
-Do not support any particular political party	Jul 28 p4 c3
-Only follow God's commandments	Aug 11 p2 c1 ed.
-Are awakening to their political duties through the ballot box; New York abolitionists resolve not to vote for pro-slavery candidates	Sep 15 p3 c1
-Should do all in their power to encourage husbandry and industrial work	Oct 27 p2 c1 ed.
-Have no reason to be discouraged	Oct 27 p2 c3
-Accused of allying with Loco-Focos to conspire against the Union	Oct 27 p4 c1
	1839
-Asked to consider the situation of the free black	May 18 p3 c2 ed.
-Urged to help make blacks respectable in the North	Jun 1 p2 c1 ed.
-Assailed by mobs in New Haven and Newburgh (New York)	Jun 1 p2 c5
-Accomplishments of abolitionists discussed	Jul 13 p3 c1 ed.

-Should make loans available for land purchases by free blacks — Aug 31 p2 c4 let.
-Rotten eggs thrown at speaker in Gettysburg, Pennsylvania — Sep 28 p1 c5

ABOLITIONISTS (Newark, New Jersey) (Notice)

1840

-Announce convention — Aug 8-22 p3 c4

ABOLITIONISTS (New York) (Notice)

1841

-Announce convention — Oct 16 p3 c3

ABOLITIONISTS (Southern)

1837

-Southern minister wishes success to New York Colored American — Sep 9 p3 c3
-Death of Lovejoy McKeown, Kentucky abolitionist, eulogized — Dec 9 p3 c1

1838

-View that southern abolitionists are doing Christ's work — May 3 p2 c1 ed.

ABOLITIONISTS
-See also Garrison, William Lloyd; Lovejoy, Elijah P.; Remond, Charles Lenox; Renshaw, Charles Stuart; Tappan, Arthur; Tappan, Lewis; Thompson, George; VanRensselaer, Thomas; Weld, Theodore Dwight

ABRAHAM

1839

-View that biblical figure was not a slaveholder — Feb 2 p1 c1

ABYSSINIAN BAPTIST CHURCH

1841

-Plans benefit supper — Apr 10 p3 c4

"ABYSSINIAN RELIGIOUS SOCIETY" (Maine)

1840

-Affairs and activities discussed — Dec 26 p1 c4 let.

ADAMS, JOHN QUINCEY

	1837
-Adams' support for right of petition and freedom of debate praised	Jul 8 p2 c4
	1838
-Defends woman's right to political activity; praised for his defense	Jul 28 pl cl ed.
-Takes stand against admitting Texas as a slave state	Aug 11 pl c4
-Praises aims and activities of Anti-Slavery Society	Aug 11 p2 c2 let.
-Called "brightest living statesman" by Colored American	Dec 22 pl cl
-Recommended as the best hope for next President	Dec 29 p3 c2
	1839
-Anti-Slavery speech printed, discussed and praised	Feb 9 pl c2
-Pushed for Presidential nomination by the Colored American	May 18 p3 c3 ed.
-Speech celebrating anniversary of Washington's inauguration printed	Jun 15 pl cl
	1840
-Description of his lecture on faith	Nov 28 p2 c2
-His activities in the Amistad case described	Dec 19 p2 c3
-Urges that fraud in Amistad case be investigated	Dec 19 p3 cl
	1841
-Will plead Amistad case before the Supreme Court	Jan 16 p2 c4 let.
-Submits abolition petitions to the House of Representatives	Jan 30, Feb 20 p3 cl let.
-Pleads on behalf of Amistad captives before the Supreme Court; praised by Colored American	Mar 6 p3 c2
-Receives letter from Amistad captive, Ka-le	Mar 27 p2 cl let.
-Discusses Amistad case	May 8 pl c4 let.
-Praised for action in Amistad case; thanks people for praise and support	May 22 p3 c2 let.
-Attempts to rescind gag rule in Congress	Jun 12 p3 cl

-Announces intention to retire from Congress — Nov 20 p3 c2
-See also The Amistad

ADAMS, SAMUEL

1839

-Praised for part played in freeing America from Britain — Sep 28 p1 c1

ADVERTISEMENTS AND NOTICES
-See Abolition Discussion; Abolitionists; Alderman, A.; Alexander, John; Allen, L.B.; American Anti-Slavery Society; Anthony, Joseph; Anti-Colonization Meeting; Appo, Mrs. E.; Appo, William; Asbury Colored Methodist Church

Baptist Anti-Slavery Society; Barker, Purdy and Co.; Barker, J.W.; Bell, Philip A.; Bellville (New Jersey); Benedict, S.W.; Bethel Methodist Church; Bishop, Joshua; Board Wanted; Boarding House; Bodee, George A.; Bodine, Lewis; Booms, Mrs. P.; Borden, Nathaniel A.; Bowens, B.; Bowers, John C.; Boy Wanted; British West India Emancipation; Broadway Tabernacle Church; Bronson, Professor; Brooklyn (L.I.) Mass Meeting; Brown, E.; Brown, J.B.; Bryce, William C.; Budd , Mrs. Hester; Burdell, John; Burton, James; Bush, David.

Campbell, A.R.; Carroll, Richard; Carter, John; Carthaginian Beneficial Society; Chard, William and Co.; Cheap Apartments; Christian Library; Cills, Edward and Co.; City Conventions; Clark, Edward V.; Clarkson Association for the Instruction of Colored Women; Coal; Collins, J.; Colored Methodist Church; Colored Orphan Asylum; Colored People's State Temperance Society (Connecticut); Colored Young Men;

Committee of Free Discussion; Congress Hotel; Convention of Colored Inhabitants of New York (Albany); Convention of Colored (Jamaica, Long Island); Conyers, John; Cornish, Reverend Samuel; Cosby, Edmund; Cowes, James C.; Crummell, Catherine; Cultivator, The.

Death Notices; Dembye, George R.; Dennison, Isaac; Directory for the People of Color, A; Dixon, G. H.; Doolittle, Dr. A.; Douglass, William P.; DuBois, Alexander

Esteve, John L.

Female Baptist Association; Female Companion; Female Trading Association; Fields, James; First African Methodist Episcopal Church; First Colored Presbyterian Church; First District Meeting; Flamer, John; Fourteenth Ward Hotel; Fourth Free Church; Francis, W.H.; Frankfort Street Church; Fraser, James; Free People of Color; Freeman, Nancy; Friends of a Fugitive Slave; Friends of Liberty;

Gardner, W.F.; Gayle, Anthony; Gaylord, Willis; General Meeting of Colored Citizens; Gibbons, Mr.; Gibbons, George W.; Gibbs, William A.; Girl Wanted; Gloucester's Church; Godwin, Mrs. A.; Goodwell, William A.; Goodwin, William A.; Graham's Biblical Lectures; Grain, Nathaniel; Green, James

Hairdresser; Hall, Priscilla; Hallock, Simney; Hamilton Lyceum; Hayes, Peter B.; Hazzard, Ebenezer; Health Almanac; Hedden, Elijah; Henderson, James H.; Hicks, Joseph; Hicks Society; Hill, J.W.; Hodges, William J.; Hoffman, T.; Hogarth, George; Hopper, Josiah; Housekeeper;

Humane Mechanics Society; Hunt, Reverend Mr.; Huntington, David; Hutson's Intelligence Office

Indian Medicines

J.M.D.; Jackson, J.M.; Jeffers, William L.; Jinnings, Thomas; Jobs, Charles; Johnson, Bennet; Johnson, Mrs. H.; Johnson, R.C.; Johnson, W.P.; Johnston, J.; Johnston, William; Jones, Mr.; Juvenile Daughters of Rush

Kinsman, Rufus

Ladies Literary Society; Lawrence, Mrs. G.; Legree, Joseph; Leonard, Isaac; Lewis, Joel W.; *Liberator* Subscribers; Lippins, John; Literary and Library Union; Lively, Dr.; Lively, W.M.; Lovering, P.; Lyon, Caesar; Lyon, Lyman

Man and Wife Wanted; Marine Benevolent Society; Marriages; Marshall, Edward F.; Meeting Room; Meetings (Misc.); Mental and Corporeal Feast; Methodist Episcopal Conference; Methodist Protestant Church; Michael, Mrs. D.; Michael, Joseph; Miller, John H.; Mitchell, John; Money Request; Monthly Concert of Prayer; Moreton, George B.; Morrison, Miss Rita; Morton, George B.; Myers, F.

National Reform Convention; Natt, George; Nelson, Liberty H.; New England Colored Temperance Society; New Jersey Anti-Slavery Society; New York Association for the Political Elevation and Improvement of the People of Color; New York *Colored American*; New York Committee of Vigilance; New York Literary and Library Union; New York Reform Society; New York Select Academy; New York State Anti-Slavery Society;

New York Union Commercial Association; New York Union Society; New York Wholesale Prices; Nicholas, W.L.

Offices and Rooms to Let; Ogden, Henry; Osborn, J.; Osborn, John

Parker, Mrs.; Parker, L. and H. and Company; Parkis, John; Parsons, Dr.; Pell, George; Perkins and Towne; Peterson, Peter A.; Philadelphia Reading Room; Phoenix High School; Plet, Cherry; Political Improvement Association; Pontou, Paul; Potter, Anthony; Potts, Reverend Dr.; Powell, Edward; Powell, William P.; Pratt, William Wylls; Prayer for the Slave; Presbyterian Church; Printing and Book Binding; Protestant Episcopal Free Church; Protestant Methodist Meeting House; Public Discussions; Public Schools

Quonn, Mark

Rawlings (Rollings), Mr.; Read, Timothy; Reading Room; Reason, Patrick H.; Reese, Dr.; Refectory to let; Robinson, E.; Rochester Colored Total Abstinence Association; Rogers, Mr.; Ruggles, David;

Sacred Concert; Saint Mark's School; Saint Matthew's Free Church; Saint Peter's; Saint Philip's Church; Scott, H. and Company; Scott, Henry; Sears' Chart of the World; Sears, Robert; Second Colored Presbyterian Church; Seneca Indian Cough Syrup; Shields, Frances Maria; Simson, S.; Sr. Cecelia's Society; Slavery As It Is; Slee, Samuel; Smith, Dr.; Smith, James McCune; Smith, Serena; "Societe Des Amis Reuni";

Spillet, John; State Convention of the Colored Freemen of Pennsylvania; Stationery Store; *Superior, The* (Steamboat)

Tappan, Lewis; Taylor, J.; Teacher; Teacher (Colored School); Thomas, G.W.; Thompson, Richard Jr.; Thompson, William; Tilman, Levin; Tompkins, Miss Fanny; Towne and Perkins; Townsend, Reverend J.B.; Trinidad; Troy and Michigan Six-Day Line

Union Coffee House; Union Evangelical Missionary Society; Union Hall; Union Prayer Meeting; Union Sunday School; United Female Assistant Benefit Society

Van Renssalaer, Thomas; Views of the Holy Land

Ward, S.R.; Webster, William C.; Weekly Report of Interments; Welch, John Robinson; Wells and Gomott; *Western Reserve Cabinet and Family Visiter*; White, George H.; Wiles, Francis; Williams, Margaret; Williams, P.; Williams, Mrs. Peggy; Wilson and Ray; Wilson, George; Wilson, William J.; Wood Mechanics; Wood, S.L.

Young, John; Young Ladies' Domestic Seminary; Young Men's Anti-Slavery Society; Young Men's Standing Correspondence Committee; Young Woman; *Youth's Cabinet*

Zion Baptist Church

AFRICA

	1837
-Notes successful completion of exploration of African interior	Mar 25 p4 cl
-Of interest to whites	Apr 29 p2 cl
-First claim goes to the free blacks in the United States	Apr 29 p2 c3
	1838
-Notes archeological discoveries in Carthage	Oct 20 pl c4
	1840
-Description of superstitious practices	Apr 11 p4 c2
-Inquiry as to how Africa shall be civilized and christianized	Jul 4 pl c3 let.
	1841
-English abolitionist emphasizes its humane civilization	Feb 27 pl cl let.
-Niger expedition noted	Feb 27 p3 c3
-Missionary activities urged	Apr 17 p2 cl let.
-Missionary efforts encouraged, but must be separate from colonization	Apr 24 p2 c3
-American war ships go to Africa to demand settlement in damage suit with African chief	May 1 p2 c3
-Missionary efforts seen necessary; are not felt to be the same as colonization	May 15 p3 c2 let.
-Missions praised as the only way to christianize Africans	May 29 p3 cl let.
-Missions praised	Jun 5 pl cl let.
-Missionary work in Africa recommended	Jun 19 p2 cl let.
-Christians have a mandate from God to do missionary work there	Jun 26 pl c3 let.
-African missions urged	Jul 3 p2 cl let.
-Missionary work in Africa seen as a Christian duty	Jul 10 pl c4 let.
-Christians duty-bound to share the gospel with African heathen	Jul 10 p2 cl let.
-Christians have a responsibility to Africans	Jul 24 pl cl let.
-Black Christians urged to aid Africa	Jul 24 p2 cl let.
-Missionary efforts in Africa urged	Jul 31 pl cl let.
-Objections to African missions dismissed	Aug 7 pl cl let.

-Ministers urged to encourage missions there — Aug 7 p1 c2 let.
-Letters from two Ashanti boys, with introductions — Sep 4 p1 c1 let.
-African missions have an important bearing on American slavery — Sep 18 p2 c1 let.
-African missions praised — Oct 9 p1 c2 let.
-Missionary work evaluated — Oct 30 p1 c1 let.
-Conditions of American and African blacks linked — Nov 20 p1 c2 let.
-See also American Colonization Society; Caffres (African Tribe); Colonization (General); Liberia; Missionary Work

AFRICAN BAPTIST CHURCH (Albany, New York)

1837

-Meeting of Union Society of Albany held — Apr 15 p1 c3

AFRICAN BAPTIST CHURCH (Boston)

1837

-Daughter of pastor (Susan Paul) leads juvenile concert — Mar 4 p4 c1

AFRICAN BAPTIST CHURCH (St. Louis)

1837

-Pastor praised for life of industry — Mar 11 p4 c2

AFRICAN CIVILIZATION SOCIETY (England)

1841

-Aims distinguished from those of the American Colonization Society — Feb 27 p1 c1 let.

AFRICAN METHODIST EPISCOPAL CHURCH

1837

-New York Zion connection plans camp meeting — Sep 9 p2 c4
-New York Zion connection lists membership statistics — Oct 14 p2 c3
-Membership statistics noted — Oct 21 p2 c2
-New York Bethel connection holds fund raising fair — Nov 11 p3 c4

1840

-Rochester, New York connection solicits building funds — Jul 18 p3 c4
-Pittsburgh, Pennsylvania connection plans regional conference — Aug 29 p2 c3

-New York connection retracts statements against Charles B. Ray — Aug 29 p2 c4 let.
-Address to the annual conference of the New York City connection on general conferences and their aims — Sep 5 p1 c4
-Rahway, New Jersey congregation requests aid — Dec 5 p2 c4 let.

1841

-Plans for annual conferences noted — Feb 20 p3 c2

AFRICAN METHODIST EPISCOPAL CHURCH MAGAZINE

1841

-Recommended and described — Sep 25 p2 c4

AFRICAN SCHOOL SOCIETY (Wilmington, Delaware)

1840

-Activities mentioned — Nov 14 p1 c2 let.

AFRICANS (Moral Qualities)

1837

-Africans kinder and more gentle — Apr 8 p4 c1

AGRICULTURE

1837

-Agricultural pursuits stressed as a possible path to prosperity — Nov 4 p2 c2

1838

-Emigration to farming communities in the West urged — Feb 17 p3 c1 ed.
-Difficulties of agricultural settlements outlined — Feb 17 p3 c3 let.
-Husbandry seen as the highway to wealth and influence — Mar 15 p2 c2
-Blacks should become farmers, but not in separate settlements — Mar 22 p3 c2 ed.
-Segregated farming settlements for blacks opposed — Mar 22 p3 c2 let.
-Farming seen as the best avenue for blacks — Apr 12 p2 c1 ed.
-Description of farming successes of Haitian blacks — Apr 12 p2 c1 let.
-Farming enterprise urged — Apr 19 p2 c2 ed.
-Congressional bill reduces price of public lands — Apr 19 p2 c4
-Samuel Cornish calls for more black farmers — Apr 19 p3 c1 ed.

-Agricultural pursuits seen to be important	May 3 p3 cl ed.
-Education necessary for the scientific cultivation of the land	May 3 p3 c2
-Wheat crop promising in Indiana	May 3 p3 c3
-No calling more healthy or beautiful than gardening	Jul 14 p3 cl ed.
-Profits can be made from gardening	Jul 14 p3 cl
-Gardens are healthy, pleasurable and profitable	Jul 28 pl c3
-Some practical gardening advice	Jul 28 pl c3
-Statement of Benjamin Franklin favoring agriculture	Sep 8 p3 c3
-Uses and properties of tomatoes	Sep 15 p4 c3
-A highly respectible profession	Oct 6 p3 c3 ed.
-Productivity of Chinese seed corn praised	Oct 13 p2 cl
-Wealth of a country depends upon farmers and mechanics	Oct 20 p4 cl
-Farming particularly suited to moral purposes of Christians	Nov 3 p4 cl
-Manufacture of the sugar beet described	Nov 17 p3 c3
-Describes three potato crops grown from the same roots	Nov 17 p3 c4
-Success of black farmers described	Dec 15 p2 c2 let.
	1839
-Love of farming seen to be innate	Jan 19 p2 c2 ed.
-Directions for planting silk trees	May 18 p4 cl
-Agricultural life best	Jun 8 p2 c2
-View that blacks should leave cities and get involved in agriculture	Jun 22 p3 cl
-Agriculture recommended for free blacks	Jun 29 p2 c5
-Formation of colored farming settlements urged	Jul 13 p2 c5 let.
-Formation of separatist settlements discouraged	Jul 13 p2 c5 ed.
-View that a farm is within everyone's reach	Jul 20 p2 c4 let.
-Success story of an immigrant farmer	Jul 27 p2 c4
-The proper education of farmers described	Jul 27 p4 cl
-Blacks encouraged to become farmers	Aug 3 p2 c3

-On the joys of a farmer's life — Aug 3 p4 c1
-Loans should be made available for the purchase of land — Aug 31 p2 c4 let.
-On the education of farmers — Aug 31 p4 c1
-On the life of a farmer — Sep 14 p3 c1
-Farming not undignified as an occupation — Sep 14 p4 c1

<u>1840</u>

-On education for farmers — Mar 21 p4 c1
-On the charms of a farmer's life — May 2 p1 c4
-On the benefits of the use of chemistry to improve the soil — Jul 4 p4 c3
-On different methods of plowing — Jul 11 p4 c3
-On the value of country life — Jul 25 p4 c3
-The farmer seen as the most independent being — Oct 17 p4 c3
-Prayer seen as the duty of the Christian farmer — Oct 24 p4 c3
-On the true use of the vine — Nov 28 p4 c2

<u>1841</u>

-Hints to the farmer — Feb 6 p4 c3
-How to kill caterpillers and worms — Jul 17 p4 c4
-Advice on making butter — Aug 28 p4 c3
-Advice on sowing wheat, selection of seed, etc. — Sep 18 p4 c3
-People advised to settle in the country and cultivate the soil — Dec 4 p1 c3
-See also American Free Produce Association; Silk Culture

ALBANY CONVENTION (Black)

<u>1840</u>

-Plans for state-wide convention in New York noted; convention call issued — Jun 6 p3 c1
-Members of Convention Committee listed — Jun 6 p3 c2
-Call for attendance issued — Jun 13 p2 c1
-Endorsed by colored citizens of Albany — Jun 13 p2 c2
-Supported by colored citizens of Poughkeepsie, New York — Jul 4 p1 c1 let.
-Colored citizens of Buffalo elect delegates — Jul 4 p1 c2 let.
-Blacks urged to assemble at Albany — Jul 4 p3 c2
-Committee of Correspondence listed — Jul 4 p3 c3; Jul 11 p3 c2

-Call for attendance issued	Jul 18 p3 c2
-New York communities urged to send delegates	Jul 25 p2 c3
-Call for attendance issued	Jul 25 p3 c3
-Discussed at public meeting in New York City	Aug 8 p2 c2
-Meeting in New York City appoints delegates	Aug 8 p2 c4
-New York City delegates appointed	Aug 15 p2 c2
-Instructions to delegates	Aug 15 p2 c4
-Objections to convention listed and discussed	Aug 15 p2 c4
-Call for attendance issued	Aug 15 p3 c2
-Description	Aug 22 p2 c3
-Description of pre-convention meetings	Aug 22 p3 cl
-Described and praised	Aug 29 p2 c2
-Proceedings outlined	Sep 12 pl c4
-Plan to publish minutes noted	Nov 14 p3 cl
-Foreign attitudes noted	Nov 14 p3 c2
-Address to black citizens	Nov 21, Dec 19 pl cl
	1841
-Extracts from minutes	Jan 2, 9 pl cl
-Criticized for separationism	Jan 30 pl c4 let.
-Separationism justified and explained	Jan 30 p2 c2
-Separationism vindicated	Feb 13 p2 cl let.
-Meets and adopts petition to present to State Legislature	Dec 4 p2 cl

ALBANY EVENING JOURNAL

	1841
-Praised for supporting franchise amendment for colored citizens to New York State Constitution	Mar 27 p2 c3
-Urges adaptation of universal suffrage amendment by New York legislature	Mar 27 p3 c2

ALBANY MECHANICAL INGENIOUS SOCIETY

	1841
-Aims described and praised	Jul 31 p2 cl let.

ALDERMAN, A. (Notice)

	1838
-Establishes elementary and secondary schools	Dec 1-15 p4 c4
	Dec 29 p3 c4
	1839
	Jan 12 p2 c4- Jan 26 p4 c4
	Feb 9, 16 p4 c4

ALDRIDGE, MRS. FANNY	
	1838
-Listed as Second Directress of Female Assistant Society (New York)	Mar 15 p3 cl
ALEXANDER, JOHN & GEORGE PELL (Advertisement)	
	1840
-Establish Restorateur	Nov 14-28 p3 c4 Dec 12-26 p3 c4
ALLEN, L.B. AND WILLIAM H. (Advertisement)	
	1839
-Tea, sugar, and coffee for sale; announce change of address	Jul 13-27 p3 c4 Aug 17-31 p4 c3 Sep 14, 28 p4 c3 Oct 5-19 p4 c3 Nov 2-23 p4 c4
	1840
	Mar 14, 21 p4 c4
ALGIERS	
	1839
-Wedding described	Aug 17 pl c2
-Notes Christian slaves	Aug 24 pl c2
ALLEN, REVEREND RICHARD	
	1837
-Praised as Methodist clergyman	Oct 14 p2 c3
-Listed as agent for the Colored American	Dec 30 p3 c4
ALSTINE, WILLIAM VAN (Hudson, New York)	
	1837
-Listed as agent for the Colored American	Sep 16 p3 cl
AMALGAMATION	
	1837
-Abolitionists do not advocate amalgamation, while planters seem to since they father children by slaves	Sep 2 p4 cl
	1838
-Abolitionists do not support amalgamation, nor do blacks want it	Jun 23 p3 c2

-Blacks want no part of amalgamation; more a southern problem	Jun 30 p2 c1
-Slaveholders are the real amalgamators because of an adulterous passion for black women	Jul 7 p3 c2
-Anecdote ridiculing miscegenation fears	Jul 14 p3 c3
-Seen as a false issue to stir up racial hatred	Jul 28 p2 c1 ed.
-Article praises colonization since it will prevent amalgamation (from Mobile, Alabama <u>Advertiser</u>)	Aug 11 p3 c3
	<u>1839</u>
-Lynn, Massachusetts Petition calls for repeal of racial intermarriage Law	Feb 23 p2 c3
	<u>1840</u>
-Racial Intermarriage Law and Lynn, Massachusetts Petition discussed	Apr 25 p1 c1
	<u>1841</u>
-Denial that amalgamation is the wish of abolitionists	Jul 3 p2 c2 let.

AMBLERMAN, HENRY (Jamaica, New York)

	<u>1837</u>
-Elected secretary of the Jamaica Benevolent Society	May 27 p2 c4

AMERICAN AND FOREIGN ANTI-SLAVERY SOCIETY

	<u>1840</u>
-Organized due to division in the American Anti-Slavery Society	May 23 p2 c3
-Necessity for its formation deplored	May 30 p2 c3
-Protests against disapproval of political action by the American Anti-Slavery Society	May 30 p2 c3
-Account of debate over differences with the American Anti-Slavery Society	May 30 p3 c3 let.
-Resolutions passed at meeting printed	Jun 27 p2 c2
-Begins publication of new anti-slavery periodical	Jul 4 p2 c3

	1841
-First anniversary meeting planned	Apr 10-24 p3 c4
-Holds anniversary meeting	May 15 p2 c3
-Annual report praises black conventions	Jun 5 p1 c2
-Passes resolution in support of equal rights movement	Jun 19 p3 c1

AMERICAN ANTI-SLAVERY SOCIETY

	1837
-Stresses the Anti-Slavery Society as the only hope for blacks	Mar 4 p2 c4 ed.
-Fourth anniversary meeting to be held in New York City in May	Apr 8 p3 c2
-800-1,000 people expected for anniversary meeting	May 6 p2 c2
-4,000 present at anniversary meeting	May 13 p3 c1
-Resolutions relating to free blacks passed	May 20 p2 c1
-Other resolutions printed in the <u>Colored American</u>	Jun 10 p1 c1
-Executive committee awards $1,000 to Reverend Theodore Wright	Dec 16 p2 c3
	1838
-Prepares to publish work on <u>Laws of American Slavery</u>	Mar 22 p3 c1
-Publishes <u>Emancipation in the West Indies</u>	Mar 22 p3 c2
-Plans to hold anniversary celebration noted	Mar 22,29 p3 c4
-Successful business meeting hoped for	May 3 p3 c1
-Seen correct in its ideas	May 3 p4 c2
-Description of anniversary meeting and celebration	Jun 2 p2 c1 ed.
-Extracts from fifth annual report and proceedings	Jun 2 p3 c3
-Letter describes debate over the "peace question" and whether Congress has the power to legislate against slavery in the states	Jun 2 p4 c1 let.
-Praised for placing blacks on the Executive Committee	Jun 9 p3 c3 ed.
-Sympathetic encouragement from the British Anti-Slavery Society	Jul 14 p2 c3 let.
-Viewed as one of the most important institutions of the age	Oct 13 p3 c3 let.

-Receives sympathetic letter from John Gridley	Oct 20 p4 c2 let.
	<u>1839</u>
-Sixth anniversary meeting; problem over schism with New England members	May 11 p3 c2
-Holds meeting concerning power of free states to abolish slavery in the United States	May 18 p1 c1 ed.
-Criticized for ignoring plight of northern free blacks	May 18 p2 c2 ed.
-Convention noted	Jun 15-29 p3 c4
-Discouraged from forming political party	Aug 31 p3 c1 ed.
-Would become corrupted by becoming a political party	Sep 7 p3 c1 ed.
-Offers to pay blacks less than whites	Nov 9 p3 c4
	<u>1840</u>
-Seventh anniversary meeting to be held	Apr 4 p3 c3
-<u>Colored American</u> discusses blacks attending	May 2 p3 c2
-Attendance at anniversary meeting urged	May 9 p2 c3
-Proceedings of anniversary meeting	May 23 p2 c2
-Divisions in anti-slavery movement deplored	May 23 p2 c3
-Passes resolutions disapproving of political action; criticized for its stand by the American and Foreign Anti-Slavery Society	May 30 p2 c3
-Resolutions passed at seventh anniversary meeting	May 30 p2 c4
-Anti-slavery petition to Congress	May 30 p3 c1
-List of officers	May 30 p3 c1
-Account of debate over the differences with the American and Foreign Anti-Slavery Society	May 30 p3 c3 let.
-Report discourages emigration to Trinidad and British Guiana	Jun 6 p3 c3
-Letter of support from Jamaica read at the convention	Jun 20 p3 c1

-Begins publication of new periodical	Jul 4 p2 c3
	1841
-Eighth annual meeting to be held	Apr 10-24 p3 c4
-Holds anniversary meeting	May 15 p2 c3
-See also Burleigh, Charles B.; Juvenile Anti-Slavery Society; Roger Williams Anti-Slavery Society; United Anti-Slavery Society; Young Men's Anti-Slavery Society	

AMERICAN COLONIZATION SOCIETY

	1837
-Criticizes Colonization Society	Mar 4 p2 c4 ed.
-Notes postponement of meeting of the American Society for the Promotion of Education in Africa	Mar 4 p3 c2 let.
-Praises the aims of the American Society for the Promotion of Education in Africa	Mar 4 p3 c2 ed.
-Defines colonization	Mar 4 p3 c4 ed.
-Mr. Goodell accuses the American Colonization Society of racism	Mar 11 p1 c1
-Efforts of Colonization Society praised	Mar 18 p2 c4 let.
-Criticizes Colonization Society	Mar 18 p2 c4
-Cites healthy environment of African interior; critical of Liberian colonization	Mar 25 p4 c3
-Samuel Cornish questions value of colonization	May 13 p2 c2
-Criticism of colonization by James Forten	May 13 p2 c3
-Holds anniversary and is criticized by the Colored American	May 13 p3 c1
-Looking for government money to destroy abolition and persecute blacks	May 27 p2 c3
-Member of Society says blacks are not fit for freedom	May 27 p3 c3
-Black opposition to colonization noted	Jun 10 p3 c1
-Colonization seen as impractical due to expense	Jun 24 p3 c2

-Colonization seen to perpetuate slavery and allay consciences	Jul 29 p2 c3
-Colonization efforts seen to be malicious	Dec 16 p3 c2
	<u>1838</u>
-Colonization sinful	Jan 20 p3 c1
-View that the Colonization Society has been involved in the loss of black suffrage in Pennsylvania	Jan 27 p3 c2 let.
-Colonization scheme founded in prejudice	Mar 15 p3 c2 ed.
-Convention suggested to show opposition to colonization	Mar 15 p3 c3 ed.
-View that the Colonization Society had nothing to do with the loss of black suffrage in Pennsylvania (from the <u>Colonization Herald</u>); <u>Colored American</u> disagrees	Mar 29 p3 c2
-Describes poor conditions in Liberia (from the <u>Liberia Herald</u>)	Apr 5 p2 c2
-Linked with racist attitudes	Apr 19 p2 c3 let.
-Seen to be a society of exile, not emigration	May 3 p2 c2 let.
-Description of Society's supporters	Jun 2 p2 c1 ed.
-Colonization convention noted	Jun 2 p2 c2
-View that members should find better things to do	Jun 2 p2 c2 ed.
-Colonizationists seen to misrepresent and persecute abolitionists	Jun 2 p2 c3 ed.
-Society criticized for not admitting blacks	Jun 9 p3 c3 ed.
-View that Philadelphia meeting is likely to incite violence	Jun 16 p2 c1 ed.
-Society's meeting seen as an anti-abolitionist force that ignored black problems completely	Jul 7 p2 c3
-Inconsistencies and misconceptions pointed out	Jul 21 p2 c3 let.
-Absence of colonization movement in the West Indies pointed out	Jul 28 p1 c3
-Viewed as a dead, Godless institution	Aug 11 p2 c1 ed.
-Particulars of colonization plan published	Oct 13 p3 c1
-Preaches a false doctrine	Oct 20 p2 c1

-One man's justification given for withdrawing support Oct 27 p1 c4 let.
-Society accused of hypocrisy Oct 27 p3 c1 let.
-Objections to colonization scheme listed Dec 8 p1 c1 let.
-Duplicity and hypocrisy of Society declared exposed by Liberian colonist Dec 8 p2 c1 ed.
-Necessity of free black colonists to Christianize and civilize Africa denied as a justification for the colonization scheme Dec 8 p3 c2 ed.

1839

-Denounced by James McCune Smith at a New York anti-colonization meeting Jan 19 p1 c1
-Denounced by James Fields at a New York anti-colonization meeting Jan 19 p1 c2
-Ministers denounced as principal agents of colonization by Samuel Cornish Jan 19 p1 c2
-Denounced by Philip A. Bell at a New York anti-colonization meeting Jan 19 p1 c4
-Efforts abhorred by inhabitants of New Jersey Jan 19 p2 c2 let.
-Destructiveness of colonizationists discussed Jul 13 p3 c1 ed.

1840

-Disavowed by the American Anti-Slavery Society May 30 p2 c4
-Has its foundations in prejudice against blacks Oct 31 p2 c2

1841

-Seen as a means of persecution and oppression of blacks Jan 30 p4 c1 let.
-Distinguished from the African Civilization Society of England Feb 27 p1 c1 let.
-Condemned by meeting of free blacks of New Bedford, Massachusetts Jul 10 p2 c3 let.
-Condemned at meeting of free blacks of Albany, New York Jul 10 p3 c1 let.
-Need to change methods seen Oct 2 p1 c3 let.
-Society does great evil Oct 2 p2 c3 ed.
-See also Carey, Matthew; Cary, Lott; Clay, Henry; Colonization (General);

Fields, James; Hodgkin, Thomas; Liberia; Masonic Work; Racism; Randall, Dr. Richard; United States Congress

AMERICAN FREE PRODUCE ASSOCIATION

	1839
-First annual meeting planned in Philadelphia, Pennsylvania	Oct 5,12 p3 c4

AMERICAN LIBERTIES AND AMERICAN SLAVERY (S.B. Treadwell)

	1838
-Book given favorable review as a convincing abolitionist appeal	Jun 30 p3 c2
-Extract from favorable review	Sep 1 p3 c2
-Favorably reviewed and recommended	Oct 27 p3 c2

AMERICAN MAGAZINE AND RESPOSITORY OF USEFUL LITERATURE

	1841
-Described and recommended	Sep 11 p3 c2

AMERICAN MORAL REFORM SOCIETY (Philadelphia, Pennsylvania)

	1837
-History and purpose of Society given	May 13 p1 c3
-Total abstinence from liquor a principle of the Society	May 20 p2 c1
-Many small societies around the country	May 20 p2 c2
-Will hold its annual convention in August	Jun 3 p3 c4 Jul 29 p3 c1
-Samuel Cornish attends convention and praises it	Aug 19 p3 c1
-Colored American criticizes society for not doing anything	Aug 26 p2 c1
-Meeting criticized by Frederick Hinton	Sep 2 p2 c4 let.
-William Whipper protests Colored American's attacks	Sep 9 p2 c2 let.
-Newspaper's criticisms reasserted	Sep 9 p2 c3 ed.
-Reasons for not publishing convention's communications explained	Sep 9 p3 c1

1838

-William Whipper and the Colored American debate the Society's merits — Feb 10 p2 c3; Mar 3 p2 c2 let.; Mar 3 p2 c3 ed.; Mar 24 p2 c4
-Second anniversary meeting planned; topics of discussion noted — Jul 21 p2 c4 let.
-Society's convention well attended — Aug 25 p4 c1
-Society criticized for overly broad aims and plans to start a newspaper — Aug 25 p4 c2 let.
-Its constitution and aims considered misconceived; Society's views not black people's views — Sep 15 p2 c1 ed.
-Criticisms of exclusively black organizations refuted — Sep 15 p2 c1 let.
-Society planning to publish a newspaper, the National Reformer — Sep 22 p3 c2

1840

-Plans to hold fourth annual meeting — Jul 11 p3 c2
-Society criticized — Sep 5 p2 c3

1841

-Fifth annual meeting planned — Jul 3 p3 c3-Aug 7 p3 c4

-See also Bowers, John C.; Brown, Joshua; Brown, Reverend Morris; Burr, John P.; Butler, Thomas; Forten, James; Forten, James Jr.; Gloucester, Stephen H.; Hinton, Frederick A.; Purvis, Robert; Roberts, John B.; Watkins, Reverend William; Whipper, William; White, Jacob C.

AMERICAN SOCIETY FOR THE PROMOTION OF EDUCATION IN AFRICA
-See Free Blacks (Education)

AMERICAN UNION FOR RELIEF AND IMPROVEMENT OF THE COLORED RACE

1837

-Organization criticized — Mar 25 p2 c3

AMERICAN WARS (Black Participation)

	<u>1837</u>
-Andrew Jackson calls free blacks of Louisiana to fight in the War of 1812 (September 21, 1814); participation praised	Mar 4 p1 c1
	<u>1841</u>
-Blacks should support America against Britain	Feb 6 p2 c1 let.
-Blacks should remain neutral in American wars	Feb 13 p1 c4 let.
-Non-participation by blacks seen to be traitorous	Feb 13 p2 c3
-Blacks should maintain neutrality until equal rights are guaranteed	Feb 27 p3 c2 let.

<u>AMISTAD, THE</u>

	<u>1839</u>
-Shipboard meeting and trial described	Sep 7 p3 c2
-Spanish request surrender of captured slaves	Sep 7 p3 c5
-Many lawyers involved in defense of slaves	Sep 7 p3 c5
-Appeal for aid	Sep 14 p2 c5
-One of the captured slaves dies	Sep 14 p3 c4
-Questions the authority of the brig <u>Washington</u> to capture the <u>Amistad</u>	Sep 28 p1 c3 ed.
-Much public interest in the case; trial described	Sep 28 p2 c1
-Some papers criticized for their stand on the case	Oct 5 p2 c2
-Much interest in the case, but some black churches ignore it	Oct 5 p2 c4
-Preacher defends actions of <u>Amistad</u> rebels	Oct 5 p2 c4
-Case and background of rebels discussed	Oct 12 p1 c3
-Slave traders arrested for mistreating <u>Amistad</u> slaves	Oct 19 p3 c1
-Appeal for justice; certain newspapers criticized for their positions	Nov 2 p2 c2
-One of the Spaniards escapes	Nov 9 p3 c4
-Date of trial announced	Nov 16 p3 c4
-Captured slaves being educated in jail	Nov 23 p1 c2
-Homeland of <u>Amistad</u> prisoners described	Nov 23 p1 c2

1840

-British government plans to intercede on behalf of the slaves	Mar 7 p3 c2
-Case held over, pending Supreme Court appeal	May 23 p3 cl
-Extended dialogue over controversial aspects of the case	Jun 6 pl cl
-Wax figures made of the rebels	Jun 27 p3 cl
-United States government accused of using its influence in the case	Jul 25 p2 c4
-Report on the trial of the defendants	Nov 14 p3 cl
-Report on the education of the defendants and a plea for defense aid	Nov 28 pl c3 let.
-Public appeal of the defense committee	Nov 28 pl c4
-Government memoranda concerning the case and the prisoners	Nov 28 pl c4 let.
-Presidential warrant for the transfer of the prisoners	Nov 28 p2 cl let.
-Final adjudication of the case to take place before the Supreme Court	Dec 19 p2 c3
-Interest of the British government in the case noted	Dec 26 p2 c3

1841

-Judge William Jay's letter defending the prisoners accuses the owner of fraud	Jan 2 pl c3 let.
-Public meeting raises money for defense expenses	Jan 2 p2 cl
-Adjudication postponed	Jan 30 p3 cl let.
-Meeting held in Wilmington, Delaware to raise defense funds	Feb 6 p2 c4
-Hearing begins in the Supreme Court	Feb 27 p3 cl let.
-John Quincey Adams' plea before the Supreme Court seen to be effective	Mar 6 p3 c2
-Captives freed by the Supreme Court	Mar 13 p2 c2
-Description of prisoners' reactions to news of successful trial outcome	Mar 27 p2 cl let.
-Supreme Court applauded for its decision; future disposition of freed captives discussed	Mar 27 p2 c3
-Female captives freed and taken in by a family	Mar 27 p2 c4

-Freed prisoners may go to New York City	Apr 3 p3 c1
-Cabin boy runs away from custodian	Apr 10 p2 c4
-Buffalo citizens hold congratulatory meeting for freed <u>Amistad</u> prisoners	Apr 17 p2 c1
-Meeting to be held to introduce the freed Africans to the public	May 1 p2 c3 May 8 p3 c3
-John Quincy Adams discusses the case	May 8 p1 c4 let.
-Resolutions passed praising the rebels at a public meeting on the case	May 22 p2 c1
-Rebels attend meetings	May 22 p2 c2
-Mendians help find drowned boy	Sep 4 p2 c2 let.
-Mendians plan return to Africa	Sep 11 p3 c3
-Mendians to return to Africa	Oct 9 p2 c4
-Appeal for funds	Oct 9 p3 c2
-Continued contributions requested for Mendian Mission	Dec 25 p1 c1 ed.
-See also Adams, John Quincy; Cinquez (Cinque), Joseph; Jay, William; Jocelyn, Simeon S.; Ka-le; Leavitt, Joshua; New Haven Committee; Ruiz, Don Jose; Tappan, Lewis; United States Supreme Court	

ANDERSON, JOSEPHINE

	<u>1839</u>
-Marries William Bradford	May 18 p3 c5

ANIMALS

	<u>1838</u>
-Description of the Peruvian Llama	Sep 15 p3 c3
	<u>1840</u>
-Description of Birds of Paradise	Aug 29 p4 c1

ANTHONY, JOSEPH (Advertisement)

	<u>1840</u>
-Gentlemen's boots for sale	Nov 13, 20 p3 c4 Dec 4, 25 p3 c4
	<u>1841</u>
	Aug 21 p3 c3- Oct 16 p3 c4

ANTI-COLONIZATION
-See American Colonization Society; Colonization (General)

ANTI-COLONIZATION MEETING (Notice)

	1838
-Meeting open to the public announced	Dec 15 p3 c4

ANTI-SLAVERY ALMANACK

	1837
-Published by Nathaniel Southard	Nov 4 p3 c2
	1839
-Praised by the Colored American	Jan 12 p2 c2

ANTI-SLAVERY ART AND MUSIC

	1837
-Songs sung in church concert	Mar 4 p4 c1
	1839
-Window blinds described	Jun 29 p1 c5
	1840
-Book of songs and hymns	Sep 26 p3 c1

-See also Poems (Anti-Slavery)

ANTI-SLAVERY CONVENTIONS
-See American Anti-Slavery Society; London Anti-Slavery Convention

ANTI-SLAVERY MAGAZINE

	1838
-Magazine will be enlarged and will focus on conditions under slavery	Feb 10 p1 c3

ANTI-SLAVERY NOMINATING CONVENTION (Liberty Party)

	1840
-Resolutions approving the nominations of James G. Birney and Thomas Earle for President and Vice-President	May 30 p3 c2

-See also Liberty Party

ANTI-SLAVERY POETRY
-See Poetry (Anti-Slavery)

ANTI-SLAVERY SOCITIES

	1839
-View that more are needed	Oct 12 p3 c4

ANTI-SLAVERY SOCIETIES (Female)
-See Female Anti-Slavery Societies

ANTI-SLAVERY SOCIETY (New York)
-See New York Anti-Slavery Society

APPO, MRS. E. A.(157 Church Street, Philadelphia) (Advertisement)

1839

-Milliner and dress maker wants several apprentices
Jun 1 p3 c4
Jun 8, 15 p4 c3
Jun 22, 29 p4 c4
Jul 13 p3 c4
Jul 20, 27 p4 c4
Aug 17-31 p4 c4

-Milliner
Sept 14, 28 p4 c4
Oct 5, 12 p4 c3
Oct 19 p4 c4
Nov 2-23 p4 c4

1840

-Milliner
Mar 14, 21 p3 c4

-Apprentices wanted
Apr 11 p4 c3-Jul 11 p4 c4
Jul 25 p4 c4-Oct 3 p4 c4
Nov 13, 20 p3 c4
Dec 4, 25 p3 c4

1841

Oct 30 p3 c4

APPO, MRS. E. AND MRS. H. JOHNSON (Philadelphia) (Advertisement)

1837

-Ten apprentices for milenary (sic) work wanted
Sep 30 p3 c4-Nov 11 p4 c4

APPO, WILLIAM (Advertisement)

1837

-Music instructor
Sep 2 p3 c4
Sep 16-30 p4 c3

APPRENTICESHIP
-See Emancipation (West Indies)

ASBURY COLORED METHODIST CHURCH (Notice)

1841

-Plans exhibition of work by Sunday school scholars
Feb 13 p3 c3

ASIA

	1840
-Archeological discoveries noted	Nov 28 p4 c2

ASSOCIATION FOR THE BENEFIT OF COLORED ORPHANS

	1837
-Annual report printed	Dec 30 p3 c3
	1838
-Praised by the Colored American	Dec 22 p2 c1
-Physician to the association asserts that blacks are physically inferior	Dec 22 p2 c1
-Annual report printed	Dec 29 p2 c4
	1840
-Fourth anniversary to be celebrated	Dec 12 p3 c3

ASSOCIATION FOR THE POLITICAL ELEVATION AND IMPROVEMENT OF PEOPLE OF COLOR (The Political Association)

	1838
-Organization established	Jun 16 p2 c3
-Address by Peter Vogelsang regarding enfranchisement	Jul 14 p1 c1
-Holds public meeting on enfranchisement; goals praised by Frederick Hinton	Jul 14 p3 c2
-Proceedings of public meeting on suffrage	Sep 1 p3 c3
-Considered the most important civil institution	Sep 8 p3 c1 ed.
-Proceedings of public meeting	Sep 8 p3 c3
-Address by Augustus W. Hanson on unconditional emancipation and equality	Sep 15 p1 c1
-Preamble and resolutions passed at special meeting	Oct 6 p3 c2
-First regular meeting to be held	Oct 6 p3 c4
-List of officers and ward committeemen	Oct 20 p3 c3
-Goal is to advance New York free blacks' political rights	Nov 17 p3 c2
-Political associations throughout the state called for	Dec 8 p3 c3 let.
-Meeting announced	Dec 15 p3 c3

	1839
-Meeting announced	Mar 16 p3 c4
-Urged to take action through a general convention	Jul 27 p2 c1 ed.
-August 1st meeting urged to plan actions	Jul 27 p2 c5 let.
-August 1st meeting planned	Jul 27 p3 c5
-Meeting held	Aug 17 p3 c4
-Public meeting planned to resist disfranchisement	Oct 12, 19 p3 c5
-See also Brown, Dr. John; Brown, Joseph; Downing, Thomas; Elston, Daniel; Hanson, Augustus William; Hardenbrugh, Samuel; Harris, Thomas; Hinton, Frederick A.; Jinnings, Thomas L.; Jinnings, William S.; Johnson, William P.; Peterson, John; Reason, Charles; Sidney, Thomas S.; Sipkins, Henry; Tyson, William A.; Wake, Ransom; Zuille, John J.	

ASTRONOMY

	1838
-Moon described and speculated about	Dec 15 p1 c4
	1840
-Moon seen to have many uses and benefits	Sep 25 p1 c4
	1841
-Description of moon's eclipse	Jan 9 p3 c3
-Lectures to begin	Feb 20 p3 c3

ASYLUM FOR COLORED ORPHANS

	1837
-Society formed	Apr 22 p2 c4
-Criticized for wanting to separate black and white orphans	Apr 29 p2 c2
-Aims and accomplishments praised and contributions to its maintenance urged	Oct 28 p3 c2 ed.
	1838
-Seen to be in a prospering state	Oct 20 p3 c2 ed.
-Second anniversary celebration described	Dec 15 p2 c4 ed.
	1839
-Inquiry concerning the dismissal of a black matron	Jan 19 p2 c4 let.

-Inquiry reveals no prejudice Feb 2 p3 c2

ATHENS

1838

-Description of the city and its architecture Sep 1 p1 c4

ATHERTON, CONGRESSMAN (New Hampshire)

1838

-Introduced pro-slavery resolutions in Congress and called a traitor by the Colored American (from the New York American) Dec 22 p3 c2

ATKINS, SAMUEL

1841

-Marries Mary Edwards Oct 16 p3 c3

AUBURN CONVENTION

1841

-Description of its topics for discussion and list of delegates Jul 3 p2 c4 let.

AUBURN, NEW YORK

1840

-Short history of Auburn Oct 31 p4 c1

AVERY, REVEREND E. K. (Pittsburgh)

1837

-Accuses Christian ministers of apathy and prejudice toward slaves Nov 4 p4 c3

1841

-Exonerated from murder charge Jul 31 p2 c4

AVERY, GEORGE A. (Rochester, New York)

1838

-Praised by Charles B. Ray Nov 17 p2 c4

B

BACON, REVEREND LEONARD

1837

-Expresses the view that blacks can never improve themselves — Mar 18 p2 c4

BAKER, ALEXANDER

1841

-Marries Frances Brooks — Oct 9 p3 c3

BALL, MARTHA V. (Boston)

1837

-Secretary of the Boston Female Anti-Slavery Society laments the death of a fellow Society member — Apr 22 p3 c2

BALTIMORE, GEORGE H. (Albany, New York)

1837

-Attends the first meeting of the Union Society of Albany — Apr 15 p1 c3
-Listed as the recording secretary of the Moral and Mental Improvement Society of Troy, New York — Oct 14 p3 c4
-Delivers address on education to the Mental and Moral Improvement Association of Troy (New York) — Oct 21 p1 c2

BANKS

1837

-Need for a national bank noted — Jul 1 p3 c2

1839

-View that banks save time and are very useful; Western banks open to blacks — Mar 2 p2 c3
-Their use encouraged — Mar 16 p2 c2 let.

1841

-United States Bank seen as a tyrant — Feb 20 p2 c2
-New York City group favors a national bank — Jul 31 p2 c3

BANKS, ROBERT (Buffalo, New York)

1837

-Listed as agent for the Colored American — Mar 4 p4 c4

BANNEKER, BENJAMIN

	1837
-Prints old letter from Benjamin Banneker to Thomas Jefferson	May 20 p1 c3

BAPTIST ANTI-SLAVERY CONVENTION

	1840
-Appeals to slaveholders	Jun 20 p1 c1
-Convention report	Jun 20 p2 c3
	1841
-Meeting to be held	May 1 p2 c3

BAPTIST ANTI-SLAVERY SOCIETY (Notice)

	1840
-Meeting announced	Sep 26 p3 c3

BARBADOS

	1838
-Slaves to be freed August 1st	Jun 9 p2 c3
-Speech of the Lord Bishop to the legislature on the abolition of apprenticeship	Jun 23 p1 c3

BARBARY, ZACHARIAH S.

	1838
-Appointed treasurer of the Political Association	Jun 16 p2 c3

BARBER, E. D. (Vermont)

	1839
-Extract of anti-slavery speech	Jul 20 p1 c5

BARKER, PURDY AND COMPANY (Advertisement)

	1840
-Cheap goods for sale (Silks, domestic goods)	Apr 18 p3 c3 Apr 25 p2 c3
-Recommended by the <u>Colored American</u>	Apr 25 p3 c4
-Cheap goods for sale (Silks, domestic goods)	May 2-23 p3 c4 Jun 6 p3 c4-Jul 11 p4 c4 Jul 25 p4 c4-Aug 8 p3 c4 Aug 22-Sep 12 p3 c4 Sep 26 p3 c4

BARKER, J.W. AND S. (Also Barker and Purdy) (Advertisement)

	1840
-Dry goods	Oct 3 pp3, 4 c3

	Oct 10 p3 c4- Dec 26 p3 c4
	1841
-Dry Goods	Jan 9 p3 c4 Jun 26 p3 c4- Aug 14 p3 c4 Sep 11, 18 p3 c4
BARNARD, MR.	
	1837
-Speaks at Temperance Jubilee	Apr 1 p3 c1
BARRETT, ANTHONY (Columbus, Ohio)	
	1838
-Listed as agent for the <u>Colored American</u>	Jan 13 p4 c4
BATES, S. (Hopewell, New York)	
	1837
-Praises the <u>Colored American</u> and calls for wider distribution; donates $5.00 to the paper	Dec 23 p3 c2, 3
BATTLER, THOMAS	
	1837
-Listed as a member of the "Philadelphia Committee"	Dec 9 p3 c2
BEEHLET, JACOB	
	1839
-Commits suicide	May 18 p3 c5
BELL, PHILIP A.	
	1837
-Details aims of the <u>Colored American</u> and calls for support	Mar 11 p3 c4 ed.
-To tour New York to find agents and obtain subscriptions	Apr 8 p3 c1
-Looks for petition support for black voting rights	Aug 12 p2 c1
-Tours upstate New York to arouse young blacks to action concerning voting rights	Aug 19 p3 c3
-Relinquishes proprietorship of the <u>Colored American</u>	Nov 4 p3 c4
-Listed as a member of the lecture committee for the Philomathean Society	Dec 16 p3 c4
	1838
-Supports civil agitation to gain enfranchisement	Mar 15 p1 c3

-Appointed to the executive committee of the "Political Association" Jun 16 p2 c3
-Requests additional aid from subscribers for the third volume of the Colored American Dec 8 p3 c1 ed.

1839

-Denounces colonization at the New York anti-colonization meeting Jan 19 p1 c4
-Accusations against him made by David Ruggles Sep 7 p3 c5

1841

-Plans to lecture on female influence before the Philomathean Society Apr 17 p3 c3
-See also Smith, Gerritt; Voting Rights (Free Blacks) (New York)

BELL, PHILIP A. (Advertisement)

1838

-Store for rent Apr 12 p3 c4
-Large room available for Sunday School and store Apr 19 p3 c4
May 3 p4 c3

1839

-Part of house to let in Jamaica, Long Island Mar 2-16 p3 c4

1840

-Two rooms to let to a small family; store also Nov 13 p3 c3

1841

-Notice to landlords and tenants Feb 13, 20 p3 c4
-Lecture on "Female Influence" announced Apr 24 p3 c4
-Room and store to let Oct 9 p3 c3

BELLVILLE (New Jersey) (Advertisement)

1839

-Several building lots for sale; inquire at Colored American office Jun 15 p3 c4-
Jun 29 p4 c4
Jul 13-27 p4 c4
Aug 17-31 p4 c4
Sep 14, 28 p4 c4
Oct 5-19 p4 c4
Nov 2-23 p4 c4

	<u>1840</u>
	Mar 21 p4 c3
	Mar 28 p4 c4
	Apr 11 p4 c4- Jul 11 p4 c4
	Jul 25 p4 c4- Oct 24 p4 c4
	Nov 7 p4 c4- Nov 28 p3 c4
	Dec 12 p3 c4- Dec 26 p3 c4
BEMAN, AMOS GERRY (Hartford and New Haven, Connecticut)	
	<u>1837</u>
-Listed as an agent for the <u>Colored American</u>	Apr 1 p3 c1
-Sends $10.00 to the paper	Aug 19 p3 c1
	<u>1840</u>
-To visit Frankfort and William Street Church in New York	Sep 12 p3 c3
-Describes conditions in New England	Nov 7 p2 c1 let.
-Praises educational accomplishments of the Female Benevolent Society	Nov 14 p2 c2 let.
-Urges mental self-improvement	Nov 21 p2 c1 let.
-Remarks concerning churches of Portland, Maine	Nov 28 p2 c1 let.
-Encourages debating societies	Dec 5 p3 c1 let.
-Stresses the Bible as the best means of self-improvement	Dec 12 p2 c2 let.
-Discusses affairs of the Abyssinian Religious Society	Dec 26 p1 c1 let.
	<u>1841</u>
-Parental indifference to blame for the failure of the mental improvement of children	Jan 2 p2 c1 let.
-His thoughts for the Christmas season	Jan 16 p1 c1 let.
-Stresses the evils of alcohol	Jan 23 p3 c3 let.
-Underscores the evils of disunity among blacks	Feb 6 p2 c1 let.
-Speech at the anniversary meeting of the New York Vigilance Committee	May 22 p1 c1
-Recommends domestic economy and the mechanical arts	Jun 5 p2 c1 let.
-Bible study recommended	Jun 19 p2 c2 let.
-Maintains virtue is the greatest human quality	Jul 3 p2 c2 let.

-Says moral virtue is more important than intellectual attainment	Jul 10 p2 c3 let.
-Urges spiritual improvement through Christianity	Jul 17 p2 c1 let.
-Urges men to take up moral responsibilities	Aug 28 p2 c1 let.
-Deems the education of children to be necessary to moral uplift	Sep 18 p2 c2 let.
-Installed as pastor of the Black Congregational Church of New Haven	Oct 9 p3 c1 let.
-See also Wright, Reverend Theodore S.	

BEMAN, JEHIEL C.

	1839
-Will work for the Massachusetts Abolition Society on projects to improve situation of Blacks	Sep 28 p3 c4
	1840
-Praises the lectures of Stephen Gloucester and encourages useful study	Jul 4 p2 c4 let.

BENEDICT, S. W. (and Lewis Tappan) (Advertisement)

	1841
-Announces the sale of anti-slavery books	May 1, 8 p3 c4

BERRY, JOHN

	1837
-Attests to the guilt of Israel Williams as a thief	Oct 14 p3 c1

BERRY, SAMUEL (Jamaica, Long Island, New York)

	1837
-Listed as an agent for the Colored American	Apr 15 p3 c4
-Elected president of the Jamaica Benevolent Society	May 27 p2 c4

BETHEL METHODIST CHURCH (Notice)

	1837
-Public meeting announced	Dec 30 p3 c4

BETHEL METHODIST CONNEXION (Philadelphia, Pennsylvania)

	1837
-Will hold conference	May 20 p2 c2
-Extracts from minutes given	Oct 14 p2 c4

BETTS, JUDGE

	1837
-Decision in slave case severely criticized by New York free blacks	Dec 9 p4 cl

BIAS, JAMES C.

	1837
-Listed as a member of the "Philadelphia Committee"	Dec 9 p3 c2

BIBLE

	1837
-Held to be a pro-slavery book	Nov 4 p4 cl
-Religion of the Bible seen as the only hope for emancipation	Dec 9 p2 c2
	1838
-View that the Bible does not sanction slavery	Jan 27 pl c4
-The importance of studying the scriptures emphasized	Jul 21 pl c2
-Seen as the best abolition book	Jul 28 p2 cl
-Contains everything that needs to be known	Nov 17 p2 c4
	1839
-New Testament does not sanction slavery	Feb 9 p2 cl
	1840
-Viewed as the best means of self-improvement	Dec 12 p2 c2 let.
-How to ascertain its meaning	Dec 19 p4 cl
-Story illustrating the second commandment	Dec 19 p4 c2
	1841
-Anecdote illustrating the importance of supplying Bibles to sailors	Jan 16 p4 c3
-Seen as a good source of amusement for children	Apr 17 p3 c2
-Its study recommended	Jun 19 p2 c2 let.
-Seen as food for the soul	Aug 28 p4 c3
-Its usefulness discussed	Sep 18 p4 c2

BIDDLE, JAMES C.

	1838
-Public meeting held to express regret at his death	Sep 8 p2 c4

BIGLEY, CAPTAIN (Brig *Canonicus*)

	1838
-Accused of racial prejudice toward black passengers	Feb 17 p2 c2 let.

BIRNEY, JAMES G.

	1837
-Speaker at Fourth Anniversary Meeting of the American Anti-Slavery Society	May 13 p3 c1
	1838
-Sustains serious injury in carriage accident	Dec 15 p3 c1 let.
	1839
-Frees slaves given to him after father's death	Nov 2 p3 c4
	1840
-Presidential nomination favored by Colored Citizens of Albany (New York)	May 23 p3 c2 let.
-Presidential nomination supported by the Anti-Slavery Nominating Convention	May 30 p3 c2
-Birney's response to his nomination	Jun 27 p1 c1 let.
-Participates at London Anti-Slavery Convention	Jul 25 p2 c1
-Presides over the London Convention	Aug 1 p1 c4
-Nominated for President by the Ohio Anti-Slavery Convention	Sep 19 p3 c1
-*Colored American* supports Birney for President	Oct 3 p2 c2
-Seen to be the best man for President	Oct 10 p2 c1
-Returns from the London Convention	Nov 28 p3 c1
-Plans a public report of his journey to England	Dec 5 p2 c4
-Plans to speak at the New York Anti-Slavery Society meeting	Dec 12 p3 c3
	1841
-Nominated for President	May 22 p2 c3

BISHOP, JOSHUA (and George H. White) (Advertisement)

	1838
-Co-dentistry practice	Dec 15 p3 c3- Dec 29 p4 c3
	1839
	Jan 12 p2 c4- Jan 26 p4 c4
	Feb 9 p4 c4- Mar 16 p4 c4
	May 11 p4 c3
	May 18 p4 c4

-Co-dentistry practice dissolved — Jun 1 p3 c4-
Jun 29 p4 c4
Jul 13-27 p4 c4
Aug 17-31 p4 c4
Sep 14, 28 p4 c4
Oct 5-19 p4 c4
Nov 2-23 p4 c4

1840
Mar 21 p4 c3
Mar 28 p4 c4

BLACK, CHAUNCEY B.

1841

-Arraigned for distributing Bibles to slaves — Oct 16 p3 c1

BLACK, THOMAS

1837

-Listed as a member of the "Philadelphia Committee" — Dec 9 p3 c4

BLACK MINISTERS
-See Christian Ministry (Black)

BLACK NEWSPAPERS
-See Newspapers (Black)

BLACKS (Connecticut)

1838

-State legislature refuses to remove suffrage restrictions — Jun 16 p4 c2

1840

-Restricts education of blacks — Mar 14 p1 c1

BLACKS (General)

1837

-Letters testifying to the self-sufficiency of free blacks in Canada — Mar 4 p4 c1
-Literary societies praised as a means to show black self-improvement — Mar 11 p2 c1
-Blacks possess more self-respect than they are given credit for; abilities praised by Dr. Proudfit — Mar 25 p2 c4
-Strong domestic attachments affirmed — Apr 1 p2 c2
-Should come forward as one against slavery — Apr 8 p2 c1 ed.
-Blacks not inferior; credited with many ancient discoveries — Apr 22 p2 c1
-Black achievements listed — May 13 p4 c1

-Letter of Benjamin Banneker to Thomas Jefferson printed as proof of the abilities of blacks	May 20 p1 c3
-Mott's <u>Biographical Sketches</u> seen to give good accounts of black achievements	Jun 3 p2 c4
-Black settlement's property valued at $39,497	Jun 10 p2 c4
-Blacks with intelligence and character respected more than similar whites	Jun 24 p2 c1
-Talents of young New York free blacks noted	Oct 28 p3 c1 ed.
	<u>1838</u>
-Unity among blacks stressed	Mar 3 p2 c4
-Testimonial on blacks' ability to care for themselves sent to the Ohio Legislature	Mar 15 p2 c2
-Blacks' spirit unbroken by suffering and oppression	Apr 12 p3 c1 ed.
-View that free blacks in Trinidad and Brazil are self-sufficient	Apr 12 p4 c1
-Evils attributed to blacks denied	Apr 12 p4 c1
-Philadelphia <u>Spirit of the Times</u> sees blacks as a cross between a monkey and a devil	Aug 18 p3 c2
-Short story about a Mulatto artist	Sep 8 p1 c1
-Anecdote illustrating the humility and gratitude of blacks	Sep 15 p4 c1
-View of indignities and outrages blacks have suffered	Oct 6 p3 c3
-Anecdote concerning the success of a black navigator	Oct 27 p4 c1
	<u>1839</u>
-Doctor's view that blacks are physically inferior to whites refuted by the <u>Colored American</u>	Jan 26 p2 c1
-View that improvement of conditions for blacks will lead to higher intellectual attainments	Jul 13 p4 c2
-Examples of black successes cited	Aug 24 p1 c1
-Conditions improving; slavery seen nearing its end	Sep 14 p2 c1
-View that every member of an oppressed race must set a good example	Sep 14 p2 c1

-Honesty of a black maid praised | Sep 28 p4 c2
-Heroic nature of Africans noted | Oct 19 p1 c1

1840

-Good religious character of blacks stressed | Apr 11 p2 c1 let.
-High moral character of blacks stressed | Apr 25 p3 c1 let.
-Lack of literary abilities among blacks seen due to lack of cultivation | May 16 p2 c1
-Blacks seen physically equal to whites | Aug 22 p2 c1

1841

-Blacks seen equal to whites in moral character | May 15 p2 c2
-Denial of view that blacks cannot care for themselves | Aug 14 p1 c2
-See also Africa; Slavery

BLACKS (Hartford, Connecticut)
-See Convention Movement

BLACKS (Legal Descrimination)

1837

-Attack against New Jersey Legislature's passage of a restrictive law | Apr 8 p2 c4
-List of legal disabilities blacks face in New York | Sep 30 p3 c2 let.

1838

-Laws prohibiting blacks from testifying against whites criticized | Mar 22 p1 c4
-Restrictions on voting rights seen to be immoral and unconstitutional | Mar 22 p2 c1 ed.
-Testimonials to unconstitutionality of suffrage restrictions | Mar 22 p2 c1
-Work on <u>Laws of American Slavery</u> published | Mar 22 p3 c1
-Description of discriminatory legislation in Michigan | Apr 12 p1 c3 let.
-Connecticut repeals black act (denying the right to attend school) and grants trial by jury to accused fugitive slaves | Jun 16 p2 c2
-Florida codes make slaves of free black debtors | Oct 13 p2 c4

1839

-Maryland Law forbids residence to blacks — Jul 13 p1 c5
-Comments on inequalities in Mississippi law — Jul 20 p3 c2
-Alabama law described — Aug 3 p4 c2
-View that disenfranchisement dehumanizes blacks — Oct 12 p2 c1
-Blacks cannot be citizens, vote, or testify in courts in Ohio — Nov 2 p2 c5

1840

-Free states restrict blacks' right of movement — Mar 7 p1 c3
-Ohio Legislature rejects petition from blacks — Mar 14 p1 c1
-Blacks may be seized as runaway slaves — Mar 21 p1 c1
-New York City blacks denied pushcart licenses — May 9 p2 c1 let.
-Text of Maryland law prohibiting settlement of free blacks — May 30 p1 c4
-Legal and moral right to pushcart licenses asserted — May 30 p2 c2 ed.
-Free blacks in Georgia taxed exhorbitantly — Dec 12 p3 c1
-Ohio's oppressive settlement laws noted — Dec 19 p2 c3
-Ohio's legal hazards for blacks discussed — Dec 26 p2 c2

1841

-Bill introduced in Congress to prohibit legal testimony of blacks in military and naval courts — Jan 2 p2 c4
-Excluded from public schools in Ohio although taxed for them — Jan 16 p2 c2
-Prohibited from testifying in courts in Ohio — Jan 23 p2 c2
-Blacks excluded from preempting public lands — Jan 23 p2 c3
-State legislatures accused of invading rights of blacks — Feb 13 p2 c2
-Massachusetts repeals law prohibiting intermarrige — Mar 27 p2 c4
-"Nine Months Law" may be removed from New York statutes — Apr 10 p2 c3
-Ohio fails to repeal oppressive black laws — Apr 17 p2 c4

BLACKS (New Haven, Connecticut)
-See Convention Movement

BLACKS (Ohio)
-See Convention Movement

BLACKS (Orphans)
-See Asylum for Colored Orphans

BLACKS (Philadelphia, Pennsylvania)

	1837
-Of 549 on alms in the city, only twenty-two are black	Aug 19 p4 cl
-See also Convention Movement	

BLACKS (Pittsburgh, Pennsylvania)
-See Convention Movement

BLACKS (Politics)

	1837
-Blacks elected to the House of Assembly in Nassau	Jun 10 p2 c4
-See also Voters (Black); Legal Discrimination	

BLACKS (Self-improvement)

	1837
-Pride seen as an evil passion	May 27 p3 cl
-Should develop high character	Jun 24 p2 cl
-Blacks need education and black teachers	Jun 24 p3 cl
-Blacks must raise their level of education to be fully emancipated	Jun 24 p3 c3
-Blacks should buy land	Jul 15 p3 cl
-Blacks need mental improvement	Jul 29 p2 c3
-Must be careful of fraud when buying land	Aug 5 p3 c2
-Must stop regarding lighter skinned blacks as better	Aug 19 p2 c3
-Blacks have to show appreciation of the rights they have	Aug 19 p2 c4
-Moral virtue and merit make a man; blacks should be virtuous	Aug 26 p2 c2
-Blacks should pay ministers and teachers	Sep 2 p2 cl
-Farming seen to be a good occupation	Sep 23 pl c2
-Blacks have to learn self-respect	Sep 23 p2 cl
-Blacks should be industrious	Sep 23 p2 c3
-Blacks should change their family life	Sep 30 p2 cl
-Blacks need education	Sep 30 p2 c2
-Virtue seen to be its own reward	Oct 7 p2 c2
-Letter stresses knowledge as the way to attain power	Oct 7 p2 c3 let.

	1838
-View that blacks should buy land in the West	Jan 27 p3 cl let.
-A national organization of blacks needed	Feb 10 p2 c2 let.
-Reading seen as the key to knowledge	Nov 18 p2 cl
-Stephen Gloucester (Philadelphia) opens a reading room; calls for larger attendance	Nov 18 p2 c2
-Mechanical arts seen to be important	Dec 22 p2 c4 let.
	1839
-Blacks must act on principle	Jan 12 p2 cl ed.
-Blacks must be pious and virtuous	Jan 12 p2 c2 ed.
-Seen possible to learn on one's own without academies and colleges	Jan 26 pl cl
-Example of a blacksmith who has learned languages on his own	Jan 26 pl c2
-Blacks should buy some of the large tracts of government land in the west	Jan 26 p3 c2
-Family reading seen to be important	Feb 2 pl c4
-Dignity of agricultural occupations discussed	Feb 2 p4 cl
-Opportunities in the western United States discussed	Feb 9 p2 c3
-Small amounts of knowledge are valuable, and time should be set aside for study	Feb 16 p3 c3
-To be free, blacks must possess equal national, moral and intellectual advantages	Feb 23 p3 cl
-Education is the road to freedom (Cleveland Observer)	Mar 2 pl cl
-Early rising, a plain diet, and plain living praised	Mar 2 p4 cl
-Parents must teach children to work hard for future rewards; training is important	May 11 p2 c2
-Children should be educated to industrious habits; agriculture is best; life in the country better than in the city	Jun 8 p2 c2
-Religion is an aid to self-improvement	Jun 8 p2 c5
-Religion, temperance and moral reform societies are good for blacks	Jun 22 pl cl

-Strict morality important — Jun 22 p2 c3
-Religion, education, and mechanical skills are necessary — Aug 3 p2 c1
-Education is important; racisim makes it hard to attain — Aug 3 p2 c2
-Rewards come to those who work for them — Aug 3 p2 c4
-Blacks must unite to improve their condition — Aug 24 p2 c1

1840

-Idleness is bad for people physically and mentally — Apr 25 p2 c1
-Lack of literary attainments deplored — May 16 p2 c1
-See also Agriculture; American Moral Reform Society; Blacks (General); Free Blacks (Education); Free Blacks (Education-Women); Free Blacks (Self-Improvement); Philadelphia Moral Reform Society

BLACKS (Worcester, Massachusetts)
-See Convention Movement

BLAKE, DR.

1837

-Gives address to Colored Young Men of New York — Sep 16 p1 c1

BLOUNT, REVEREND N. (Poughkeepsie, New York)

1837

-Listed as agent for the Colored American — Jun 3 p3 c4

1840

-Addresses colored citizens of Buffalo, New York on behalf of the New York Colored American — Aug 29 p2 c1

BOARD WANTED (Advertisement)

1837

-In a private family home for a gentleman and lady — Sep 2 p3 c4; Sep 16 p4 c4; Sep 23 p3 c4

BOARDING HOUSE (50 Beach Street) (Advertisement)	
-One or two gentlemen with their wives	1838 Dec 29 p4 c3
	1839 Jan 12 p2 c4
BOARDING HOUSE (62 Leonard Street) (Advertisement)	
-Rooms	1838 Jun 16 p4 c3
BOARDING HOUSE (North 12th Street) (Advertisement)	
-Rooms	1837 Jun 17 p3 c4 July 1, 8, 22 p4 c3
BOARDING HOUSE (33 Sullivan Street) (Advertisement)	
-Rooms	1840 Jun 6 p3 c4 Jun 20 p3 c4- Jul 18 p3 c4
BOARDING HOUSE (43 Thomas Street) (Advertisement)	
-Rooms	1837 Jun 24 p3 c4 Jul 1-15 p4 c4 Jul 29 p3 c4 Aug 19 p1 c4 Sep 16, 23 p4 c3
BODEE, GEORGE A. (and William R. Powell) (Advertisement)	
-Colored seamen's boarding house	1840 Jun 6 p3 c4- Jul 11 p4 c4 Jul 25 p4 c4- Oct 3 p4 c4
-Partnership dissolved	1841 Jul 10 p3 c4- Sep 4 p3 c4 Sep 18 p3 c4
BODINE, LEWIS (Advertisement)	
-Boarding House	1838 Jun 2 p3 c4 Jun 23 p4 c4- Oct 6 p4 c4

	Oct 20 p4 c4- Nov 17 p4 c3 Dec 1 p4 c3 Dec 8 p4 c4
BOND, ROBERT (Virginia)	
	1837
-Writes address to Virginians portraying evils of slavery	May 27 p1 c3
BOOKS	
	1839
-Most novels and romances have no value because they are immoral	Feb 16 p1 c3
	1840
-_Pictorial Illustrations of the Bible_ advertised	Oct 31 p3 c4
	1841
-_The Cultivator_ described and advertised	Jan 2 p3 c3
-_Origin and History of the Colored People_ advertised	Jan 9 p3 c3
-_The Hour and the Man_ reviewed	Feb 20 p2 c4
-_Christian Love_ or _The Duty of Personal Efforts For the Immediate Conversion of the Impenitent_ by John S. Taylor; reviewed and recommended	Mar 27 p3 c1
-_Correspondence Between Oliver Johnson and George F. White_ noted	Mar 27 p3 c1
-_Pictorial Illustrations of the Bible_ advertised	Apr 10 p2 c2
-_Illustrations of Prophecy_ by David Campbell advertised	Apr 24 p3 c1
-_A Scripture Manual_ by Charles Simmons described and recommended	Jun 12 p3 c1
-_Fourth of July Book_ by J. W. Seaton advertised	Jun 19 p3 c1
-_Sketches of the Higher Classes of Colored Society in Philadelphia_ advertised	Sep 25 p2 c4
-_An Argument on the Unconstitutionality of Slavery_ by G.W.F. Mellen reviewed and recommended	Sep 25 p3 c1
-_Health Almanack_ advertised	Sep 25 p3 c4
BOOMS, MRS. P. (Notice)	
	1840
-Religious worship at her home	Jun 27 p3 c4 Jul 4 p3 c4

BORDEN, NATHANIEL A. (and William P. Powell) (Advertisement)

1841

-Owners of sailor's home — Jul 24 p3 c3- Sep 4 p3 c3; Sep 18 p3 c3

BOSTON

1838

-Letter describes city — Jun 23 p3 c1
-Letter describes citizens as industrious and intelligent, but prejudiced — Jul 7 p2 c4

BOSTON FEMALE ANTI-SLAVERY SOCIETY
-See Chapman, Ann G.

<u>BOSTON REGISTER AND OBSERVER</u>
-See Worcester, Noah

BOSTON, URIAH (Poughkeepsie, New York)

1840

-Chosen president of the Poughkeepsie committee to support the general Convention — Jul 4 p1 c1 let.
-Praises the actions of the New York *Colored American* — Nov 28 p3 c1 let.

1841

-Urges self-examination and reflection — Jan 16 p1 c3 let.
-Describes Poughkeepsie August 1 celebration — Aug 21 p1 c1 let.

BOSTON YOUNG MEN'S SOCIETY

1840

-Addressed on the evils of the lottery system — Nov 14, 21 p1 c3; Nov 28 p1 c1

-See also Gordon, George William

BOURNETT, ABRAHAM (New Rochelle, New York)

1837

-Sends $1.50 to the *Colored American* — Jun 17 p3 c4

BOWENS, B. (Advertisement)

1838

-Store for cheap dry goods — Sep 29 p3 c4; Oct 6 p4 c3; Oct 20 p4 c4- Nov 17 p4 c3; Dec 1 p4 c3- Dec 29 p4 c4

	<u>1839</u> Jun 15 p3 c4- Jun 29 p4 c3 Jul 13-27 p4 c3 Aug 17-31 p4 c5 Sep 14 p4 c5 Sep 28 p4 c5- Oct 19 p4 c5
BOWERS, JOHN C. (Philadelphia)	
	<u>1837</u>
-Listed as agent for the New York <u>Colored</u> <u>American</u>	Mar 11 p4 c4
-Speaks on temperance at the convention of the Philadelphia Moral Reform Society; praised by the <u>Colored American</u>	Aug 26 p3 c1
-Listed as president of the Philadelphia Library Committee	Dec 23 p2 c1
	<u>1839</u>
-Advertises wholesale and retail clothing	Jan 26 p3 c4 Feb 9 p4 c4- Mar 16 p4 c4 May 11, 18 p4 c4 Jun 1 p4 c4- Jun 29 p4 c5 Jul 13-27 p4 c5 Aug 17-31 p4 c5 Sep 14 p4 c5 Sep 28 p4 c5- Oct 19 p4 c5 Nov 2-23 p4 c5
	<u>1840</u> Mar 14-28 p4 c4
BOY WANTED (Advertisement)	
	<u>1837</u>
-Colored lad, 12-15, to make change and tend bar	Nov 18 p3 c4
	<u>1838</u>
-Colored, age 14, to live on a farm	Apr 12 p3 c4 Apr 19 p4 c2 May 3 p4 c3 Jun 2 p4 c4
	<u>1839</u>
-To learn barber's trade	Jun 1 p3 c4- Jun 29 p4 c4 Jul 13 p4 c4

-Colored, as printer's apprentice — Jul 20 p3 c4
Aug 17-31 p4 c3
Sep 14, 28 p4 c3
Oct 5 p4 c3

1840

-To assist waiter and attend carriage — Nov 21 p3 c4
Mar 6, 13 p3 c4

BOYD, HENRY

1839

-Advancement of ex-slave described — Aug 17 p1 c4

BOYER, PRESIDENT (Haiti)

1838

-London newspaper describes him; calls him a remarkable man — Jun 30 p3 c3

BRADFORD, WILLIAM

1839

-Marries Josephine Anderson — May 18 p3 c5

BRADISH, L. (Candidate for Governor of New York)

1838

-Affirms abolitionist sentiments to Utica black citizens — Nov 3 p1 c1
-Supported by colored free-holders of New York City — Nov 3 p3 c4
-Ridicules attack of southern slaveholder upon British M.P. who supported British abolition — Nov 3 p4 c2 let.

BRECKENRIDGE, REVEREND R.J.

1838

-Accused of taking equivocal stance on abolition — Apr 19 p3 c2 ed.
-Statement on slavery — Apr 19 p3 c2

BREWER, HENRY (Troy, New York)

1839

-Commits suicide — May 18 p3 c5

BREWER, WILLIAM (Wilkesbarre, Pennsylvania)

1837

-Listed as agent for the Colored American — Mar 4 p4 c4

BRIGGS, JOHN (New Bedford)

1837

-Secretary of the Colored Citizens Organization of New Bedford, Massachusetts — Nov 18 p3 c3

BRIGGS, OLNEY	
	1837
-Spoke against slavery at the 1821 New York Constitutional Convention	Mar 11 p2 c2
BRIGHT, MARY ADAMS	
	1837
-Praises the _Colored American_ for inspiring blacks	Oct 21 p3 c2 let.
BRITISH AMERICAN _JOURNAL OF LIBERTY_	
	1839
-Prospectus printed	Jun 22 p3 c3
BRITISH AND FOREIGN ANTI-SLAVERY SOCIETY	
	1839
-Society formed to fight slavery and the slave trade around the world	Jun 29 p2 c5
	1840
-States opposition to general emigration to crown colonies	Apr 4 p1 c3
-Proceedings of anniversary meeting; speeches	Aug 29 p1 c1
	1841
-Anti-slavery address to President Tyler	Jun 26 p1 c1 let.
-Extracts from speeches of Daniel O'Connell and Charles Remond at its anniversary meeting	Jul 10 p1 c1
-See also West Indies (Jamaica)	
BRITISH GUIANA	
	1840
-Affirmation of recent positive improvements in agriculture and industry	Jul 25 p1 c2
BRITISH WEST INDIA EMANCIPATION (Notice)	
	1837
-Jubilee celebration announced	Jul 22 p1 c4
BROADWAY TABERNACLE CHURCH (Notice)	
	1837
-Evening School for Colored People	Sep 30 p3 c4- Nov 11 p4 c4

	Nov 25 p4 c4- Dec 16 p4 c4
	<u>1838</u>
-Gentlemen expected to take part in church exercises	Jul 28 p3 c4
-Evening school for colored people	Dec 1 p3 c4- Dec 29 p4 c4
	<u>1839</u>
	Jan 12 p2 c4- Jan 26 p4 c4 Feb 9, 16 p4 c4
BRONSON, PROFESSOR (Notice)	
	<u>1840</u>
-Recitation announced	Mar 21, 28 p2 c4
BROOKLYN, NEW YORK MASS MEETING (Notice)	
	<u>1841</u>
-In support of an unrestricted franchise	Jan 2 p3 c3 Jan 9 p3 c4
BROOKS, CHARLES (Brooklyn, New York)	
	<u>1837</u>
-Listed as agent for the <u>Colored American</u>	Dec 23 p3 c3
BROOKS, FRANCES	
	<u>1841</u>
-Marries Alexander Baker	Oct 9 p3 c3
BROUGHAM, LORD (England)	
	<u>1839</u>
-Demonstrates interest in the lower classes	Sep 14 p1 c4
	<u>1840</u>
-Speaks at London Anti-Slavery Convention	Jul 25 p2 c2
-See also Wilberforce, William	
BROWN, ANSON C.	
	<u>1841</u>
-Arrested after committing robbery	Oct 2 p3 c3
BROWN, BENJAMIN	
	<u>1837</u>
-Teaches in black Sabbath School	Jul 29 p2 c4

BROWN, E. (Advertisement)	
	1838
-Accomodations; lodging	Sep 8 p3 c4- Sep 29 p4 c3
BROWN, MRS. FLORINDA	
	1838
-Marries Aaron Wood	Aug 4 p3 c4
BROWN, GEORGE L. (Utica, New York)	
	1837
-Listed as agent for the Colored American	Sep 16 p3 cl
BROWN, J.B. (and S. L. Wood) (Advertisement)	
	1840
-Confectionary and fruit store; family supplies	Jul 4 p3 c3- Jul 18 p3 c4 Aug 1 p3 c4- Oct 17 p4 c4
BROWN, DOCTOR JOHN	
	1837
-Inaugurated as Philomathean Society Prefect; delivers address at anniversary meeting	Nov 4 p3 cl
	1838
-Reports on Committee of Investigation of Colored Citizens of New York City	Feb 17 p2 c4
-Appointed to the Political Association's executive committee	Jun 16 p2 c3
	1839
-Opens school for blacks	May 18 p3 c2
	1840
-Obituary	Mar 7 p3 c2
-Eulogy	Mar 28 pl cl
	1841
-Tribute from Phoenixonian Society	Mar 27 p3 c2
BROWN, JOSEPH (New Haven, Connecticut)	
	1838
-Listed as agent for the Colored American	Feb 3 p3 c4
-Appointed to executive committee of Political Association	Jun 16 p2 c3

BROWN, JOSHUA

	1837
-Director of the American Moral Reform Society issues a call to meeting	Aug 5 p3 c3

BROWN, J.B.

	1841
-Obituary	Apr 24 p3 c2

BROWN, REVEREND MORRIS

	1837
-Issues a call to meeting for the American Moral Reform Society	Aug 5 p3 c3
-Elected an honorary member of the Mental and Moral Improvement Association (Troy, New York)	Oct 21 pl c2

BROWN, MOSES (Providence, Rhode Island)

	1837
-Freed his slaves in 1773	Apr 22 pl cl

BROWN, WILLIAM L. (Rochester, New York)

	1838
-Listed as agent for the <u>Colored American</u>	Jan 13 p4 c4

BRUSHELL, EMELINE

	1841
-Marries Benjamin C.S. Littlefield	Oct 30 p3 c4

BRYAN, THOMAS

	1837
-Confined to prison in Vicksburg; to be sold for jail fees	Mar 11 p3 c4

BRYANS, RICHARD (Pittsburgh, Pennsylvania)

	1837
-Elected president of the Pittsburgh Moral Reform Society	May 13 pl c4
-Elected president of an all-black meeting to discuss a permanent constitutional convention and the proposed disfranchisement of blacks	Jul 1 p2 cl

BRYCE, WILLIAM C. (Advertisement)	
	1837
-Upholsterer	May 27 p3 c4 Jun 10 p3 c4 Jun 24 p4 c3 Jul 1,8, 22 p4 c3 Aug 12 p4 c4
BUCKINGHAM, MR.	
	1837
-Lectures on Egypt	Nov 11 pl cl Nov 25 pl cl Dec 2 pl cl Dec 9 pl cl Dec 16 pl cl
-Lectures on Palestine	Dec 23 pl cl Dec 30 pl cl
	1838
	Jan 13 pl cl Jan 20 pl cl Jan 27 pl cl
-Lectures on Edom	Feb 3 pl cl Feb 10 pl cl
-Lectures on Syria	Feb 17 pl cl
-Lectures on Lebanon	Mar 3 pl cl
BUDD, MRS. HESTER (Saratoga Springs, New York) (Advertisement)	
	1840
-Rooms to let	Apr 11 p4 c3
-Taken over by proprietors W. H. Francis and P. Williams	May 16 p3 c3
	1841
-Accommodations by Mrs. Budd	Jun 5 p3 c4 Jun 19 p3 c4- Jul 24 p3 c4 Aug 21 p3 c4- Sep 4 p3 c4
BUEL, JUDGE	
	1837
-Spoke against slavery at the 1821 New York Constitutional Convention	Mar 11 p2 c2
BUFFALO, NEW YORK	
	1841
-Blacks meet to discuss Cincinnati riot	Nov 13 pl cl
-See also Colonization (General); Female Dorcas Society (Buffalo, New York); Free Blacks (New York)	

BUFFALO LIBRARY ASSOCIATION (Buffalo, New York)

	1841
-Eulogy for Thomas Harris delivered before it	Mar 27 p1 c1

BUGBEE, PROFESSOR (Bridgeport, Connecticut)

	1839
-Accidently killed	May 18 p3 c5

BURCHELL, JOHN

	1839
-Dies and is praised for his work	Mar 2 p3 c2
-Poetic tribute	Mar 9 p2 c4

BURDELL, JOHN (Advertisement)

	1837
-Dentist	May 6 p3 c4-Jun 24 p4 c3

BURLEIGH, CHARLES B.

	1837
-Speaker at the Fourth Anniversary meeting of the American Anti-Slavery Society	May 13 p3 c1
	1841
-Addresses the Temperance and Moral Reform Society (Wilmington, Delaware)	May 1 p3 c1 let.
-See also <u>Christian Witness</u> (Pittsburgh, Pennsylvania)	

BURNLEY, WILLIAM H.

	1839
-Disperses apprehensions about emigration to Trinidad	Oct 12 p3 c1 let.
	1840
-Extracts from letter favoring immigration of free blacks to Trinidad	Jul 11 p2 c3 let.
-His assertions about immigration denied	Jul 11 p2 c3

BURR, JOHN P.

	1837
-Issues call for August convention of the American Moral Reform Society	Jun 3 p3 c4

BURTON, JAMES (New Brunswick, New Jersey) (Advertisement)

	1841
-Boarding and lodging	Jul 3 p3 c4-Sep 4 p3 c4

BUSH, DAVID (Jamaica, New York)
(Advertisement)

1840
-House to let — Mar 14 p3 c3-Mar 28 p4 c4; Apr 11-25 p4 c4

BUTTLER, THOMAS

1837
-Issues a call to a meeting of the American Moral Reform Society — Aug 5 p3 c3

1838
-Dies and is eulogized — Dec 29 p3 c3

BYRON, LORD

1841
-Examined as a reform poet — Apr 17 p4 c3

BUXTON, THOMAS FOWELL (England)

1841
-Distinguishes between the aims of the American Colonization Society and the African Civilization Society — Feb 27 p1 c1 let.
-Anti-slavery work praised — Feb 27 p2 c2

C

CABILL, ELIZA

1841
-Marries Charles Smith — Oct 9 p3 c3

CAFFRES (African Tribe)

1837
-Attack white colonists — Apr 15 p1 c2

CAIRO (Illinois)

1839
English development project discussed — Feb 16 p4 c2

CALHOUN, MR.

1840
-Praised — Dec 26 p2 c4 let.

CALHOUN, REVEREND S.H.

1838
-Describes Athens and its architecture — Sep 8 p1 c4

CAMPBELL, A.R. (Boston)
(Advertisement)

1840

-Temperance eating room Aug 15 p2 c4

CANADA

1837

-Afraid of emancipation for fear that all blacks will move to Canada Nov 18 p2 c3
-Black citizens warned against supporting Canadian rebels too strongly Dec 16 p3 c2
-Insurrection in Canada noted and black citizens requested to remain loyal Dec 23 p3 c1
-View that the United States is better off if Canada stays under British control Dec 30 p3 c2

1838

-President VanBuren promises to keep Americans out of the Canadian situation Jan 13 p3 c2
-Offers a good example of equality and integration Oct 20 p3 c2 ed.
-Offers opportunities to blacks Dec 1 p1 c1
-Letter sides with British in dispute; view that if Canada became part of the United States, fugitive slaves would be tracked down Dec 1 p3 c3 let.

1840

-Many blacks go to Canada through Ohio Apr 25 p3 c2
-Ties of friendship affirmed by the American Anti-Slavery Society May 30 p2 c4

1841

-Much racism toward blacks; (e.g., separate church pews) Mar 13 p1 c1
-The problem of racism in Canada should be dealt with by British, not Americans Mar 13 p2 c2
-View that Americans should help solve problems of racism in Canada Mar 20 p1 c1
-View that Americans should not give money to help Canadians fight against prejudice Mar 20 p3 c2 ed.

-Poor conditions of refugee blacks denied — Aug 14 p2 c3

CANADA MISSION

1841

-Separate schools and churches for fugitive slaves decried — Feb 6 p2 c2
-Report on well-being of Canada refugees — Feb 27 p3 c1
-Usefulness examined — Apr 3 p2 c3
-New York Colored American denies refusing help, but feels it detracts from American philanthropies — Apr 10 p2 c2

CAPLES, C.V.

1837

-People warned to stay away from him — May 27 p3 c4

CARMEN

1837

-Blacks denied licenses as carmen or porters in New York City — Sep 16 p2 c1

CARROL, RICHARD (Advertisement)

1840

-Bathing establishment; no regard to color or sex — Jul 11, 18 p3 c4
Aug 1 p3 c4-
Oct 17 p3 c4
Nov 7 p4 c4-
Dec 26 p4 c4

1841

Jan 9, 16 p4 c4

CARTER, JOHN (Advertisement)

1837

-Family groceries — Jan 14-28 p3 c4
Feb 11 p2 c4-
Mar 18 p4 c4

CARTHAGINIAN BENEFICIAL SOCIETY (Philadelphia) (Notice)

1841

-Seeking new members — Jun 12 p3 c3-
Aug 28 p3 c4

CARY, GEORGE (Cincinnati, Ohio)

1837

-Listed as agent for the Colored American — Jun 3 p3 c4
-Resigns as agent because he is too busy; sends in $20 — Sep 2 p3 c3

CATHOLIC TELEGRAPH (Bardstown, Kentucky)

1841

-Praised for anti-slavery statements — Jun 19 p2 c4

CATHOLICS

1838

-United States upset about the corrupting influence of Catholics; yet condones slavery and the slave trade — Sep 22 p3 c3

CENTRAL AMERICA

1841

-Visits to ancient Indian ruins described — Jun 12 p4 c2

CHANDLER, HENRY A.

1840

-Supports the Colored American — Nov 21 p2 cl let.

CHANNING, WILLIAM E.

1839

-Letter to Jonathan Phillips, with remarks on slavery printed — May 11 p4 cl let.

CHAPMAN, ANN G. (Boston)

1837

-Death of a member of the Boston Female Anti-Slavery Society lamented — Apr 22 p3 c2

CHARD, WILLIAM AND COMPANY (Advertisement)

1840

-Ohio canal (Cleveland to Portsmouth) — Jun 13 p3 c3-Jul 18 p3 c4; Aug 1 p3 c4-Sep 12 p3 c4; Sep 26 p3 c4-Oct 24 p4 c4; Nov 7-28 p3 c4

CHARITY

1838

-Charity a check against the evils of extravagance — Jun 2 pl c4

CHASE, ALFORD (Fitchburg, Massachusetts)

1838

-Listed as agent for the Colored American — Aug 11 p3 c4

CHASE, SOLOMON P.

1837

- -Paper prints his agrument in the case of the colored woman, Matilda (Hamilton County, Ohio) — Jul 15 p1 c1-Aug 5 p1 c1

CHEAP APARTMENTS (Wall Street and Broadway) (Advertisement)

1839

- -Apartment rental — May 11 p4 c4

CHEROKEE INDIANS
- -See Indians (Cherokee)

CHILD,DAVID LEE

1838

- -Authors work on *Laws of American Slavery* — Mar 22 p3 c1

CHILDREN

1837

- -One successful resistance to parental authority will undo a year's obedience — Apr 1 p4 c3
- -Children must be polite — Apr 15 p4 c2
- -Children put out to trades at age fourteen — Jun 3 p3 c3
- -Children imitate parents; parents should set a good example — Jun 17 p4 c2

1840

- -Anecdote demonstrates the true meaning of obedience — Aug 29 p3 c2
- -Anecdote about a mischievous boy — Nov 7 p3 c2
- -See also Children's Department (*Colored American*); *Youth's Cabinet* (*Colored American*)

CHILDREN'S DEPARTMENT (*Colored American*)

1840

- -*Colored American* starts series of articles aimed at the moral education of children — Mar 21 p2 c4
- -Religion — Mar 21 p3 c1
- -Temperance — Mar 21 p3 c1
- -Pride — Mar 21 p3 c2
- -Religion — Mar 28 p3 c2
- -Children need parents for support and instruction — Mar 28 p3 c2

-Use of libraries	Apr 4 p3 c2
-Temperance	Apr 4 p3 c2
-Benefits of reading and religion	Apr 11 p3 c2
-Temperance	Apr 11 p3 c2
-Hard work	Apr 18 p3 c2
-Children should not worry about what siblings do	Apr 18 p3 c2
-Sabbath	Apr 25 p3 c2
-The Lord watches over children	Apr 25 p3 c3
-Parents know best what is right for children	May 2 p3 c2
-On lying	May 2 p3 c3
-Love of parents	Jun 20 p3 c2
	Aug 8 p3 c1
-Love of Bible	Aug 8 p3 c2
-Obedience to parents	Aug 22 p3 c2
-Tell troubles to God	Sep 12 p3 c2
-Story about lying	Sep 19 p3 c2
-Man should not eat meat	Sep 26 p3 c2
	Oct 3 p3 c1
-Mother saves her children	Sep 26 p3 c2
-Prayer	Oct 3 p3 c2
-Be kind	Oct 17 p3 c2
-On the sin of forgetting God in times of health	Nov 14 p3 c3
-Children's story noted	Nov 14 p3 c3
-On children's cunning falsehoods	Nov 21 p3 c2
-Story of a little blind boy	Dec 12 p3 c2
-One bad word draws another	Dec 19 p3 c2
-Children's story illustrating the second commandment	Dec 26 p4 c1
	<u>1841</u>
-Grandfather counsels respect for parents	Jan 2 p3 c2
-Sandwich Islands described	Jan 16 p3 c3
-On the child's duty to obey the parents	Feb 27 p3 c2
-Story illustrating the golden rule	Mar 27 p3 c2
-On the wickedness of deceit	Apr 3 p3 c3
-Bible a good source of amusement for children	Apr 17 p3 c2
-Story about a deceitful child	May 1 p3 c2
-Children should be industrious	May 22 p3 c3
-Virtues of patience and resignation stressed	Aug 28 p3 c2
-Story about a sinner's refuge	Oct 9 p4 c1
-Prayer for a child	Oct 9 p4 c1
-Story about neatness	Oct 30 p4 c1
-Story about thoughtfulness	Oct 30 p4 c1
-Story about stinginess	Nov 20 p4 c1

<u>CHRISTIAN ADVOCATE AND JOURNAL</u>

	<u>1839</u>
-Editor criticized for rejecting copies of the <u>Colored American</u>	Mar 9 p3 c3 ed.

CHRISTIAN LIBRARY (Advertisement)

	<u>1838</u>
-Books	Jun 9 pp3,4 c3,4- Jul 14 p2 c3 Sep 22 p4 c3- Dec 29 p4 c3
	<u>1839</u>
	Jan 12 p2 c4 Jan 19 p4 c4
	<u>1840</u>
	Apr 11, 18 p3 c4 May 2 p3 c4

CHRISTIAN MINISTRY (Black)

	<u>1837</u>
-Lack of respect shown black ministers in white congregations	Mar 11 p2 c4
-Memoirs of Reverend Leonard Haynes published	Mar 11 p4 c1
-Black ministers are in many cases incompetent	Jun 17 p2 c2 let.
-Too easy to become a black minister	Jun 24 p2 c2
-Need to raise requirements for admittance to the ministry	Jul 1 p2 c3
-Black ministers realize the problems; pass resolutions to deal with them at Bethel Methodist Convention in Philadelphia	Jul 1 p2 c4
-Letter pleads case of impoverished black ministers	Sep 9 p1 c1 let.
-Stresses sinfulness of color prejudice against black ministers in white congregations	Oct 7 p2 c4
	<u>1838</u>
-Ministry incompetent in many cases; should have higher standards	Jan 27 p2 c2
	<u>1840</u>
-Black preaching at a camp meeting is a success	Sep 26 p3 c1

1841

-Temptations of ministers noted — Jul 17 p4 cl

CHRISTIAN MINISTRY (White)

1837

-Accused of apathy and prejudice toward slaves — Nov 4 p4 c3
-Methodist ministers criticized for stand on slavery — Dec 16 p2 cl
-Ministers supporting Colonization Society accused of abetting sin — Dec 16 p3 c2

1838

-Objects of Christian ministry closely connected with anti-slavery — Mar 22 p2 c3 ed.
-Where were the clergy during the August 1st celebration? — Aug 25 p3 cl
-Ministers should legislate slavery out of the church — Sep 1 p3 c3 ed.

1839

-How southern ministers absorb planter values and close their eyes to slavery — Jul 20 pl c5
-Those who accept slavery commit a sin — Sep 7 p2 c3

1841

-Temptation of ministers noted — Jul 17 p4 cl

<u>CHRISTIAN REFLECTOR</u>

1838

-Baptist church anti-slavery paper begins publication — Aug 4 p3 cl let.

<u>CHRISTIAN WITNESS</u> (Pittsburgh, Pennsylvania)

1838

-Inaugural editorial of Charles Burleigh printed; call for an end to slavery — Aug 25 p2 cl

CHURCHES (Baptist)
-See <u>Christian Reflector</u>

CHURCHES (Black)

1837

-Seen necessary until color prejudice is generally eliminated — Jul 1 p3 c4
-Should support divinity students — Sep 2 p2 c3 let.
-New multidenominational church consecrated — Oct 28 p3 c3 let.

	1838
-Separate churches opposed	Aug 4 p2 cl ed.
	1840
-New York churches described	May 28 p2 c2
-See also Abyssiniam Baptist Church; Abyssinian Religious Society (Portland, Maine); African Baptist Church; African Methodist Episcopal Church; Asbury Colored Methodist Church; First Colored Presbyterian Church; Saint Matthew's Episcopal Church; Saint Phillips Church; Zion Baptist Church; Zion's Methodist Connexion	

CHURCHES (Christian)

	1837
-Accuses Christian churches of being strongholds of color prejudice	Mar 11 p2 c4
-Churches are prejudiced	Mar 18 p2 c2
-Racism exists most prominently in churches; ministers responsible	Mar 25 p2 c3
-Should eliminate racism	Mar 25 p3 cl
-Sends questionnaire to churches in New York City	Mar 25 p3 c2
-Lists churches in each ward in New York City	Mar 25 p3 c3
-Making heathens of thousands	Apr 8 p2 c3
-Black preachers not allowed to preach in white churches	Apr 18 p2 c3
-Questions whether blacks can belong to Christian churches	Apr 15 p3 c2 let.
-Church schools will not admit black children	Apr 22 p2 c2
-Calls for purification of the church	Apr 29 p3 c3 let.
-Blacks have many claims against churches	May 6 p2 c3
-Churches too fancy and expensive; also racist	May 27 p2 c2
-Churches indifferent to slavery	Jun 3 p2 cl
-Book, <u>Negro</u> <u>Pew</u>, praised by paper for attack on racism in the churches	Jun 3 p2 c3
-Churches desert their mission by supporting slavery	Jun 17 pl cl
-Prejudice is the crying sin of the church	Jun 24 p3 c2 let.
-How can Christian ministers be neutral on slavery?	Aug 19 pl c2

-Blacks who go to a white church should refuse to sit in black pews	Aug 19 p2 cl
-Ministers will do nothing to aid abolition; churches racist	Sep 23 p2 c2
-New church consecrated for multi-denominational use	Oct 28 p3 c3 let.
-No revival of religion possible until the church rids itself of racism	Nov 18 p3 c2
-Churches, especially ministers, should work against slavery	Dec 2 p2 cl
-The church is the main pillar of racism	Dec 30 p4 c2
	1838
-Slavery, the sin of the nation, is the fault of the churches	Feb 3 p2 c2
-American churches have failed in their anti-slavery duty	May 3 p2 cl ed.
-Segregated sections for blacks criticized	Jun 30 p2 cl
-The business of the church should be to oppose slavery	Jul 28 pl c2
-Moral impurity of the church is a major stumbling block	Sep 1 p3 c3 ed.
-Justification of criticism of churches	Sep 8 p2 cl ed.
-Caste distinctions abolished by the English Church in India	Oct 6 pl c2
-Turkish musselman has more consistant faith than a Christian	Oct 6 p3 c2
	1839
-Colored American explains why it dwells so much on the impurities of the church	Jun 8 p3 c2 ed.
-The church forgets that the colored man is also made in the image of God	Sep 14 p3 cl
-On the difficulties of blacks gaining admission to white seminaries	Dec 7 p2 c3 let.
	1840
-Church disavowed for toleration of slavery by the American Anti-Slavery Society	May 30 p2 c4
-Methodist convention fails to take on anti-slavery position	Jun 20 p2 c2
-Churches of Portland, Maine described	Nov 28 p2 cl let.

	1841
-Churches do nothing to aid black people	Jan 30 p4 c1 let.
-First Congregational Church (Fall River, Massachusetts) passes anti-slavery resolutions	Feb 13 p3 c1 let.
-On the history of Saint Peter's Basilica in Rome	Apr 10 p4 c2
-Those who have split from the church are urged to rejoin the main body	Jul 10 p1 c3 let.

CHURCHES (Congregational)

	1838
-Meeting of ministers passes anti-slavery resolutions; attempts to purify church of sin of slavery	Oct 6 p2 c1
	1839
-Should be consistant regarding the rights of man	Mar 9 p3 c2 ed.

CHURCHES (Episcopal)

	1839
-Saint Matthew's Free Church opens	May 18 p3 c2

CHURCHES (Methodist)

	1838
-Orders removal of blacks from its college	Aug 4 p2 c1 let.
	1841
-Minutes of eleventh annual church conference	Jun 19 p3 c2
-Methodists urged to support abolition convention	Aug 21 p1 c3

CHURCHES (Presbyterian)

	1837
-Seen to be pro-slavery	Jun 17 p2 c1
-Reverend Cornish appeals to New York Presbyterians to aid in educating black children	Oct 7 p3 c1 ed.
	1838
-Plans to divide into white and black branches applauded	Jun 2 p3 c2 ed.
-Testimonies on slavery by ten presbyteries	Sep 1 p3 c3
-Concert of prayer	Oct 27 p3 c4

1839

-Lack of interest of white church members in blacks deplored — Mar 16 p3 c2
-Southern church pro-slavery — Jun 1 p2 c3 ed.
-Divisions in the church result from its pro-slavery stand — Jun 1 p3 c1 ed.

CILLEY, CONGRESSMAN (Maine)

1838

-Congressional investigation of his murder called for — Mar 3 p3 c2

CILLS, EDWARD AND COMPANY (Advertisement)

1837

-Tin, sheet, iron, and copper workers — Sep 16, 23 p4 c3

CINCINNATI (Ohio)

1839

-City and its inhabitants praised — Oct 12 p2 c5 let.
-See also Colonization (Ohio); Free Blacks (Ohio)

CINQUEZ, JOSEPH (Cinque)

1839

-Led rebellion aboard the _Amistad_ — Sep 7 p3 c2
-Lawyer retained for him — Sep 14 p3 c4

1841

-Engraved portrait offered for sale — Feb 27 p2 c4
-His reaction to news of a successful trial — Mar 27 p2 c1 let.
-Allowed to decide where _Amistad_ prisoners will settle — Mar 27 p2 c3
-Praised by the _Colored American_ — Mar 27 p2 c4
-See also _Amistad_

CITY CONVENTIONS (Notice)

1841

-Series of public meetings and county conventions to build up support for extension of the franchise — Sep 18, 25 p3 c4; Oct 2-16 p3 c3

CIVIL RIGHTS

1839

-On the difference between civil and natural liberty — Sep 7 p1 c5

CLAPP, OTIS (Palmyra, New York)	
	<u>1837</u>
-Listed as agent for the <u>Colored American</u>	Jun 10 p3 c3
CLARK, EDWARD V. (Advertisement)	
	<u>1837</u>
-Boot and shoemaker	Apr 15 p3 c4- Jul 22 p4 c4 Aug 5, 19 p4 c3
-Appointed vice-president of the Colored Young Men of New York City	Sep 2 pl cl
-Boot and shoemaker	Sep 2 p4 c4- Oct 14 p4 c3 Oct 28 p4 c4 Nov 4 p4 c4 Nov 18 p4 c4- Dec 9 p4 c3
-Member of Philomathean Society lecture committee	Dec 16 p3 c4
-Boot and shoemaker	Dec 30 p4 c4
	<u>1838</u>
	Jan 13 p4 c3- Feb 17 p4 c3 Apr 12, 19 p4 c3
CLARKE, ROBERT	
	<u>1837</u>
-Spoke against restriction of black franchise at 1821 New York Constitutional Convention	Mar 4 pl c2
-Goes to Ohio as agent of <u>Colored American</u>; heads meeting	Jul 22 p2 cl
	<u>1838</u>
-Testimonial against restrictions on black voting rights	Mar 22 p2 cl
-Denies refusal of free blacks to serve in the military	Mar 22 p2 c3
CLARKSON ASSOCIATION FOR THE FREE INSTRUCTION OF COLORED WOMEN (Notice)	
	<u>1839</u>
-Opens evening school	Nov 23 p3 c4
CLAY, HENRY	
	<u>1837</u>
-Gave speech in favor of colonization; criticized by James Forten	May 13 p2 c3

	1838
-Presents petitions for National Bank before Congress	Jun 16 p3 c4
-Hopes of colonizationists fixed on electing Clay to the Presidency	Sep 22 p2 c3
	1839
-Speech on abolitionists and slavery criticized	Feb 16 p2 c1 ed.
-Concerning a prophecy that the races would one day be merged	May 18 p2 c3
-Clay's ownership of slaves criticized	Jun 1 p1 c1 let.
-Endorsed by Moroccan Emperor for American Presidency	Jul 13 p1 c3 let.
-His Moroccan endorsement ridiculed	Jul 13 p1 c4 ed.
-Accused of a political sell-out to slaveholders	Jul 13 p1 c5
-Plans campaign trip in the North	Jul 20 p3 c2
-Criticized for pro-slavery stance	Oct 19 p2 c2 let. Nov 2 p1 c3
-Praised for his oratory in Congress	Dec 26 p2 c4 let.
	1841
-Senate speech praised	Feb 6 p3 c1 let.
-Speaks before Supreme Court on Mississippi slave case	Feb 27 p3 c1

CLEVELAND (Ohio) OBSERVER
-See Blacks (Self-Improvement)

CLOTHING
-See Dress

CLUBS

	1838
-No true family man will patronize them	Nov 17 p4 c1 ed.

COAL (Advertisement)

	1838
-For sale (161 Duane Street)	Jun 2 p3 c4- Sep 15 p4 c3 Nov 3 p3 c4- Nov 17 p3 c4 Dec 1 p4 c3- Dec 29 p4 c3

	<u>1839</u>
	Jan 12 p2 c4- Jan 26 p4 c4
	Feb 9 p4 c4- Mar 2 p3 c4
	Mar 16 p4 c4
	Jul 20 p3 c4
	Aug 24, 31 p4 c3
	Sep 14 p4 c3
	Sep 28 p4 c3- Oct 5 p4 c3
COLDER, MR. (Pittsburgh, Pennsylvania)	
	<u>1837</u>
-Praised for closing his shop on the Sabbath	Apr 1 p2 c2
COLE, THOMAS (Boston, Massachusetts)	
	<u>1840</u>
-Urges blacks to support the <u>Colored American</u>	Mar 7 p2 c1 let.
-Says political parties are hostile to the interests of slaves and free blacks	Dec 12 p1 c4 let.
-Criticizes free blacks for failure to vote whenever possible	Dec 26 p1 c2 let.
COLEMAN, EDWARD	
	<u>1838</u>
-Murders his wife	Aug 4 p3 c4
COLES, JAMES	
	<u>1841</u>
-Marries Mary Ann Huntington	Oct 30 p3 c4
COLLEGES	
	<u>1837</u>
-Many will not admit blacks; Dartmouth College an exception	Apr 22 p2 c2
	<u>1838</u>
-Methodist college orders removal of black student	Aug 4 p2 c1 let.
-Girard College is described	Nov 17 p3 c3
COLLINS, J. (Advertisement)	
	<u>1841</u>
-Rooms	Jul 3 p3 c4
COLMAN, GABRIEL (Saint Catherine's, Canada)	
	<u>1838</u>
-Listed as agent for the <u>Colored American</u>	Jan 13 p4 c4

COLONIZATION (General)

	1837
-Recommends that blacks move to more hospitable countries	Jul 22 p2 c2
-Black people in Philadelphia came out against colonization in 1817	Jul 22 p2 c3
	1838
-Colonization scheme founded in prejudice	Mar 15 p3 c2 ed.
-Colonization seen the twin sister of slavery	Mar 29 p1 c1 ed.
-Free blacks should remain in America with enslaved brethren	Apr 12 p3 c1 ed.
-Anti-colonization convention called for	Apr 12 p3 c3 let.
-Colonization attacked as no answer for blacks (from <u>Herald of Freedom</u>)	Jul 7 p2 c1
-Inconsistencies and misconceptions pointed out	Jul 21 p2 c3 ed.
-Lack of colonization movement in West Indies pointed out	Jul 28 p1 c2
	1838
-Blacks would rather die than be transported	Jul 28 p3 c1 ed.
-Difficulties of emigrating to West Indies outlined	Aug 11 p3 c1
-Mass talk of migration to a foreign country is nonsense	Aug 11 p3 c1 ed.
-Praised as preventing amalgamation (Mobile <u>Advertiser</u>)	Aug 11 p3 c3
-Colonization would have to be achieved by law, but blacks would never agree to it	Aug 18 p2 c3
-Colonizers in Africa struck with health problems	Sep 1 p4 c3 let.
-Hopes of colonizationists fixed on electing Henry Clay to the Presidency	Sep 22 p2 c3 let.
-The morality and immorality of accepting expatriation	Oct 6 p2 c3 let.
-A moral right to hazard life to maintain a principle	Oct 6 p2 c3 ed.
-Ministers who support colonization are trafficking in human flesh	Oct 13 p3 c1
-Canada offers better opportunities than Africa	Oct 20 p3 c2 ed.

-Expatriation to Africa viewed as a valid means of elevation	Oct 27 p2 cl let.
-Pro-colonization sympathizer criticized	Oct 27 p2 cl ed.
-A hypocritical scheme	Oct 27 p3 cl let.
-Colonization not a terrible thing, if people can find happiness through it; a misguided philanthropy	Nov 17 p2 c3 let.
-Missionary efforts acceptable, but not colonization	Dec 15 p2 c2 ed.
-Public anti-colonization meeting announced	Dec 15 p3 c4
-Blacks oppose colonization because it is not the answer	Dec 22 pl c2 let.
-Colonizationists feel blacks are physically inferior	Dec 22 p2 cl
	1839
-Colonization criticized by Charles B. Ray	Jan 12 p2 c3 let.
-Large anti-colonization meeting held; resolutions printed	Jan 12 p3 cl
-Report of New York anti-colonization meeting	Jan 19 pl cl
-Reverend Theodore Wright denounces colonization as heresy at anti-colonization meeting	Jan 19 pl c3
-Denounced as positive evil by Thomas Van Renssalaer at New York anti-colonization meeting	Jan 19 pl c4
-Denounced by John Steward at New York anti-colonization meeting	Jan 19 p2 cl
-Denounced by Peter Vogelsang at New York anti-colonization meeting	Jan 19 p2 cl
-Colonization undergoing a rebirth as certain people try to palm it off on America	Feb 23 p2 c2
-Free blacks in Cleveland pass many resolutions against colonization	Mar 2 pl c2
-Colonizationists claim to love blacks, but love them in Africa, not the United States	May 11 p2 c3
-Slaves liberated if they agree to go to Liberia	Aug 24 p2 c5
-One hundred and one United States emigrants reach Puerto de Plato, Haiti	Sep 28 p3 c3

-Trinidad encourages black emigration from the United States	Oct 5 p1 c1
-*Colored American* criticizes excitement over Trinidad	Oct 5 p3 c3 ed.
-Colonization would never work	Nov 16 p1 c4 let.
-Difference seen between voluntary emigration and colonization	Nov 16 p2 c4
	1840
-Bad conditions in Liberia described	Mar 28 p1 c4
-Blacks are American by character	May 9 p2 c2
-Generally condemned by New York City colored citizens meeting	Jun 26 p3 c1
-Anti-colonization meeting condemns Maryland Colonization Convention	Jul 3 p2 c4
-Condemned at meeting of Buffalo blacks	Jul 31 p1 c3
-Distinguished from missionary work	Aug 21 p2 c1 let.
	1841
-Seen unsuccessful in Liberia	Oct 2 p1 c3 let.
-Called a cold-blooded scheme of expatriation	Dec 4 p1 c2 let.
-See also American Colonization Society; Clay, Henry; Hezlett, George; Hodgkin, Thomas; Liberia; Wilkinson, Samuel	

COLONIZATION (Maryland)

	1841
-Leading colonizationists take a bold stand; form a special convention	Jun 19 p2 c3
-Colored citizens of Maryland warned against colonization efforts	Jun 26 p3 c1
-See also Free Blacks (New York)	

COLONIZATION (New Jersey)

	1838
-State Colonization Society formed as an auxiliary to the Slaveholders Negro Shipping Company	Jul 21 p2 c1
-Strongly criticized	Jul 21 p2 c1 ed.
-View that Colonization Society leads to a worsening condition for blacks	Sep 1 p3 c1
-Colonizationist efforts in vain	Oct 13 p2 c1

COLONIZATION (Ohio)

1841

-Free blacks of Cincinnati declare their opposition to emigration to Africa — Nov 20 p2 c2

COLONIZATION (Pennsylvania)
-See Colonization Herald

COLONIZATION HERALD

1838

-Paper published by the Pennsylvania Colonization Society full of hypocrisy — Jan 27 p3 c1
-See also American Colonization Society

COLOR PREJUDICE
-See Racism

COLORED AMERICAN
-See New York Colored American

COLORED CITIZENS OF ALBANY (New York)

1840

-Proceedings of meeting; resolutions favoring political action — May 23 p3 c1 let.

COLORED CITIZENS OF BOSTON

1840

-Express faith in William Lloyd Garrison and the Massachusetts Anti-Slavery Society — Apr 11 p2 c1
-Resolutions supporting decisions of the American Anti-Slavery Society — Jun 6 p2 c3 let.

COLORED CITIZENS OF FLUSHING (New York)

1840

-First great mass meeting — Dec 19 p3 c3

COLORED CITIZENS OF NEW BEDFORD (Massachusetts)

1837

-Hold meeting and set up committee to study slavery in Washington, D.C. — Nov 18 p3 c3

COLORED CITIZENS OF NEW YORK
-See Elston, Daniel; Fields, James; Peterson, John; Sidney, Thomas S.; Smith, Dr. James McCune; Wake, Ransom; Zuille, John J.

COLORED CITIZENS OF NEWARK (New Jersey)
-See Ward, Samuel Ringgold

COLORED MAN'S JOURNAL

1838

-Characterized as deceitful due to pro-colonization stance — Mar 3 p3 c1
-See also Vashon, John B.

COLORED METHODIST CHURCH (Newark, New Jersey) (Notice)

1841

-Meeting of colored citizens — Apr 17 p3 c3

COLORED ORPHAN ASYLUM (Notice)

1840

-Teacher wanted — Sep 19 p3 c4
Sep 26 p3 c3
Nov 7 p3 c4-
Nov 28 p4 c4

COLORED PEOPLE OF TROY (New York)

1837

-Letter describes meetings to promote improvement of free blacks' situation — Apr 1 p1 c4 let.

1840

-Resolutions in support of state convention — Jun 6 p3 c3 let.

COLORED PEOPLE'S STATE TEMPERANCE SOCIETY (Connecticut) (Notice)

1837

-Gives notice of meeting — Sep 9 p3 c4-
Sep 23 p4 c3

COLORED YOUNG MEN OF NEW YORK CITY

1837

-Public meeting scheduled — Aug 19 p3 c3
-Holds first meeting and appoints officers; for petition drive favoring enfranchisement of blacks — Sep 2 p1 c1
-Group addressed by Dr. Blake — Sep 16 p1 c1

	1838
-Public meeting	Feb 10 p3 c4
-See also Clark, Edward V.; Downing, George; Garnet, Henry Highland; Seaman, Timothy; Zuille, John J.	

COLORED YOUNG MEN OF PHILADELPHIA

	1838
-Resolve to work for improved public school attendance	Oct 13 p4 c1

COMMERCIAL ADVERTISER
-See Smith, Dr. James McCune

COMMITTEE OF FREE DISCUSSION (Notice)

	1838
-To meet	Feb 3 p3 c4

CONCERT OF PRAYER FOR THE ABOLITION OF SLAVERY (Philadelphia, Pennsylvania)

	1837
-Reverend Samuel Cornish speaks at meeting; group praises the Colored American	Dec 2 p3 c2

CONGRESS HOTEL (Saratoga Springs, New York) (Advertisement)

	1839
-Rooms	Jun 1 p3 c4- Jun 29 p4 c4 Jul 13 p4 c4- Jul 27 p4 c4 Aug 17 p4 c4- Aug 31 p4 c4 Sep 14 p4 c4

CONOVER, S. (New York, New York)

	1837
-Listed as agent for the Colored American	Mar 11 p4 c4

CONVENTION OF COLORED INHABITANTS OF NEW YORK (Albany) (Notice)

	1840
-Meetings to be held	Jun 27 p3 c2,3- Jul 25 p3 c3,4
-Public meetings announced	Jul 25 p3 c4 Aug 8 p2 c4
-Notices about convention from other newspapers; delegates appointed	Aug 8 p3 c4- Aug 15 p2 c3,4 p3 c2-4

CONVENTION OF COLORED (Jamaica, Long Island, New York) (Notice)

1840

-Convention soliciting colored population — Apr 18,25 p3 c3
-Notice to colored freemen of Long Island — Nov 20 p3 c4

CONVENTION MOVEMENT (BLACK)

1837

-Development traced — Oct 7 p3 c3 let.
-National convention for blacks called for — Oct 30 p2 c4 let.

1838

-Anti-colonization convention suggested — Mar 15 p3 c3
-Utility of conventions for mobilizing efforts discussed — Mar 22 p3 c1 let.
-Conventions viewed as means of opposing colonization and elevating blacks — Apr 12 p3 c3
-Praised as best method for blacks to attain rights — Jun 16 p3 c3 let.
-Conventions viewed as a means of strengthening black solidarity — Jul 21 p2 c3 let.
-Valuable in giving blacks political importance — Aug 4 p2 c4 let.

1840

-Colored American endorses black conventions — May 2 p3 c1 ed.
-General convention urged for purposes of establishing black high school or college — May 23 p2 c4 let.
-Value and influence of general conventions affirmed — May 30 p3 c4 let.
-General conventions viewed as useless — Jun 6 p2 c3 let.
-National convention called for — Jun 13 p1 c4
-Need for nation-wide convention noted — Jun 13 p2 c1 let.
-Nation-wide convention seen as unifying force — Jun 13 p2 c2 let.
-State conventions called useful and urged before national ones — Jun 13 p2 c3
-Call for New York State Convention signed by black leaders — Jun 13 p3 c2
-Conventions deemed necessary for blacks — Jun 20 p2 c1 let.
-Opposition to separate black conventions voiced and answered — Jun 27 p2 c3

-Objections to separate black conventions refuted; general convention should be postponed until financially feasible	Jul 4 p1 c2 let.
-Colored citizens of Worcester, Massachusetts recommend a general convention	Jul 4 p1 c3 let.
-National convention should be postponed until blacks achieve more unity	Jul 18 p1 c4 let.
-Blacks of Pittsburgh, Pennsylvania approve plans for a general convention	Jul 18 p2 c1
-Concurrent state and national conventions deemed impractical	Jul 18 p2 c2 let.
-<u>Colored American</u> disapproves of an immediate national convention	Jul 25 p2 c3 ed.
-National convention considered inexpedient	Jul 25 p2 c4
-National convention strongly urged	Jul 25 p3 c1 let.
-Plans for national convention deemed too hasty	Aug 1 p3 c3
-State conventions should consider question of a national convention	Aug 8 p2 c1 let.
-Hartford, Connecticut blacks defer call for a national convention until 1841	Aug 8 p3 c1
-National convention in 1840 deemed a mistake	Aug 15 p2 c1
-Slaveholders considered beneath the notice of national conventions	Aug 29 p2 c1 let.
-National conventions disapproved	Aug 29 p2 c4
-New Haven, Connecticut citizens oppose national conventions	Sep 5 p2 c3 let.
-State conventions deemed valuable if conditions are right	Sep 12 p2 c3
-Conventions should include whites	Sep 26 p2 c1 let.
-National anti-slavery convention proposed	Nov 21 p2 c4
	<u>1841</u>
-National convention of black people urged	Feb 27 p1 c4 let.
-<u>Colored American</u> against a national convention	Mar 13 p2 c3 ed.
-Call for national convention issued	Mar 20 p1 c2
-Separate black national convention deemed necessary	Apr 3 p3 c2

-Connecticut blacks favor state conventions over national convention	Apr 17 pl c4
-Ohio blacks call for state convention	Apr 24 p2 c3
-Philadelphia blacks consider state convention	May 8 pl cl
-<u>Colored American</u> doubts usefulness of a national convention	May 8 p2 c3 ed.
-National convention not needed	May 22 p3 cl
-National convention advocated	Jun 5 p2 cl
-Plans for an exclusively black convention criticized	Jun 12 pl cl let.
-Another New York convention deemed necessary to secure rights	Jun 12 p2 c3
-Controversy over national conventions discussed	Jun 19 p2 c2 let.
-Another New York convention urged	Jun 19 p3 cl
-Call for another New York state convention issued	Jun 19 p3 c3
-Need for another New York state convention seen	Jun 26 p2 c4 let.
-Call for another New York state convention issued	Jun 26 p3 c3
-Missionary convention planned	Jul 3 pl c2 let.
-Blacks of Portland, Maine call for a state convention	Jul 3 pl c4
-Call for Pennsylvania state convention issued	Jul 3 p3 cl
-Call for New York state convention issued	Jul 3 p3 c3
-Call repeated for New York convention	Jul 10 p3 c2
-Objections to national convention stated	Jul 17 pl cl let.
-Call for missionary convention issued	Jul 17 pl c4 let.
-Various conventions mentioned and evaluated	Jul 17 p2 c3
-Call for Pennsylvania state franchise convention issued	Jul 24 p4 cl
-Missionary convention urged	Jul 24 p4 cl let.
-Reasons for missionary convention listed	Jul 31 p4 cl let.
-Reasons for missionary convention listed; date set	Aug 14 pl c4 let.
-Missionary, Troy, and Pennsylvania conventions discussed	Aug 14 p2 cl
-Call for convention in Maine issued; topics discussed	Sep 4 pl c4
-Philadelphia blacks call for a national convention	Oct 16 pl c3

-Criticized by <u>Colored American</u>	Oct 16 p2 c2 ed.
-Need to fix upon a plan of action	Nov 13 p2 c2 let.
-Long Island blacks call for convention on education and temperance	Nov 20 p3 c4
-Need for united action cited	Dec 4 p1 c4 let.
-See also Albany Convention; Convention of Disfranchised Commissioners; Free Blacks (Connecticut); Free Blacks (New York); London Convention; Maine Anti-Slavery Convention; Methodist Abolition Convention; Missionary Convention; Moral Reform Convention; National Convention; New England Convention; New Haven Reform Convention; New York City Abolition Convention; New York Convention; Ohio Convention; Pennsylvania Convention; Rensselaer County Convention; Rhode Island Suffrage Convention; Troy (New York) Convention	

CONVENTION OF THE COLORED INHABITANTS OF BUTLER COUNTY, OHIO

	<u>1840</u>
-Proceedings of organization meeting and list of delegates and officers	Jul 11 p2 c2 let.

CONVENTION OF DISFRANCHISED COMMISSIONERS

	<u>1841</u>
-Accused of being aristocratic movement	Sep 18 p2 c3
-50% vote disapproval of <u>Colored American</u>	Sep 18 p2 c4

CONYERS, JOHN (Notice)

	<u>1841</u>
-Notice that Hannah Conyers, age 12, has left home; all persons forbidden to harbor her	Jan 9 p3 c3 Jan 16 p3 c4

COOLEY, DOCTOR

	<u>1837</u>
-Brings out memoirs of Reverend Lemuel Haynes	Mar 11 p4 c1

CORNISH, JAMES

1837

-Sends invitation to meeting of Philadelphia Association for Mental and Moral Improvement of People of Color	May 20 p2 c3

CORNISH, REVEREND SAMUEL

1837

-Eulogizes Mrs. Henrietta B. Ray in sermon	Mar 4 p3 c2
-Delivers petitions of New York free Negroes to New York State Legislature	Mar 11 p3 c2
-Details aims of New York Colored American and calls for support	Mar 11 p3 c4 ed.
-Listed as member of committee of arrangements for 4th anniversary American Anti-Slavery Society meetings	Apr 8 p3 c2
-Praised in letter	Jun 24 p3 c4 let.
-Refused tea at Pattinson's Eating House	Aug 12 p2 c4
-Appeals to colored and white readers for monetary contributions to the Colored American	Oct 7 p3 c1 ed.
-Appeals to New York Presbyterians to aid in educating black children	Oct 7 p3 c1 ed.
-Writes from Philadelphia describing his trip there and conditions in church he attended	Nov 25 p3 c1

1838

-Second quarter of evening school for colored people	Jan 13 p2 c4 adv.
-Explains his move from New York City to the country	Apr 19 p3 c1 ed.
-Calls for more black farmers	Apr 19 p3 c1 ed.
-Describes benefits of life in the country	Jun 2 p2 c2 ed.
-Subscribers to Colored American inquire of his health and request more editorials	Dec 8 p3 c1 let.
-Defends himself against charge of negligence in editorship	Dec 8 p3 c1 ed.
-Health of family and domestic responsibilities require absence from editorial chair temporarily	Dec 8 p3 c3 ed.

-Offers services to President VanBuren	Dec 15 p3 c2 let.
	1839
-Denounces ministers who support colonization scheme at New York Anti-Slavery meeting	Jan 19 pl c2
-Stresses need to save New Jersey from corrupting influence of the American Colonization Society	Jan 19 p2 c2 ed.
-Confirms validity of anti-colonization letter	Jan 19 p2 c3 ed.
-Resigns as editor of the Colored American	Jun 22 p2 cl ed.
-Accused by David Ruggles of causing his persecution	Jul 27 p2 c2 ed.
-Says political abolition will corrupt the movement	Oct 5 p3 cl
-Called a leader of the old school	Nov 9 p2 c2
-States his stand against political action	Nov 9 p3 cl let.
	1840
-Publishes ant-colonization pamphlet	May 9 p3 c2
	1841
-Plans to lecture before Phoenixonian Society noted	Feb 27 p3 c4
-See also American Moral Reform Society; Concert of Prayer for the Abolition of Slavery (Philadelphia)	
COSBY, EDMUND (Advertisement)	
	1840
-Administrates the sale of books and other property	Nov 7, 14 p3 c4
COLVER, NATHANIEL	
	1837
-Speaker at annual meeting of Anti-Slavery Society	Aug 5 p3 cl
COTTEN, LOUISA	
	1840
-Marries Jason Cuffee	Sep 19 p3 c4
COWES, JAMES C. (Advertisement)	
	1837
-Elected vice-president of the Mutual Relief Society of New York	Sep 9 p2 c4

	1839
-Upper part of house to let	Mar 16 p3 c4
-Boarding House	Sep 14 p3 c4
	Sep 28 p4 c3
	Nov 2 p3 c4
	Nov 9 p4 c3
	Nov 23 p4 c3
	1840
	Mar 14 p3 c4
	Apr 11 p3 c4-
	May 2 p3 c4
	May 16 p3 c4-
	May 23 p3 c4
	Jul 4 p4 c4
	Jul 25 p4 c4-
	Aug 15 p3 c4
	Nov 7 p3 c4-
	Dec 26 p3 c4
	1841
	Jan 9,16 p3 c4
	Feb 13-27 p3 c4
	Mar 27 p3 c4
	Apr 10 p3 c4-
	Sep 18 p3 c4
	Oct 2-16 p3 c4
	Nov 13, 20 p3 c4
	Dec 4 p3 c4
	Dec 25 p3 c4
COX, REVEREND DOCTOR	
	1837
-Lectures at Auburn meeting	Mar 25 p4 c2
CRANBERRY MORAL REFORM SOCIETY	
	1837
-Formed to promote moral elevation of blacks	Aug 12 p4 c1
	1839
-Constitution printed; officers listed	Jan 12 p1 c1
-See also Ditmus, Edward; Ditmus, Lewis F.; Higgins, Caesar; Styke, Francis; Trindall, George; Valentine, Richard	
CREDIT BUYING	
	1837
-People should not buy on credit	Aug 26 p3 c1

CROOM, H.

	1837
-Letter describes tragic death of Croom and family in steamship accident	Nov 4 p1 c4 let.

CROSS, MARTIN (Catskill, New York)

	1837
-Listed as agent for the <u>Colored</u> <u>American</u>	Mar 4 p4 c4
-Sends in $3.00 to the paper	Apr 15 p3 c4
-Composes poem calling for emancipation	Oct 7 p2 c4

CRUMMELL, ALEXANDER

	1839
-Relates difficulties of blacks gaining admission to theological seminaries	Dec 7 p2 c3 let.
-See also Racism (Churches)	

CRUMMELL, CATHARINE (and Edward Powell) (Notice)

	1840
-Information on the above requested by a relative	Oct 17 p3 c3- Nov 7 p3 c4

CUFFEE, JASON

	1840
-Marries Louisa Cotten	Sep 19 p3 c4

CUFFEE, WILLIAM

	1837
-Listed as Mate of New Bedford (Massachusetts) brig owned by free blacks	Mar 11 p4 c2

<u>CULTIVATOR</u>, <u>THE</u> (Willis Gaylord and Luther Tucker, editors) (Advertisement)

	1841
-Agricultural journal described and advertised	Jan 2 p3 c3

CUBA

	1837
-Blacks warned to stay away	Oct 21 p3 c3 let.

CUTLER, J.B.

	1837
-Denounced for attacking the <u>Colored</u> <u>American</u>	Oct 14 p3 c2

CUSHING, MR.

	1840
-Describes journey to Albany by steamer	Jun 6 p2 c2 let.

D

DARTMOUTH COLLEGE

	1837
-Will admit blacks	Apr 22 p2 c2
-Has abolition society of 88 members	Apr 22 p3 cl

DAUGHTERS OF ABYSSINIA

	1837
-Gives notice of fifth anniversary meeting	Sep 9 p3 c4

DAVIS, JOHN

	1841
-Elected Governor of Massachusetts	Nov 13 p3 c2

DAVIS, JOHN (New York)

	1837
-Picked up by Negro-catchers; $300 raised in churches to free him	May 27 p3 c4

DAVISON, GEORGE

	1837
-Barbarously murdered by Governor of Havana	Oct 28 p3 cl
	1838
-Released from prison; never murdered as feared	Jun 16 p2 c4 let.

DAVISON, HENRY W.

	1838
-Informs _Colored American_ of his brother's release from prison (George Davison)	Jun 16 p2 c4 let.
-Accuses American Colonization Society of hypocrisy	Oct 27 p3 cl let.

DEATH

	1839
-Preparation for it is to set one's house in order	Feb 2 p3 c4

DEATH NOTICES

	1837
-Ann G. Chapman	Apr 22 p3 c3
-Peter Smith, Samuel Saulters, Harriet Carroll, Dennis Hedden	Apr 29 p3 c4
-John Moore, Francis Peckhan	May 6 p3 c4
-Harriet Coles, Susan Fenwick	May 13 p3 c4
-William Louder	Jun 10 p3 c3

-Margaretta VanStay	Jun 17 p3 c4
-Amberdore Elsworth, Martha A. Strong	Jul 8 p3 c4
-Harriet Lee	Jul 15 p3 c4
-William Levington, James Miller	Aug 5 p3 c4
-Elizabeth Collins, Arabella B. Esteve, John M. VanStay	Aug 26 p3 c4
-David Fields	Sep 2 p3 c4
-William Willard	Sep 16 p3 c4
-John Denby, George Plato, Martha E.M. Smith	Sep 23 p3 c4
-Mary Seaman	Sep 30 p3 c4
-Henry Nichols	Oct 28 p3 c4
-James C. Anderson, Nancy Spencer	Nov 18 p3 c4
-Theodore Montonio, John Valentine	Dec 2 p4 c4
-Elizabeth Mitchell Reason	Dec 16 p3 c4
-Elizabeth Jerred	Dec 30 p3 c4
	<u>1838</u>
-Susan Ann King	Jan 27 p3 c4
-Mrs. Susan E. McClain	Feb 3 p3 c4
-William Brown, John Lee	Feb 10 p3 c4
-Cornelius Brooks	Mar 3 p3 c4
-Francis Cook, Anna Keating	Mar 15 p3 c4
-Catharine S. West	Mar 22 p3 c4
-Isaiah H. Ward	Apr 19 p3 c4
-Hannah Greene, John Hogarth, Enos Payne	Jun 2 p3 c4
-Richard Levingston	Jun 23 p3 c4
-Ishmael Bartho	Jun 30 p3 c4
-John E. Battis	Jul 21 p3 c4
-Dennis Rand	Aug 4 p3 c4
-Caroline Richards Morel	Aug 11 p3 c4
-George C. Lamas, Lewis Henry Tappan	Aug 18 p3 c4
-Isaac Hedden	Sep 1 p3 c4
-Elizabeth Ann Day, Richard Purnell	Sep 8 p3 c4
-James B. Cills, Edward Stewart, Margaret VanSurley	Sep 22 p3 c4
-Richard Seaman	Sep 29 p3 c4
-Lettitia Garribrance, Henry Sipkins	Oct 6 p3 c4
-Golden Lyons, Jane Ann Pier	Oct 20 p3 c4
-James C. Thomas	Nov 3 p3 c4
-Thomas Butler, Jr.	Dec 8 p3 c4
-Margaret Amelia Garrison	Dec 29 p3 c4
	<u>1839</u>
-George Downing	Jan 19 p3 c4
-James W. Simpson	Jan 26 p3 c4
-Caesar Smith	Feb 9 p3 c4
-John Birchell, Theodore Garrison	Feb 23 p3 c4

-Susan Black	Mar 2 p3 c4
-Harriet B. King	Mar 9 p3 c4
-John W. Carroll, Richard Ebrezer, John Frenin, Sarah A. Gray	Mar 16 p3 c3,4
-Amelia Ann Vattab	May 11 p3 c4
-Prince Saunders	Jun 8 p3 c4
-Elizabeth Ann Mitchell	Jul 27 p3 c4
-Charles W. Coyes, Margaret Green, Samuel C. Hatchings, Mary Louisa Hughes	Aug 17 p3 c4
-Mary Elizabeth Hall	Aug 24 p3 c4
-Julia Graham	Aug 31 p3 c4
-Emma V. Green	Sep 14 p3 c4
-George Washing	Oct 12 p3 c4
-Julia Brooks	Oct 19 p3 c4
-Peter Barron	Nov 2 p3 c4
-William Thompson	Nov 9 p3 c4
-Laura Crawford	Nov 16 p3 c4
-Mathias Dorsey	Nov 23 p3 c4
	1840
-Dr. John Brown (Eulogy)	Mar 7, 14 p3 c2,3
-Elizabeth Brown	Mar 21 p3 c3
-William Henry Caldwell	Apr 18 p3 c3
-Maria B. Jinnings, Martha Yates	May 2 p3 c3
-John Thompson	Jun 6 p3 c4
-Margaret Sands	Jun 13 p3 c4
-Thomas Simpkins Sidney	Jun 20 p3 c3
-Isabella Julius, Henry Jackson	Jul 4 p3 c3
-Adam K. Young	Aug 15 p3 c2
-Letty Wallace	Sep 5 p3 c3
-William S. Jinnings, Harriet Taylor	Oct 3 p3 c2,3
-Mary Ann Elizabeth	Oct 10 p3 c3,4
-David E. Conyers, Eliza E. Conyers, Sarah Rugg, Peter Slocum	Oct 17 p3 c4
-Jane Bartlett, Mary Robinson Howard, Reverend Peter Williams	Oct 24 p3 c4
-Andrew Brady	Nov 7 p3 c3
-Margaret Green	Nov 14 p3 c4
-Horace Crawford	Nov 21 p3 c3
-Jane Drayton	Dec 12 p3 c3
-William Garnet, Eliza Jane Philips	Dec 26 p3 c3
	1841
-John Aaron Day	Jan 16 p3 c3
-Matilda Cills	Jan 23 p3 c4
-William Mills, Joseph Legree, William Augustus Smith	Feb 27 p3 c4
-Sarah Gardner	Mar 6 p3 c4

-Elizabeth Payne (Mrs. Henry Bell)	Mar 13 p3 c3,4
-Harriet Jamieson	Mar 20 p3 c4
-Mary Ann Freeman, Samuel Smith	Mar 27 p3 c4
-Mary Ann Willis, Frederick Willis	Apr 3 p3 c3
-Reverend Isaiah G. DeGrasse, John Hamilton, Ezra Morris	Apr 10 p3 c3
-William Lloyd Garrison, Jr.	May 1 p3 c3
-Susan Paul, Ann Read	May 8 p3 c3
-William Fisher	May 15 p3 c4
-Joseph C. Caples, Charlotte Ann Graham	May 22 p3 c4
-Jane DeWitt, George Foster, Matilda Jane Harris, William Jeffers	Jun 5 p3 c3,4
-Lydia Grant	Jul 10 p3 c3
-Samuel L. Townsend	Jul 17 p3 c3
-Emeline Bishop, Peter Johnson	Jul 24 p3 c3
-Jacob Dubois Richardson	Aug 7 p3 c3
-Martha W. Alden Robinson	Aug 21 p3 c3
-William Henry Henderson	Aug 28 p3 c3
-Catharine Willingman	Sep 25 p3 c4
-Mary Jane Morgan	Oct 9 p3 c3
-Charles Hamilton	Oct 16 p3 c3
-James B. White	Oct 30 p3 c4
-Laura Brooks, Hannah Downing, Jeremiah Beman Gloucester	Nov 13 p3 c3
-Rebecca Berry, Robert Pogue, James W. Smith	Dec 4 p3 c4
-Enoch McBlenan, Ellen Almirah Scott	Dec 25 p3 c4

DEBATING INSTITUTIONS

	1837
-Praised as a valuable method of education	Jul 8 p3 c1 let.

DEBT

	1838
-Debt should be avoided, since it causes hardships	Dec 1 p1 c3
	1840
-On being in debt	Jun 27 p4 c2

DECKER, SARAH

	1837
-Married to Samuel Hardenbrugh by the Reverend Theodore S. Wright	Apr 1 p3 c3

DECLARATION OF SENTIMENTS (Anti-Slavery Convention 1834)

1838

-Praised as an example of outstanding anti-slavery literature — Jun 9 p1 c1 ed.

DE GRASSE, ISAIAH

1837

-Named to aid the editorial department of the Colored American — Nov 11 p3 c2

1838

-Course of lectures on the evidences of Christianity noted — Mar 22 p3 c4
-Lectures on evidence of Christianity praised — Apr 19 p3 c1 ed.
-Ordained as Episcopal minister — Jul 21 p3 c2
-Begins duties as missionary in Jamaica — Aug 11 p2 c4
-Becomes minister of Second Colored Episcopal Congregation (New York) — Oct 20 p3 c4

1839

-Preaches sermon on education — Mar 16 p3 c4

1840

-Resigns as pastor of the Saint Mathews Epsicopal Church — Jul 4 p2 c4 let.

1841

-Arrival in Jamaica noted — Jan 30 p2 c4
-Death noted — Mar 13 p2 c4
-Life work reviewed and praised — Apr 3 p2 c1
-Last days described — Apr 3 p2 c1 let.
-Obituary — Apr 10 p3 c3
-Poem on his death — May 1 p3 c2

DELAWARE

1837

-Conditions of slaves and free blacks described — Aug 12 p1 c1 let.

DEMBYE, GEORGE R. (Advertisement)

1838

-Boarding and victualing house — Jan 13 p4 c4-Feb 17 p4 c3
Mar 3 p4 c3
Mar 22, 29 p4 c3
Apr 12, 19 p4 c3
May 3 p4 c2
Jun 2 p4 c3

DEMONSTRATIONS (Black)

1837

- -Demonstrations against fugitive slave trials criticized — Apr 15 p3 c1 ed.
- -Crowds of illiterates are prey to their passions — Apr 29 p2 c3

DEMOSTHENIAN INSTITUTE

1841

- -Its origin and aims described; praised as a moral and mental improvement society — Apr 24 p2 c1

DEMOSTHENIAN SHIELD

1841

- -Begins publication and is recommended — Jul 24 p2 c3

DENNISON, ISAAC (Notice)

1840

- -Funeral sermon for Dennison open to the public — Apr 11 p3 c3

DEPRESSION OF 1837

1837

- -A help if the rich would spend their money — May 13 p3 c1
- -Depression caused by southern slavery — May 13 p3 c2
- -Not caused by death of National Bank, but by love of fast profit — Jun 17 p3 c2
- -The South owed $1,000,000 to people in Philadelphia — Jul 29 p4 c1
- -Winter of '37 - '38 will bring much hardship to the poor — Nov 25 p2 c4

DETOCQUEVILLE, ALEXIS

1839

- -Comments on differences between Americans and Russians — Nov 23 p1 c5

1840

- -His comments on the expansion of the Anglo-American race — May 16 p4 c1

1841

- -Review of his work, Democracy in America — Jan 23, 30 p2 c1; Feb 6 p3 c2
- -Criticized for misjudging black Americans — May 1 p2 c1 let.
- -Review of his sections on blacks — May 15 p2 c4

DICKSON (Dixson), WILLIAM

1837

-Tried as a fugative slave — Apr 15 p3 c3
-Judge in trial criticized — Apr 22 p3 c1
-Attempt made to free Dickson fails; view that most blacks do not support such attempts — Apr 29 p2 c4
-New York Times mentions demonstration for Dickson which really was a parade of the Clarkson Benevolent Society — Apr 29 p3 c1
-Case postponed; Dickson remains in jail — Apr 29 p3 c1
-Dickson freed on bail — Jul 8 p3 c3
-Meeting held to raise money — Jul 15 p2 c4
-Supreme Court of New York sent case back to lower court — Aug 5 p3 c3
-See also Griffin, Mr.; Palmer, Mr.; Ruggles, David

DIET
-See Health (Diet)

DIRECTORY FOR THE PEOPLE OF COLOR, A

1837

-Residences, occupations and names listed of colored — Jan 28 p3 c3
-Also to list churches, ministers, benevolent and literary institutions — Feb 4,18,25 p3 c4

DITMUS, EDWARD

1837

-Elected First Vice-President of the Cranberry Moral Reform Society — Aug 12 p4 c1

DITMUS, LEWIS F.

1837

-Elected Recording Secretary of the Cranberry Moral Reform Society — Aug 12 p4 c1

DIXON, G . H. (and Osborn J.) (Advertisement)

1840

-Land for sale in Brooklyn — Apr 11 p4 c3- Jul 4 p4 c4; Jul 25 p4 c4- Sep 12 p3 c4; Sep 26 p3 c3; Oct 3 p3 c3

	1841
-Paul Pontou also noted	May 22, 29 p3 c4
-Pontou no longer mentioned	Aug 7 p3 c3- Sep 18 p3 c4
DIXON, GEORGE W.	
	1839
-Sentenced to prison for 1½ years for libel	May 18 p3 c5
DOLTON, MARGARET	
	1840
-Marries Henry Emery	Sep 19 p3 c4
DOOLITTLE, DOCTOR A. (Notice)	
	1841
-Cures cancer	May 1-15 p3 c4
DORSEY, BASIL (Doylestown, Pennsylvania)	
	1837
-Freed of charge of being a fugitive slave	Sep 2 p4 c2
DOUGE, MICHAEL (Albany, New York)	
	1837
-Attends meeting of the Union Society of Albany	Apr 15 p1 c3
DOUGLASS, FREDERICK	
	1841
-Chairmen of free blacks of New Bedford (Massachusetts) condemns the American Colonization Society	Jul 10 p2 c3 let.
-Forcibly removed from a railroad car in Massachusetts	Oct 30 p1 c2 let.
DOUGLASS, ROBERT JR.	
	1838
-Describes Haitian Independence Day celebration	Mar 3 p2 c3 let.
-Describes attempted assassination of General Iuginac in Haiti	Jun 16 p2 c2 let.
DOUGLASS, SARAH (Philadelphia)	
	1837
-Runs school for blacks	Dec 2 p3 c1
DOUGLASS, REVEREND WILLIAM (Philadelphia, Pennsylvania)	
	1837
-Elected honorary member of the Troy (New York) Mental and Moral Improvement Association	Oct 21 p1 c2

-Listed as chairman of the Philadelphia Committee — Dec 9 p3 c2

1838

-August 1st speech printed — Aug 18 p4 c1

1839

-Dies and is eulogized by resolutions passed by Young Mens' Philadelphia Literary Association — Oct 5 p3 c3

DOUGLASS, WILLIAM P. (Philadelphia) (Advertisement)

1838

-Sign writer — Sep 8 p3 c4- Oct 6 p4 c4; Oct 20 p4 c4- Nov 17 p3 c4; Dec 1 p4 c3

DOWNING, GEORGE

1837

-Appointed Secretary of the Colored Young Men of New York City — Sep 2 p1 c1

1841

-Abused by Harlem Railroad Agents — Jan 16 p3 c2

-Loses suit against Harlem Railroad — Feb 20 p2 c4

DOWNING, THOMAS

1838

-Appointed Vice-President of the Political Association — Jun 16 p2 c3

DRESS

1837

-Necessity of cleanliness and neatness of dress stressed — Aug 12 p2 c3 let.

-Extravagance criticized — Aug 26 p2 c2 let.

-Stresses the importance of respectable clothing — Sep 9 p3 c3 let.

-The extravagance of dress decried — Oct 14 p3 c3 let.

1841

-Mourning attire deemed an unnecessary expense — Jul 31 p2 c3

DRESSER, MR.

1837

-Counsel for Ben Thompson, an escaped slave — Apr 8 p3 c1

DUBOIS, ALEXANDER (New Haven)
(Advertisement)

	1837
-House for sale	Sep 9 p3 c4- Nov 11 p4 c4 Dec 2 p4 c3- Dec 16 p4 c3

DUFFIN J. W. (Geneva, New York)

	1837
-Listed as agent for the _Colored American_	Mar 11 p4 c4
-Describes August 1st celebration in Geneva	Jul 29 p2 c4 let.
-Describes episode of pre-judicial treatment in Presbyterian lecture room	Dec 9 p2 c2 let.
	1838
-Opposes all-black farming settlements	Mar 22 p3 c2 let.
	1839
-Praises and defends _Colored American_'s stand on political abolition; calls for a convention	Nov 2 p2 c3
	1841
-Agrees on the need for a new convention in New York	Jun 26 p2 c4

DUKE OF SUSSEX

	1840
-Speaks in favor of the abolitionist cause	Aug 29 p1 c2

DUMAS, ALEXANDER (France)

	1841
-Criticized for being a mulatto by a European newspaperman; criticism of Dumas ridiculed	Aug 21 p2 c2
-About to be elected a member of the French Institute	Oct 16 p3 c1

DUNBAR, A. (Syracuse, New York)

	1838
-Listed as agent for the _Colored American_	Jan 13 p4 c4

DUNLAP, CAPTAIN R. G.

	1837
-Testifies as to self-sufficiency and responsibility of free blacks	Mar 4 p4 c2

DUNN, JOHN H.

1837

-Testifies to self-sufficiency and responsibility of blacks in Canada — Mar 4 p4 c3

E

EARLE, THOMAS

1840

-His nomination for vice-president favored by the Colored Citizens of Albany — May 23 p3 c2 let.
-Vice-presidential nomination supported by the Anti-Slavery Nominating Convention — May 30 p3 c2
-His letter of acceptance of vice-presidential nomination stating his anti-slavery views — Jul 18 p1 c1 let.
-Nomination supported by the Ohio Convention — Sep 19 p3 c1

EAST INDIES

1840

-Description of people of Borneo — Dec 5 p4 c1

EASTON, REVEREND HOSEA

1837

-Publishes a book on the civil and moral conduct of blacks in the United States — Jun 3 p2 c4

EDDY, REVEREND (Newark, New Jersey)

1840

-Accused of being an apologist for slavery — Nov 21 p2 c2

EDINBURGH REVIEW
-See Slavery (General)

EDUCATION (Free Blacks)
-See Free Blacks (Education)

EDUCATION (General)

1837

-Important in building and preserving democracy — Aug 26 p3 c1

	1838
-More money should be spent on education and less on jails; education reduces crime	Dec 1 p3 c1
	1839
-Education without religious education does not reduce crime	Jan 26 p2 c4
-School at Newtown, Long Island examined	Sep 7 p3 c5
-Early experiences educate people; physical education important	Sep 7 p4 c1
-John S. Copley's success used to illustrate the results of education	Oct 5 p1 c5
	1840
-Table relating education to crime	Mar 14 p4 c1
-Separatist high school and college called for	May 23 p2 c4 let.
-Separatist educational institutions viewed as wrong in principle, right in practice	May 23 p2 c4 ed.
-Memoirs of a common school master	Jul 25 p2 c4
-On the poor effects of too much study	Sep 5 p2 c1
-On the evils of showing partiality	Nov 7 p2 c2 let.
	1841
-Holland's educational system praised	Sep 25 p4 c2

EDWARD, COL. MONROE

	1841
-Arrested for forgery	Oct 9 p3 c3

EDWARDS, MARY

	1841
-Marries Samuel Atkins	Oct 16 p3 c3

ELECTION OF 1840

	1840
-Both sets of candidates are felt to be pro-slavery	Sep 12 p1 c2
-Tyler accused of being a slaveholder	Sep 26 p3 c1
-Johnson accused of being a slaveholder	Oct 3 p2 c1
-Candidates discussed	Oct 3 p2 c2

-Readers urged to support the Liberty Party — Oct 10 p1 c1
-People urged to support the Liberty Party — Oct 24 p1 c4
-Coming election noted, slate given — Oct 31 p3 c3
-Partial election returns — Nov 7 p2 c4
-Election of Harrison confirmed — Nov 14 p3 c2
-Full election returns discussed — Nov 14 p3 c3
-Unfavorable result of independent nominations noted — Dec 5 p2 c2

1841

-Presidential and vice-presidential ballots counted in Congress — Feb 27 p1 c3 let.

ELLENBOROUGH, LORD (England)

1841

-Appointed Governor General of India — Nov 13 p3 c2

ELSTON, DANIEL

1837

-Listed as one of the secretaries of Colored Citizens of New York — Oct 28 p1 c3

1838

-Appointed to the executive committee of the Political Association — Jun 16 p2 c3

ELSTON, EDGAR

1837

-Elected secretary of the Mutual Relief Society of New York — Sep 9 p2 c4

ELSWORTH, AMBERDORE

1837

-Dies — Jul 8 p3 c4

EMANCIPATION (United States)

1837

-If not granted, terrible changes will take place in the United States — Mar 25 p2 c2
-A most prominent subject — Mar 25 p2 c3
-Should be a major objective — Mar 25 p3 c2
-Emancipation should be immediate, but slaves should not receive their political rights immediately — Jun 17 p1 c1 ed.

-Black have to raise their level of education in order to be fully emancipated	Jun 24 p3 c3
-Plea for immediate emancipation	Jul 8 p2 c3 let.
-Argument for universal and immediate emancipation	Jul 8 p4 cl
-Defines emancipation and says the only way is for the masters voluntarily to free their slaves	Aug 26 p4 c2
-Group from Wales urges the United States to rid itself of the curse of slavery	Dec 2 p4 c2
	<u>1838</u>
-Blacks must use all lawful means	Jan 20 p3 cl
-Immediate emancipation necessary and good for all concerned	Feb 10 p4 cl
-Only immediate emancipation can rid slaveholders of sin	May 3 p4 c2
-Immediate emancipation supported by history	Jun 9 p2 c3
-Anecdote in favor of immediatism	Jul 14 p2 c2
-Universal emancipation seen certain	Sep 22 p2 cl
	<u>1839</u>
-Argument in favor of immediate emancipation	Mar 9 p2 c2 let.

EMANCIPATION (West Indies)

	<u>1837</u>
-Cites increased educational opportunities as a practical result of emancipation	Apr 1 pl cl
-Describes the effects of emancipation upon religious observance	Apr 1 pl cl
	<u>1838</u>
-Apprentice system should be abolished along with slavery	Mar 3 p3 c2
-Description of conduct of blacks upon emancipation in Antigua	Apr 12 pl cl
-Reimbursement arrangements for Haitian colonists	Apr 12 p2 c2 let.
-Apprenticeship terminated in Montserrat	Apr 19 p3 c3
-Slaves on Barbadoes to be freed August 1st	Jun 9 p2 c3

-Immediate and unconditional emancipation soon to occur on all the Islands	Jun 16 p2 cl ed.
-Bill for total emancipation passes Jamaican colonial assembly; apprenticeship ended	Jul 7 p3 c4
-England praised for West Indian policy	Jul 21 p3 cl ed.
-American blacks should rejoice in West Indian emancipation	Jul 21 p4 c3 ed.
-Civil condition of freed apprentices described	Jul 28 p4 cl
-Seen as a moral example which will start a world revolution against slavery	Jul 28 p4 cl let.
-Has proved both safe and right	Jul 28 p4 c2 let.
-Lack of enthusiasm for West Indian emancipation among Americans decried	Aug 11 p2 c3
-Emancipation Proclamation	Aug 11 p2 c4
-Emancipation working well	Sep 8 p3 c2
	1839
-Emancipation anniversary should be celebrated soberly	Jul 20 p2 c3 ed.
-Political Association should celebrate August 1st	Jul 27 p2 c5 let.
-Celebration plans for August 1st noted	Jul 27 p3 c4
-Boston celebration of August 1st emancipation day described	Aug 31 p3 c3 let.
-August 1st celebrated with temperance dinner	Aug 31 p3 c3
-Reports of adverse results refuted	Sep 7 p2 c4
	1840
-Emancipation day a memorable event in the British empire (Illustration)	May 9 p4 cl
-August 1st considered the birthday of freedom	Jul 25 p2 c4
-Celebration of August 1st urged	Aug 1 p3 cl
-Emancipation in the British West Indies is influencing other islands	Dec 26 p2 c3

EMANCIPATOR

	1838
-British anti-slavery sympathiser praises its principles	Mar 15 p4 cl let.

	<u>1840</u>
-Responsibility for publication assumed by the American Anti-Slavery Society	May 30 p2 c4
-See also Religion (General)	

EMERY, HENRY (Albany, New York)

	<u>1840</u>
-Marries Margaret Dolten	Sep 19 p3 c4

EMIGRATION (West Indies)

	<u>1839</u>
-Inquiry into possibilities of Trinidad	Aug 31 p3 c4
-Apprehensions about emigration to Trinidad refuted	Oct 12 p3 cl let.
-Emigrants urged to reach understanding with the Trinidad government before leaving	Oct 12 p3 c2
	<u>1840</u>
-Advantages of Trinidad and British Guiana	Mar 7 p2 c4
-British and Foreign Anti-Slavery Society discourages emigration to crown colonies	Apr 4 pl c3
-Contradictory reports on Trinidad emigrants reviewed	Apr 4 p2 c2
-Importance of labor market to emigrants discussed	Apr 11 p3 cl
-Abandonment of emigration plans to Trinidad urged	May 16 p2 c4
-Group sails for Trinidad	May 30 p3 c4
-American Anti-Slavery Society discourages movement to Trinidad or British Guiana	Jun 6 p3 c3
-Disadvantages of emigration to Jamaica stressed	Jul 18 pl c3 let.
-Discouraged by the <u>Colored American</u>	Oct 17 p2 c2
-New York City blacks do not favor moving to Trinidad	Oct 31 p2 c3
-Baltimore envoys are fooled by Trinidadian planters	Nov 7 p3 cl
	<u>1841</u>
-Sufferings of Trinidadian emigrants described	Jan 16 p3 cl
-Viewed critically	Feb 6 p2 c2
-Would be a mistake	May 29 p3 c2
-Criticized as a failure	Nov 13 p2 c3 ed.
-Criticized as a money-getting scheme	Dec 4 pl c3 let.

EMIGRATION (Western United States and Canada)

	1837
-Settlement in Indiana encouraged by tales of prosperity	Oct 28 p4 c2
	1838
-Free blacks urged to settle low-priced western lands	Apr 19 p2 c2
-Exodus from cities to country urged	Apr 19 p3 c1
-Considered sound and good when voluntary	May 3 p2 c1 let.
-Must not be compared with the aims of the American Colonization Society	May 3 p2 c2 let.
-Country settlements of free blacks encouraged	Jul 28 p2 c1 let.
	1839
-Defended	Jan 19 p2 c3 let.
-Movement to country encouraged	Mar 16 p3 c1
-Westward exodus encouraged	Jul 13 p2 c1
-Description of educational system in western settlements	Jul 13 p2 c2 let.
-Seen not always bad	Jul 27 p3 c1
-Western lands highly desirable	Aug 31 p2 c2 let.
-Formation of separatist colony in West suggested	Aug 31 p3 c3
	1840
-Good prospects in Canada noted; many have gone	May 16 p3 c1
-Description of Ohio's oppressive settlement laws	Dec 19 p2 c3
	1841
-Iowa described as an advantageous place to settle	Apr 3 p3 c1
-Movement beyond the Rocky Mountains viewed as humbug	Apr 24 p2 c4
-Blacks urged to buy Ohio lands	Aug 31 p2 c3

EMIGRATION
-See also Colonization; West Indies

EMLIN, SAMUEL

	1838
-Death eulogized; praised for contribution to education of black youth	Mar 3 p2 c1

ENGLAND

	1837
-Inundation of Thames Tunnel described	Oct 28 p1 c3
	1838
-Anti-slavery meeting held in Exeter; bill to amend Apprentice Act read in Parliament	Apr 19 p3 c3
-Rural serfdom seen to exist in Northern England	Jun 16 p3 c2
-Description of Queen Victoria	Oct 27 p2 c3
	1839
-Concludes commercial treaty with Haiti	Mar 9 p2 c2
-Summary of Parliamentary debates on Jamaica	Jul 13 p3 c4
-State of early Briton tribes described	Jul 27 p1 c5
	1840
-Southern states will prevent boundary war with Canada	May 9 p1 c3
-Description of city of London	Aug 1 p4 c1
-Mortality and disease in London	Aug 1 p4 c2
	1841
-Domestic conditions of United Kingdom evaluated	Aug 14 p1 c3
-Purchases islands from Spain	Oct 2 p3 c2

ENGLISH LANGUAGE

	1841
-Essay on its origins	Apr 24 p4 c3

ENGLISH NAVY

	1838
-Cruisers capture three slave ships off Montevideo	Aug 4 p3 c4

ENNALS, SAMUEL

	1837
-Elected president of the Mutual Relief Society of New York	Sep 9 p2 c4

ESTEVE, JOHN L. (Advertisement)

	1838
-Opens the Tivoli Garden; sells ice cream	Jun 30 p4 c4- Sep 22 p4 c4

	<u>1839</u>
	May 18 p3 c3
	Jun 8 p4 c3
	Jun 22 p3 c4
	Jun 29 p4 c3
	Jul 13 p4 c3- Jul 27 p4 c4
	Aug 17-31 p4 c4
	Sep 14, 28 p4 c4
EUROPE	
	<u>1840</u>
-Political situation described	Apr 25 p4 c2
-Description of the Alps	May 9 p1 c4
-Parisian Sabbath described	Nov 7 p4 c1
	<u>1841</u>
-City of Rome and its ancient architecture described	Jan 2 p4 c1
-See also England; France	
EVANS, ALEXANDER	
	<u>1838</u>
-Severely beaten	Jun 16 p3 c1
EVERETT, EDWARD	
	<u>1841</u>
-Initially refused nomination as minister to England	Sep 4 p3 c1
-Confirmed as minister to England	Sep 18 p3 c1

F

<u>FACTS FOR THE PEOPLE</u>	
-See Depression of 1837	
FAIRCHILD, DANIEL M. (Westfield, New York)	
	<u>1838</u>
-Listed as agent for the <u>Colored American</u>	Sep 29 p3 c4
FALL RIVER (Massachusetts)	
	<u>1837</u>
-People in factories much happier than slaves	Aug 5 p2 c3
FAMILY LIFE	
	<u>1838</u>
-Family members should strive for accord	Jul 7 p4 c1

-Questions regarding family religious devotions — Jul 7 p4 c2
-How parents should be truly honored — Jul 14 p2 c4
-Mothers must instruct daughters in how to sustain the misfortunes of life — Jul 14 p2 c4
-Children should be raised by appealing to their conscience — Jul 14 p4 c2
-Good habits must begin in childhood — Jul 14 p4 c2
-Anecdote recommends parental forgiveness — Jul 21 p1 c1
-Advice to women on governing a family; submission to the husband counselled — Sep 8 p4 c2
-Extent of a mother's moral influence and responsibility — Oct 6 p1 c3
-Proper upbringing of an eldest daughter — Oct 6 p4 c2
-Joys of responsible family life vindicated — Nov 3 p1 c4
-List of rules for wives — Nov 3 p4 c2
-General rules for husbands and wives — Dec 8 p3 c3

1839

-Influence of marriage on health and life — Jan 19 p4 c3
-On the necessary subservience of women — Oct 12 p3 c3 let.

1840

-Story stresses the importance of sibling love — May 16 p3 c2
-On the significance of marriage — Aug 1 p4 c3
-On the importance of kindness to siblings — Sep 5 p3 c2
-On the errors made by parents — Dec 19 p2 c2

1841

-Never punish a child in anger — Apr 3 p4 c4
-On maternal influence — Apr 10 p4 c3
-Anecdote regarding filial affection — Apr 24 p4 c4
-Anecdote illustrating the responsibilities of parents — Jun 19 p4 c4
-Exhortations to parents — Jul 17 p4 c1
-Discussion of the importance of parental influence — Aug 28 p3 c3
-Warning to young men — Aug 28 p3 c3

FARMING
-See Agriculture

FEMALE ASSISTANT SOCIETY

	1838
-Proceedings of annual meeting	Mar 15 p2 c4
-Henry H. Garnet addresses meeting on theme of charity	Mar 15 p2 c4
-See also Mumford, Mrs. Janet; Thomas, Mrs. Rachel; United Female Assistant Benefit Society	

FEMALE BAPTIST ASSOCIATION (Notice)

	1839
-Meeting announced	Aug 24 p3 c4

FEMALE BEHAVIOR
-See Family Life; Women (Black); Women (General); Women (White)

FEMALE BENEVOLENT SOCIETY (Troy, New York)

	1837
-Description of the fourth anniversary celebration meeting	Apr 1 p1 c3 let.
	1840
-Educational accomplishments praised and described	Nov 14 p2 c2 let.
-See also Harris, Andrew; Miter, John J.; Vandevere, Reverend Daniel	

FEMALE BRANCH OF ZION

	1837
-Fifth anniversary meeting	Apr 1 p3 c3
-Holds meeting; address published	Jun 3 p4 c1

FEMALE COMPANION (Nelsonville, Ohio) (Notice)

	1840
-Wanted	May 2 p3 c4-May 23 p3 c4 Jun 6 p3 c4-Jul 4 p3 c4

FEMALE DORCAS SOCIETY (Buffalo, New York)

	1837
-Receive thanks for monetary donation to salary of Colored American editor	Nov 4 p3 c2

FEMALE EDUCATION SOCIETY

	1840
-Celebration of anniversary noted; annual report notes	

group's philanthropic successes — Oct 31 p2 c1

-See also Free Blacks (Education)

FEMALE MITE SOCIETY

1837

-Fourth Anniversary planned — Oct 14 p3 c4

FEMALE SINKING FUND SOCIETY

1841

-Founding noted — May 1 p2 c4

FEMALE SOCIETY FOR COLORED ORPHANS

-See Free Blacks (Education, Women)

FEMALE TEMPERANCE SOCIETY (Troy, New York)

1837

-Formed — Apr 1 p2 c1

FEMALE TRADING ASSOCIATION (Advertisement)

1840

-Dry Groceries for sale — Nov 13 p3 c4

1841

May 1 p3 c3
Jul 10 p3 c3-
Oct 16 p3 c4

-Aims described and commended — Jul 31 p2 c4

FEMALE WESLEYAN ANTI-SLAVERY SOCIETY

1839

-Third Anniversary Meeting announced — Mar 2 p3 c4-
Mar 16 p4 c4

1840

-Fourth Anniversary meeting announced — Mar 14 p3 c3
Mar 21 p3 c4

1841

-Fifth Anniversary meeting announced — Mar 20 p3 c4
Mar 27 p3 c4

FIELDS, JAMES (Advertisement and Notice)

1837

-Listed as agent for the Colored American — Mar 11 p4 c4

-Listed as one of four vice-presidents of the Colored Citizens of New York — Oct 28 p1 c3

	<u>1838</u>
-Clothes dresser and tailor	Dec 8 p3 c4- Dec 22 p4 c3 adv.
	<u>1839</u>
-Addresses New York anti-colonization meeting; denounces the American Colonization Society as destructive to true patriotism	Jan 19 p1 c2
	<u>1840</u>
-Proposes opening an evening school; looking for applicants	Nov 21, 28 p3 c4 Dec 12, 19 p3 c4

FIJI ISLANDS

	<u>1840</u>
-Description of cannibalism practised there	Dec 5 p4 c3

FIRST AFRICAN METHODIST EPISCOPAL CHURCH (New York City) (Notice)

	<u>1837</u>
-Indian lecturer	Apr 22 p3 c4
-Camp meeting	Sep 9 p2 c4
	<u>1840</u>
-Open for services	Apr 18 p3 c3
-Public exhibition	Oct 3 p3 c3 Nov 13 p3 c3
	<u>1841</u>
-Conference	Jun 5 p3 c4

FIRST AFRICAN METHODIST EPISCOPAL CHURCH (Rochester, New York) (Notice)

	<u>1840</u>
-The church's only authorized minister is the Reverend Thomas James	Jul 11, 18 p3 c4 Aug 1 p3 c4- Sep 12 p3 c4 Sep 26 p3 c4 Oct 3 p3 c3

FIRST COLORED PRESBYTERIAN CHURCH (Notice)

	<u>1839</u>
-Celebration of the 1st of August (West Indies emancipation)	Jul 27 p3 c4

	<u>1841</u>
-Holding a fair	Feb 13 p3 c3 Feb 20 p3 c4 Mar 20 p3 c4 Apr 10, 17 p3 c3 May 1 p3 c3
FIRST DISTRICT MEETING (Notice)	
	<u>1840</u>
-Mass meeting of colored citizens concerning blacks' political situation	Nov 20 p3 c3
FLAMER, JOHN (Advertisement)	
	<u>1839</u>
-Wants a boy as an apprentice in the boot-making business	Feb 23 p3 c3- Mar 16 p4 c4
FLORIDA	
	<u>1839</u>
-Armed occupation and emigration ridiculed	Jan 19 p3 c1 ed.
-War with Indians appears imminent	Mar 9 p2 c2 ed.
-Approaching war deplored	Mar 16 p3 c3
-War a source of money-making for speculators	Oct 12 p4 c2
-Men who die in the Florida war fall in the service of slavery	Nov 23 p1 c4
FORD, HUGH (Harper's Ferry, Virginia)	
	<u>1839</u>
-Drowns	May 18 p3 c5
FORTEN, JAMES (Philadelphia)	
	<u>1837</u>
-Criticizes colonization and Clay's speech in praise of it	May 13 p2 c3 let.
-Chairman of Moral Reform Convention (Philadelphia)	Aug 19 p3 c1
-<u>Colored American</u> feels he should resign from the Moral Reform Society of Philadelphia	Aug 26 p2 c1 ed.
FORTEN, JAMES JR.	
	<u>1837</u>
-Secretary of the Moral Reform Convention (Philadelphia)	Aug 19 p3 c1
-Speaks on education	Aug 26 p3 c1
-Praised by the <u>Colored</u> <u>American</u>	Aug 26 p3 c1
FORTEN, VIRGINIA	
	<u>1840</u>
-Obituary	Aug 29 p3 c3

FOSTER, HENRY

1838

-President of the Connecticut State Temperance Society — Oct 13 p3 c2

FOURTEENTH WARD HOTEL (Advertisement)

1837

-Holding fair — Nov 11 p3 c4

FOURTH FREE CHURCH (Notice)

1837

-Sermon on the Sabbath's desecration, by the Reverend E. A. Fraser — Oct 21 p3 c4

FRANCE

1838

-Blockades Mexican ports — Aug 4 p3 c4

1841

-Chamber of Deputies discusses scandalous treatment of slaves in French colonies — Jul 24 p2 c4

-Attempted assassination of one of the royal family — Oct 9 p3 c3

FRANCIS, W. H. (and P. Williams) (Saratoga Springs, New York) (Advertisement)

1840

-New proprietors for Mrs. Budd's boarding house; will continue to accommodate colored people — May 16 p3 c3; May 23 p3 c4; Jun 6 p3 c4-Sep 12 p3 c4

FRANKFORT STREET CHURCH (Advertisement and Notice)

1838

-Pews to let — Sep 8 p3 c4-Oct 6 p4 c4

1840

Jun 13 p3 c3-Jul 18 p3 c4

-Musical association of the church commemorating emancipation in the British West Indies — Aug 1 p3 c4

FRANKLIN, BENJAMIN

1838

-Statement favoring agriculture — Sep 8 p3 c3
-Short biographical note — Sep 8 p4 c2

1839

-Character sketch by Lord Brougham — Jul 20 p1 c1

FRASER, JAMES (Advertisement)

1837

-Desires new colored apprentices; will also furnish same — Apr 15 p3 c4- May 13 p4 c4

FREE AMERICAN
-See Massachusetts Abolitionist

FREE BLACKS (Alabama)

1839

-Possibly to be enslaved after 1 August 1840 — Sep 28 p4 c2

FREE BLACKS (Brazil)

1838

-Testimonial as to their self-sufficiency — Apr 12 p4 c1

FREE BLACKS (Canada)

1837

-Self-sufficiency and responsibility of free blacks described — Mar 4 p4 c2

1838

-Hold meeting; pass resolutions condemning treatment of blacks in the United States and murder of Elijah Lovejoy — Mar 29 p1 c4

1839

-Blacks have no say in the Toronto government — May 11 p3 c4

1841

-Much prejudice against blacks; separate schools, churches, etc. — Mar 13 p1 c1

FREE BLACKS (Connecticut)

1839

-New Haven conditions described as good; no poor blacks — Jun 29 p2 c1

1840

-Colored Citizens of New Haven opposed to national convention	Aug 1 p3 cl let.
-Citizens of New Haven refute statements by David Ruggles	Aug 29 p3 cl let.
-Citizens of New Haven reassert opposition to national convention	Sep 5 p2 c3 let.

1841

-Blacks of Hartford hold public meeting about the spread of the Gospel to Africa	May 15 pl c4

FREE BLACKS (Delaware)

1839

-Portrayal of poor conditions of colored citizens there	Mar 9 p3 cl

1840

-Wilmington citizens pledge support to the Colored American	Nov 1 p2 cl let.
-Wilmington community described	Nov 14 pl cl let.

FREE BLACKS (Education)

1837

-Praise for free black school in Newport, Rhode Island	Mar 4 p2 cl let.
-Stresses vocational education	Mar 4 p2 c3
-Postponement of a meeting of the American Society for the Promotion of Education in Africa	Mar 4 p3 c2
-Praises the aims of the American Society for the Promotion of Education in Africa	Mar 4 p3 c2 ed.
-Cites successful educational institutions of Haiti	Mar 11 p3 cl
-1,200 - 1,300 out of 3,000 black youths educated in New York City; disappointing number	Mar 25 p3 cl
-Cites increased educational opportunities as a practical result of emancipation in the West Indies	Apr 1 pl cl
-Black school in Utica, New York cited as a good example of what black children are capable of	Apr 1 p4 c3
-Qualified teachers needed	Apr 8 p2 c2
-Blacks must take interest in schools	Apr 15 p2 c2
-School opened in New London, Connecticut	Jun 3 p3 c4

-School boards willing to help blacks, but blacks must send their children to school	Jun 24 p3 c1
-Education a necessity for children	Aug 26 p2 c4
-Many blacks realize the value of education	Sep 16 p3 c2
-Providence, Rhode Island has three schools for blacks	Sep 23 p2 c4
-Blacks need education	Sep 30 p2 c2
-Lists twenty colored schools successfully operating in Ohio	Oct 14 p1 c4
-Notes teachers wanted for Ohio schools	Oct 14 p2 c1
-Cornish praised for encouraging education among free blacks	Oct 28 p1 c1 let.
-Education of free blacks urged as method of increasing the popularity of the abolitionist cause	Oct 28 p1 c2
-Inconsistent attitude of white Americans toward education of colored race pointed out	Nov 4 p3 c1
-Dr. Lively announces course in physiology and hygiene	Nov 4 p3 c4
-A more liberal education should be sought by free blacks	Nov 11 p3 c3
-Education must include language	Dec 2 p2 c2
-Black schools in Philadelphia not as good as in New York	Dec 2 p3 c1
-Miss Sarah Douglass runs a black school in Philadelphia	Dec 2 p3 c1
-Dr. James McCune Smith lectures on the importance of classical and mathematical studies	Dec 16 p3 c3
	1838
-Mutual education suggested as a good method	Jan 27 p2 c3
-Education viewed as a powerful transforming agency	Feb 17 p1 c1
-Appeal to Christian churches of New York to help educate black children	Feb 17 p3 c1 ed.
-Eulogy praises Samuel Emlin for contributions to education of black youth	Mar 3 p2 c1
-Lack of educational opportunity for New York City black children decried	Mar 3 p3 c2
-Exhibition of black school described	Mar 22 p3 c1 let.

-Description of examinations in New York Colored Free Schools	Apr 19 p2 c3 let.
-Vocational training seen as important as the professions	May 3 p3 c1 ed.
-Farmer's children also need education	May 3 p3 c2
-Formation of a colored education society urged	Jun 2 p3 c1 let.
-Educated blacks should be voluntary teachers to the uneducated	Jun 2 p3 c1 let.
-Higher education important	Jun 2 p3 c1 let.
-Need for teachers in Ohio; Separation of schools opposed	Aug 4 p2 c1 ed.
-Facts respecting pro-slavery colleges and seminaries	Oct 13 p1 c1
-Meeting discusses a woman's duty to stress the importance of a public school education	Oct 13 p4 c1
-Colored Young Men of Philadelphia stress the importance of education	Oct 13 p4 c1
-Success of black children at school exams described	Oct 20 p2 c2 let.
-One is never too old to learn	Oct 20 p2 c4
	1839
-New York City black children are not going to public schools; many possibly closed for this reason	Jan 26 p3 c3
-Black lack of attendance discussed	Feb 9 p3 c1
-Augustus Wattles teaches school in Ohio (26 blacks and 4 whites)	Mar 2 p3 c1
-Education of colored citizens of Delaware neglected	Mar 9 p3 c1 ed.
-Statistics on education in Delaware	Mar 9 p3 c2
-Essay on pedagogical methods	Mar 9 p4 c1
-Condition of New York City public schools discussed	Mar 16 p3 c1 ed.
-Oppressive treatment in New Jersey schools discussed	Mar 16 p3 c1 ed.
-School opened by Dr. Brown	May 18 p3 c2
-Lack of education a major cause of the blacks' situation	May 18 p3 c3 let.
-Description of educational system in western settlements	Jul 13 p2 c2 let.
-Children should learn trades	Oct 5 p3 c2
-Children should not be burdened with too much book learning	Oct 19 p1 c3

-Lack of opportunity in New York compared with Ohio	Oct 19 p2 cl ed.
-Black teacher needed in Hartford, Connecticut	Nov 2 p3 cl let.
	<u>1840</u>
-Education for blacks restricted in Connecticut	Mar 14 pl cl
-Schools in Cincinnati described	Oct 17 pl cl
-Description of Ohio schools for black youths	Oct 31 pl cl
-Female Education Society notes successes at its anniversary meeting	Oct 31 p2 cl
-Attendance at evening schools urged	Nov 7 p2 c3
-Description of ignorance and backwardness on Long Island	Nov 14 p2 c2 let.
-Educational accomplishments of the Female Benevolent Society (Troy, New York) described	Nov 14 p2 c2 let.
-New York public schools discussed	Nov 28 p2 c3
	<u>1841</u>
-Advice on methods of study	Jan 16 p4 c2
-Parents urged to send children to public schools for colored children	Jan 30 pl cl let. Apr 3 pl cl let.
-Mistakes made by parents in educating their children	Apr 10 p2 cl let.
-Attendance at New York public schools urged	Apr 17 p2 cl let.
-Errors of parents involving education	May 8 p2 cl let.
-School in New York City wants students	May 8 p2 cl let.
-Carlisle (Pennsylvania) school described	Oct 2 p2 cl
-Exhibition of Brooklyn primary school praised	Nov 13 p2 cl
-See also Loveridge, P.; Maxon, Mrs.; Parker, Ranson; Wattles, Augustus	

FREE BLACKS (Education, Women)

	<u>1837</u>
-Need for domestic education stressed	Mar 18 p2 cl
-White women requested to aid in breaking down racial barriers in female seminaries	Oct 7 p4 c2

-Legacy donated to the Female Asylum for Colored Orphans	Dec 30 p2 c2
	1839
-Lack of girls' schools deplored	Nov 23 p3 c1
	1840
-Seminary for young black girls opened in Oneida, New York	May 2 p3 c2

FREE BLACKS (Employment)

	1838
-Lack of opportunities deplored	Jul 28 p3 c2 let.
-Slavery is at war with the interests of free laboring classes	Sep 1 p4 c2

FREE BLACKS (Georgia)

	1840
-Taxed exhorbitantly and oppressed	Dec 15 p3 c1

FREE BLACKS (Louisiana)

	1841
-Whites urged by local paper to be watchful of free Negroes	Aug 14 p2 c2
-Whites warned against mis-treating blacks	Aug 14 p2 c2

FREE BLACKS (Maine)

	1841
-Portland citizens pass resolution favoring state convention	Jul 3 p1 c4

FREE BLACKS (Maryland)

	1839
-Must have pass and manu-mission papers to travel	Jun 22 p3 c4
-Residence forbidden	Jul 13 p1 c5
	1840
-State laws restrict settlement of free blacks	May 30 p1 c4
-Baltimore Methodists criticize racial attitudes of white Methodist congregations; present petition	Jul 4 p1 c4 let.
	1841
-Warned against work of Maryland Colonization Convention	Jul 3 p3 c2 let.

FREE BLACKS (Massachusetts)

1837

- State constitution praised for making blacks equal — Mar 18 p2 c4
- Describes good living conditions of New Bedford citizens — Jul 22 p2 c4

1838

- Boston colored citizens hold meeting to protest death of Elijah Lovejoy — Jan 13 p2 c4

1840

- Colored citizens of Worcester recommend general convention — Jul 4 p1 c3 let.
- Lack of racism in Fall River noted — Jul 4 p2 c2 ed.

1841

- Citizens of New Bedford condemn the American Colonization Society — Jul 10 p2 c3 let.

FREE BLACKS (Military Duty)

1838

- Refusal of free blacks to do military duty denied — Mar 22 p2 c2

1841

- Should refuse to fight in any conflict between America and England — Jan 23 p3 c2 let.
- See also Free Blacks (United States)

FREE BLACKS (Missouri)

1841

- Accused of causing unrest among slaves by St. Louis newspaper; accusation refuted — Sep 4 p3 c2

FREE BLACKS (New Jersey)

1837

- Restricted by new law — Apr 8 p2 c4

1838

- Colored citizens of Newark meet to plan celebration of West Indian Emancipation — Jul 21 p3 c3

1840

- Colored citizens of Newark plan public meeting to plan first of August celebration — Jul 25 p3 c1

FREE BLACKS (New York)

	1837
-Petitions of New York blacks delivered to state legislature	Mar 11 p3 c2
-Petitions of New York blacks rejected by state legislature	Mar 11 p3 c3
-Only one-third of black youths eligible to be educated in New York City	Mar 25 p3 c1
-New York City mayor calls for more aid to free black immigrants	Jun 17 p3 c1
-Description of colored communities in Buffalo and Lockport (New York)	Nov 4 p2 c2 let.
	1838
-Colored Citizens of Buffalo protest their treatment	Jan 27 p1 c4 let.
-Economic problems of urban blacks described	Mar 3 p3 c2
-Meet to discuss political enfranchisement; form a political association	Jun 16 p2 c3
-Colored Citizens of New York City plan to celebrate West Indian enfranchisement	Jul 21 p3 c1
-New York City schools for blacks described by a visitor	Sep 1 p2 c2 let.
-New York City black leaders, associations, and congregations described	Sep 15 p2 c3 let.
	1839
-Description of Poughkeepsie schools (1835-1839)	Sep 28 p3 c2
	1840
-Colored Citizens of Poughkeepsie support a state convention	Jul 4 p1 c1 let.
-Colored Citizens of Buffalo appoint delegates to a general convention	Jul 4 p1 c1 let.
-Community in Troy described	Jul 11 p2 c1 let.
-Colored Citizens of Poughkeepsie appoint delegates to state convention	Jul 25 p2 c4
-Colored Citizens of New York City plan a meeting to appoint delegates to a state convention	Jul 25 p3 c4
-Colored Citizens of Oswego choose delegate to the New York state convention	Aug 1 p3 c1

-Colored Citizens of Rochester approve New York state convention	Aug 1 p3 c2 let.
-Hold meeting to discuss state convention of blacks	Aug 8 p2 c2
-Hold meeting in Lansingburg to discuss convention	Aug 8 p3 cl
-Colored Citizens of Buffalo plan to form a total abstinence society	Aug 29 p2 cl
-Citizens of New York City meet and approve plans adopted at the State Convention to obtain the franchise	Sep 5 p2 c2
-Description of August 1st celebration among Rochester citizens	Sep 5 p2 c2
-New York City citizens welcome reappearance of the <u>Mirror of Liberty</u>	Sep 5 p2 c4 let.
-New York City citizens plan to petition the state legislature for the elective franchise	Nov 14 p3 c2
-New York City citizens petition New York State Legislature for the franchise	Nov 21 p3 cl
-Rochester citizens pass a resolution to support the <u>Colored American</u>	Nov 21 p3 c2 let.
-General meeting of New York City citizens called	Nov 28 p3 c3
-Text of New York City petition to New York Legislature requesting franchise	Dec 5 pl cl
-New York City citizens plan to raise funds to publish their petition requesting the franchise	Dec 5 p3 c2
-Mass meeting planned in New York City to support the franchise petition	Dec 5 p3 c4
-Proceeding of New York City mass meeting to support the franchise petition	Dec 12 p2 cl
-New York blacks plea for political equality	Dec 19 pl cl
-Citizens of Flushing, Long Island plan a mass meeting for the franchise	Dec 19 p3 c3
-Public meetings held in Schenectady, Troy and Albany to declare support for the franchise petition	Dec 26 p2 cl

1841

-Colored citizens of Buffalo hold meeting to congratulate freed Amistad captives	Apr 17 p2 cl
-Syracuse blacks lack education	May 15 p2 cl
-New York City citizens meet to celebrate New York law prohibiting slavery	Jun 19 p3 c2
-Meeting of New York City citizens called to consider Maryland Colonization Convention	Jun 19 p3 c4
-New York City citizens hold anti-colonization meeting	Jun 26 p3 cl
-Williamsburgh citizens pass a resolution to start a school	Jul 3 p2 cl
-Citizens of Albany warn those of Maryland against the work of the Colonization Convention	Jul 3 p3 c2 let.
-Citizens of Albany meet and condemn the American Colonization Society and the Maryland Colonization Convention	Jul 10 p3 cl let.
-Citizens of Buffalo condemn the Maryland Colonization Convention; endorse the Troy Convention	Jul 31 pl c3
-New York City citizens approve the Troy Convention	Aug 7 p2 c3
-Troy blacks elect delegates to the Troy Convention	Aug 14 p2 cl
-Buffalo blacks meet to discuss the Cincinnati riot	Nov 13 pl cl
-New York blacks meet to consider the franchise question	Nov 20 p2 cl

FREE BLACKS (Ohio)

1837

-Under many legal restrictions; lack the franchise	Jul 22 p2 cl

1838

-Description of black settlements and accomplishments	Mar 22 p4 cl Mar 29 p4 cl Apr 5 p4 cl

1839

-Colored Citizens of Cleveland pass resolutions against colonization	Mar 2 pl c2
-Cincinnati Colored Citizens in good financial condition	Oct 5 p2 c5 let.

-Are upright, respectable, and skillful farmers	Nov 2 p2 c5
-Barred from citizenship and voting	Nov 2 p2 c5
	1840
-Their petition for the franchise rejected by the state legislature	Mar 14 pl cl
-Colored Citizens of Butler County organize a convention to redress grievances	Jul 11 p2 c2 let.
-Free blacks in Cincinnati described	Oct 17 pl cl
-Description of colored settlements	Oct 31 pl cl
-Civil disabilities noted	Dec 12 p2 c3
-Oppressiveness of Settlement Laws noted	Dec 19 p2 c3
-Legal hazards discussed and deplored	Dec 26 p2 c2
	1841
-Discussion of "black laws"	Jan 9 p2 c4
-Taxed to support schools from which they are excluded	Jan 16 p2 c2
-Discussion of the "Oath Law"	Jan 23 p2 c2
-Citizens of Mercer County prospering	Jan 23 p3 cl

FREE BLACKS (Pennsylvania)

	1837
-Financial conditions in general	Aug 19 p4 cl
	1838
-Criticized for over-reaction to term "colored American"	Mar 15 p3 c2
-Urged to agitate for civil rights	Mar 15 p3 c3
-Send memorial to constitutional reform convention pleading for civil rights	Apr 5 pl c4
-Their appeal to white citizens regarding enfranchisement	May 3 pl cl
-New York Colored American endorses appeal	May 3 p3 cl
-Appeal continued	Jun 2 pl cl
-Philadelphia blacks urged to avoid violence	Jun 16 p3 c4
-Proceedings of meeting of Colored Citizens of Pennsylvania	Sep 8 p4 cl
-Colored citizens of Philadelphia praised for attitude toward the black press	Sep 8 p4 cl

	1839
-Criticized as being too timid	Aug 17 p2 c5
-Colored citizens of Philadelphia meet to protest remarks made in a southern newspaper	Sep 7 p3 c3
-Considered generally well-off; a source of jealousy	Sep 28 p2 c4
	1840
-Colored citizens of Philadelphia pass resolutions honoring Dr. Joseph Parrish	Mar 28 p3 cl
-Colored citizens of Pittsburgh approve plans for a national convention	Jul 18 p2 cl
-Philadelphia churches and community described	Nov 14 pl cl let.
	1841
-Public meeting in Philadelphia considers a state convention	May 8 pl cl
-Philadelphia citizens approve Pennsylvania Convention; also call for a national convention	Sep 25 p2 c2

FREE BLACKS (St. Thomas, West Indies)

	1837
-Cites achievements of the free black population on St. Thomas	Mar 11 p4 cl

FREE BLACKS (Self-Improvement)

	1837
-Notes need for good use of leisure time	Mar 18 p2 c3
-Notes need to keep Sabbath	Mar 18 p2 c3
-Must be perfect people	Mar 25 p3 c2
-Meeting of Troy, New York Colored People to promote the improvement of free blacks	Apr 1 pl c4 let.
-Should avoid extravagance	Apr 1 p4 c3
-Should be taught self-respect, not abasement	Apr 8 p2 c3
-Blacks must develop themselves	Apr 8 p3 cl let.
-Blacks must become involved with agriculture	Apr 15 p2 c3
-Blacks should not demonstrate at fugitive slave trials	Apr 15 p3 cl
-Black youths should become mechanic's apprentices	Apr 15 p3 cl ed.

-Blacks must change long-standing habits and become thrifty, intelligent	May 6 p2 c2
-Blacks must be equal to whites in every aspect if they want to be treated equally	May 27 p2 c4
-Young men of New York should form an organization for self-improvement	Jun 3 p3 c3
-Calls on colored brethren to renew efforts toward self-improvement	Sep 9 p3 c2
-Importance of respectable clothing stressed	Sep 9 p3 c3 let.
-Idleness a vice	Oct 21 p2 c4 ed.
-Self-improvement through education stressed	Oct 28 p1 c2
-Mental and moral qualifications stressed as prerequisites to equality	Nov 4 p2 c1
-Indebtedness viewed as a source of temptation to black Christians	Dec 16 p4 c1
-Organization of all free blacks proposed in order to concentrate efforts on self-improvement	Dec 23 p2 c2 let.
	1838
-Blacks called on to contribute to the cause of abolition	Jan 27 p2 c1
-Story discourages idleness	Feb 17 p1 c3
-Reading of history encouraged	Feb 17 p4 c1
-Blacks must be virtuous, wise, and wealthy to be respected	Mar 15 p3 c1
-Special efforts should be made to represent the true moral and mental character of blacks to the public	Mar 22 p2 c4 let.
-More frugal living urged	Apr 19 p2 c1 ed.
-More enterprising and well-directed activities necessary to elevate blacks from misery	Apr 19 p2 c2 ed.
-Establishment of permanent and unified organizations for the betterment of free blacks called for	Apr 19 p3 c3 let.
-Mechanical trades seen as important means of uplifting blacks	May 3 p3 c1 ed.
-General plan for the formation of Councils of Associations	May 3 p3 c3 let.
-Extravagance a harmful temptation	Jun 2 p1 c4
-Conduct crucial to the anti-slavery question	Jun 2 p3 c1 let.

-Virtues of thrift discussed	Jun 16 p1 c3
-Gambling condemned	Jun 16 p3 c1 ed.
-Blacks should move to the country	Jun 30 p2 c2
-Benefits of agriculture described	Jun 30 p3 c1
-Blacks must wake up and rouse themselves with great enterprise	Jul 7 p3 c1
-Anecdote demonstrates the value of hard work and tenacity	Jul 21 p4 c1
-Should maintain self-respect in their relationships with whites	Aug 4 p2 c3 let.
-Energy of character needed	Aug 4 p4 c2
-Young men urged to preserve their character	Aug 4 p4 c3
-Hope is an important part of life	Aug 11 p2 c1
-No way to make a living the easy way; gambling is not the answer	Sep 1 p2 c2
-Necessity of planning for future needs stressed	Sep 8 p4 c3
-Blacks need economy, enterprise, and husbandry	Sep 22 p3 c1
-German families commended as examples of frugality and temperance	Oct 6 p1 c2
-Blacks must increase their moral and intellectual abilities in order to be considered truly American	Oct 6 p3 c1 ed.
-Free blacks gain nothing from a haughty attitude	Oct 13 p2 c2 let.
-Education the key to respectability and true equality	Oct 13 p4 c1
-Blacks must beome practical and efficient to attain standing	Oct 27 p2 c1 ed.
-Story demonstrates that there is no shame in poverty	Oct 27 p2 c4
-Free blacks can do more to elevate themselves	Oct 27 p3 c2
-Industry is rewarded by success	Oct 27 p4 c2
-Tact and talent are important virtues	Nov 17 p2 c4 ed.
-Important to maintain one's dignity	Nov 17 p3 c4
-Success depends upon individual effort	Dec 8 p2 c2
-Money spent on tobacco would be more profitably applied to periodical subscriptions	Dec 15 p2 c4 let.

	1839
-Principle cause of depression among blacks is disunity	Jan 19 p2 c4 let.
-Employment in mechanical trades should be encouraged	Mar 9 p1 c2 ed.
-Benefits of early rising noted	Mar 9 p1 c2
-Labor and talent can overcome prejudice	Mar 9 p2 c1 ed.
-Industry, honesty, and wisdom can counteract prejudiced public sentiment	Mar 9 p2 c4 let.
-Energy and faith will lead to elevation	Mar 9 p3 c1 ed.
-Detrimental qualities of garrulous talkers	Mar 16 p2 c1 ed.
-List of virtues necessary to become appreciated and loved	Mar 16 p2 c3 let.
-The oppressed must make public their grievances	Mar 16 p2 c4 let.
-Ignorant blacks should not speak publicly	Mar 16 p2 c4 ed.
-Must unite to accomplish goals	May 18 p3 c2 ed.
-Warned against quacks	May 18 p3 c3
-Lectures on housewifing and domestic economy valuable; slavery and caste prejudice hold back advancement	Jun 22 p1 c1
-Real estate companies owned by blacks will help advance the race	Jun 22 p1 c1
-Advice on how to get rich	Jul 20 p1 c3
-Money should not be wasted on traveling	Jul 27 p3 c2 ed.
-One should not anticipate evil	Aug 3 p1 c5
-Education, religion, and mechanical skills necessary	Aug 3 p2 c1
-Commercial ventures advantageous	Aug 17 p2 c1
-Industry and hard work necessary	Sep 28 p2 c2
-Blacks are divided by petty things; waste money	Oct 5 p3 c2
-Children should learn trades	Oct 5 p3 c2
-On the pleasures of hard work	Oct 19 p1 c2
-Mechanics are the ablest men	Nov 2 p1 c4
-Education is the only way to advance	Nov 2 p2 c1
-The press is a means of elevation	Nov 16 p3 c4
-Some are made poor by domestic extravagance	Nov 23 p1 c5

-Various means of elevation listed — Nov 23 p2 c2
-Moral principles must be raised by proper education — Dec 7 p2 c2

1840

-Address on the acquisition of property and knowledge — Sep 26 p1 c1
-Address continued on moral elevation — Oct 3 p1 c1

1841

-Must not be slothful in business — Jan 30 p4 c4
-Essay on the nature and attainment of happiness — Feb 6 p1 c1
-Unity essential to the elevation of blacks — Apr 24 p2 c2
-Real advancement is the product of combined effort — Apr 24 p4 c2
-Cultivation of the mind is a means of elevation — May 1 p2 c2
-Honest industry is the best means to gain wealth — Jun 26 p2 c2
-Discourse on human judgement — Jul 10, 17 p2 c4; Jul 31 p2 c2
-Blacks retain love of learning for its own sake — Jul 17 p1 c3
-Urged to follow intellectual pursuits rather than gambling — Nov 13 p2 c4
-See also Agriculture

FREE BLACKS (Trinidad)

1838

-Testimonial to their self-sufficiency — Apr 12 p4 c1

FREE BLACKS (United States)

1837

-Should dedicate their lives to winning emancipation — Mar 25 p2 c3
-Warned against travel to Cuba — Oct 21 p3 c3 let.

1838

-Need seen to inquire into the history of blacks — Jun 16 p2 c3 ed.
-Various forms of segregation discussed — Aug 4 p1 c1 ed.
-Address on the treatment of free colored people — Aug 11 p1 c1
-Conditions free blacks face seen to be terrible; abolitionists should be more concerned — Sep 1 p2 c3 let.

1840

-Disabilities and oppressions suffered in non-slaveholding states — Mar 7 p1 c1
-Conditions described; seen better off than slaves — Mar 7 p1 c1
-Conditions described; forbidden to participate in the militia — Mar 14, 21 p1 c1

1841

-Seen much better off than southern slaves — Nov 20 p1 c1 ed.

FREE BLACKS (Voting Rights)
-See Voting Rights (Free Blacks) (General)

FREE LABOR
-See Labor (Free)

FREE PEOPLE OF COLOR (New York)

1839

-Agency established in their behalf — Nov 9 p3 c4

FREELAND, SAMUEL W. (New Jersey)

1841

-Marries Mary E. Oscar — Oct 30 p3 c4

FREEMAN, AMOS (New Brunswick, New Jersey)

1837

-Listed as agent for the Colored American — Apr 1 p3 c1

1838

-Describes success of black children at school examinations — Oct 20 p2 c2 let.

1841

-Ordained as a minister — Sep 18 p3 c2
-Account of his ordination and installation — Oct 16 p2 c3

FREEMAN, NANCY (New Haven, Connecticut) (Advertisement)

1841

-Boarding house — Jun 26 p3 c4-Sep 18 p3 c4
-Marries John Mosely — Oct 16 p3 c3

FREEMAN'S NATIONAL CONVENTION

1841

-To convene for nominations of abolitionist political candidates — May 1 p3 c1 let.

FRENCH ANTI-SLAVERY SOCIETY

	<u>1840</u>
-Presents report at London Convention	Aug 1 p2 c1

FRENCH, T.G.

	<u>1838</u>
-His doctor found guilty of manslaughter as a result of his death	Jan 27 p1 c4

FRIENDS OF A FUGITIVE SLAVE (Notice)

	<u>1838</u>
-Notice of who pledged money	Sep 22 p3 c4

FRIENDS OF LIBERTY (Notice)

	<u>1839</u>
-Appeal	Oct 12, 19 p4 c3 Nov 2-16 p4 c3

FUBBARD, JAMES

	<u>1837</u>
-Attends first meeting of the Union Society of Albany	Apr 15 p1 c3

FUGITIVE SLAVE LAWS

	<u>1837</u>
-Free blacks of New York request jury trials for persons arrested as fugitive slaves	Mar 11 p3 c2
-Criticized by the <u>Colored American</u>	Apr 29 p3 c1
-Called unconstitutional	Aug 12 p2 c2
-Description of fugitive slave trial in Philadelphia	Oct 7 p4 c2
	<u>1838</u>
-Florida codes examined	Oct 13 p2 c4
-Colored Freeholders of New York City demand jury trial for fugitives	Nov 3 p3 c3
	<u>1841</u>
-Federal government has no right to intervene in any way	Apr 3 p1 c2

FUGITIVE SLAVES

	<u>1837</u>
-William Dickson tried as a fugitive slave	Apr 15 p3 c3
-Attempt to free him criticized and <u>Colored</u> <u>American</u> agrees with criticism	Apr 29 p2 c4

-New Jersey grants blacks charged as being fugitives the right to trial by jury	Jun 17 p2 c4
-Basil Dorsey held by the court	Sep 2 p4 c2
-Description of a fugitive slave trial in Philadelphia	Oct 7 p4 c2
-Alfred Canada arrested and shipped to North Carolina as a fugitive slave	Dec 2 p3 c4
-Henry Metcher returned to slavery by decision of Judge Betts	Dec 9 p4 c1
-Wife of Gabriel Johnson abducted in Ohio as run-away slave of Kentucky man	Dec 16 p4 c2
	1838
-William Stewart jailed in Louisiana as a slave (a free black from New York)	Jan 27 p2 c4
-Connecticut grants jury trial to accused fugitive slaves	Jun 16 p2 c2
-Sample advertisement for runaway slave	Jul 7 p3 c2
-David Ruggles requests aid in freeing three young men	Jul 28 p3 c4 let.
-Two frenchmen arrested illegally as fugitive slaves	Sep 8 p3 c2
-Audubon relates encounter with runaway slaves	Oct 20 p1 c1
	1839
-Man jailed in Virginia as a fugitive slave, but freed by money and testimony of friends in New York	Feb 2 p2 c3
-Black in Marion, Ohio found innocent	Sep 14 p3 c4
-Futher description of Marion, Ohio incident	Sep 28 p1 c4
-Woman escapes from court room	Sep 28 p4 c1
-Comment on the attempted Marion kidnapping	Oct 19 p1 c5
	1840
-One thousand escape through Ohio to Canada	Mar 21 p2 c1
-Account of New York custody case involving an imported Puerto Rican Slave	Apr 4 p1 c1
-New York blacks warned against kidnappers	Apr 4 p2 c4
-Henry Metscher wrongfully convicted	Apr 18 p1 c1

-Account of an unjustly reclaimed runaway	May 9, 16 p1 c1
-United States law passed granting jury trial to accused runaways	May 23 p3 c1
-New York State passes law granting jury trial to accused runaways	May 30 p3 c3
-Account of aged runaway	Jun 13 p1 c1
-Account of free white woman who spent forty years in slavery before running away	Jun 20 p1 c2
-Account of runaway eventually manumitted	Jul 11 p1 c1
-Account of two women who successfully established their claim to freedom	Jul 11 p1 c3
-Slave imported into New York from Delaware freed	Aug 1 p3 c4
-North-South railroads helpful to escaping slaves	Sep 26 p2 c2
	1840
-New Jersey policy described	Nov 21 p2 c3
-Narrative of a man accused as a fugitive	Dec 5 p1 c2
	1841
-Freedmen unlawfully kidnapped in Louisiana; names listed	Jan 2 p2 c3
-Maine and Georgia in conflict over slave case	Jan 9 p3 c1
-Discussion of plans to aid fugitives in Canada; appeal for funds	Feb 20 p2 c3
-Report on well-being of Canada refugees	Feb 27 p3 c1
-Woman slave flees successfully to Canada	Mar 20 p2 c1
-Three slave-catchers arrested in Ohio	Mar 27 p3 c1
-Federal government has no right to interfere in fugitive slave cases (Joshua Giddings speech)	Apr 3 p1 c2 Apr 10 p1 c1
-New York Governor William Seward's letter to Virginia concerning his refusal to return fugitive slave	May 15 p1 c1
-Black man seized by whites with no trial or legal action	May 22 p2 c4
-Black escapes to Canada	Jun 5 p1 c3
-Example of advertisements for runaways; criticized	Jun 12 p1 c4
-Successful outcome for one runaway reported; case described	Jun 12 p2 c4 Jun 12 p3 c1

-Slaveholder accidentally kills wife while attempting to catch runaway slave — Jun 26 p2 c3
-Success story of two runaways — Jun 26 p2 c3
-Attempted arrest of two children; blacks warned against traps — Jul 31 p2 c3
-Dispute between governors of New York and Georgia — Nov 13 p2 c3
-See also Georgia

G

GAG RULE

1839

-Senator Morris (Ohio) introduces anti-slavery petition; gag rule used — Mar 2 p1 c3

1841

-John Quincy Adams attempts to rescind the gag rule — Jun 12 p3 c1

GAMBLING

1837

-Gambling seen evil that slows emancipation efforts — Mar 11 p1 c3
-Calls on women to work against gambling — Mar 18 p4 c1
-Describes negative effects of gambling — Mar 25 p4 c2
-One of the greatest vices — Nov 11 p2 c1

1838

-Gambling stands in the way of self-improvement — Feb 17 p3 c1
-Horseracing has no practical value — Jul 28 p1 c3
-Visitation of young black men to gambling houses deplored — Sep 8 p2 c3 let.
-Gambling criticized — Sep 29 p3 c2
-Evil fate of gambler and drunkard described — Oct 13 p3 c2

1839

-Gambling a waste of money — Feb 23 p2 c1
-Purchasing lottery tickets leads to ruin — Nov 9 p2 c5

1840

-Lottery playing extensive and costly — Apr 18 p2 c2
-Lottery playing is a fraud and a deception — Oct 31 p2 c3
-Lecture on evils of lottery systems — Nov 14 p1 c3
-Readers urged not to purchase lottery tickets; evils noted — Nov 14 p2 c3; Nov 21 p1 c3; Nov 28 p1 c1
-Lottery gambling illegal in New York — Dec 19 p2 c4

1841

-Lottery gambling a waste of time and money — Mar 6 p2 c4
-Attorney General of New Orleans declares war on lotteries — Apr 17 p2 c4
-Gambling rife in Southern society — Apr 24 p2 c4
-View that District Attorney should crack down on gambling — May 8 p2 c3

GARDNER, REVEREND CHARLES

1837

-Speaks at fourth anniversary of the American Anti-Slavery Society — May 13 p3 c1
-Speaks against the disenfranchisement of blacks at constitutional convention in Pennsylvania — Jun 10 p3 c4
-Elected honorary member of the Mental and Moral Improvement Association (Troy, New York) — Oct 21 p1 c2

GARDNER, W.F. (or S.R. Ward) (Bellville, New Jersey) (Advertisement)

1839

-House for rent — Jun 29 p3 c4; Jul 13 p3 c4-Jul 27 p4 c3; Aug 24 p4 c3

GARNET, HENRY HIGHLAND

1837

-Appointed vice-president of the Colored Young Men of New York City — Sep 2 p1 c1

1838

-Addresses the Female Assistant Society on the virtue of charity — Mar 15 p2 c4

	1840
-Speaks at the seventh anniversary meeting of the American Anti-Slavery Society on black contributions	May 23 p2 c2 May 30 p1 c1
-Appointed secretary of the Colored Citizens of Troy, New York	Jun 6 p3 c3 let.
-His congregation in Troy, New York described	Jul 11 p2 c1 let.
-Suffers amputation of a limb; recovers	Dec 12, 19 p3 c2
	1841
-Urges blacks to sign franchise petitions	Jan 16 p2 c1 let.
-Reports on the New York Legislature's reception of franchise petitions	Feb 13 p1 c3 let.
-Addresses New York City blacks on slavery, prejudice and colonization	Jun 12 p3 c3 let.
-Addresses Albany blacks on political action	Jul 10 p3 c1 let.
-Urges black Christians to aid Africa	Jul 24 p2 c1 let.
-His plan for Troy Convention to aid the *Colored American* revealed	Sep 18 p3 c1

GARRISON, WILLIAM LLOYD

	1837
-Learned from Samuel Cornish	May 13 p2 c2
	1838
-Speech given at the Broadway Tabernacle (August 1, 1838) printed	Aug 18 p1 c1- Sep 1 p1 c1 Sep 22 p4 c2
	1840
-The *Liberator* praises the *Colored American*	Mar 21 p3 c1
-His efforts and motives praised by the Colored Citizens of Boston	Apr 11 p2 c1
-The *Colored American* calls on the *Liberator* to stop backing emigration to Trinidad	Apr 18 p2 c4
-Appointed a delegate to the London Anti-Slavery Convention	May 30 p3 c1
-Praised for his anti-slavery efforts at the London Convention	Jul 18 p3 c1

-His position on the women question at the London Convention discussed — Aug 8 p3 c3

GAVINO, JOSEPH

1837

-Reports the attempted sale of black slaves — Oct 7 p2 c4

GAYLE, ANTHONY (Advertisement)

1837

-Boarding house — Jan 21 p3 c4
Feb 4 p1 c4-
Mar 4 p4 c4
Apr 29 p4 c4
May 20 p3 c4
Jun 10-24 p4 c3

GAYLORD, WILLIS (and Luther Tucker) (Advertisement)

1841

-Editors of The Cultivator; for agricultural improvement — Jan 2 p3 c3

GAZZAM, J.P. (Pittsburgh, Pennsylvania)

1837

-Thanked for his contribution to the salary of the Colored American's editor — Dec 16 p3 c4

GENERAL MEETING OF COLORED CITIZENS (Jamaica, Long Island, New York) (Advertisement)

1841

-Meeting called — Jan 2 p3 c3

GENERAL MEETING OF COLORED CITIZENS (New York) (Notice)

1840

-For extension of the franchise — Nov 28 p3 c3

GENERAL THEOLOGICAL SEMINARY OF THE PROTESTANT EPISCOPAL CHURCH

1839

-Extracts of minutes of the Board of Trustees' meeting — Sep 7 p1 c1
-Comments on its refusal to admit a black student — Sep 7 p2 c1 ed.
-Condemned for racism by the Colored American

GENEVA (New York) COLORED ANTI-SLAVERY SOCIETY

1839

-Holds meeting; resolutions printed — Feb 2 p3 c1

GENIUS OF UNIVERSAL EMANCIPATION

1838

-Published by Benjamin Lundy — Dec 22 p3 c1

GEOLOGY

1839

-Definition of terms — May 18 p4 c4

GEORGIA

1839

-Gorvernor calls on the legislature to get fugitives back from Maine — Jan 12 p3 c2

GIBBONS, MR. (Notice)

1840

-Lecture postponed — Dec 19 p3 c3

GIBBONS, GEORGE W. (Advertisement)

1840

-Carpenter and builder — Nov 21 p3 c4
Dec 5 p3 c4
Dec 26 p3 c4

1841

Sep 4- Oct 16 p3 c4

GIBBS, WILLIAM A. (Advertisement)

1837

-House carpenter and joiner — Dec 9 p3 c4

1838

Jan 13 p4 c4- Feb 17 p4 c3
Mar 3 p4 c3
Apr 12, 19 p4 c3
May 3 p4 c3
Jun 2 p4 c4

GIDDINGS, JOSHUA

1841

-His congressional speech against the Seminole Indian War — Mar 27 p1 c3- Apr 24 p1 c1

-Congressional speech opposing federal intervention regarding fugitive slaves — Apr 3 p1 c2

GILMER, GOVERNOR (Virginis)

1841

-Resigns after refusing to extradite a criminal to New York — Apr 3 p2 c2

GIRL WANTED (Advertisement)

1838

-For chamber work — Apr 12, 19 p4 c3
May 3 p4 c3
Jun 2 p4 c4

1840

-To work for small family — Nov 14, 21 p3 c4

1841

-To work as waitress — May 22 p3 c4

GLASGOW, ISAAC C.

1837

-Cited as an example of good work habits and financial success — Mar 11 p4 c1

GLASGOW EMANCIPATION SOCIETY

1838

-Committee enrolls James McCune Smith as an honorary member — Feb 17 p2 c4 let.

GLOUCESTER, STEPHEN H. (Philadelphia, Pennsylvania)

1837

-Issues call for a convention — Jun 3 p3 c4
-Holds a fair to raise money for his church — Sep 30 p3 c1
-Fund-raising praised — Oct 21 p3 c1 ed.
-Thanks New York citizens for their participation in a fund-raising fair for the Second Presbyterian Church — Nov 4 p3 c3
-Listed as an agent for the Philadelphia Committee — Dec 9 p3 c2
-Listed as a general agent for the Colored American (Pennsylvania, Delaware, Maryland and west Jersey) — Dec 23 p4 c2
-Opens reading room with abolitionists newspapers; letter calls for larger attendance — Nov 18 p2 c2 let.

	<u>1840</u>
-Temperance lectures praised	Jul 4 p2 c4 let.
GLOUCESTER'S CHURCH (Notice)	
	<u>1837</u>
-Fair	Oct 7 p3 c4
GODWIN, MRS. A. (and Mr. William) (Advertisement)	
	<u>1840</u>
-Rooms and bedrooms to let	Mar 14 p3 c3 Mar 21 p3 c4 Apr 11-25 p3 c4
GOODELL, WILLIAM	
	<u>1837</u>
-Describes and compares the extent of color prejudice in America, Europe and India	Mar 11 p1 c1
-Argues against the idea of black inferiority	Mar 18 p1 c1
-Stresses the bad influence of Northern color prejudice upon southern attitudes toward slavery	Mar 18 p1 c2
-Receives a letter calling for people to petition the New York legislature	Mar 18 p4 c2
	<u>1839</u>
-Calls for political action to gain abolition	Oct 19 p3 c2
-Criticized for advocating political intrigue	Oct 19 p3 c2 ed.
-See also American Colonization Society; Racism (United States)	
GOODRICH, WILLIAM (Little York, Pennsylvania)	
	<u>1838</u>
-Listed as agent for the <u>Colored American</u>	Jan 13 p4 c4
GOODWELL, WILLIAM A. (Goodwill) (Advertisement)	
	<u>1838</u>
-Rooms to let	Apr 12 p3 c4 Apr 19 p3 c4 May 3 p4 c3 Jun 2 p4 c4
	<u>1841</u>
-Apartments to let	Jul 24 p3 c3
GOODWIN, WILLIAM A. (Advertisement)	
	<u>1840</u>
-Rooms and bedrooms	Aug 1 - Sep 12 p3 c4

	1841
-Rooms and bedrooms to let	Mar 27-Apr 24 p3 c4
GORDON, GEORGE WILLIAM	
	1840
-Addresses the Boston Young Men's Society on the evils of the lottery system	Nov 14 pl c3 Nov 21 pl c3 Nov 28 pl cl
	1841
-Describes his visit to Philadelphia	Jan 23 pl c4 let.
GORDON, ROBERT C.	
	1837
-Listed as a member of the Philadelphia Committee	Dec 9 p3 c4
GRAHAM'S BIBLICAL LECTURES (Notice)	
	1840
-To be delivered	Dec 4 p4 c4
	1841
	Oct 16 p3 c3 Oct 30 p4 c4
GRAHAM'S LADY'S AND GENTLEMAN'S MAGAZINE	
	1841
-Praised	Jun 12 p3 cl
GRAHAM, CHARLES	
	1838
-Death eulogized	Feb 17 p3 cl
GRAIN, NATHANIEL (Advertisement)	
	1837
-Gentlemen's shaving and hair dressing	Jul 8, 15 p4 c4
GRANT, THEODORE (Oswego, New York)	
	1837
-Praised as a true abolitionist	Aug 26 p3 c4
-Listed as an agent for the <u>Colored American</u>	Sep 16 p3 cl
GRANVILLE, JONATHAN (Port au Prince, Haiti)	
	1839
-Death eulogized	Jul 27 pl cl
GRAVES, HENRY	
	1840
-Denied a pushcart license in New York City	May 9 p2 cl let.
-On the injustice of his treatment	May 30 p2 c2 ed.

GRAY, ALONZO (Sanquoit, New York)

1838

-Listed as an agent for the Colored American — Sep 29 p3 c4

GREECE
-See Athens

GREEN, JAMES (and John Osborne) (Advertisement)

1837

-Dry goods store — Jan 14 p3 c4-
Jun 24 p4 c4
Sep 30 p3 c4-
Dec 9 p4 c3

1838

Jan 13 p4 c3
Jan 20 p4 c2
Feb 17 p4 c3
Oct 27 p4 c3-
Dec 29 p4 c3

1839

Jan 12 p2 c4-
Mar 16 p4 c4
May 11 p4 c4
Jun 8 p4 c3-
Nov 23 p4 c4

GREEN, WILLIAM (Springfield, Massachusetts)

1841

-Marries Parthena Peters — Oct 30 p3 c4

GREEN, WILLIAM P.

1839

-Accuses the Colored American of encouraging support from pro-slavery politicians — Oct 19 p3 c4 let.
-His accusations refuted — Oct 19 p3 c4 ed.

GREENE, LOWLAND (Plainfield, Connecticut)

1837

-Cites benefit of good work habits — Mar 11 p4 c1

GREW, HENRY (Philadelphia)

1840

-Participates at the London Convention — Aug 1 p1 c1

GRIDLEY, JOHN

	1838
-Expresses sympathy with the anti-slavery movement	Oct 20 p4 c2 let.

GRIFFIN, MR.

	1837
-Attempted to free William Dickson who was on trial as a fugitive slave	Apr 29 p2 c4

GRIFFIN, WILLIAM P. (Albany, New York)

	1837
-Listed as an agent for the Colored American	Mar 11 p4 c4

GRIMKE, ANGELINA E. (and Sarah)

	1837
-Writes a reply to Clarkson on slavery in Washington, D.C.; criticizes Congress's support for the slave trade	Aug 26 p1 c1
	1838
-Angelina holds meetings on the subject of memorials to the Massachusetts Legislature	Mar 3 p3 c2
-Abolitionist efforts praised by a British sympathiser	Mar 15 p4 c1 let.
-Reply to Sarah Grimke's "Duties of Woman" which is critical	Sep 22 p4 c1 let.

GUIGNON, PETER

	1837
-Elected treasurer of the Societie des Amis Reunis	Dec 23 p3 c4

GUNNISON, J.

	1837
-Criticizes the church	Apr 29 p3 c3

GURNEY, JOSEPH J.

	1841
-English philanthropist on an anti-slavery visit to France	Oct 2 p3 c1

H

HAGUE, MR.	
	<u>1837</u>
-Speaks at Temperance Jubilee	Apr 1 p3 c1
HAIR-DRESSER (Advertisement)	
	<u>1838</u>
-Apprentice wanted	Jan 20 p3 c4 Feb 17 p4 c3 Mar 3 p4 c3- May 3 p4 c2
HAITI	
	<u>1837</u>
-Praised for achievements as an independent republic	Mar 11 p3 c1
-Successful educational institutions cited	Mar 11 p3 c1
-United States criticized for not recognizing Haitian independence	Mar 18 p2 c4
-Beauty of the island praised	May 13 p2 c4
-Trade, manufactures, and exports discussed	Jul 1 p1 c1
-Three Haitian businessmen face racism in New York City	Jul 1 p1 c1
-Room in Haiti for United States blacks	Jul 1 p1 c1
-Haitians lack the Christian religion	Aug 5 p4 c2
	<u>1838</u>
-Independence Day celebration described	Mar 3 p2 c3 let.
-Southern slaveholder comments favorably on political and social conditions	Mar 15 p1 c1 let.
-Haitian example to the world of universal emancipation	Mar 15 p2 c1 ed.
-Trip through the country described	Mar 22 p1 c1 let.
-Lack of color prejudice noted	Mar 22 p1 c2 let.
-Description of Haiti's legal requirements regarding immigration	Mar 29 p1 c1
-Treaty with France described; $400,000 annual indemnity included	Apr 5 p1 c2
-Description of the agricultural successes of the black population	Apr 12 p2 c1 let.
-Reimbursement arrangements for Haitian colonists following independence	Apr 12 p2 c2 let.

-Restrictions on trade to be removed by Great Britain	Aug 4 p3 c1 let.
-Commercial relations between the United States and Haiti would be advantageous - low prices described	Aug 25 p4 c1
-Crew of a Haitian vessel scandalously treated by America	Sep 15 p2 c4
-August 1st celebration described	Sep 22 p2 c1
-Lack of a commercial treaty with Haiti deplored	Oct 20 p1 c4
-United States government criticized for not acknowledging Haitian independence; Haitian government unhappy	Nov 3 p2 c1 ed.
-<u>Colored American</u> calls for diplomatic recognition	Nov 18 p3 c1
	<u>1839</u>
-Memorials presented to the House of Representatives request recognition	Jan 19 p3 c2
-<u>Colored American</u> calls for diplomatic recognition; lists the amount of trade	Feb 2 p2 c2
-A short history of the Haitian revolution and a call for diplomatic recognition	Feb 23 p1 c2
-Britain concludes a commercial treaty with Haiti	Mar 9 p2 c2
-One hundred and one United States emigrants reach Puerto de Plato	Sep 28 p3 c3
-Rumors of political disorder received	Nov 23 p2 c4
	<u>1841</u>
-Recognized by England	Jan 23 p3 c1
-Haitians show great charity to German castaways	May 1 p1 c4
-Lecture on the Haitian Revolution	Aug 7 p1 c3 Aug 21 p1 c1 Sep 18 p1 c1- Oct 16 p1 c1
-See also Boyer, President; Granville, Jonathan; Jinnings, William S.; L'ouverture, Toussaint	

HAITIAN ABOLITION SOCIETY

	<u>1837</u>
-Letter cites social and political progress of Haitian people	Mar 11 p3 c1 let.

HALL, PRISCILLA (MRS.)(Advertisement)	
	1839
-Dress and cloak maker	Jun 29 p3 c4 Jul 13 p3 c4- Nov 23 p4 c4
HALLOCK, SIMNEY (Advertisement)	
	1839
-Will cut, make, and repair children's clothes (also repair gentlemen's clothes)	Jun 8 p3 c4- Oct 5 p4 c4
HAMBLETON, WILLIAM	
	1837
-Listed as the second Mate of the New Bedford brig owned by free blacks	Mar 11 p4 c2
HAMILTON, CHARLES	
	1841
-Dies	Oct 16 p3 c3
HAMILTON LYCEUM (Notice)	
	1840
-Formerly the New York Phoenixonian Literary Society	Dec 4 p3 c3
HAMILTON, ROBERT	
	1837
-Traces development of the convention movement	Oct 7 p3 c3-4 let.
HANCOCK, JOHN	
	1839
-Praised for the part played in freeing America from Britain	Sep 28 p1 c1
HANSON, AUGUSTUS WILLIAM	
	1838
-Appointed agent for the <u>Mirror of Liberty</u> and the New York Committee of Vigilance	Sep 29 p3 c4 Oct 6 p4 c3 Oct 20 p4 c2
-Address to the Political Association on unconditional emancipation and equality	Sep 15 p1 c1
	1841
-Urges a missionary convention	Jul 3 p1 c2 let.
-Calls for a missionary convention	Jul 17 p1 c4 let. Jul 24 p4 c1 let

HARDENBRUGH, SAMUEL

1837

-Married to Sarah Decker by the Reverend Theodore S. Wright — Apr 1 p3 c3

1838

-Reports on a person wrongly accused of attempted kidnapping — Feb 17 p2 c4
-Appointed vice-president of the Political Association — Jun 16 p2 c3

1841

-Urges public expression of gratitude for a new anti-slavery law in New York — Aug 28 p2 cl let.

HARMONY TEMPERANCE ASSOCIATION (Westchester, Pennsylvania)

1840

-Meeting held to encourage the cause of Temperance — Dec 5 p3 cl

HARRIS, ANDREW (Burlington, Vermont)

1837

-Addresses the fourth anniversary celebration of the Female Benevolent Society of Troy (New York) — Apr 1 pl c3
-Speaks on the observance of the Sabbath — Apr 1 pl c4
-Speaks on temperance — Apr 1 p2 cl
-Attends the first meeting of the Union Society of Albany — Apr 15 pl c3
-Listed as an agent for the Colored American — Sep 30 p3 c4

1841

-Ordained in Philadelphia — May 8 pl c3
-Urges blacks to elect representatives who reflect their interests — Dec 4 pl cl

HARRIS, HENRY

1840

-Marries Maria Thomas — Sep 19 p3 c4

HARRIS, THOMAS

1838

-Appointed a vice-president of the Political Association — Jun 16 p2 c3

	1841
-Eulogy	Mar 27 p1 c1
-See also Buffalo Library Association	

HARRIS, WILLIAM (Toronto, Canada)

	1838
-Listed as an agent for the Colored American	Jan 13 p4 c4

HARRISON, WILLIAM HENRY

	1840
-Declared unworthy of the votes of American abolitionists	May 28 p2 c2
-Many true abolitionists plan to vote for him	Aug 29 p2 c3
	1841
-Visit to Pittsburgh noted	Feb 20 p3 c2
-Arrival in Washington noted	Feb 27 p1 c3 let.
-Inaugural address criticized	Mar 13 p2 c3
-Inauguration described	Mar 13 p3 c1
-Eulogy	Apr 10 p3 c1
-His funeral in New York City described	Apr 17 p2 c3
-Day of national fasting and prayer proclaimed to mourn him	Apr 17 p2 c4

HATCH, SAMUEL (Chelsea, Vermont)

	1837
-Sends $1.50 to the Colored American	Jun 17 p3 c4

HAWES, REVEREND J.

	1838
- Supports the views of the American Anti-Slavery Society	Feb 10 p4 c2

HAYES, PETER B. (or Samuel Slee) (Notice)

	1839
-School teacher wanted for Poughkeepsie colored school	Mar 16 p3 c4

HAYNES, REVEREND LEMUEL

	1837
-Memoirs published by Dr. Cooley	Mar 11 p4 c1
-Biography published	Apr 8 p1 c4

HAZZARD, EBENEZER (Advertisement)

	1837
-Listed as a member of the lecture committee of the Philomathean Society	Dec 16 p3 c4

	1839
-Rooms to let	Feb 23 p3 c4 Mar 2, 16 p4 c4
HEALTH (Diet)	
	1838
-Advice regarding diet	Apr 19 p1 c4 May 3 p4 c1
-Vegetarian diet recommended	Jul 14 p4 c1
	1839
-Injurious effects of tea discussed	Mar 9 p2 c3
-Uses of fruit	Aug 31 p3 c5
	1841
-How to cook green peas	Jul 17 p4 c4
HEALTH (General)	
	1839
-Woolen clothing aggravates rheumatism	Feb 16 p3 c1
-Advantages of bathing	Mar 16 p1 c1 ed.
-On how to remove foreign bodies from the eye	Dec 7 p1 c2
-On the cure of a club-foot and rhinoplasty	Dec 7 p4 c2
	1840
-Many diseases are incurred by intemperance	Apr 4 p4 c2
-A cure-all recipe for childhood afflictions	Sep 5 p3 c1
-How to avoid and care for colds; cures for the deaf	Nov 14 p4 c3
-Reduction in lifespan of man noted	Dec 5 p3 c2
	1841
-Improvements in surgical techniques noted	Jan 16 p4 c3
-Story of a strangulated hernia	Feb 6 p4 c3
-Discoveries on cancer noted	May 1 p3 c4
-Consumption a major cause of death; remedy for lightning shock given; cure for deafness	Jul 3 p3 c2
-Remedy for diarrhea	Aug 14 p4 c4
HEALTH ALMANAC (Advertisement)	
	1840
-For sale	Nov 13 p3 c4 Dec 4 p3 c4
	1841
	Sep 25 p3 c4- Oct 16 p3 c4

HECTER, THOMAS (Lowell, Massachusetts)

1837

-Listed as agent for the Colored American — Sep 30 p3 c4

HEDDEN, ELIJAH (Advertisement)

1841

-Apartments to let — Mar 27 p3 c4- Apr 24 p3 c4

HENDERSON, JAMES H. (Advertisement and Notice)

1839

-Boot and shoe manufactory — May 11 p4 c4- Sep 14 p4 c3

1840

-Evening school at the Second Presbyterian Church of Color — Oct 17 p3 c4; Nov 7 p3 c4

HERALD OF FREEDOM
-See Colonization (General)

HEZLETT, GEORGE

1838

-Justifies withdrawal of support for colonization — Oct 27 p1 c4 let.

HICKS, AARON

1841

-Marries Frances Ann Highland — Nov 13 p3 c3

HICKS, JOSEPH (and Caesar Lyon) (Advertisement)

1838

-China, glass, earthenware — Jun 2 p3 c4- Jul 14 p2 c4

1839

May 11 p4 c3- Nov 23 p4 c4

1840

Mar 14 p3 c4- Jul 4 p3 c4

HICKS SOCIETY (Notice)

1837

-Regular monthly meeting — Feb 4 p3 c4

HIGGINS, CAESAR

1837

-Elected second vice-president of the Cranberry Moral Reform Society — Aug 12 p4 c1

HIGHLAND, FRANCES ANN

1841

-Marries Aaron Hicks — Nov 13 p3 c3

HILL, J.C.

1837

-Sends $3.00 to the Colored American — Apr 15 p3 c4

HILL, J.W. (Advertisement)

1840

-Wood turning — May 9 p3 c4-Sep 12 p4 c4

HILTON, J.H.

1837

-Denounced for attacking the Colored American — Oct 14 p3 c2

HINDUISM

1837

-The caste system is the main barrier to improvement among Hindus — Nov 11 p1 c3

-Hindu caste system compared to color prejudice in the United States — Nov 11 p1 c4

HINTON, FREDRICK A.

1837

-Speaks against the disenfranchisement of blacks at a constitutional convention in Pennsylvania — Jun 10 p3 c4

-Issues a call to a meeting of the American Moral Reform Society — Aug 5 p3 c3

-Criticizes the convention for refusing to recognize its "color" — Sep 2 p2 c4

-Encourages use of the term "colored man" — Nov 11 p2 c2

-Listed as a member of the Philadelphia Committee — Dec 9 p3 c4

1838

-Praises the pursuits of the Political Association — Jul 14 p3 c2

HISTORY (United States, Colonial)

1840

-Colonists of Plymouth and Jamestown compared — Apr 11 p1 c3

HOCKNEY, JOSEPH (Virginia)	
	1837
-Attends the annual Virginia Abolition Convention	May 27 p1 c3
HODGES, WILLIAM J. (Advertisement)	
	1839
-Part of a house to let (williamsburgh, Long Island)	Jun 8 p3 c4- Nov 23 p4 c3
HODGKIN, THOMAS (London)	
	1840
-Criticized for attempting to vindicate the American Colonization Society	Oct 31 p2 c2
HOFFMAN, T. (Advertisement)	
	1841
-Rooms to let	Mar 6, 13 p3 c4
HOGARTH, GEORGE (Advertisement)	
	1840
-Upper part of house to let	Nov 13 p3 c4
	1841
	Oct 30 p3 c4
HOLCOMB, J. (Brandon, Vermont)	
	1841
-Distinguishes African missionary work from colonization	Aug 21 p2 c1 let.
HOLIDAY (Emancipation Day, British West Indies)	
	1837
-August 1st seen as a great holiday; celebrates the emancipation of British slaves	Jul 29 p3 c1
	1838
-Descriptions of celebrations in New York City, Boston, Fall River, and Newark	Aug 11 p3 c2
-Descriptions of celebration in New York City, Albany, Madison (New York) and Lynn (Massachusetts)	Aug 18 p3 c2
-Description of celebration and resolutions passed at Utica (New York) and Cincinnati (Ohio)	Aug 25 p2 c2

-Description of celebration and speeches in Haiti	Sep 22 p2 c1
	<u>1839</u>
-Celebration in Detroit (Michigan)	Aug 17 p3 c2
-Celebrations described	Aug 17 p3 c3
-Preparations in Detroit (Michigan)	Aug 17 p3 c4
-Celebration in Wilmington (Delaware)	Aug 24 p2 c2
-Celebrations in Newark (New Jersey)	Aug 24 p2 c3
-Celebration in Troy (New York)	Sep 28 p2 c3
	<u>1840</u>
-Celebration in Wilmington (Delaware)	Aug 15 p2 c2
-Celebrations around the United States	Aug 15 p2 c3
	<u>1841</u>
-Celebrations urged	Jul 17 p3 c1
-Public meetings urged to commemorate emancipation	Jul 17 p3 c2 let.
-Description of Williamsburg celebration	Jul 24 p2 c3 Aug 14 p1 c2
-Should be honored by Americans	Jul 24 p2 c4 let.
-Poughkeepsie (New York) celebration described	Aug 21 p1 c1 let.
-Wilmington (Delaware) celebration described	Sep 28 p1 c4 let.
HOLIDAYS (Independence Day)	
	<u>1838</u>
-4th of July deemed a hypocritical celebration	Jul 14 p3 c3
-Description of a celebration by a church congregation	Jul 21 p3 c2 let.
	<u>1839</u>
-Meaning of celebrations evaluated	Jul 13 p2 c1 ed.
	<u>1841</u>
-Plans for celebrations noted	Jul 3 p3 c1
-Celebration in Schenectady (New York) described	Jul 24 p1 c2 let.
HOLLAND	
	<u>1838</u>
-Very few in jail there due to their educational system	Dec 1 p3 c1
	<u>1841</u>
-Educational system described and praised	Sep 25 p4 c2

HOLMES, J.N. (New York, New York)

1837

-Listed as an agent for the Colored American — Mar 11 p3 c4

HOLMES, CHRISTIAN (Virginia)

1837

-Writes an address to Virginians portraying the evils of slavery — May 27 p1 c3

HONDURAS

1839

-Description of emancipation there — Jun 15 p3 c3

HOPEWELL, MRS. PAULINA

1838

-Death eulogized — Jun 9 p3 c4

HOPPER, JOHN

1837

-Attacked in Savannah (Georgia) because he is an abolitionist — Apr 29 p3 c2

-Story of his trip to Savannah — May 6 p4 c1

HOPPER, JOSIAH (and John) (Advertisement)

1837

-Drugs and medicines — May 6 p3 c4- Jul 15 p4 c4; Aug 12 p4 c3; Sep 2 p4 c3- Sep 23 p4 c3

HORNER, J.M.

1837

-Elected corresponding secretary of the Roger Williams Anti-Slavery Society — Apr 15 p3 c3

HORTON, MR.

1837

-Speaks at a Temperance Jubilee — Apr 1 p3 c1

HOUSEHOLD EXPENSES

1839

-Can be reduced by putting the wife in charge — Aug 17 p1 c3

HOUSEKEEPER (Advertisement)

1839

-Wanted — Mar 16 p3 c4

HOVEY, SYLVESTER

	1838
-Extract of letters from the West Indies	Jul 14 p1 c4 let.
-Maintains that the success of West Indian emancipation is more threatened by planters than by the conduct of blacks	Jul 14 p1 c4

HUMANE MECHANICS SOCIETY (Philadelphia) (Notice)

	1838
-Oration	Jun 30 p3 c4

HUNT, REVEREND MR. (Newark, New Jersey) (Advertisement)

	1838
-Accommodations (Recommended by the Colored American)	Aug 4,11,25 p3 c4

HUNT, REVEREND THOMAS

	1841
-Brings news of poor conditions for blacks on Trinidad	Jan 16 p3 c1
-Welcomed on arrival from Trinidad and praised	Feb 6 p2 c2
-Gives evidence of poor treatment of blacks on Trinidad	Feb 6 p2 c3
-Returns to Newark, New Jersey to speak on Trinidad	Feb 13 p3 c1

HUNTINGTON, MARY ANN

	1841
-Marries James Coles	Oct 30 p3 c4

HUNTINGTON, DAVID (Advertisement)

	1838
-Watch and clock maker	Mar 22, 29 p3 c4 Apr 19 p4 c2 May 3 p4 c3 Jun 2 p4 c4- Dec 29 p4 c4
	1839
	Jan 12 p2 c4- Mar 2 p4 c4 May 11 p4 c4- Nov 23 p4 c5
	1840
	Mar 21 p4 c4- Dec 26 p4 c4
	1841
	Jan 9 p4 c4- Dec 25 p3 c4

HUTSON'S INTELLIGENCE OFFICE (Advertisement)	
	1837
-Two small girls wanted for hair-working business	Oct 14 p3 c4- Nov 11 p4 c2
	1839
-Change of address	Jun 1 p3 c4- Jun 29 p4 c4 Jul 20 p4 c4 Aug 17 p4 c4 Nov 23 p4 c4
	1840
-Clocks for sale	Sep 5 p3 c4- Nov 7 p3 c4
-Colored waiters (male and Female); agency advertisement	Nov 13 p3 c3 Nov 20 p3 c4
-Clocks for sale	Dec 12 p3 c4
	1841
-Two story house to let	Jan 30 p3 c4
-Rooms to let; house to let	Feb 13, 20 p3 c4
-Cooks and waiters wanted; apartments to let	Apr 3 p3 c3,4- May 22 p4 c4
-Clocks for sale	Aug 21 p3 c4
-Advertisement for agency; waiters	Oct 9,16 p3 c3
-Advertisement for agency	Dec 4,25 p3 c4

I

IMMIGRANTS (New York City)	
	1837
-Mayor calls them a burden on the city	Jun 24 p1 c1
IMMORTALITY	
	1839
-Discussed	Sep 14 p1 c2
INDEPENDENCE DAY	
-See Holidays (Independence Day)	
INDIA	
	1838
-Caste distinctions abolished in English churches there	Oct 6 p1 c2

1840

-Hindu school described Mar 21 p4 c2
-View of slaves-agricultural and domestic Apr 25 p3 c3
-Calcutta described Sep 26 p4 c2

1841

-Slavery tolerated by the British government there Sep 18 p2 c2
-See also Hinduism

INDIAN MEDICINES (Advertisement)

1838

Sep 29 p3 c4-Dec 8 p4 c3

INDIANS (American, General)

1838

-General Jessup's treatment of them criticized Feb 3 p2 cl

1840

-Whites encourage them to drink liquor Mar 28 p4 cl

INDIANS (American, Cherokee)

1838

-Their appeal to the Senate is printed; calls for abrogation of the treaty of New Echota Apr 5 pl cl
-Their appeal to the citizens of the United States for justice in the sale of tribal lands Apr 12 pl cl
-Passing through Nashville, Tennessee Dec 1 p3 cl

INDIANS (American, Seminole)

1841

-Cannot be legally forced by the United States government to pay owners for runaway slaves Mar 27 pl c3
-Speech on their oppression in the Florida War over fugitive slaves Apr 3 pl c2
Apr 10-24 pl cl
-Being moved to new homes in the west Apr 24 p3 cl
-Take over Tampa May 1 p2 c4
-Frontier settlers reported killed by them Aug 21 p3 c2

INDUSTRY

1839

-Mechanical trades and domestic industry should be encouraged — Mar 9 p1 c2 ed.

1840

-Protectionism of American manufactures is the only road to prosperity — May 23 p2 c1

INTEGRATION

1837

-Blacks can integrate if they have money — Jul 29 p2 c1

-Blacks should not be cut off from their own people by integration — Jul 29 p2 c1

1838

-Blacks must intermix in order to enjoy full rights and priveleges — Mar 22 p3 c2 ed.

-Blacks should not establish separatist communities — Jul 28 p2 c3

-See also Separation of the Races

INTERMARRIAGE (Racial)

-See Marriage (Interracial)

IOWA

1839

-Proposed as an area for colonization by free blacks — Aug 31 p3 c3 let.

1841

-Advantages of settlement listed — Apr 3 p3 c1

IRISH

1838

-Joke refers to Irish as "Hard drinkers" — Aug 18 p2 c4

IRVING, JUDGE

1837

-Judge in case of alleged fugitive slave, George Thompson (alias Ben) — Apr 8 p3 c1

-See also Thompson, George (alias Ben); Wilkinson, General

ISAACS, JOHN

1840

-Marries Hennetta Welden — Sep 19 p3 c4

J

J.M.D. (Advertisement)

	1840
-Wants room and bedroom	Oct 31 p3 c3- Nov 14 p3 c4

JACKSON, ANDREW

	1837
-Calls free blacks of Louisiana to fight in War of 1812, September 21, 1814; praises black participation after War of 1812	Mar 4 p1 c1

JACKSON, J.M. (Advertisement)

	1839
-House to let	Feb 23 p3 c4 Mar 2,16 p4 c4

JACKSON, JOHN

	1837
-Married to Hagar Olives by the Rev. Theodore S. Wright	Apr 1 p3 c3

JACKSON P. (Pittsburgh, Pennsylvania)

	1837
-Elected vice-president of the Pittsburgh Moral Reform Society	May 13 p1 c4

JACKSON, THOMAS S.

	1838
-Marries Martha L. Peterson	Jun 9 p3 c4

JAMAICA
-See Renshaw, Charles Stewart; Smith, Sir Lionel; West Indian; West Indies (Jamaica)

JAMAICA BENEVOLENT SOCIETY
-See White, Samuel

JAMAICA CONVENTION

	1840
-Resolves to remedy abuses against blacks and calls for a general convention; recommendations seconded	May 9 p3 c1-2

JAMES, REVEREND JOHN ANGEL (Birmingham, England)

	1840
-Anti-slavery activities noted	Nov 21 p2 c2

JANNEY, DANIEL (Virginia)

1837

-Writes address to Virginians portraying the evils of slavery — May 27 p1 c3

JAY, JOHN

1841

-Unjust biography criticized — Feb 27 p4 c1

JAY, PETER

1837

-Spoke against the restriction of the black franchise at the 1821 New York Constitutional Convention — Mar 4 p1 c2

1838

-Testimonial against the restriction of black voting rights — Mar 22 p2 c2

JAY, JUDGE WILLIAM

1837

-Gives ten dollars to the Colored American — Apr 1 p3 c4

1841

-Defends the Amistad prisoners and accuses the owner of fraud — Jan 2 p1 c3 let.
-Honored in England; his address at the ceremonies printed — Mar 27 p4 c2

JEFFERS, WILLIAM L. (and Reverend I.G. DeGrasse) (Notice)

1841

-Memoirs of and eulogies for each — Sep 18 p3 c3

JEFFERSON, THOMAS

1837

-Paper prints Jefferson's reply to letter from Benjamin Banneker — May 29 p2 c1

1839

-Quote from his Notes on Virginia about man's quest for freedom — Jun 15 p3 c1

1840

-Advocated liberty for whites; a tyrant toward blacks — Mar 21 p2 c1

JESSUP, GENERAL

1838

-His treatment of the Indians criticized — Feb 3 p2 cl

JEWS

1838

-Prejudice against Jews discussed — Jun 9 p3 c4 ed.

JINNINGS, THOMAS L. (Boston, Massachusetts) (Advertisement)

1837

-Moves a resolution in praise of the Colored American — Mar 18 p3 cl

1838

-Elected vice-president of the Political Association — Jun 16 p2 c3

1840

-Dentist — Aug 22 p3 c4-Oct 10 p3 c4; Nov 28 p3 c4; Dec 26 p3 c4

1841

Feb 13 p3 c4

-Abused on a Massachusetts railroad — Jun 19 p2 c4

JINNINGS, WILLIAM S. (Boston, Massachusetts)

1837

-Listed as an agent for the Colored American — Mar 4 p4 c4
-Sends $5.00 to the paper — Jul 15 p3 c4
-View that all must support the Colored American — Jul 22 p2 c3

1838

-Describes farming successes of Haitian blacks — Apr 12 p2 cl let.
-Describes reimbursement arrangements for Haitian colonists following independence — Apr 12 p2 c2 let.
-Chairman of public meeting of "Political Association" New York — Jul 14 p3 c2
-Vice-president of the Political Association — Oct 20 p3 c3

1840

-Dies and is eulogized — Oct 3 p3 c2

JOBS, CHARLES (Shrewsbury, New Jersey) (Advertisement)

1841

-Board and lodging — Jul 3 p3 c4-Sep 11 p3 c4

JOCELYN, SIMEON S.

1837

-Praises the Colored American as an important auxiliary to the cause of abolition and the advancement of colored Americans — Mar 11 p3 c2
-Praised the Colored American as a powerful means of elevating blacks — Mar 18 p3 c1
-Listed as a member of the committee of arrangements for the fourth anniversary meetings of the American Anti-Slavery Society — Apr 8 p3 c2

1839

-Appeals for donations to the Amistad defense fund — Oct 19 p4 c3

JOHN W. RICHMOND, THE (Steamboat)
-See Shipping Industry

JOHNSON, MR. (Elmira, New York)

1837

-Sends $2.25 to the Colored American — Apr 5 p3 c4

JOHNSON, BENNET (Advertisement)

1838

-Furs dyed, cleaned and repaired — Dec 8 p3 c4-Dec 29 p4 c3

JOHNSON, EZRA R. (New Bedford, Massachusetts)

1837

-Elected to the committee to study slavery in Washington, D.C. — Nov 18 p3 c3

JOHNSON, MRS. H. (Philadelphia) (Advertisement)

1837

-Fancy millenary and dress-making — Jun 24 p3 c4-Sep 30 p4 c3

JOHNSON, MRS. H. (and Mrs. E. Appo) (Philadelphia) (Advertisement)

1837

-Want ten apprentices for milenary (sic) work — Sep 30 p3 c4- Nov 11 p4 c4

JOHNSON, JOHN H.

1837

-Attends the first meeting of the Union Society of Albany — Apr 15 p1 c3

1840

-Speaks at London Convention — Aug 1 p1 c1

JOHNSON, NATHAN (New Bedford, Massachusetts)

1837

-Elected to the committee to study slavery in Washington, D.C. — Nov 18 p3 c3

JOHNSON, RICHARD (New Bedford, Massachusetts) (Advertisement)

1837

-Listed as an agent for the Colored American — Mar 4 p4 c4
-Listed as an agent for the New Bedford brig owned by free blacks — Mar 11 p4 c2
-Sends $4.50 to the Colored American — Apr 22 p3 c4
-Chairman of the Colored Citizens of New Bedford — Nov 18 p3 c3

1840

-Five or six first-rate tailors wanted — May 9 p3 c4- Jun 20 p3 c4 adv.

JOHNSON, VICE-PRESIDENT RICHARD M.

1837

-Recognizes the power of Congress to abolish slavery in the District of Columbia — Aug 26 p1 c4 ed.

1840

-Visit to New York noted; criticized for sanctioning slavery — Jul 18 p2 c4

JOHNSON, W.P. (Advertisement)

	<u>1837</u>
-Swamp leather and French calf-skins	Jan 14 p3 c4- Sep 23 p4 c4
	<u>1838</u>
-Boot and shoemaker	Dec 15 p3 c3- Dec 29 p4 c3
	<u>1839</u>
	Jan 12 p2 c4- Mar 16 p4 c4
	May 11 p4 c4
	<u>1841</u>
-Authorized to sell Sears' Pictorial Illustrations of the Bible	Jan 9 p3 c3

JOHNSON, WILLIAM P. (New York)

	<u>1837</u>
-Secretary of the People of Color; group passes a resolution in favor of the <u>Colored American</u>	Mar 18 p3 c1
-Listed as an agent for the <u>Colored American</u>	Nov 18 p3 c4
	<u>1838</u>
-Appointed a vice-president of the Political Association	Jun 16 p2 c3
-Discussion with Thomas Van Renssalaer	Dec 22 p3 c3
	<u>1839</u>
-Elected president of the New York Anti-Colonization Meeting	Jan 19 p1 c1
-Denies implication of the New York Vigilance Committee in its libel suit against the <u>Colored American</u>	Aug 31 p2 c1 let.
	<u>1840</u>
-Listed as a general agent for the <u>Colored American</u>	Apr 25 p2 c2
-Describes journey to the Jamaica Convention	May 16 p2 c1 let.
-Describes the free black community of Troy, New York	Jul 11 p2 c1 let.
-Addresses the colored citizens of Wilmington, Delaware	Nov 7 p2 c1 let.
-Tours the Philadelphia area	Nov 7 p2 c4

-Describes the colored community in Philadelphia and Wilmington, Delaware	Nov 14 p1 c1 let.
-Will speak on the character of the New York Colored American	Dec 5 p3 c1
-Addresses a temperance meeting in Westchester, Pennsylvania	Dec 5 p3 c1
-Describes his trip to Westchester, Pennsylvania	Dec 12 p1 c3 let.
-Describes Philadelphia trip and meetings he attended	Dec 26 p1 c1 let.
	1841
-Describes his stay in New Jersey	Jan 30 p1 c2 let.
-Describes his visit to the black communities in Morristown, New Jersey	Jun 19 p1 c2 let.
-Reports on travels in New York	Jul 17 p1 c1 let.
-Describes July 4th celebrations in Schenectady, New York	Jul 24 p1 c2 let.
-Describes and praises the work of the Albany Mechanical Society	Jul 31 p2 c1
-Lectures Albany citizens on abolition	Jul 31 p2 c1
-Extract from his letter	Sep 25 p2 c1 let.
-Criticizes the New York and Harlem Railroad for racial prejudice	Sep 25 p2 c2 let.
-See also New York Vigilance Committee	

JOHNSTON, J.

	1840
-Information wanted about Horace Hitchcock, in New Orleans; held as a slave but claims he is free	Jun 6 p3 c4- Sep 12 p4 c4

JOHNSTON, WILLIAM (Advertisement)

	1841
-Boarding	May 29 p3 c4 Jun 19 p3 c4- Sep 18 p3 c3

JONES, MR. (Notice)

	1840
-Lecture on sacred music	Dec 5 p3 c3

JONES, ALEXANDER

1837

-Praises the idea of blacks moving to more hospitable countries — Jul 22 p2 c2

JONES, REVEREND HENRY

1838

-New York Colored American praises his book, Principles of Interpreting the Prophesies — Mar 15 p2 cl

JONES, REVEREND JOHN

1837

-Elected an honorary member of the Mental and Moral Improvement Association Troy, New York — Oct 21 pl c2

JOURNAL OF COMMERCE
-See Phrenology

JOURNAL OF EDUCATION AND WEEKLY MESSENGER

1841

-Begins publication and is recommended by the Colored American — Jun 26 p2 c3
-Critically evaluated — Aug 14 pl cl let.
-Its errors pointed out — Sep 11 p3 c2
-See also Pennington, Reverend James W.C.

JUVENILE ANTI-SLAVERY SOCIETY

1838

-Plans a public meeting — Oct 27 p3 c4

1839

-Donates $5.00 to support the Colored American — Nov 23 p3 c2 let.

JUVENILE DAUGHTERS OF RUSH (Notice)

1837

-Anniversary noted — Sep 16 p3 c4

K

KA-LE

	1841
-Letter of Amistad prisoner to John Quincy Adams printed	Mar 27 p2 c1 let.

KAPITEIN, JAN

	1839
-Memoir printed about life in Africa	Feb 9 p4 c1

KENT, CHANCELLOR JAMES

	1837
-Spoke against slavery at the 1821 New York Constitutional Convention	Mar 11 p2 c2

KENT, LUCIA ANN (Concord, New Hampshire)

	1838
-Dies and is eulogized by the Colored American	Mar 29 p3 c3

KENTUCKY

	1839
-Governor Clarke urges capital punishment for those who help slaves escape	Jan 12 p3 c2
-Sends two ambassadors to Ohio to discuss the problem of runaway slaves	Feb 2 p3 c4

KILBURN, D.

	1837
-Issues anti-slavery resolutions passed at a Methodist conference	Jun 10 p1 c3

KIMBALL, JOSEPH

	1837
-Arrival on St. Thomas noted	Mar 18 p1 c2
-Denies validity of criticisms of newly liberated West Indies blacks	Nov 4 p1 c1
	1838
-Co-authors Emancipation in the West Indies	Mar 22 p3 c2

-Retires and is eulogized by the <u>Colored American</u>	Apr 5 p2 c1
-Anti-slavery work praised	May 3 p2 c4 ed.
-His last days described	May 3 p2 c4 let.
-Describes his missionary work in Kingston, Jamaica	Jul 21 p1 c3

KING, RUFUS

	<u>1837</u>
-Spoke against slavery at the 1821 New York Constitutional Convention	Mar 11 p2 c2

KING, THOMAS (Norwich, Connecticut)

	<u>1837</u>
-Listed as an agent for the <u>Colored American</u>	Sep 16 p3 c1

KINSMAN, RUFUS (Notice)

	<u>1841</u>
-Information wanted on the above freeman	Feb 6,13 p3 c4

KNAPP, ISAAC (Boston)

	<u>1838</u>
-Prepares a book on the history of the slavery controversy	Mar 29 p1 c3

KOHNE, FREDERICK

	<u>1838</u>
-Eulogized for his philanthropic bequests	Jul 14 p2 c1

L

LABOR (Free)

	<u>1837</u>
-Endangered by the slave system; John C. Calhoun's speeches cited as proof	Apr 1 p3 c2
-Slavery seen at war with the interests of free laborers	Sep 1 p4 c2
	<u>1839</u>
-Erie canal listed as a triumph of free labor	Jun 15 p2 c4
-Northern workers urged to beware of both slaveholders and capitalists	Aug 3 p1 c3

	1841
-Report of London Anti-Slavery Convention	Jan 23 p1 c1
	Feb 13 p1 c1
	Feb 20 p1 c1
-Description of European laboring class	Apr 24 p4 c1
-See also London Anti-Slavery Convention	
LADIES BOOK	
-See The Lady's Book	
LADIES LITERARY SOCIETY	
	1837
-Holds meeting	Sep 23 p3 c2
-Holds fair for the benefit of the New York Colored American and the New York Vigilance Committee	Dec 23 p3 c4
	1840
-Holds lecture	Dec 25 p3 c4
LADY'S BOOK, THE	
	1841
-Praised and described	Apr 24 p3 c1
-Contents praised	Aug 7 p2 c2
LAND	
	1839
-Amount of public land listed by the state	Jan 26 p3 c2
LARNED, MR.	
	1837
-Speaks in favor of temperance	Apr 1 p1 c4
LATIMER, BENJAMIN (Albany, New York)	
	1837
-Vice-president of the Union Society; attends meeting	Apr 15 p1 c3
LAWRENCE, MRS. G. (Advertisement)	
	1840
-Boarding house	May 23 p3 c4
LEAVITT ANTI-SLAVERY SOCIETY	
	1838
-Stresses need for black peoples' efforts to gain emancipation	Jun 16 p2 c4

LEAVITT, JOSHUA (Philadelphia)

1837

- -Praises the New York Colored American as an important auxiliary to the cause of abolition and the advancement of colored Americans — Mar 11 p3 c2
- -Praises the Colored American as a powerful means of elevating blacks — Mar 18 p3 c1
- -Praised by William Yates as a great force behind black unity — Jun 24 p2 c3 let.

1838

- -British sympathiser praises abolition efforts — Mar 15 p4 c1 let.

1839

- -Appeals for donation to Amistad defense fund — Oct 19 p4 c3

1840

- -Deplores divisions in the American Anti-Slavery Society — May 23 p2 c2 let.

1841

- -Plans to lecture on English corn laws to Phoenixonian Society noted — Apr 3 p3 c4

LEBANON

1838

- -Buckingham lecture — Mar 3 p1 c1

LEE, REVEREND JOHN (Bellville, New Jersey)

1837

- -Listed as an agent for the Colored American — Sep 16 p3 c1

LEGAL DISCRIMINATION (Blacks)

- -See Blacks (Legal Discrimination)

LEGGETT, WILLIAM

1839

- -Appointed Charge des Affaires at Guatemala — May 18 p3 c5
- -Dies and is eulogized — Jun 15 p3 c2
- -His deeds seen as his best monument — Aug 3 p1 c3

1840

- -On running for political office — Apr 18 p1 c3 let.

LEGREE, JOSEPH (Advertisement)

1837

-Tailoring and steam scouring — May 27 p3 c4-Jul 8 p4 c3

1838

-Clothes dressing, tailoring and repairing — Oct 27 p3 c4

LEONARD, ISAAC (and John Parkis) (New Haven, Connecticut) (Advertisement)

1839

-Boarding House — Jun 29 p3 c4-Nov 23 p4 c4

1840

Mar 14 p3 c4-Apr 25 p4 c4

LEWIS, A.D. (Pittsburgh, Pennsylvania)

1837

-Elected Vice-president of the Pittsburgh Moral Reform Society — May 13 p1 c4

LEWIS, ISRAEL

1839

-Raised money for the Wilberforce Colony, but did not give it to the colony — Feb 16 p1 c1

-Letter requests verification of his credentials as agent of the Wilberforce Colony — Jul 13 p3 c2 let.

-Repudiated by the Wilberforce Colony as an imposter — Jul 13 p3 c2 let.

-Committee of Colored Citizens of New York repudiates his fund-raising activities — Jul 13 p3 c3 let.

-Repudiated by the New York Colored American — Jul 13 p3 c3 ed.

-Members of the Wilberforce Colony criticize him — Aug 24 p3 c5

LEWIS, JOEL W. (Boston, Massachusetts) (Advertisement)

1838

-Temperance boarding house — Jul 7 p3 c4-Nov 17 p4 c4

1840

Aug 15 p2 c4

LEWIS, REVEREND JOHN	
	<u>1841</u>
-His anti-slavery work praised	Jan 23 p2 c3
-Discussed controversies within the New Hampshire Anti-Slavery and Abolition Societies	Feb 13 p3 c2 let.
-Discusses the state of anti-slavery feeling in Maine	Jul 3 p1 c3 let.
LEWIS, THOMAS	
-See Ruggles, David (General)	
<u>LIBERATOR</u> SUBSCRIBERS (Notice)	
	<u>1838</u>
-Notice to those who intend to move	Mar 22, 29 p3 c4 Apr 19 p3 c4 May 3 p4 c3
LIBERIA	
	<u>1838</u>
-Poor living and health conditions in Liberia described (from the <u>Liberia Herald</u>)	Apr 5 p2 c2
-Colonist describes poor social and physical conditions	Dec 8 p1 c3 let.
-Departure of missionaries to Liberia noted	Dec 15 p2 c1
-Missionary efforts praised; but colonization criticized	Dec 15 p2 c2 ed.
-Gerrit Smith suggests chartering ships to bring back dissatisfied Liberian colonists	Dec 15 p3 c1 let.
-Must stop slave trade	Dec 22 p2 c3
-Agriculture not developed	Dec 22 p2 c3
	<u>1839</u>
-Poor state of agriculture discussed	Feb 23 p1 c1
-Ship returns with progress report of colony	Jul 20 p3 c2
-People who emigrate there become sickly	Aug 24 p2 c5
-Criticized for proposing to help stop slave trade	Nov 2 p1 c5
	<u>1840</u>
-Health conditions bad	Mar 28 p1 c4
-News of hostilities between natives and colonists received	Jun 6 p2 c4 Jun 13 p1 c3

-Immigrants die Oct 24 p3 c1
-Report received of bad conditions in the colony Dec 5 p3 c2 let.
-May be involved in the slave trade Dec 26 p2 c3

1841

-Assertion that blacks want to go there is a hoax Apr 24 p3 c1
-Colonization unsuccessful Oct 2 p1 c3 let.
-See also American Colonization Society; Colonization; Smith, Gerrit; Sheridan, Louis; Tappan, Lewis

LIBERIA HERALD
-See American Colonization Society; Liberia

LIBERTY

1839

-Blessings described Aug 17 p2 c2

LIBERTY PARTY

1840

-Nominates Gerrit Smith for governor of New York Aug 22 p2 c4
-In general disrepute for presidential election Aug 29 p2 c3
-Colored American says to vote for the Liberty Party for all offices Oct 3 p2 c2 ed.
-Support should be given to the party Oct 10 p1 c1
-Tickets for New York, Vermont and Massachusetts Oct 10 p2 c2
-People urged to support the Liberty Party Oct 24 p1 c4 ed.
-Election returns show lack of support except by pure abolitionists Dec 5 p2 c2

1841

-Supported by the Colored American Oct 2 p2 c3 ed.
-See also Anti-Slavery Nominating Convention; Birney, James; The Tocsin of Liberty

LIBRARIES

1837

-Philadelphia library has 1,000 volumes Dec 2 p3 c1

	1838
-Advice on building home libraries	Jul 7 p4 c1
	1840
-Dialogue on their value	Apr 4 p3 c2
LIGHTFOOT, MADISON (Detroit, Michigan)	
	1838
-Listed as agent for the Colored American	Jul 14 p4 c4
LINCHCUM, NIMROD	
	1840
-Death eulogized	Sep 19 p2 c3
LIPPINS, JOHN (Newark, New Jersey) (Advertisement)	
	1839
-Boarders wanted	Jun 8 p3 c4- Nov 23 p4 c4
LITERACY	
	1837
-"English Shepherd's Story" stresses value of literacy	Mar 25 p4 c2
LITERARY AND LIBRARY UNION (Notice)	
	1841
-Meeting noted	Apr 10 p3 c4 Jun 5 p3 c4 Oct 2,9 p3 c3
LITERARY SOCIETIES	
	1837
-Praised as a means of demonstrating mental self-improvement for free blacks	Mar 11 p2 c1
	1839
-Praised as important institutions	Oct 5 p2 c1 ed.
LITTLEFIELD, BENJAMIN C.S.	
	1841
-Marries Emeline Brushell	Oct 30 p3 c4
LIVELY, DOCTOR (Notice)	
	1837
-Lecture on physiology and hygiene	Nov 4 p3 c4

	1839
-Will preach	Jun 8 p3 c4- Jun 22 p4 c4
-Lectures on Hebrew	Jul 13 p3 c4- Nov 23 p4 c3
	1840
-Wants to purchase herbs	Jul 18 p3 c4 Aug 1 p3 c4 Aug 15, 22 p4 c4
LIVELY, W.M. (Advertisement)	
	1837
-Cures rheumatism	Apr 8 p3 c4- Jun 24 p4 c3
LOCKPORT, NEW YORK	
	1839
-Blacks send compliments and money to the <u>Colored American</u>	May 11 p3 c4
LOCO-FOCOS	
	1838
-Accused of allying with abolitionists to conspire against the union	Oct 27 p4 c1
LONDON ANTI-SLAVERY CONVENTION	
	1840
-Importance of world anti-slavery convention stressed	Apr 4 p2 c3
-Idealized in prose portrait	Jul 18 p3 c1
-Praised	Jul 25 p2 c1
-Account of its proceedings and speeches	Jul 25 p2 c1 Aug 1 p1 c1 Aug 8 p1 c1
-Women not admitted as delegates	Aug 8 p2 c3
-Speeches at conference	Aug 15 p1 c1 Aug 22 p1 c1
-Efforts praised by Lord Palmerston	Nov 7 p2 c4 let.
-Efforts praised by Governor Pennington of New Jersey	Nov 7 p3 c4 let.
	1841
-Report on free labor	Jan 23 p1 c1 Feb 13 p1 c1 Feb 20 p1 c1
-Replies to its circulars express abhorrence of slavery	Apr 17 p2 c3
-Account of its addresses to sovereign powers	Apr 24 p1 c3 May 1 p1 c1

L'OUVERTURE, TOUSSAINT

	1841
-Lionized; exploits praised	Jul 24 p1 c4
-See also Haiti	

LOVEJOY, REVEREND ELIJAH P.

	1837
-Account of the destruction of his presses	Sep 16 p2 c2
-Account of his murder	Nov 25 p2 c2
-Meeting of black citizens held in Lovejoy's behalf	Dec 2 p3 c3
-Meeting planned to express sympathy for his widow and orphans	Dec 16 p3 c4
-Martyrdom of Lovejoy viewed as a source of inspiration	Dec 23 p3 c1
-Proceedings of meeting to sympathize with widow recounted	Dec 23 p3 c1
	1838
-Article eulogizes his death (from the Boston Recorder)	Jan 13 p4 c1
-Lovejoy's last speech	Jun 9 p2 c1
	1839
-Letter of condolence to his widow from Haiti	Jul 20 p1 c4 let.
-His sacrifice praised	Jul 20 p1 c4 let.

LOVERIDGE, P. (Agent of Schools For Colored Children) (Notice)

	1838
-School Reopening	Sep 1 p3 c4
	1841
-Urges attendance at public schools	Apr 3 p1 c1 let.
	Apr 24 p2 c1 let.
	Aug 21 p1 c1 let.
-Urges children to prepare for the new school year	Aug 28 p2 c1 let.

LUNDY, BENJAMIN (Hennepin, Illinois)

	1838
-Thanked for his great services	Aug 4 p3 c3
-Publishes the Genius of Universal Emancipation; Colored American says no living man has done more for blacks	Dec 22 p3 c1 ed.
	1839
-Dies and is eulogized	Sep 14 p3 c5

	1841
-Sonnet to his memory	Apr 3 p3 c2
LUSHINGTON, DOCTOR	
	1840
-Speaks against slavery	Aug 29 p1 c3
LYNCH LAW	
	1841
-Two runaways in Arkansas lynched for murdering their master	Jan 23 p3 c1
-Many criminals put to death in Mississippi	Sep 11 p3 c3
-See also Mob Violence	
LYNN (Massachusetts)	
	1839
-Citizens sign petition calling for repeal of law banning interracial marriages	Feb 23 p2 c3
	1840
-Law and petition described	Apr 25 p1 c1
-See also Methodist Anti-Slavery Society	
LYON, CAESAR (and Joseph Hicks)	
	1838
-China, glass and earthenware advertised	Jun 2 p3 c4-Jul 14 p2 c4
LYON, LYMAN (Advertisement)	
	1840
-Garden open for refreshments	Jun 20 p3 c4-Aug 22 p3 c4

M

MADISON COUNTY ABOLITIONIST	
	1841
-New paper recommended by the Colored American	Oct 16 p2 c3
MAHAN, J.B.	
	1838
-Letters from prison printed; claims he is in prison because of his temperance reform activity	Nov 18 p1 c3
	1839
-Praised for his abolitionist activities	Nov 16 p3 c5
MAINE ANTI-SLAVERY CONVENTION	
	1837
-Color prejudice prevailing there noted	Mar 25 p4 c2
	1841
-Convention call issued; topics discussed	Sep 18 p4 c1 Sep 25 p4 c1
MAMMOTH CAVE (Danville, Kentucky)	
	1837
-Description of cave	Sep 23 p1 c2
MAN AND WIFE WANTED (Colored) (Advertisement)	
	1837
-To take charge of small home	Dec 30 p3 c4
	1838
	Jan 13-27 p4 c3
MANUMISSION	
	1840
-Slave family freed in Virginia	Apr 4 p1 c4
-South Carolinian frees eleven slaves	Jul 4 p2 c4
-Runaway slave obtains manumission	Jul 11 p1 c1
MARINE BENEVOLENT SOCIETY (Notice)	
	1839
-Meeting of stewards and cooks	Sep 28 p3 c4

MARRIAGE (Interracial)

	1837
-Blacks and whites should be allowed to intermarry	Aug 26 p3 c3

MARRIAGES (Notice)

	1837
-John Butler to Mary Ennalls	Jan 14 p3 c4
-John Jackson to Haver Parkens; Marcus A. Dye to Julia A Ray	Apr 15 p3 c3
-John Brown to Jane Johnson	Aug 26 p3 c4
-Hercules White to Bulah Gilbott; Charles Warmsly to Elmira Duncan	Sep 23 p3 c4
-Abner Clarkson to Eliza Firman	Oct 14 p3 c4
-Henry Wilson to Mary Carter (Lancaster, Pennsylvania); George Cork to Susannah Neilson (Columbia, Pennsylvania); Stephen Jackson (Clarkstown, New York) to Martha Ann Wells (Newark, New Jersey)	Oct 28 p3 c4
-Thomas Smith (Philadelphia, Pennsylvania) to Elizabeth Conner; Theodore C. Breshow Vedat to Henrietta W. Boot	Nov 11 p3 c4
-H. C. Turner to Rachel Sanders (Carlisle, Pennsylvania); Horace Stevenson (Williamstown, Massachusetts) to Violetta S. Swain (Trenton, New Jersey); William J. Wilson to Mary Anne Garrett Marshall	Nov 18 p3 c4
-James Durkin to Clementa Young (Washington)	Nov 25 p3 c4
	1838
-Henry Carter to Catharine Jane Fields; William Randall Peal to Elizabeth Ann Brown	Jan 13 p3 c4
-Henry Stevens to Ellen Canumn; Robert J. Cowes to Ann Churl (Bethlehem, Pennsylvania)	Jan 27 p3 c4
-Samuel R. Ward (Maryland) to Emily E. Reynoldson; Edward Landrick to Sarah Ann Carold (Washington)	Feb 3 p3 c4
-George F. Robinson to Mary Salisbury (Providence, Rhode Island); Sylvester Daily to Hoppy Watt	Feb 10 p3 c4
-Thomas C. Graham to Eliza Day; James Brown (Pennsylvania) to Eliza Brown (Maryland)	Mar 3 p3 c4

-Thomas Johnson to Jane Ann Garrison	Apr 12 p3 c4
-Stephen A. Poussien to Maria M. Joseph; John H. Millar to M. Anderson (Philadelphia); Abraham Grosse (Delaware) to Ann Majors (Lynchburgh, Virginia)	Apr 19 p3 c4
-Peter Nott (Hartford, Connecticut) to Ann DeGruder (Baltimore, Maryland); Francis Prince Graham (Charlestown, South Carolina) to Judah Jackson (New York)	Jun 2 p3 c4
-George Roberts to Ann Whopper (Philadelphia, Pennsylvania); Thomas S. Jackson to Martha Louisa Peterson	Jun 9 p3 c4
-William Jewell (New Jersey) to Nancy Day	Jun 30 p3 c4
-Immanuel Edwards to Jane Eliza Butler	Jul 7 p3 c4
-Aaron Wood to Florinda Brown	Aug 4 p3 c4
-Reason Hopkins to Mary Jane Coles (Philadelphia)	Aug 11 p3 c4
-Mr. Jennifer McKeel (Philadelphia) to Mary M. Bonswell; Caesar Lyons to Dianah Beckers	Aug 18 p3 c4
-Nathan Smith (Barbadoes) to Ann Bradford (Baltimore, Maryland); Thomas Smith to Elvina Smith (Washington); William Green (Philadelphia) to Susan Francis (Connecticut)	Aug 25 p3 c4
-Cyrus Mitchell to Caroline Tuel; Francis Champion (Pennsylvania) to Sarah Stevens (Delaware)	Sep 1 p3 c4
-Thaddeus Jackson to Ann Smith; Eli Avery to Rachel Edgar; Arthur Dawson to Lucy Seaman	Sep 8 p3 c4
-Reverend Hiram Wilson to Hannah Maria Hubbard; William S. Jinnings (Boston) to Maria Smith	Sep 22 p3 c4
-Peter Morgan to Emma Wilson	Oct 6 p3 c4
-Mr. Murray (Elizabethtown, New Jersey) to Elizabeth Ming; John Davis to Diana Hutherson	Oct 20 p3 c4
-William Mann to Amelia Armstrong; John Paul Vatab to Amelia Ann Campbell (Fall River, Massachusetts) in Newport, Rhode Island;	

Elias Conover (Monmouth, New Jersey) to Margaret B. Davis (Shrewsbury, New Jersey)	Nov 3 p3 c4
-James Peterson to Julia Ann Brinckerhoff	Nov 10 p3 c3
-Miller Pierce to Elizabeth Ann Charwick; John Odle to Mary Nichols; Allen Cook to Mary Elizabeth Peterson; Elwer Michael Reason to Marie Louisa Coulier; Frederick Woodston to Martha Judson	Dec 29 p3 c4
	1839
-George H. Dixon to Tamar Sharp; Lewis Payne to Rachel Bell (Washington)	Feb 9 p3 c4
-Henry Amberman to Halda Ana Acley; John Scott to Barbery Broekenbary (Westerly, Rhode Island)	Feb 23 p3 c4
-Diana Cisco to Samuel Armstrong; Henry Jackson to Elizabeth Southard	Mar 2 p3 c4
-Thomas Jackson to Leah Downing	Mar 9 p3 c4
-Samuel A. Smith (Philadelphia) to Sarah C. Jinnings;	Mar 16 p3 c4
-Thomas Jackson to Charlotte Ellis	May 11 p3 c4
-William Bradford to Josephine Anderson (Baltimore)	May 18 p3 c4
-Richard P. Jinnings (Boston) to Christiana Butler (Troy, New York)	Jun 8 p3 c4
-William Thompson to Susan Sears	Jun 15 p3 c4
-John Givens(Tampa, Florida) Margaret Hamilton (Richmond, Virginia)	Jun 29 p3 c4
-James Arfa (Canton, China) to Ann Josephine Kneeland	Jul 13 p3 c4
-Issac Evans to Martha Chapman; Mr. Scudder to Dianah Augustus; Caesar C. Jenson to Hester Cassidy (New Jersey); Thomas A. Innes to Frances S. Duffield	Jul 20 p3 c4
-Thomas Thompson to Mary Smith; John Holbert (Delaware) to Catherine Graham	Jul 27 p3 c4

-Thomas Willis to Sarah Harris; Francis Hasbrock to Clarissa Jefferson	Aug 17 p3 c4
-John S. Vincent (Nantucket, Massachusetts) to Frances D. Johnson; Henry Green (Nantucket, Massachusetts) to Nancy Cuffee; Peter Lewis to Sarah Jane Peterson	Aug 31 p3 c4
-Elizabeth Le B. Stuckney (Newburyport, Massachusetts) to Lewis C. Gunn (Philadelphia)	Oct 5 p3 c4
-George Borde (Nassau, New Brunswick) to Mary Ann Winte (Liverpool, England)	Oct 12 p3 c4
-Jacobs F. Platt to Amelia B. Matthews; John L. Esteve to Clorice Duplessy; John Williams to Nancy Miller; John M. Dolanto to Felila Francis; John Dolphin to Jane N. Green; Charles I. S. Goodrich to Caroline Virginia Brooks; William H. Nobel to Harriet Jones Brooks	Nov 9 p3 c4
-Luther Bradish to Mary E. Hart; Enoch E. Mills to Elizabeth O'Brien	Nov 23 p3 c4
	1840
-John J. Zuille to Rachel Ann Nichols	Mar 14 p3 c2
-H. Primus(North Branford) to Lydia Phillips (New Haven); Peter Williams (Middletown, Connecticut) to Sarah M. Brown (Norwich, Connecticut); George H. Rogerson to Rebecca Anna Carrs	Mar 21 p3 c3
-Jacob McCoy (Somerville, New Jersey) to Elizabeth Follett (Bound Brook, New Jersey)	Apr 11 p3 c3
-Charles Mosley (New Haven, Connecticut) to Caroline Smith (Patterson, New Jersey)	Apr 18 p3 c3
-Thomas Johnson to Eliza Bunn	May 2 p3 c3
-Abraham T. Abrahams to Jane Mitchell (Charleston, South Carolina)	May 16 p3 c3
-Alto Lyons to Mary Marshall	May 23 p3 c4

-Henry Wolcott to Hannah Mott	Jun 13 p3 c4
-Edward B. Lawton to Eliza A. Logan	Jul 11 p3 c4
-Charles W. Downer to Sarah Collier	Jul 11 p3 c4
-Isaac J. Honeywell to Susan Johnson; Henry Thomas to Julia Ann Campbell; Moses Burke to Violet Solix; James Bowers to Betty Jane Hammond; John Wilson (Baltimore) to Jane James	Jul 18 p3 c3
-Peter Vogelsang to Theodocia B. DeGrasse	Aug 1 p3 c4
-Aaron Cisco to Rosetta C. Livingston (Charleston, South Carolina); Tunis E. Campbell to Harriet Nelson (Boston); Archibald Call to Betsy Heyman; Peter Sampson to Ellen Mercer	Sep 5 p3 c3
-John Isaacs to Hennetta Welden; Henry Emery to Margaret Dolton; Henry Harris to Maria Thomas; Jason Cuffee to Louisa Cotten	Sep 12 p3 c4
-James Hall to Catharine Mott	Sep 26 p3 c3
-Samuel Barber to Maria Hart; Albert Dixon to Sophia Navilett Pior	Oct 3 p3 c3
-Henry L. Reavels to Ann Closson; Stephen Barrell to Elizabeth Johnson	Oct 10 p3 c4
-Isaac Sailor to Rachel Ann Cox; David Anderson to Mary Predegross; Peter Taylor to Mary Ann Montgomery; Henry Bell to Ann F. Jackson; John Trecel to Julia Caesar	Oct 17 p3 c4
-Reverend John Lyle to Elizabeth Williams	Oct 31 p3 c3
-Wilson Lewis to Elizabeth Craig; Robert Simms to Hetty Ann Ward	Nov 7 p3 c3
-Jarmin Wesley Logues to Caroline E. Storum	Nov 14 p3 c4
-George Robinson to Malinda Johnson; Cornelius T. Hendrickson to Amelia Cufferson; Thomas Woods to Elizabeth Douglass	Nov 21 p3 c3

James Jones to Jane Armstrong; T. George Washington to Margaret Lyons; Jeremiah Simmons to Phoebe Basco; Nathaniel Weeks to Sarah Harris; Peter Demond to Rebecca Thompson; Erastus Jenkins to Eliza Thompson; Reverend P. Proll to Louisa Freeman (Newark, New Jersey) — Dec 5 p3 c3

-Dr. Merriwether to Jane Butler; John Demack Revalpons to Harriet Elizabeth Rowe; Edward H. Snider to Mary A. Grimes — Dec 19 p3 c3

-John Topp, Jr. to Eliza Johnson — Dec 26 p3 c3

1841

-John Bly to Ann Harden; John Marshall to Ann Jones; John Hansbrook to Sarah Brown; Peter Domenus to Emmaretta Cooke; John Stephens to Isabella Servents; Zachariah Brogden to Matilda Ireland; Lawrence Beckman to Rebecca Brown — Jan 2 p3 c3

-William Mason to Mary Ellis; Lewis Powers to Mercy Ann Deming; Isaac Powers to Elisabeth Omsto — Jan 9 p3 c3

-Charles James to C. Howe; David B. Snowden to Catharine Thompson; William Nicholsen to Catharine Mendiney — Jan 16 p3 c3

-Samuel Burns to Mary Williams; Anthony Phillips to Tamer Wood; Littleton Stockeley To Rachel Briskus; Francis Barnes to Mary Jane Screwmaker; George Washington Myers to Diana Fuller — Jan 23 p3 c4

-Abner Brown to Ann Butler; John Brinkoff to Ellen Harris; Joseph Holden to Mary Ann Roberson; Joseph Watkins to Ann Hicks; William Wilberforce to Eliza Marker; James Thompson to Matilda D. Jennings — Feb 27 p3 c4

-Peter Jackson to Sarah Ward — Mar 6 p3 c4

-Peter Johnson to Eileen Freeman — Apr 10 p3 c3

-Titus Strong to Mary Ann Richards; Samuel Wyckoff to Mary A. Williams; Robert Banks to Caroline Dickson;

Jacob Zimerson to Ellen A. Decker; D. S. Thomas to Mary Yorks; Joseph Gale to Hannah Jackson	May 1 p3 c3
-Nathaniel Galligo to Sarah Eliza Jackson; Nathaniel Smith to Mary Benjamin; Abraham Houston to Susan Franklin; Joseph Thomes to Jane Thomes; Peter Johnson to Lydia Johnson; Jeremiah Brown to Elizabeth Ward; Timothy Hampton to Hester Haines	May 8 p3 c3
-Lewis S. Robinson to Caroline Copover; W. Simmons to Rachel Ward; Samuel S. Woods to Abigail Elizabeth Rankins; Joseph Lawrence to Jane Cornell; Thomas Kershaw to Mary C. Welsh; John Dickson to Eliza Sansers; George Wilson to Mary Jane Scudder	May 15 p3 c4
-John Peterson to Eliza Glasco; William Brown to Edith Ann Depee	May 22 p3 c4
-Francis Smith to Sarah Vandaveer (Albany, New York); John Huffton to Sarah Root (Albany, New York); John Shepherd to Jane Cease (Albany, New York); William Francis Pashay to Susan Cooley; William H. Conner to Antoinette Roberts	May 29 p3 c4
-George Pilpot to Catharine Botts	Jun 5 p3 c3
-Henry Williams to Elizabeth Wheeler; John Parker to Julia Ann Clark; Edward Johnson to Pheobe Winston	Jun 12 p3 c3
-George Nott to Theodocia Freeman (Hartford, Connecticut); Benjamin Steadman to Henrietta Offley (Boston, Massachusetts); William LaCroix to Lucy A. Reed; Hugh Hinson to Deborah Simmons	Jun 26 p3 c3
-James Davis to Sarah Chase	Jul 3 p3 c3
-Benjamin Decker to Lydia Curl (See July 17); Francis Brewer to Mary Green	Jul 10 p3 c3
-Benjamin Dixon to Julia Curl (Correction)	Jul 17 p3 c3

-John Hudson to Emily Doughty; Abram M. Nahar to Elizabeth S. Ray; P. Robinson to Edvina Franklin; James Pierce to Emeline Turner; Henry Fields to Cornelia Anthony; Henry Chellis to Mary Sargent; Aaron Potter to Maria Jones	Jul 24 p3 c3
-Silas Harris to Ann Francis; George Roberts to Carr Bell; Moses Anderson to Abby Jane Bennett; Clement C. Fraser to Mary Ann Seaborne	Jul 31 p3 c3
-Thoms Harris to Jane Johnson	Aug 7 p3 c3
-Reverend H. H. Garnet to Julia Williams; Elympus P. Rogers to Harriet E. Sherman; John Francis to Jennette Creaser; Joseph Martin to Mary Ann Smith	Aug 21 p3 c3
-William Stevenson to Ann Jones; Theodore Dalton to Susan Latting; Peter S. Potter to Eliza W. Graham	Aug 28 p3 c3
-William Newton to Cynthia Clarke	Sep 4 p3 c3
-Henry Hicks to Elizabeth Simpson	Sep 11 p3 c3
-Moses K. Harris to Louisa Jane Smith; George Russell to Susan Brough; Richard Williams to Nancy Cornell; John Mead to Charlotte Cornell	Sep 18 p3 c3
-Henry Artis to Ann Elizabeth Steuben Charles Arden to Martha Francis; Francis Bird to Jane Burnet; Alexander Duncan to Henrietta M. Collins; Issac Duncan to Harriet Scudder; Samuel Duncan to Mary Ann Conover; John Nevious to Eve Scudder	Sep 25 p3 c3
- Alexander Baker to Frances Brooks; Charles Smith to Eliza Cabill; Gilbert Walker to Sarah Phillips	Oct 9 p3 c3
-John Mosely to Nancy Freeman; Samuel Atkins to Mary Edwards	Oct 16 p3 c3
-Samuel W. Freeland to Mary E. Oscar; William Green to Parthena Peters; James Cowes to Mary Ann Huntington; Benjamin G.S. Littlefield to Emeline Brushell; George L. Freeman to Sophia Jane Mitchell	Oct 30 p3 c4

-Aaron Hicks to Frances Ann Highland; Henry Williams to Abby Seaman; Stephen Brooks to Cornelia Sniffen; Henry W. Eggains to Margaret Phillips; Henry Shaw to Phoebe Armstrong — Nov 13 p3 c3

-Theodore Wright to Harriet B. Sammons — Nov 20 p3 c3

-George T. Downing to Serena L. DeGrasse; John Weeks to Mary Spellman; John Berry to Elizabeth Berry; Charles Wilson to Elizabeth Plain; John Butler to Martha Ann Fuller; David Robinson to Elizabeth Gardner; Isaac Clayton to Mary K. Smith; George A. W. Gibbons (Philadelphia) to Ann B. Poole; Charles Sandford to Charlotte M. Bevard; Charles H. Crool to Mary Jane Conberry — Dec 4 p3 c4

-Isaac Wright (Philadelphia) to Rosetta Morrison (Hartford, Connecticut); Moses K. Harris to Louisa Coal; Joseph Pierson to Ann Martin; Henry Peu to Phoebe Armstrong; Henry P. Hall to Eliza Ann Loudon — Dec 25 p3 c4

MARS, S.S.

1837

-Pledges support for the Colored American — Jul 8 p2 c2 let.

MARSHALL, EDWARD F. (Notice)

1839

-Opening evening school — Sep 14 p3 c4-Nov 23 p4 c4

MARTHA'S VINEYARD

1838

-Described — Jun 30 p1 c4

MARTINEAU, HARRIET

1837

-Exerpt of her work published — Sep 9 p4 c2

1841

-Her book, The Hour and the Man, reviewed — Feb 20 p2 c4

MARYLAND

1839

- Governor says abolition has influenced free blacks in Maryland against colonization — Jan 12 p3 c2

MARYLAND COLONIZATION CONVENTION

1841

- Formed by Maryland ministers; criticized — Jun 19 p2 c3
- Meeting of New York citizens called to consider it — Jun 19 p3 c4
- Colored citizens of Maryland warned against the Colonization Convention — Jun 26 p3 c1 let.
- Condemned by anti-colonization meeting in New York City — Jul 3 p2 c4 let.
- Colored citizens of Maryland warned against its work — Jul 3 p3 c2 let.
- Condemned at meeting of Albany blacks — Jul 10 p3 c1 let.
- Condemned by meeting of Buffalo blacks — Jul 31 p1 c3

MASON, JOSEPH (Painesville, Ohio)

1837

- Listed as agent for the <u>Colored American</u> — Dec 23 p3 c3

MASSACHUSETTS

1840

- Legal actions against slavery — Mar 14 p1 c4

1841

- Railroads discriminate against blacks — Sep 4 p3 c1

MASSACHUSETTS ABOLITION SOCIETY

1839

- Establishes department headed by Jehiel C. Beman to improve situation of blacks — Sep 28 p3 c4
- Creates special department to benefit colored youth — Nov 23 p4 c3 let.

<u>MASSACHUSETTS ABOLITIONIST</u>

1839

- Newspaper edited by A.A. Phelps, but soon to be edited by Elizur Wright seen to be a good paper — May 11 p3 c3

1841

- Changes name to <u>The Free American</u> — Mar 27 p3 c1
- See also Wright, Elizur

MASSACHUSETTS ANTI-SLAVERY SOCIETY

1837

-Convention resolutions call for Christian ministers to uphold the cause of human freedom — Oct 7 p3 c3

1840

-Efforts and motives praised by Colored Citizens of Boston — Apr 11 p2 c1

MASSACHUSETTS LEGISLATURE

1837

-House of Representatives passes a resolution attacking denial of right of petition by the United States Congress — Apr 1 p3 c2

-House of Representatives passes resolution calling for abolition in Washington, D.C. — Apr 1 p3 c2

-Senate calls for abolition in Washington, D.C. — Apr 8 p3 c2

1838

-Passes anti-slavery resolutions — May 3 p2 c4

1841

-Criticized for tolerating racist marriage laws — Feb 13 p2 c2

MASSILLON (Ohio) COLORED ASSOCIATION

1840

-Pledges moral and financial aid to the _Colored American_ — Mar 7 p2 c2 let.

-Praised by the _Colored American_ — Mar 7 p2 c2

MAXON, MRS. (Utica, New York)

1837

-Her school for blacks rated highly — Apr 1 p4 c3

MAY, JOHN N.

1838

-Appointed chairman of the Colored Citizens of Newark, New Jersey — Jul 21 p3 c3

MCDONALD, GOVERNOR (Georgia)

1841

-Involved in dispute with Governor of New York over a fugitive slave — Nov 13 p2 c3

MCKEOWN, LOVEJOY

1837

-Death in Kentucky eulogized — Dec 9 p3 cl

MCKIM, J.M.

1838

-Relates incidents during journey through a slave state — Mar 3 pl c2 let.

MEACHUM, REVEREND JOHN BARRY

1837

-Praised for industry in advancing himself and buying freedom for enslaved blacks — Mar 11 p4 c2

MEDICINE

1839

-Successful operation for new nose performed — Jan 19 p2 cl

MEDITERRANEAN

1838

-Home of great civilizations now in decline — Jul 21 pl c4

MEETING ROOMS (Advertisement)

1840

-Rooms for society meetings — Jul 18 p3 c3
Sep 12 p3 c3
Sep 26 p3 c4
Oct 3 p3 c3-
Oct 17 p3 c4
Nov 7 p3 c4-
Dec 26 p4 c4

1841

Jan 9 p4 c4

MEHEMET ALI (Pasha of Egypt)

1840

-Opposes slavery — Nov 14 p2 c4
-Described — Nov 21 pl c4

MENDIANS
-See The Amistad

MENTAL AND CORPOREAL FEAST (Notice)

1841

-Open to the public — Apr 24 p3 c3

MENTAL AND MORAL IMPROVEMENT ASSOCIATION (Troy, New York)

1837

-Meeting in honor of Dr. James McCune Smith — Oct 14 p3 c3 let.
-Holds meeting — Oct 21 pl c2
-See also Douglass, Reverend William; Gardner, Reverend Charles; Jones, Reverend John; Miller, Reverend William; Payne, Reverend Daniel A.; Rush, Reverend Christopher; Seldon, Clarence; Thuey, Alexander; Underwood, Reverend Daniel; Vanlere, Moses F.; Waters, Reverend Edward; Watkins, Reverend William; Williams, Reverend Peter

MENTAL AND MORAL REFORM SOCITY (Troy, New York)
-See Mental and Moral Improvement Association; Thuey, Alexander

MERRIMAN, H.N.

1837

-Advocates immediate emancipation — Jul 8 p2 c3 let.

METHODISM
-See Churches (Methodist); Religion (Methodism)

METHODIST ABOLITION CONVENTION

1841

-Plans discussed — Aug 21 pl c4

METHODIST ANTI-SLAVERY SOCIETY

1837

-Holds convention in Lynn, Massachusetts; discusses slavery and the slave trade — Nov 18 p4 cl

1838

-Holds convention in Utica, New York; officers listed; events described — Jun 2 p4 cl

	1840
-Calls for meeting in response to General Conference's support of slavery	Aug 22 p1 c4
METHODIST EPISCOPAL CONFERENCE (Philadelphia) (Notice)	
	1839
-Convention and appointments	Jun 29 p3 c4
METHODIST PROTESTANT CHURCH (Notice)	
	1841
-Meeting for colored ministers	Jul 24 p3 c1,2
-Camp meeting in Hackensack, New Jersey	Sep 4 p3 c3
METSCHER, HENRY	
	1837
-Returned to slavery by trial decision of Judge Betts	Dec 9 p4 c1
MEXICO	
	1838
-Ports blockaded by the French fleet	Aug 4 p3 c4
	1839
-Fight with French discussed	Feb 2 p3 c2
-French will teach Mexicans necessity of union	Feb 23 p3 c3
-Mexico in the days of Montezuma described	Oct 12 p1 c4
	1840
-Federalists defeated	Mar 14 p3 c2
	1841
-Plans to invade Texas noted	Jan 30 p2 c4
-Indian antiquities described	Aug 14 p4 c1
-Revolution breaks out	Oct 16 p3 c2
MICHAELS, MRS. D. (Advertisement)	
	1837
-Board and lodging	Jan 14 p3 c4-Mar 18 p4 c3
	1838
	Oct 20 p4 c4-Dec 1 p4 c3
MICHAELS, JOSEPH	
	1837
-Listed as agent for the <u>Colored American</u>	Mar 11 p4 c4

-Wants old metals and glass; will furnish floormats for churches, halls, etc; services as teacher advertised	Jan 14 p3 c4- Mar 18 p4 c4
MICHIGAN	
	1838
-Description of discriminatory laws	Apr 12 pl c3 let.
	1839
-Life there described	Nov 2 p4 cl
MIDDLE EAST	
	1837
-Lectures on geography and antiquities of Egypt	Nov 11 pl cl
	Nov 25 pl cl
	Dec 2 pl cl
	Dec 9 pl cl
	Dec 16 pl cl
-Lectures on geography and antiquities of Palestine	Dec 23 pl cl
	Dec 30 pl cl
	1838
	Jan 13 pl cl
	Jan 20 pl cl
	Jan 27 pl cl
	1839
-Description of Egyptian system of bathing	Mar 16 pl cl
	1840
-Jerusalem's holy places	Mar 7 p4 c2
-History, geography, and climate described	May 2 p4 cl
-Description of Babylonian antiquities	May 9 p4 cl
-Geography and history of Syria	Jun 6 p4 cl
	Jun 13 p4 cl
-Destruction of Babylon described	Jun 20 p4 cl
-Description of Jerusalem	Nov 21 p4 c2
	1841
-Description of beyrout (Beirut)	Jan 9 pl c4
-Ancient Ephesus described	Jun 19 p4 c2
-Ancient Smyrna described	Jun 26 p4 c2

-Ancient churches described — Jul 3 p4 c2
Jul 10 p4 c2
Jul 17 p4 c2
Jul 31 p4 c2
Aug 7 p4 c2
-Ancient ruins of Baalbec described — Aug 21 p4 c2
-Ancient ruins of Patmos described — Aug 28 p4 c2
-History of Jerusalem — Sep 11 p4 c2

MILLER, A. (New York)

<u>1837</u>

-Elected Recording Secretary of the Roger Williams Anti-Slavery Society — Apr 15 p3 c3

MILLER, JOHN H. (Hoboken, New Jersey) (Notice)

<u>1839</u>

-Hoboken social retreat — Jun 1 p3 c4-Sep 14 p4 c4

MILLER, REVEREND WILLIAM

<u>1837</u>

-Elected honorary member of the Mental and Moral Improvement Association (Troy, New York) — Oct 21 p1 c2

MINGO, JONATHAN (Flushing, Long Island, New York)

<u>1837</u>

-Listed as agent for the <u>Colored American</u> — Apr 1 p3 c1
-Sends in $13.00 to the paper — Apr 15 p3 c4

MINIFEE, ADAM

<u>1838</u>

-Dies — Jun 9 p3 c4

MINISTRY
-See Christian Ministry (Black); Christian Ministry (White)

<u>MIRROR OF LIBERTY</u>

<u>1838</u>

-Begins publication — Jul 21 p3 c4
-New quarterly published by David Ruggles — Aug 11 p3 c4
-Public meeting to introduce quarterly — Sep 1,8 p3 c4
-New York citizens meet to pledge support — Oct 20 p3 c3

-Meeting Nov 10 p3 c3
-New agent appointed Dec 8 p3 c4
Dec 15 p4 c3

1840

-Praised by New York Colored Citizens; reappearance welcomed Sep 5 p2 c4
-To extend patronage Sep 26 p3 c4
-See also Free Blacks (New York); Hanson, Augustus William

MISCEGENATION
-See Amalgamation

MISSIONARY CONVENTION

1841

-Plans discussed Aug 14 p2 c1
-To take place at Hartford, Connecticut; officers chosen Aug 28 p2 c4
-Abstract of proceedings Sep 4 p2 c2

MISSIONARY WORK

1840

-Description of Christian missions in South Pacific Sep 5 p4 c2
-Story of martyred missionary in Africa Nov 7 p4 c1

1841

-Urged for Africa Apr 17 p2 c1 let.
-Christianizing of Africa encouraged if separate from colonization scheme Apr 24 p2 c3
-African missions encouraged Jun 19 p2 c1 let.
-Christians have a mandate from God to do work in Africa Jun 26 p1 c3 let.
-Missionary convention planned Jul 3 p1 c2 let.
-African missions urged Jul 3 p2 c1 let.
-Missionary work to Africa is a Christian duty Jul 10 p1 c4 let.
-Christians are duty-bound to give the gospel to the heathen in Africa Jul 10 p2 c1 let.
-Call for missionary convention issued Jul 17 p1 c4 let.
-Christians have a responsibility to Africans Jul 24 p1 c1 let.
-Black Christians urged to aid Africa Jul 24 p2 c1 let.
-African missionary work urged Jul 31 p1 c1 let.
-Reasons for missionary convention listed Jul 31 p4 c1

-Objections to African missions dismissed	Aug 7 p1 c1 let.
-Ministers urged to encourage African missions	Aug 7 p1 c2 let.
-Reasons for missionary convention listed; date set	Aug 14 p1 c4 let.
-Distinguished from colonization efforts	Aug 21 p2 c1 let.
-Missionary to European Jews appointed	Aug 21 p3 c1
-African missionary work has important bearing on slavery	Sep 18 p2 c1 let.
-Work in Africa praised	Oct 9 p1 c2 let.
-Evaluated	Oct 30 p1 c1 let.
-African missions need assistance	Nov 20 p1 c2 let.
MITCHELL, JOHN (Advertisement)	
	1840
-Boarding house	Aug 15 p2,3 c4- Sep 12 p3 c4 Nov 28 p3 c4- Dec 26 p3 c4
	1841
	Mar 20 p4 c4 Mar 27 p3 c4
MITCHELL, JOHN (Advertisement)	
	1837
-Tailor	Oct 7 p3 c4- Dec 30 p4 c3
	1838
	Jan 13 p4 c3- May 3 pp3,4 c3,4 Jun 2 p4 c3
MITCHELL, JOHN (Advertisement)	
	1838
-Union refectory	Jun 2 p3 c4- Dec 29 p4 c3
	1839
	Jan 12 p2 c4
-Refectory change of address	May 18 p3 c4 Jun 8 p4 c3- Nov 23 p4 c4
	1840
	Mar 21, 28 p4 c4
MITER,JOHN J.	
	1837
-Describes fourth anniversary celebration of the Female Benevolent Society (Troy, New York)	Apr 1 p1 c3

-Describes aims and financial condition of United Sons and Daughters of Zion's Benevolent Society of Troy, New York — Apr 1 p1 c4
-Describes meeting of Colored People of Troy, New York, for improvement of free blacks — Apr 1 p1 c4
-Sends five subscription names to the Colored American — May 27 p3 c1

MOB VIOLENCE

1837

-Criticized by the Colored American — Jun 23 p2 c1 ed.
-Mob rule ruins a town (from the National Philanthropist) — Nov 18 p3 c2
-Encouraged by merchants when it was against abolitionists — Dec 22 p2 c3

1838

-Philadelphia mob attacks abolitionists — Jan 2 p3 c3

1840

-New York mob destroys black homes — Mar 21 p1 c1

1841

-Mob in Dayton, Ohio breaks up anti-slavery meeting — Feb 13 p2 c3
-Report on Dayton riots — Feb 27 p2 c4
-Judge Helfenstein's arguments regarding self-defense for blacks threatened with violence in Dayton riots — Apr 3 p2 c4
-No white men indicted in Dayton riot case — Apr 10 p3 c1
-Lynching of four Missouri blacks reported — Sep 11 p3 c1
-Riot in Cincinnati reported — Sep 11 p3 c2
-Cincinnati riot described and decried — Sep 18 p2 c4
-Sentiments of Cincinnati newspapers against riots — Sep 25 p3 c1
-Narrative of Cincinnati riot — Sep 25 p3 c1

MOBILE ADVERTISER
-See Colonization (General)

MONEY REQUEST (Notice)

1841

-Capital of $500-$1,000 needed — Mar 27 p3 c4-May 29 p3 c4

MONTHLY CONCERT OF PRAYER

	1837
-"To Enslaved and Free People of Color"	Oct 28 p3 c4 Nov 18 p4 c4 Nov 25 p3 c4

MONTSERRAT
-See West Indies (Montserrat)

MOORE, GEORGE (New Haven, Connecticut)

	1837
-Listed as agent for the Colored American	Mar 4 p4 c4
-Sends $3.00 to the paper	Apr 15 p3 c4

MORAL REFORM (Children)
-See Youth's Department (Colored American)

MORAL REFORM (General)

	1837
-Seen as the best way to convince the nation of the error of oppression	Aug 26 p2 c2 ed.
-Virtue is its own reward	Oct 7 p2 c2
-Blacks must take responsibility for their own moral elevation	Dec 9 p2 c3 let.
-Indebtedness viewed as a source of temptation	Dec 16 p4 c1
	1838
-Conscientious and moral young men praised	Jul 7 p3 c3
-Neatness and taste in the home have a moral effect	Jul 7 p4 c1
-Good moral habits must begin in childhood	Jul 14 p4 c1
-Moral maxims	Jul 14 p4 c2
-Juvenile delinquency shocking	Jul 21 p4 c3
-Model boarding house cited for good moral influence	Sep 15 p4 c1
-Dissolute young men require a Christian lecture	Oct 6 p1 c1
-Swearing is a vice	Oct 6 p4 c3
-A sense of right and wrong makes all men equal	Oct 20 p1 c3
-Virtue never decays	Oct 27 p2 c4
-God requires purity in principle and practice	Oct 27 p4 c2

	1838
-Social dancing for amusement is wrong	Dec 15 p1 c1 let.
-Spiritual time misspent creates remorse	Dec 15 p4 c1
	1839
-Disorderly conduct of young men condemned	Mar 9 p1 c1
-Good intentions do not excuse bad conduct	Dec 12 p1 c2
-Falsehood one of the greatest sins	Dec 12 p4 c3
	1841
-On the importance of punctuality in payment	Apr 3 p4 c4
-On the temptations of popularity	Apr 10 p4 c3
-Regular employment is the price of happiness	Apr 10 p4 c4
-Slavery hinders moral elevation	Apr 17 p2 c4
-An ambitious man is his own worst enemy	Jun 19 p4 c1
-Rules to regulate jesting	Sep 4 p4 c1
-On the necessity of energy of character	Sep 4 p4 c4
-Description of an honest man	Sep 11 p4 c3
-See also American Moral Reform Society; Cranberry Moral Reform Society; Gambling; Pittsburgh Moral Reform Society; Sabbatarianism; Temperance (United States); Temperance and Moral Reform Society (Wilmington, Delaware); Thuey, Alexander; Young Men's Literary and Moral Reform Society (Pittsburgh)	

MOREL, JUNIUS

	1837
-Encourages usage of term "colored"	Nov 11 p2 c2 let.
-Expresses sorrow over inability to contribute to the economic support of the Colored American	Dec 9 p2 c3 let.
	1838
-Apathy toward the anti-slavery cause must be combatted by an independent black press	May 3 p2 c2 let.

1840

-Affirms value and influence of general conventions — May 30 p3 c4 let.

MORETON, GEORGE B. (Advertisement)

1840

-Manufactures and repairs gentlemen's shoes and boots — Sep 26 p4 c3

MORGAN, MARY JANE

1841

-Dies — Oct 9 p3 c3

MORMONS

1839

-Horribly attacked and persecuted in Tennessee — Jan 19 p3 c3
-Claim to divine origin called unfounded — May 18 p4 c3 let.

1841

-Are increasing in Illinois — Jun 12 p3 c1

MORRIS, THOMAS (Ohio)

1839

-Senator introduces anti-slavery petition which was "gagged" in the Senate — Mar 2 p1 c3
-Supported for Vice-President by the <u>Colored American</u> — May 18 p3 c3 ed.

1841

-Speaks at anti-slavery convention in Ohio — Jun 5 p1 c3

MORRISON, MISS RITA (Notice)

1841

-Primary school for colored children — May 8 p4 c4-Jun 5 p4 c4

MORSE, MR.

1837

-Praises the Colonization Society — Mar 18 p2 c4 let.

MORTON, GEORGE B. (and Thomas VanRensselaer) (Notice)

1840

-Public meeting of colored voters — Oct 17 p3 c4

MOSELY, JOHN

1841

-Marries Nancy Freeman — Oct 16 p3 c3

MOSES

1839

-View that Moses did not support slavery — Feb 2 p1 c3

MOTT, LUCRETIA

1840

-Appointed a delegate to the London Anti-Slavery Convention — May 30 p3 c1

MOTTS' BIOGRAPHICAL SKETCHES AND INTERESTING ANECDOTES OF PERSONS OF COLOR

1837

-Praised by the Colored American — Jun 3 p2 c4

MOUNT, C.I.B. (Brockport, New York)

1837

-Listed as agent for the Colored American — Apr 15 p3 c3

-Sends $5.00 to support the editor of the Colored American — Aug 19 p3 c2, Aug 26 p3 c4

-Praises Theodore Grant as a true abolitionist — Aug 26 p3 c4

MUMFORD, MRS. JANET

1838

-Listed as secretary of the Female Assistant Society — Mar 15 p3 c1

MURRAY, J.H.(New York, New York)

1837

-Listed as agent for the Colored American — Apr 15 p3 c4

MURRAY, JOHN (Glasgow, Scotland)

1838

-Accuses American ship captain of racial prejudice toward a black passenger — Feb 17 p2 c2 let.

MUSIC

1838

-Advice on how to enjoy music — Aug 4 p4 c2

1841

-Address on sacred music — Feb 6 p4 c1

MUTUAL RELIEF SOCIETY

	1837
-Regular monthly meeting	Mar 11 p3 c3
	Apr 8 p3 c4
	Aug 12 p3 c4
-Cites annual election of officers	Sep 9 p2 c4
	1838
-Twenty-eighth anniversary	Mar 22 p3 c4
-Monthly meeting	Jul 7 p3 c4
	Aug 11 p3 c4
-Election of officers	Sep 8 p3 c4
-Meeting	Oct 6 p3 c4
-Meeting and eulogy	Oct 20 p3 c4
	1839
-Meeting	Mar 9 p3 c4
	Jun 8 p3 c4
	1841
-Meeting	Mar 20 p3 c4
-See also Cowes, James C.; Elston, Edgar; Ennals, Samuel; Robertson, John	

MYERS, F. (and P.A. Bell) (Advertisement)

	1840
-Large room to let (Myers only)	Nov 14 p3 c4-Dec 19 p3 c4
	1841
-Store to let (Myers and Bell)	Nov 13 p3 c3

MYERS, FRANCIS

	1837
-Elected secretary (<u>Societie des Amis Reunis</u>)	Dec 23 p3 c4

N

NASH, DANIEL

	1837
-Leads mob against John Hooper	May 6 p4 c1

NASSAU (Bahamas)

	1837
-Blacks elected to the House of Assembly	Jun 10 p2 c4

NATIONAL ANTI-SLAVERY STANDARD

1840
-Begins publication Jul 4 p2 c3
-Criticized for opposing general convention of blacks Jul 11 p3 c1
-Criticized for articles opposing separate convention of blacks Jul 18 p2 c3

NATIONAL PHILANTHROPIST
-See Mob Violence

NATIONAL REFORM CONVENTION (Notice)

1840
-Meeting Aug 1 p3 c3-4
Aug 15 p3 c1-2

NATIONAL REFORMER

1838
-Praised by the Colored American Dec 22 p3 c1
-See also American Moral Reform Society (Philadelphia)

NATT, GEORGE (Notice)

1837
-Information desired about missing young colored man May 13 p3 c4-
May 27 p4 c4

NEEDHAM, JAMES

1837
-Listed as a member of the Philadelphia Committee Dec 9 p3 c2

NEGRO PEW

1837
-Book praised for criticism of racism in the churches; preface published in paper Jun 3 p2 c3

NELSON, LIBERTY H. (Advertisement)

1837
-Listed as agent for the Colored American Mar 11 p4 c4
-Grocer and tea dealer Jan 14 p3 c4-
Mar 4 p4 c4
Apr 8 p4 c4
Apr 15 p3 c4
May 13 p3 c4
Jun 17 p4 c4-
Jul 22 p4 c4

NEVIS
-See West Indies (Nevis)

NEW AGE (Providence, Rhode Island)	
	1840
-Devoted to the extension of the franchise; begins publication	Dec 26 p2 c3
NEW BEDFORD (Massachusetts)	
	1837
-Notes color prejudice in the shipping industry	Mar 11 p4 c2
-See also Free Blacks (Massachusetts)	
NEW ENGLAND (General)	
	1838
-People, especially farmers, are very industrious	Aug 18 p2 c2
NEW ENGLAND CHRISTIAN ADVOCATE	
	1840
-New Methodist paper begins publication	Dec 19 p3 c2
NEW ENGLAND COLORED TEMPERANCE SOCIETY (Boston) (Notice)	
	1838
-Third annual meeting to be held	Sep 15 p4 c2
-Calls for delegates and cooperation	Oct 6 p4 c3
	1839
-Annual meeting	Sep 14 p3 c4
NEW ENGLAND CONVENTION	
	1838
-Criticizes Northern apologists of slavery	Jun 16 p3 c1
NEW ENGLAND WESLEYAN ANTI-SLAVERY SOCIETY	
	1841
-Passed resolutions against slavery and colonization	Jul 31 p3 c1
NEW HAMPSHIRE ANTI-SLAVERY SOCIETY	
	1840
-Member expresses support for a national organization for blacks	Jul 25 p1 c4 let.
	1841
-Controversy with the New Hampshire Abolition Society discussed	Feb 13 p3 c2 let.

NEW HAVEN (Connecticut)

1841
-City described Jun 5 p2 c2

NEW HAVEN COMMITTEE (for the defense of the Amistad prisoners)

1840
-Report on education of Amistad defendants and plea for defense aid Nov 28 p1 c3 let.
-Their appeal to the public on behalf of the Amistad prisoners Nov 28 p1 c4

NEW HAVEN REFORM CONVENTION

1840
-Held Aug 15 p3 c2
-Called a failure Sep 19 p3 c1
-Criticized Oct 10 p2 c4 let.

NEW JERSEY ANTI-SLAVERY SOCITY (Essex County) (Notice)

1841
-Meeting held Apr 17 p3 c3

NEW JERSEY (Legislature)

1837
-Criticized for new restrictive bill on black freedoms Apr 8 p2 c4
-Passed law granting trial by jury to blacks charged with being fugitive slaves Apr 22 p4 c2
Jun 17 p2 c4

1838
-Receives petition supporting legislation abolishing slavery in Washington, D.C. Jan 20 p4 c2

NEW JERSEY (Slaves)

1837
-2,254 slaves in New Jersey in 1837 Apr 8 p3 c2

NEWSPAPERS (General)

1840
-Penny presses discussed Aug 8 p2 c4

NEWSPAPERS (Black)

1837
-Appropriate objectives of the press discussed Oct 28 p2 c3

	1838
-<u>Colored Man's Journal</u> criticized for pro-colonization views	Mar 3 p3 c1
-Establishment of <u>West Indian</u> in Jamaica noted	Mar 3 p3 c2
-Independent black press seen crucial to the anti-slavery cause	May 3 p2 c2 let.
-Blacks must have their own periodical	May 3 p3 c1 **ed.**
-Subscriptions to periodicals urged instead of use of tobacco	Dec 15 p2 c4 let.
	1839
-Reading public corrupted and led away from good periodicals	Jul 20 p2 c1 ed.
-Several anti-slavery papers compelled to close for lack of subscription payments	Jul 20 p3 c2
	1840
-New anti-slavery papers begin publication	Jul 4 p2 c3

NEW YORK <u>AMERICAN</u>
-See VanBuren, Martin

NEW YORK ANTI-SLAVERY SOCIETY

	1837
-Addressed by Reverend Theodore S. Wright on color prejudice	Jul 8 p1 c1 ed.
-Daniel Payne expresses regret at inability to address meeting	Oct 7 p2 c2
-Reverend Wright addresses convention on acceptance of annual report	Oct 14 p1 c1
-Reverend Wright addresses anniversary meeting on color prejudice	Nov 11 p3 c1
	1838
-Lack of colored office holders deplored	Jul 28 p3 c2 let.
	1839
-Holds convention; proceedings discussed	Feb 9 p3 c3
-Report on activities and methods of improving blacks' welfare	Jun 22 p1 c1

-_Colored American_ comments on recommendations for improving blacks' welfare	Aug 3 p2 c1 ed.
-Comments on recommendations about commercial ventures	Aug 17 p2 c1 ed.
-Criticized for its attitude toward the _Colored American_	Oct 5 p2 c2
-President of the Society vows no more support for the _Colored American_ until it backs political abolition	Oct 5 p3 c1
-Society member pledges support for the _Colored American_ if it loses money because of president's action	Oct 5 p3 c2
-Praise for _Colored American_'s stand on political abolition	Nov 2 p2 c3,4 let.
-_Colored American_ feels a convention would convince political abolitionists of their errors	Nov 2 p2 c5 ed.
-Address of committee on political action	Nov 2 p3 c2
	1840
-Meeting planned	Apr 4 p3 c3
-Meeting planned	Dec 12 p3 c3
	1841
-Sixth annual meeting planned	Sep 4 p3 c3
-Holds annual meeting	Oct 2 p2 c4

NEW YORK ASSOCIATION FOR POLITICAL ELEVATION AND IMPROVEMENT OF PEOPLE OF COLOR (Notice)

	1838
-Constitution printed	Jun 23 p3 c2
-Public meeting	Aug 25 p3 c3

NEW YORK CITY ABOLITION CONVENTION

	1839
-Announced	Jan 19 p3 c1
-Evaluated	Mar 9 p2 c1
-Proceedings discussed	Feb 9 p2 c2
	1841
-To meet	Oct 9 p2 c3
-County committees urged to canvass state	Oct 9 p2 c4 ed.
-Delegates elected to City Convention	Oct 9 p3 c1

NEW YORK COLORED AMERICAN

	1837
-Justifies establishment of the Colored American	Mar 4 p2 c2 ed.
-Justifies title of Colored American	Mar 4 p2 c2 ed.
-Calls for support of Colored American by blacks and whites	Mar 4 p3 c3 ed.
-Details aims of Colored American and calls for support	Mar 4, 11 p3 c4 ed.
-Emminent abolitionists sign petition recommending support of the New York Colored American	Mar 11 p3 c2
-Colored American praised by People of Color; aid promised	Mar 18 p3 c1
-Calls on ministers, editors and others to bring attention to the Colored American	Mar 18 p3 c2
-Colored American seen as a way to reach blacks	Mar 18 p3 c4
-Paper praised	Mar 25 p2 c1 let.
-Calls for aid in money and articles	Mar 25 p3 c2
-Calls on all blacks to subscribe to the paper	Apr 22 p2 c1 let.
-Independence of paper praised	Apr 22 p3 c2 let.
-Criticizes New York Times for racism	Apr 29 p3 c1
-Reminds people to pay postage on letters to the paper	Apr 29 p3 c4
-1,250 copies of paper circulated in New York	May 6 p3 c1
-Paper must be the work of the editor	May 6 p3 c1
-Paper praised by American Anti-Slavery Society	May 20 p2 c1
-Paper helps build organizations	May 27 p2 c4
-Paper is the public's servant	Jun 10 p2 c2
-Papers sent to Newark, New Jersey were destroyed	Jun 10 p3 c3
-Editor Samuel Cornish, says he can only work two more weeks without pay; calls for support	Jun 17 p3 c2
-Lack of funds curtails number of subscribers	Jun 24 p2 c4 let.
-Praised as an excellent paper by the Philanthropist	Jul 8 p2 c3 let.
-Paper calls on blacks to stay in the United States and help improve conditions	Jul 15 p2 c1

-Paper praised for criticizing blacks as well as whites	Jul 15 p2 c2 let.
-Traveling agents and black organizations are major sources of money for the paper	Jul 22 p3 cl let.
-Paper needs money to pay Samuel Cornish	Jul 22 p3 c4
-Editors want to know facts about black societies	Jul 29 p3 c2
-Appeals for financial support from abroad	Aug 12 p2 c3
-Bell to make a trip to upstate New York; hopes to arouse young blacks to action	Aug 19 p3 c3
-Appeals for increase in number of subscribers	Sep 16 p3 c3
-Cornish appeals for monetary contributions	Oct 7 p3 cl
-Paper praised for inspiring blacks	Oct 21 p3 c2 let.
-Paper to be run by a committee rather than by Philip Bell alone	Nov 11 p3 c2
-Paper asks for suggestions and prompt payment of subscriptions	Dec 2 p2 c2
-Small fund for salary of editor requested	Dec 16 p3 c2
-Reverend Ray urges attendance at meeting to support the Colored American	Dec 16 p3 c4
-Reverend Ray evaluates the first year of publication	Dec 23 p2 c4
-Wider distribution requested	Dec 23 p3 c2
-Paper has 1,650 subscribers; 800 from New York City	Dec 30 p4 c3
	1838
-Lists publishing committee members	Jan 13 p3 cl
-Paper has 1,800 subscribers and 10,000 read it	Jan 13 p2 cl
-Paper seen vital in circulating information and communication	Feb 3 p3 cl
-Paper will set up a reading room with all the exchange papers received	Feb 10 p2 cl
-Black Americans seen duty bound to support the Colored American	Apr 12 p2 cl ed.
-New York citizens give greatest support	Apr 12 p2 cl ed.
-Paper appeals for financial support	Jun 9 p3 cl ed.

-To issue editions in both New York and Philadelphia	Jun 9 p3 c2
-Requests support	Jun 16 p2 c2
-Paper enlarged; price raised	Jun 16 p3 c3
-Principles praised	Sep 8 p2 c2 let.
-Praised by Colored Citizens of Philadelphia	Sep 8 p4 c1
-Fined nearly $600 in libel suit	Nov 3 p3 c1 ed.
-Involved in libel suit; appeals for money	Dec 1 p3 c2 ed.
-Philip Bell requests aid from subscribers to defray costs of publication of third volume	Dec 8 p3 c1 ed.
-Requests further donations for costs of libel suit	Dec 15 p3 c2 ed.
-Objectives reviewed; support requested	Dec 15 p3 c2 ed.
-Describes forthcoming volume	Dec 15 p3 c4 ed.
-Reviews happenings of 1838; criticizes United States for failing to end slavery	Dec 29 p2 c1
	<u>1839</u>
-Sums up position of blacks in the United States	Jan 12 p2 c1
-Praised for urging the acquisition of property as a means of attaining the franchise	Jan 19 p3 c2 let.
-Requests funds to pay fine in libel suit	Jan 19 p3 c4 ed. Feb 2 p3 c4
-David Ruggles discusses his role in the libel suit	Jan 26 p3 c1
-May suspend publication unless subscription money received	Mar 9 p3 c3 ed.
-Now owns its own press and shop	May 11 p3 c1
-Begs subscribers to pay what they owe	Jun 1 p2 c4
-Samuel Cornish and Dr. James McCune Smith resign as editors of the paper	Jun 22 p2 c1
-Editors accused by David Ruggles of persecuting him	Jul 27 p2 c2 ed.
-Accuses Vigilance Committee of irresponsibility regarding libel suit	Jul 27 p2 c2 ed.
-Subscribers urged to pay bills	Jul 27 p3 c5 ed.
-Reaffirms implication of Vigilance Committee in libel suit	Aug 31 p2 c1 ed.
-Its improvements praised	Sep 7 p2 c5 let.

-Denies supporting pro-slavery politicians	Oct 19 p3 c3-4 ed.
-Asks why paper publishes irregularly	Nov 2 p3 c5 let.
-Paper will publish as finances allow	Nov 2 p3 c5
-Appeals for money	Nov 16 p3 c2
-Describes business difficulties at length; appeals for subscriptions	Nov 23 p2 c1
-May be forced to cease publication	Dec 7 p2 c1
	<u>1840</u>
-Future prospects not bright	Mar 7 p2 c3
-Should continue publishing	Mar 14 p2 c3 let.
-Starts "Youth's Department" with articles aimed at children	Mar 21 p2 c4
-Charles Ray takes over as editor and publisher	Apr 25 p2 c4
-Letters of praise on resumption of publication	Apr 25 p2 c4 let.
-Solicits subscribers	May 16 p2 c3
-Delinquent subscribers criticized	May 30 p2 c2
-Subscribers urged to pay debts	Jun 6 p3 c1
-Editor will take two week trip to settle paper's affairs	Jun 20 p2 c3
-Calls for support	Aug 22 p2 c3 let.
-Accused by David Ruggles of numerous offenses	Sep 12 p2 c4 let.
-Response to Ruggles	Sep 12 p3 c1
-Support for more discussion of religion in the paper	Oct 3 p1 c3 let.
-Deplores wars of all kinds	Oct 17 p2 c2
-In trouble financially; calls for payment of bills	Oct 17 p2 c3
-Urges Ohio subscribers to pay bills	Oct 31 p2 c4
-Supported by Rochester citizens	Nov 21 p3 c2 let.
-Notes future publication plans	Dec 5 p2 c1
-Public meeting planned to demonstrate and encourage support	Dec 5 p3 c1
-Praised for promoting temperance	Dec 5 p3 c1
-Praised for promoting cause of elective franchise	Dec 12 p2 c2 let.
-Urges that subscriptions be given as New Year's presents	Dec 19 p2 c4

	1841
-Wishes patrons a Happy New Year	Jan 2 p2 c3
-Appeals to readers for $500	Jan 9 p2 c3
	Jan 16 p3 c3
-Urges readers to fulfill pledges of financial support	Jan 30 p2 c2
-Responses to their appeal for money	Jan 30 p3 c2 let.
-Appeal repeated	Jan 30 p3 c3
-Status of financial appeal revealed	Feb 13 p2 c4
-Appeal repeated	Feb 13 p2 c4
-Encourages subscriptions; plans for next volume discussed	Feb 20 p2 c2
-Praised and supported by colored citizens of Buffalo	Feb 20 p3 c2
-Prospectus of new volume	Feb 20 p3 c3
-Reviews first volume of paper	Feb 27 p2 c2
-Starts new volume; hopes are high that paper will continue	Mar 6 p2 c2
-Paper wants 1,000 new subscriptions	Mar 20 p2 c2
-Desires payment for subscriptions	Apr 10 p2 c4
-Work praised	May 1 p2 c1 let.
-Gerrit Smith tried to silence paper because of disagreement with Philip Bell	May 22 p1 c1 let.
-Appeal for funds	Jun 12 p2 c2
-Delinquent subscribers listed	Jun 12 p3 c2
-Appeals for funds to Troy Convention	Aug 28 p2 c2
-To be financially aided by Troy Convention	Sep 4 p2 c4
-"Dollar Plan" of Troy Convention to aid New York <u>Colored</u> <u>American</u> revealed	Sep 18 p3 c1
-An appeal for its support	Sep 25 p1 c3
-Appeal for financial support	Oct 2 p3 c3
	Oct 9 p2 c2
-Opposes National Convention	Oct 16 p2 c2 ed.
-Recommends <u>Madison</u> <u>County</u> <u>Abolitionist</u>	Oct 16 p2 c3 ed.
-Calls for financial aid	Oct 23 p2 c3 ed.
-Reports financial prospects	Oct 30 p3 c3 ed.
-Asks subscribers to meet obligations	Nov 13 p3 c1 ed.

NEW YORK COLORED AMERICAN
(Advertising and Notices)

	1837
-Job printing	Mar 25 p4 c3 Apr 15,22 p3 c4 May 6 p4 c3 May 13 p3 c4 Jun 10 p3 c4
-Job printing office for sale	Jul 8 p3 c4
	1839
-Boarding inquiries to John Mitchell and James C. Cowes	Sep 18 p3 c3
	1840
-Rooms to let; inquire of Charles B. Ray	May 30 p3 c4- Jul 4 p4 c4
-Apartment to let	Feb 13 p3 c4 Mar 13 p3 c4
-Renting agency	Mar 20 p4 c4
-Rooms and bedrooms	Apr 3-17 p3 c4

NEW YORK COLORED AMERICAN
(Agent Notices)

	1837
-Use of name without approval	Mar 4-18 p4 c4
-City agents	Mar 11 p4 c4- Apr 15 p4 c4
	1838
-No subscriptions without payment	Jul 7 p4 c3
-Agent fees	Jun 2 p1 c1- Dec 29 p1 c1
	1839
	Jan 12 p1 c1- Mar 16 p1 c1 May 11 p1 c1 Jun 1 p1 c1- Nov 23 p1 c1

NEW YORK COLORED AMERICAN
(Agent Notices)

	1837
-Travelling agent, Charles B. Ray	Jul 1 p4 c4
-Individuals authorized as agents	Nov 11 p3 c4 Dec 2 p4 c4- Dec 30 p4 c4

1838
Jan 20 p4 c3-
Apr 19 p4 c2,3
Jun 2 pp3,4 c3,4

-Agents abroad — Jun 30 p4 c4-
Jul 21 p4 c4
Aug 18 p4 c4

-Individuals authorized as agents — Aug 11 p3 c4

1839
Jan 12 p3 c4
Feb 9 p4 c4

1840
Mar 28 p2 c4
Apr 25 p2 c2
May 9 p2 c2

NEW YORK <u>COLORED</u> <u>AMERICAN</u> (Agents)

-Rev. Richard Allen (Phila., Pa.) *(Dec 30,'37 p3 c4)
-William Van Alstine (Hudson, N.Y.) (Sep 16,'37 p3 c1)
-Robert Banks (Buffalo, N.Y.) (Mar 4,'37 p4 c4)
-Anthony Barrett (Columbus, Ohio) (Jan 13,'38 p4 c4)
-Amos Gerry Beman (Hartford, Conn.) (Apr 1,'37 p3 c1)
-Samuel Berry (Jamaica, N.Y.) (Apr 15,'37 p3 c4)
-Rev. N. Blount (Poughkeepsie, N.Y.) (Jun 3,'37 p3 c4)
-John C. Bowers (Philadelphia, Pa.) (Mar 11,'37 p4 c4)
-William Brewer (Wilkesbarre, Pa.) (Mar 4,'37 p4 c4)
-Charles Brooks (Brooklyn, N.Y.) (Dec 23,'37 p3 c4)
-George L. Brown (Utica, N.Y.) (Sep 16,'37 p3 c1)
-Joseph Brown (New Haven, Conn.) (Feb 3'38 p3 c4)
-William L. Brown (Rochester, N.Y.) (Jan 13,'38 p4 c4)
-George Cary (Cincinnati, Ohio) (Jun 3,'37 p3 c4)
-Alford Chase (Fitchburg, Mass.)(Aug 11,'38 p3 c4)
-Otis Clapp (Palmyra, N.Y.) (Jun 10,'37 p3 c3)
-Gabriel Colman (St. Catherine's, Canada) (Jan 13,'38 p4 c4)

*Date first listed as agent

-S. Conover (New York, N.Y.) (Mar 11,'37 p4 c4)
-Martin Cross (Catskill, N.Y.) (Mar 4,'37 p4 c4)
-J. W. Duffin (Geneva, N.Y.) (Mar 11,'37 p4 c4)
-A. Dunbar (Syracuse, N.Y.) (Jan 13,'38 p4 c4)
-Daniel M. Fairchild (Westfield, N.Y.) (Sep 29,'38 p3 c4)
-James Fields (New York, N.Y.) (Mar 11,'37 p4 c4)
-Amos Freeman (New Brunsick, N.J.) (Apr 1,'37 p3 c1)
-Stephen H. Gloucester (Philadelphia, Pa.)(Dec23, '37 p4 c2)
-William Goodrich (Little York, Pa.) (Jan 13,'38 p4 c4)
-Theodore Grant(Oswego, N.Y.) (Sep 16,'37 p3 c1)
-Alonzo Gray (Sanquoit, N.Y.) (Sep 29,'38 p3 c4)
-William P. Griffin (Albany, N.Y.) (Mar 11,'37 p4 c4)
-William Harris (Toronto, Canada) (Jan 13,'38 p4 c4)
-Thomas Hector (Lowell, Mass.) (Sep 30,'37 p3 c4)
-J. A. Holmes (New York, N.Y.) (Mar 11,'37 p3 c4)
-William S. Jinnings (Boston, Mass.) (Mar 4,'37 p4 c4)
-Richard Johnson (New Bedford, Mass.) (Mar 4,'37 p4 c4)
-William P. Johnson (New York, N.Y.) (Nov 18,'37 p3 c4)
-Thomas King (Norwich, Conn.) (Sep 16,'37 p3 c1)
-Reverend John Lee (Bellville, N.J.) (Sep 16,'37 p3 c1)
-Madison Lightfoot (Detroit, Mich.) (Jul 14,'38 p4 c4)
-Joseph Mason (Painesville, Ohio) (Dec 23,'37 p3 c3)
-Johnathan Mingo (Flushing,' N.Y.) (Apr 1,'37 p3 c1
-George Moore (New Haven, Conn.) (Mar 4,'37 p4 c4)
-C.I.B. Mount (Brockport, N.Y.) (Apr 15,'37 p3 c3)
-J.H. Murray (New York, N.Y.) (Apr 15,'37 p3 c4)
-Liberty H. Nelson (New York, N.Y.) (Mar 11,'37 p4 c4)

-Mr. Nichols (New Milford, Conn.) (Sep 16,'37 p3 c1)
-J. B. Owens (Syracuse, N.Y.) (Sep 29,'38 p3 c4)
-Charles Payne (Newburgh, N.Y.) (Mar 4,'37 p4 c4)
-George Peacock (New York Mills, N.Y.) (Sep 29,'38 p3 c4)
-John Peck (Carlisle, Pa.) (Mar 4,'37 p4 c4)
-Reverend James W. C. Pennington (Newtown, L.I., New York) (Aug 5,'37 p3 c3)
-Isaac Pinckham (West Northwood, N.H.) (Aug 11,'38 p3 c4)
-Captain Edward J. Pompey (Nantucket, Mass.) (Jul 15, '37 p3 c4)
-Reverend Charles B. Ray (New York, N.Y.) (Apr 1,'37 p3 c1)
-J. T. Raymond (New York, N.Y.) (Feb 17,'38 p3 c4)
-Charles Lenox Remond (Providence, R.I.) (Mar 4,'37 p4 c4)
-E. A. Rice (Lowell, Mass.) (Aug 18,'38 p4 c3)
-William Rich (Troy, N.Y.) (Mar 4,'37 p4 c4)
-David Roach (Pottsville, Pa) (Jan 13,'38 p4 c4)
-Sidney W. Rockwell (Hartford, Conn.) (Apr 1,'37 p3 c1)
-David Roselle (New Haven, Conn.) (May 13,'37 p4 c4)
-John Scott (Lockport, N.Y.) (Jan 13,'38 p4 c4)
-Abraham D. Shad (Chester, Pa.) (Mar 4,'37 p4 c4)
-P. Shields (New York, N.Y.) (Mar 4,'37 p4 c4)
-Asa B. Smith (Farmington, Conn.) (Jun 10,'37 p3 c3)
-Mortimer J. Smith (New York, N.Y.) (Jun 30,'38 p3 c3)
-E. Stanford (Salina, N.Y.) (Sep 29,'38 p3 c4)
-Austin Steward (Rochester, N.Y.) (Jul 13,'38 p4 c4)
-Reverend Asa Story (Hulburton, Orleans County, N.Y.) (Aug 19, '37 p3 c2)
-Edwin Thompson (Lynn, Mass.) (Jun 30,'38 p3 c3)
-Richard Valentine (Cranberry, N.J.) (Dec 15,'38 p3 c3)

-John B. Vashon (Pittsburgh, Pa.) (Mar 4,'37 p4 c4)
-Samuel R. Ward (Newark, N.J.) (Mar 4,'37 p4 c4)
-A. Washington (Trenton, N.J.) (Jan 13,'38 p4 c4)
-William Whipper (Columbia, Pa.) (Mar 4,'37 p4 c4)
-James J. Williams (London Grove, Pa.) (Sep 29,'38 p3 c4)
-A. Williams (Salem, Mass.) (Jun 30,'38 p3 c3)
-G. Woodson (Jackson, Ohio) (Sep 30,'37 p3 c4)

NEW YORK COLORED AMERICAN
(Appeals for Aid) (Notice)

	1837
-Help needed	Apr 1 p4 c4- Apr 15 p4 c3 Aug 12 p4 c4 Oct 14-28 p4 c4
-Send money to Charles B. Ray	Nov 11 p3 c4
	1838
	Jan 13 p1 c1- May 3 p1 c1
-Asking subscribers and agents to give paper money due	Mar 3 p3 c4
-Send money to Charles B. Ray	Jun 2 pp1,3 c1,4- Dec 29 p1 c1
-Need money to meet expenses	Aug 25 p3 c4
	1839
-Send money to Charles B. Ray	Jan 12 p1 c1- Mar 16 p1 c1
-Money needed or paper will be suspended	Mar 9 p3 c3
-Send money to Charles B. Ray	May 11 p1 c1
-Send money to Charles B. Ray	Jun 1 p1 c1- Nov 23 p1 c1
-Money due should be paid	Jul 27 p3 c4 Sep 14 p3 c4
	1840
	Mar 21, 28 p2 c3
-Need subscribers and donations	Apr 25 p2 c4 Oct 31 p2 c4

	1841
-Appeal for $500	Jan 16,30 p3 c3,4 Oct 30 p3 c3,4
NEW YORK COLORED AMERICAN (Notice) (Committee of Correspondence)	
	1840
-Appointed	Jun 13,27 p3 c3 Jul 4 p3 c3
NEW YORK COLORED AMERICAN (Notice) (Committee Meetings)	
	1837
-General committee meeting	Dec 16 p3 c4
	1838
	Mar 3, 10 p3 c4
-Executive committee	Apr 12, 19 p3 c4
NEW YORK COLORED AMERICAN (Contributions received)	
	1837
-$105.75	Apr 15 p3 c4
-$ 82.25	Apr 22 p3 c4
-$ 46.00	Apr 29 p3 c4
-$124.75	May 20 p3 c4
-$ 46.00	Jun 17 p3 c4
-$197.11	Aug 19 p3 c4
-$ 88.00	Sep 2 p3 c4
-$171.00	Sep 30 p3 c4
-$100.75	Oct 21 p3 c4
-$ 8.00	Dec 23 p3 c3
	1838
-$ 18.00	Jan 20 p3 c3
-$ 72.00	Jun 16 p3 c4
-$ 30.75	Jun 23 p3 c4
-$ 20.00	Aug 4 p3 c4
-$101.00	Aug 11 p3 c4
-$ 88.00	Sep 8 p3 c4
-$ 42.00	Oct 13 p3 c4
-$ 49.00	Oct 20 p3 c4
-$ 10.00	Dec 8 p3 c4
-$ 31.00 and $59.00 ($5.00 for libel suit)	Dec 15 p3 c4
	1839
-Money collected for libel suit	Jan 26 p3 c1
-Contributors to libel suit fund acknowledged	Mar 9 p3 c3 ed.
-$ 4.00	Mar 9 p3 c3
-$ 17.00	Mar 16 p3 c4
-$ 48.00	Jul 20 p3 c4
-$10.00	Jul 27 p3 c5
-$ 37.50	Aug 17 p3 c5
-$ 7.00	Aug 31 p3 c5

-$140.00	Sep 28 p3 c1
-$ 32.00	Oct 19 p3 c5
-$ 28.00	Nov 23 p3 c5
-$ 90.00 pledged	Dec 7 p3 c5
	<u>1840</u>
-$265.00 pledged	Mar 7 p3 c2
-$ 28.00 received	Mar 14 p3 c1
-$ 68.00 received for libel suit expenses	May 9 p3 c3
-$ 14.00	May 16 p3 c3
-$ 12.00	May 30 p3 c4
-$ 26.75	Jul 4 p3 c3
-$ 11.00	Jul 25 p3 c4
-$ 57.00 (From Jamaica)	Aug 1 p3 c3
-$ 25.00	Sep 5 p3 c3
-Amount of pledges noted	Oct 31 p2 c4
-$ 63.00	Nov 7 p3 c3
-$ 62.25	Nov 21 p3 c4
-$ 97.00 in cash and pledges	Dec 5 p3 c3
-$ 63.90	Dec 26 p3 c3
	<u>1841</u>
-$ 86.00	Jan 30 p3 c3
-$ 36.00	Feb 13 p3 c3
-$ 27.50	Feb 20 p3 c3
-$ 82.00	Feb 27 p3 c4
-$ 32.00	Mar 27 p3 c4
-$ 44.00	Apr 10 p3 c3
-$ 21.00	Jun 12 p3 c3
-$ 38.00	Jul 17 p3 c3
-$ 12.00	Jul 24 p3 c3

NEW YORK <u>COLORED</u> <u>AMERICAN</u>
(General Committee of Publication)

	<u>1837</u>
-Formed to replace Philip Bell as paper's proprietor	Nov 4 p3 c4
	<u>1838</u>
-List of publishing committee members	Jan 13 p3 c1
-Holds meeting regarding paper's interests	Mar 3 p3 c4
-Viewed as a means of liberation	Jun 2 p3 c1 let.
-Transfers paper to Reverend Ray, Philip Bell, and Stephen Gloucester	Jun 9 p3 c2

NEW YORK <u>COLORED</u> <u>AMERICAN</u> (Notice)

	<u>1838</u>
-Caution: Ohioans should not give William Skipworth money	Oct 27 p3 c4

	Nov 10, 17 p4 c4 Dec 1 p4 c4
NEW YORK COLORED AMERICAN (Notices to Correspondents)	
	1837
-Notice	Apr 15 p3 c3 Apr 29 p3 c4 Sep 23, 30 p3 c3,4
	1838
	Nov 3 p3 c4
	1839
	Jul 20 p3 c3 Aug 24 p3 c4 Oct 5 p3 c4 Oct 12 p3 c3 Nov 2 p3 c4
NEW YORK COLORED AMERICAN (Notices to Subscribers)	
	1837
-New York Subscribers	May 6 p3 c3
	1838
-Change of address	Mar 29 p3 c4
-Subscribers who do not receive the paper	Apr 12, 19 p3 c4 May 3 p4 c3
-Paper changing hands; price increase	Jun 16 p3 c3,4
	1839
-New York subscribers	Jul 20 p3 c4 Aug 24 p3 c4
	1840
-Subscribers moving	Apr 25 p2 c3 May 9 p2 c2
NEW YORK COLORED FEMALE VIGILANCE COMMITTEE	
	1841
-Organized	Aug 21 p2 c3
NEW YORK COMMITTEE OF VIGILANCE (Notice)	
	1837
-Meeting	Mar 11 p3 c4 Jul 8 p3 c4
-Special public meeting	Oct 21, 28 p3 c4
-Meeting adjourned	Nov 4 p3 c4
-Meeting	Dec 9 p3 c4

	1838
-Meeting	Feb 10 p3 c4
	May 3 p3 c4
-Circular and reading room	Jun 16, 23 p3 c4
-Meeting	Aug 11 p3 c4
	Aug 25 p3 c3
	Sep 8 p3 c4
	Oct 27 p3 c4
	Nov 3 p3 c4
	Nov 10 p3 c3
	Dec 8 p3 c4
	1839
-Cash received	Jun 8 p3 c4
-Meeting	Oct 12 p3 c4
-Report	Nov 9 p3 c4
	Nov 23 p4 cl,2
	1840
-Meeting	Jun 20 p3 c3
	Jul 11 p3 c4
	Sep 12 p3 c3
	Oct 24 p3 c4
	Nov 7 p3 c3
	Dec 12 p3 c3
	1841
-Meeting	Jan 9 p3 c4
	Apr 10,24 p3 c3
	May 1 p3 c3
-Celebration	Jun 12 p3 c3
-Meeting	Aug 7 p3 c3
-Acknowledgements of contributions	Oct 2 p3 c2
-Lost child	Oct 9 p3 c3
NEW YORK CONSTITUTION (1821)	
	1837
-Speeches opposing restriction of negro franchise by 1821 constitution	Mar 4 pl c2
-Speeches opposing continuence of slavery in New York by 1821 constitution	Mar 4 p2 c2
-Free blacks petition for repeal of voting restrictions embodied in 1821 constitution	Mar 11 p3 c2
-Petition to New York Legislature requests repeal of property qualification for black voters	Dec 16 p3 c3
-See also Root, General; Russell, Samuel; Talmadge, General; VanVechten, Abraham	

NEW YORK EVANGELIST
-See Racism (United States); Slave Trade (Domestic)

NEW YORK (Legislature)

1837

-Call for people to send abolition petitions to the legislature — Mar 18 p4 c2 let.
-Public meeting to build petition drive favoring enfranchisement of blacks — Aug 5 p3 c4
-Calls for more petition drives — Aug 19 p2 c4 let.
-Philip Bell to tour upstate New York to arouse young blacks to petition for voting rights — Aug 19 p3 c3
-Public meeting endorses petitions to legislature to gain voting rights — Aug 19 p3 c4
-Petition requests repeal of property qualifications for black voters — Dec 16 p3 c3

1839

-Summary of activities — May 11 p2 c4
-Act guaranteeing trial by jury printed — Jun 8 p1 c1
-Debate on jury trial law discussed — Jun 8 p2 c3
-Called on to enfranchise blacks — Nov 16 p2 c2

1841

-Forms committee to deal with black suffrage petitions — Jan 23 p2 c4
-Resolutions regarding elective franchise for blacks — Jan 23 p3 c4
-In a turmoil over the franchise petitions — Feb 6 p2 c4
-Report on its reception of franchise petitions — Feb 13 p1 c3
-Rescinds resolution which confined blacks to a special section of the legislature's gallery — Mar 6 p3 c1
-Rejects suffrage petitions of free blacks — Apr 24 p2 c4

NEW YORK LITERARY AND LIBRARY UNION (Notice)

1840

-Meeting — Dec 4 p3 c3

	1841
-Meeting	Sep 11 p3 c3
NEW YORK OBSERVER	
	1837
-Criticized for blaming blacks for their own condition	Jul 8 p2 c1 ed.
NEW YORK (Politics)	
	1838
-Election statistics for governorship and lieutenant governorship	Dec 8 p3 c4
	1841
-Results of New York City elections of 1841	Apr 17 p2 c2
NEW YORK MUTUAL RELIEF SOCIETY	
	1838
-Twenty-eighth anniversary celebration plans noted	Mar 22 p3 c4
NEW YORK REFORM SOCIETY (Notice)	
	1840
-Public discussion	Nov 28 p3 c4
	1841
-Meeting	Jan 16 p3 c4
NEW YORK SELECT ACADEMY (Notice)	
	1839
-For co-education of young children	May 11,18 p4 c3 Jun 1 pp3,4 c4- Nov 23 p4 c3
NEW YORK STATE ANTI-SLAVERY SOCIETY (Notice)	
	1839
-Convention	Jan 26 p3 c4 Feb 2 p3 c4
-Anniversary meeting	Sep 14 p3 c4
	1840
-Meeting	Dec 12 p3 c3
	1841
-Convention call for extension of franchise	Jun 26 p3 c3,4- Aug 21 p3 c3
-Meeting for society	Sep 4,11 p3 c4

NEW YORK STATE CONVENTION

1841

-Meets to discuss political disfranchisement of blacks; petitions state legislature — Oct 30 p2 cl
-See also Albany Convention; Troy Convention

NEW YORK STATE TEMPERANCE SOCIETY

1841

-Holds annual meeting — Nov 13 p2 c2

<u>NEW YORK SUN</u>

1839

-Criticized for its stand on emancipation and enfranchisement of colored citizens — Jul 13 p3 c2 ed.

1841

-Criticized for hypocrisy and bad influence on the reading public — Feb 6 p2 c3
-Accused of lacking impartiality — Sep 25 p2 c3
-Criticized for unjust reportage on Cincinnati riots — Sep 25 p2 c3

NEW YORK <u>TIMES</u>
-See Dickson, William

NEW YORK UNION COMMERCIAL ASSOCIATION (Notice)

1840

-First meeting to be held — Dec 19 p3 c4

NEW YORK UNION SOCIETY (Notice)

1837

-Meeting — Dec 2 p4 c4

1838

-Meeting — Mar 3 p3 c4
Mar 29 p3 c4
Apr 19 p3 c4
Jun 2 p3 c4
Sep 1 p3 c4
Sep 29 p3 c4
Nov 3 p3 c4
Dec 1 p3 c4

1839

-Anniversary — Feb 23 p3 c4
-Meeting — Mar 9 p3 c4

	1841
-Meeting	Apr 3 p3 c3
	May 1 p3 c3

NEW YORK VIGILANCE COMMITTEE

	1837
-Proposed meeting and program of study	Mar 11 p3 c4
-Publishes annual report	Apr 8 p4 c1
-Will hold meeting	Jul 8 p3 c4
-Will hold celebration August 1st	Jul 29 p3 c3
-Reports attempted sale of black slaves	Oct 7 p2 c4 let.
-Special meeting to be held	Oct 21 p3 c4
-David Ruggles notes meeting to discuss trial-by-jury rights	Oct 28 p3 c4
-Adjourned meeting rescheduled	Nov 4 p3 c4
	1838
-Secretary outlines purposes and activities of committee	Jan 20 p3 c2 let.
-David Ruggles requests financial aid from the public	Jul 21 p2 c1 let.
-Colored American urges patrons to aid committee	Jul 21 p2 c1 ed.
-David Ruggles requests aid for freeing fugitive slaves	Jul 28 p3 c4 let.
-Holds large meeting to discuss colonization	Aug 25 p3 c3
-Plans meeting to discuss sailors' rights	Oct 27 p3 c4
-To meet to consider seamans' rights	Nov 3 p3 c4
-Regular monthly meeting planned	Dec 8 p3 c4
	1839
-Contributions to committee listed	Jun 8 p3 c5
-Accused of irresponsibility in libel suit affecting the Colored American	Jul 27 p2 c2 ed.
-Implication in libel suit denied	Aug 31 p2 c1 let.
-Implication in libel suit affirmed	Aug 31 p2 c1 ed.
-Public meeting planned	Oct 12 p3 c5
-Repudiates David Ruggles for mismanagement of accounts	Nov 23 p4 c1 let.
-Monthly meeting planned	Dec 7 p3 c5

	1840
-Monthly meeting planned	Apr 11 p3 c2
-Call for support	Aug 22 p1 c4
-Meeting to be held	Nov 7 p3 c3
-Achievements noted and praised	Nov 14 p2 c4
-Regular monthly meeting planned	Dec 12 p2 c4
	1841
-Meeting to be held	Jan 9 p3 c4
-Will hold anniversary	May 8 p3 c1
-Anniversary held	May 15 p2 c3
-Speech of Amos Beman at anniversary meeting	May 22 p1 c1
-Description of anniversary meeting	May 22 p3 c2
-To celebrate abolition of slave law	Jun 12 p3 c3
-Plans to form female auxiliary	Aug 21 p2 c3
-See also New York Colored American	

NEW YORK WHOLESALE PRICES (Notice)

	1839
-List	Jan 19 p4 c4- Feb 2 p3 c4 Feb 23 p3 c4- Mar 16 p3 c4
	1840
-List	Mar 7-21 p3 c4- Apr 25 p3 c4 May 9,16 p3 c4
	1841
-List	Feb 13,20 p4 c4

NEWMAN, JAMES

	1837
-Listed as a member of the Philadelphia Committee	Dec 9 p3 c2

NEWPORT, RHODE ISLAND

	1837
-Cursed by the slave trade	Jul 15 p3 c3

NIAGARA FALLS

	1838
-Description and praise	Jun 7 p4 c2 Sep 22 p1 c1

NICHOLAS, W.L. (Advertisement)

	1840
-Rooms and bedrooms to let	May 9-23 p3 c4

NICHOLS, MR. (New Milford, Connecticut)

1837

-Listed as agent for the Colored American — Sep 16 p3 c1

NOAH, MAJOR

1837

-Unprincipled political doctrine called "heresy" — Oct 28 p2 c3

NON-RESISTANCE

1837

-William Whipper asserts the benefits of non-resistance over offensive aggression — Sep 9 p1 c2
Sep 16 p1 c3
Sep 23 p1 c2
Sep 30 p4 c1

NORTH, WILLIAM

1837

-Issues anti-slavery resolutions — Jun 10 p1 c3
-See also Quarterly Methodist Conference

NOVELS

1838

-Source of licentiousness — Aug 4 p1 c2 ed.
-French novels lead to loss of virtue — Dec 22 p4 c2

NUGENT, DR. (Antigua)

1838

-His kindness as a slave-holder praised — Jun 16 p4 c2

O

O'CONNELL, DANIEL

1838

-Description of his reception at Kensington Palace — Sep 8 p2 c4

1839

-Anti-slavery eloquence praised — Jul 27 p1 c5
-Anti-slavery work praised by Charles Remond — Nov 7 p1 c1 let.

	1841
-Extract of his speech to the British and Foreign Anti-Slavery Society	Jul 11 p1 c1
OCTON, L.	
	1837
-Elected Treasurer of the Roger Williams Anti-Slavery Society	Apr 15 p3 c3
OFFICES AND ROOMS TO LET (Advertisement)	
	1839
-43-47 Liberty Street	Mar 16 p3 c3 May 11 p4 c4
OGDEN, H.	
	1838
-Extracts from journal during sea voyage to Africa	Jul 21 p3 c3
OGDEN, HENRY (Advertisement)	
	1840
-Carpenter and builder	Nov 13 p3 c4- Dec 4 p3 c4 Dec 25 p3 c4
	1841
-Carpenter and builder	Jun 12 p3 c3- Oct 16 p3 c4
OHIO (General)	
	1839
-A sketch of Cincinnati	Jul 20 p1 c2
-Unjust laws are not often enforced	Aug 31 p2 c2 let.
	1840
-Excludes blacks from courts	May 14 p1 c1
-1,000 slaves escape through Ohio to Canada	Mar 21 p2 c1
-Ohio Convention supports James Birney and Thomas Earle for President and Vice-President	Sep 19 p3 c1
	1841
-Mob kills black man who married a white woman	Mar 20 p3 c1
-Supreme Court decides that as soon as a slave enters Ohio, he or she is free	May 22 p2 c4
-Large tracts of land offered for sale	Aug 21 p2 c3

OHIO (Legislature)

1837

-Petitioned to give blacks the franchise — Jul 22 p2 c1

1838

-List of petitions presented to legislature relative to blacks — Feb 17 p4 c2
-Extracts from memorials to legislature request removal of legal disabilities against blacks — Mar 15 p2 c2
-Extracts from memorial to legislature points out ability and human rights of blacks — Mar 15 p2 c2; Mar 22 p4 c1; Mar 29 p4 c1; Apr 5 p4 c1; Apr 12 p4 c1
-Abolitionists control balance of power (from Ohio Political Journal and Register) — Nov 18 p3 c2

1840

-Rejects petition from blacks — Mar 14 p1 c1

1841

-Criticized for upholding law prohibiting legal testimony by blacks — Feb 13 p2 c3
-Legislature will probably not pass bill providing alleged fugitive slaves with a jury trial — Mar 20 p3 c1
-Fails to repeal oppressive black laws — Apr 17 p2 c4

OHIO POLITICAL JOURNAL AND REGISTER
-See Ohio (Legislature)

OHIO RIVER

1839

-Trip down river in steamboat described — Oct 12 p2 c4

OHIO STATE ANTI-SLAVERY SOCIETY

1839

-Fourth anniversary celebrated — Jun 22 p3 c5

OLIVER, THEODORE (Boston)

1839

-Dies — May 18 p3 c5

OLIVER, THOMAS

1837

-Case to be discussed at a meeting of the New York Committee of Vigilance — Mar 11 p3 c4

ONEIDA INSTITUTE

1837

-Distrust in character of Institute denied — Dec 16 p2 c3 ed.

1839

-Testimonial to its noble spirit — Sep 7 p2 c4 let.
-Circular details progress — Sep 7 p2 c4

ORIGIN AND HISTORY OF THE COLORED PEOPLE

1841

-Book by James W.C. Pennington described and advertised — Jan 9 p3 c3
-Reviewed — Feb 27 p2 c3

OSBORN, J. (and G. H. Dixon) (Advertisement)

1840

-Land for sale in Brooklyn — Apr 11 p4 c3- Jul 4 p4 c4; Jul 25 p4 c4- Oct 3 p3 c3

1841

-Paul Pontou also listed — May 22, 29 p3 c4
-Pontou no longer listed — Aug 7 p3 c3- Sep 18 p3 c4

OSBORN, JOHN (and James Green) (Advertisement)

1837

-Dry goods, fancy articles, and so forth — Sep 30 p3 c4- Dec 9 p4 c3

1838

Jan 13 p4 c3
Jan 20 p4 c2
Feb 17 p4 c2

OSCAR, MARY E.

1841

-Marries Samuel W. Freeland — Oct 30 p3 c4

OWENS, J.B. (Syracuse, New York)

1838

-Listed as agent for the Colored American — Sep 29 p3 c4

P

PALLADIUM OF LIBERTY

1841

-New anti-slavery newspaper, begins publication in Cleveland, Ohio — Mar 27 p3 cl

PALMER, MR.

1837

-Made attempt to free William Dickson who was on trial as a fugitive slave — Apr 29 p2 c2

PALMERSTON, LORD

1841

-Announces to the Anti-Slavery Society that only abolitionists will be appointed to government service — Oct 9 p3 c2

PARENTS

1838

-Advised to control children at church — Jun 16 p4 c2

PARKER, MRS. (Advertisement)

1841

-Colored girl wanted for house work — May 1 p3 c3-May 15 p4 c4

PARKER, L. & H. AND COMPANY (Advertisement)

1838

-Wholesale and retail furniture warehouse — Nov 17 p3 c4; Dec 1 p4 c3-Dec 29 p4 c3

1839

Jan 12 p2 c4-Mar 16 p4 c4; May 11 p4 c3-Nov 16 p4 c5

PARKER, MARY S. (Boston)

1837

-President of Boston Female Anti-Slaver Society laments the death of a fellow member, Ann Chapman — Apr 22 p3 c2

PARKER, RANSON (Providence, Rhode, Island)

1837

-Teaches black school with eighty children — Sep 23 p2 c4

PARKIS, JOHN (AND ISAAC LEONARD) (New Haven, Connecticut) (Advertisement)

1839

-Boarding house — Jun 29 p3 c4
Jul 13 p3 c4-
Nov 23 p4 c4

1840

Mar 14 p3 c4-
Apr 25 p4 c4

PARRISH, JOSEPH
-See Free Blacks (Pennsylvania)

PARSONS, DR. (Advertisement)

1837

-Dentistry — Dec 2 p4 c4
Dec 9 p3 c4
Dec 30 p4 c4

PATRIOTISM

1840

-Its significance to an American citizen — Jul 25 p4 cl

PATTINSON, H. (Temprance House)

1837

-Refused to serve blacks — Aug 19 p2 cl

PAUL, SUSAN (Boston)

1837

-Praised for skill in directing juvenile concert at African Baptist Church — Mar 4 p4 cl

PAUL, REVEREND NATHANIEL (Albany, New York)

1837

-Attends the first meeting of the Union Society of Albany — Apr 15 pl c3

1839

-Death eulogized; funeral noted — Jul 27 p3 c4

PAYNE, CHARLES (Newburgh, New York)

	<u>1837</u>
-Listed as agent for the <u>Colored American</u>	Mar 4 p4 c4
-Sends $10.00 to the paper	Apr 15 p3 c4

PAYNE, REVEREND DANIEL A.

	<u>1837</u>
-Religious poem reproduced	Sep 9 p2 c4
-Regrets inability to address the New York Anti-Slavery Society	Oct 7 p2 c2
-Listed as President of the Mental and Moral Improvement Society (Troy, New York)	Oct 14 p3 c4
	<u>1841</u>
-Establishes a male and female seminary in Philadelphia	Apr 3 p3 cl

PEACOCK, GEORGE (New York Mills, New York)

	<u>1838</u>
-Listed as an agent for the <u>Colored American</u>	Sep 29 p3 c4

PEAS, MR. (New London, Connecticut)

	<u>1837</u>
-Opens black school	Jun 3 p3 c4

PECK, JOHN (Carlisle, Pennsylvania)

	<u>1837</u>
-Listed as an agent for the <u>Colored American</u>	Mar 4 p4 c4

PELL, GEORGE (AND JOHN ALEXANDER) (Advertisement)

	<u>1840</u>
-Restorateur set up	Nov 14 p3 c4- Dec 26 p3 c4

PENN, WILLIAM

	<u>1839</u>
-His dealing with Indians described	Jun 22 p4 c3
	<u>1840</u>
-Story of his first treaty with Indians (Picture)	Jul 18 p4 cl

PENNINGTON, REVEREND JAMES W.C. (Newtown, Long Island, New York)

	1837
-Appointed agent for the Colored American	Aug 5 p3 c3
	1840
-Plans series of articles on education	Jul 4 p2 c4 let.
-Describes beginnings of teaching career	Jul 25 p2 c4 let.
-Describes teaching experiences on Long Island	Aug 22 p2 c2 let.
-Describes prerequisites of a teacher	Oct 24 p2 cl let.
-Stresses evils of showing partiality toward some students	Nov 7 p2 c2 let.
-Describes backwardness and ignorance on Long Island	Nov 14 p2 c2 let.
-On the difficulties of teaching spoiled children	Nov 28 p3 c2 let.
-On the errors of parents	Dec 19 p2 c2 let.
	1841
-Reports floods in Hartford, Connecticut	Jan 23 p3 c2 let.
-On the errors of parents	Apr 10 p2 cl let.
-Urges missionary activities in Africa	Apr 17 p2 cl let.
-Urges school committees to support their teachers adequately	Jun 26 p2 cl let.
-Urges missionary convention	Jul 3 pl c2 let.
-Calls for a missionary convention	Jul 17 pl c4 let.
-Again urges school committees to take responsibility for teachers' salaries	Jul 17 p2 cl let.
-Calls for missionary convention	Jul 24 p4 cl let.
-Criticizes Journal of Education and Weekly Messenger	Aug 14 pl cl let.
-Advises on furniture and school supplies	Sep 4 p3 c2 let.
-See also Origin and History of the Colored People	

PENNSYLVANIA (Constitutional Convention)

	1837
-Attempt at Convention to disenfranchise blacks	Jun 10 p3 c4
-Movement to disenfranchise blacks criticized	Jun 17 p2 c2 ed.

-Disenfranchisement movement failed; blacks retain voting rights — Jul 22 p2 c2
-Disenfranchisement movement may prove successful — Dec 16 p3 cl let.

1838

-Black citizens of Pennsylvania urged to take a stand against disfranchisement — Mar 3 p2 cl ed.
-Memorial from free blacks of Philadelphia remonstrates against disenfranchisement plans — Mar 15 p2 c3
-Memorial requesting aid for colonization effort criticized — Mar 15 p3 c2
-Criticized for disenfranchising free blacks — Apr 19 p2 c2
-Citizens urged to vote for amendments — Oct 13 p2 c3 let.
-Revised constitution attacked as unrighteous for disfranchising blacks — Dec 15 p3 cl

PENNSYLVANIA FREEMAN
-See Whittier, John Greenleaf

PENNSYLVANIA (General)

1838

-Anti-slavery sentiments prevailed only fifty years previously — Jul 28 p4 c2
-Description of black communities and congregations — Oct 13 p2 c3 let.; Oct 20 p2 c3 let.
-Description of Philadelphia — Oct 27 pl cl
-Mob takes over state legislature and is attacked — Dec 22 p2 c3

1839

-Praised, but people behind those in New England and New York in education — Aug 3 p3 cl

PENNSYLVANIA HALL

1838

-Official investigation of its burning called a pack of lies — Jul 28 p3 c2 let.
-Leading men of a previous generation would have been shocked by burning — Jul 28 p4 c2

1839

-Reaction of press criticized — Aug 17 p2 c3

PENNSYLVANIA (Legislature)

1837

-Entreated not to supply state funds to colonization effort — Dec 16 p3 c2

1838

-Memorial from Pennsylvania Reform Convention requests aid for colonization effort — Mar 15 p3 c2

1841

-Criticized for tolerating racist marriage laws — Feb 13 p2 c2

PENNSYLVANIA SOCIETY FOR PROMOTING THE ABOLITION OF SLAVERY

1840

-List of members on Acting Committee — May 23 p3 c1

1841

-Attempts to free freedmen arrested in Louisiana — Jan 2 p2 c4

PENNSYLVANIA STATE CONVENTION

1841

-Planned in order to secure equal rights — Jun 12 p2 c4
-Controversy continues over whether to have it — Jul 3 p1 c1
-Election of delegates noted — Jul 31 p2 c1 let.
-Call issued — Jul 31 p3 c2
Aug 7 p3 c2
Aug 14 p3 c2
Aug 21 p3 c2
-Successfully held — Sep 11 p3 c3
-Report on its proceedings — Sep 18 p1 c4
-Approved by Philadelphia citizens — Sep 25 p2 c2 let.

PEOPLE OF COLOR (Organization)

1837

-Praises the Colored American — Mar 18 p3 c1

THE PEOPLE'S PRESS

1841

-New paper commences publication — Oct 30 p3 c3

PERKINS AND TOWNE (Advertisement)

1839

-Free labor goods — Jun 15 p3 c4-
Nov 23 p4 c5

-Free labor goods	1840 Mar 14 p4 c4- Dec 19 p3 c4
-Free labor goods	1841 Sep 18 p3 c4- Dec 25 p3 c4
PETERS, PARTHENA (Springfield, Massachusetts)	
-Marries William Green	1841 Oct 30 p3 c4
PETERSON, JOHN	
-Listed as one of the four vice-presidents of Colored Citizens of New York	1837 Oct 28 pl c3
-Appointed to tne executive committee of the Political Association	1838 Jun 16 p2 c3
PETERSON, MARTHA L.	
-Marries Thomas S. Jackson	1838 Jun 9 p3 c4
PETERSON, PETER A. (Advertisement)	
-House for sale in New Haven	1837 Dec 9, 16 p4 c3
	1838 Jan 13 p4 c4- Jan 27 p4 c3
PHELPS, AMOS A.	
-Praises the Colored American as a powerful means of elevating blacks	1837 Mar 18 p3 cl
-See also Massachusetts Abolitionist	
PHILADELPHIA ASSOCIATION FOR THE MENTAL AND MORAL IMPROVEMENT OF PEOPLE OF COLOR	
-Will hold annual meeting; sends invitations	1837 May 20 p2 c2
-Constitution printed	Jun 24 pl c3
-Annual meeting praised; unity among blacks emphasized	Jun 24 p2 c3 let.
-Holds annual meeting; events described	1839 Jun 29 p3 c2

-See also Cornish, James

PHILADELPHIA CITY AND COUNTY ANTI-SLAVERY SOCIETY

1840

-Holds meeting; calls for unity among anti-slavery forces — Jun 13 p2 c4

PHILADELPHIA COMMITTEE

1837

-Organized to aid black newspapers — Dec 9 p3 c2
-See also Douglass, Reverend William; Gloucester, Stephen H.; Gordon, Robert C.; Hinton, Frederick A.; Needham, James; Newman, James; White, Jacob C.

PHILADELPHIA LIBRARY COMMITTEE

1837

-Invites Dr. James McCune Smith to visit and lecture — Dec 23 p2 cl
-See also Bowers, John C.

PHILADELPHIA READING ROOM (Notice)

1838

-Opening announced by Mr. Gloucester — Jul 7 p3 c4
-Advertisement — Dec 15 p3 c3- Dec 29 p4 c3

1839

Jan 12 p2 c4- Mar 16 p4 c4
May 11 p4 c3

PHILANTHROPIST

1837

-Calls the Colored American an excellent paper — Jul 8 p2 c3 let.

PHILLIPS, SARAH

1841

-Marries Gilbert Walker — Oct 9 p3 c3

PHILLIPS, WENDELL (Boston)

1840

-Participates in London Anti-Slavery Convention — Aug 1 pl c2

PHILOMATHEAN SOCIETY

	1837
-Regular meeting; donations; lectures; debates	Feb 4 p3 c4
	Apr 29 p3,4 c3,4- Jul 22 p4 c3
	Sep 2 p4 c3
	Sep 30 p3 c4
	Nov 4 p3 c1
	Dec 2 p4 c4
	Dec 16 p3 c4
	Dec 23 p3 c4
	Dec 30 p4 c3
	1838
	Jan 13 pp3,4 c3,4
	Apr 19 pp3,4 c3,4
	May 3 p4 c2
	Jun 2 pp3,4 c3,4- Jun 30 p3 c4
	Aug 4 p3 c4
	Sep 1,22,29 p3 c4
	Nov 3 p3 c4
	Dec 1 p3 c4
	Dec 15 p3 c3
	1839
	Jan 26 p3 c4
	Feb 2 p3 c4
	Mar 2-16 p3 c4
	Jun 22 p3 c4
	Aug 31 p3 c4
	1840
	May 2 p2 c2
	Jul 4 p3 c3
	Oct 31 p3 c3
-Poshumous tribute to Reverend Peter Williams	Nov 14 p3 c2
	1841
-Regular monthly meeting, etc.	Jan 16 p3 c4- Apr 17 p3 c3
	May 22 p3 c4
	Jun 26 p3 c4
	Jul 3 p3 c4
	Oct 2,9 p3 c3
	Dec 4 p3 c3
-See also Brown, Dr. John; Clark, Edward V.; Hazzard, Ebenezer; Ray, Reverend Charles B.; Smith, Dr. James McCune; Wake, Ransom; Wright, Reverend Theodore S.	

PHOENIX HIGH SCHOOL (Notice)

	1837
-Forced to close due to lack of funds	Jul 1 p2 c2
-Reopens female department	Sep 16 p3 c4- Dec 16 p4 c3

PHOENIXONIAN LITERARY SOCIETY (Phoenix Society)

	1837
-Board of Directors meeting	Apr 15 p3 c4
-Holds anniversary meeting	Jul 8 p3 c3
	1838
-Description of anniversary meeting	Jul 21 p3 c1 let.
-Preamble and resolutions of special meeting	Oct 6 p3 c2
	1839
-Member requests <u>Colored American</u>'s help in getting the Phoenixonian Society's library turned over to the Literary Society	Feb 16 p2 c4 let.
-Meeting called	Mar 9 p3 c4
-Proceedings of anniversary celebration	Jul 13 p2 c4 ed.
	1840
-Pays tribute to Thomas Sidney	Jul 4 p1 c1 let.
-Seventh anniversary meeting to take place	Jul 4 p3 c3
	1841
-Lecture series noted	Jan 30 p3 c4- Apr 24 p3 c4
-Plans to offer course of public lectures noted	Feb 13 p3 c1 let.
-Debate	May 22 p3 c4
-Eighth anniversary planned	Jul 3 p3 c2
-See also Brown, Dr. John; Hamilton Lyceum; Leavitt, Joshua; Reason, Charles; Smith, Dr. James McCune	

PHRENOLOGY

	1837
-James McCune Smith lectures against phrenology	Oct 14 p3 c3
-Article critical of phrenology (from the <u>Journal of Commerce</u>)	Nov 25 p4 c3

PHYSIOLOGICAL SOCIETY (Boston)

1839

-The "Johnny Cake Society" criticized as being stupid — Jun 15 p4 c3

PICKERING, JOSEPH S.

1837

-Presents an argument on the unconstitutionality of the Fugitive Law — Aug 12 p2 c2

PIERSON, N.E. (Madison, New Jersey)

1837

-Describes blacks' feelings about colonization — Jun 10 p3 c1 let.
-Sends $3.00 to the Colored American — Jul 17 p3 c4

PINCKHAM, ISAAC (West Northwood, New Hampshire)

1838

-Listed as an agent for the Colored American — Aug 11 p3 c4

PIRACY

1841

-Pirate vessel captured off New Orleans — Jun 19 p3 c1

PITTSBURGH

1839

-City described — Sep 28 p2 c4

PITTSBURGH GAZETTE
-See Slavery (General)

PITTSBURGH MORAL REFORM SOCIETY

1837

-Praises temperance activity and criticizes failure to ensure Sabbath observance — Mar 25 p4 c3
-Meeting elects officers — May 13 p1 c4
-See also Bryans, Richard; Jackson, L.; Templeton, John N.; Vashon, John B.; Woodson, Lewis; Young Men's Literary and Moral Reform Society

PITTSBURGH TEMPERANCE SOCIETY

1837

-Holds meeting; praised by the Colored American — May 20 p2 c4

PLAYS
-See Theater

PLET, CHERRY (Advertisement)

	1839
-Phoenix Saloon and Garden	Aug 17 p3 c4- Nov 16 p4 c3
	1840
	May 23 p3 c4- Jul 4 p4 c4
	Aug 1 p3 c4- Dec 19 p3 c4
	1841
	Jul 3 p3 c4- Aug 14 p3 c4

POETRY (Anti-Slavery)

	1837
-"Ode - July 4, 1837" by Alonzo Lewis	Jul 8 p4 cl
-"Enlargement of the Kingdom of Christ"	Aug 12 p4 cl
-"Song of Liberty"	Aug 26 p2 c4
-Abolitionist poem (anonymous)	Oct 7 p2 c4
-Exalts freedom (anonymous)	Oct 7 p4 cl
-"Texas" by W. B. Tappan	Dec 9 p4 cl
-"The Press" (anonymous)	Dec 9 p4 cl
	1838
-"The Card of Oppression"	Jan 20 p2 c4
-"Massachusetts" (anonymous)	Mar 3 p4 cl
-"The Tocsin"	Jun 23 p4 cl
-"Moral War Song"	Jul 7 p2 c3
-"A Sketch" by James Henry Carleton	Jul 21 p4 cl
-"A Parody"	Jul 28 p4 cl
-"They Sing of Freedom"	Aug 11 p4 cl
-"Prayer of the Oppressed"	Aug 18 p2 c3
-"The Freed Bird"	Sep 29 p4 cl
-"The Painter's Slave" by Juan de Paresa	Oct 6 p4 cl
-"On The Total Abolition of Slavery" by James Montgomery	Oct 13 p4 cl
-"The Leper"	Dec 8 p4 cl
	1839
-There could not possibly be pro-slavery poetry	Feb 2 p2 c3
-"Columbia's Eagle"	Feb 9 p2 c4
-"Original Poetry"	Mar 16 p2 c4
-"Vermont"	May 11 p4 cl
-"The Chain"	May 18 p4 cl
-"The Slave's Prayer"	Jun 22 p4 cl
-"Thomas Morris" By A.L.B.	Jul 13 p4 cl
-"Freedom" by G.C.M.	Jul 20 p4 cl
-"The Glorious First of August"	Aug 17 p4 cl
-"Lines"	Sep 28 p4 cl

-"The Ballot Box"	Oct 19 p4 cl
	1840
-"Lines" by Mrs. M.L. Gardiner	Apr 11 p4 cl
	1841
-"The African's Dream" (anonymous)	Apr 3 p4 cl
-"Southern Scenes" (Zion's Watchman)	May 1 p4 cl
-"Freedom's Son and Daughter"	Jun 26 p2 c3
-"The Burden and the Cross" by William Tappan	Sep 4 p4 cl
-"A Picture of Patience" by Mrs. Stedman	Sep 25 p4 cl
-"Ode on the Abolition of Slavery" by Lord Morpeth	Dec 4 p4 cl

POETRY (General)

	1837
-"Drink and Away" by Reverend William Croswell	Aug 12 p4 cl
	1838
-"Joy of Spring and Morning"	Jun 16 p4 cl
-"I've Thrown the Bowl Aside" by Charles F. Ames	Aug 4 p4 cl
	1839
-"The Dying Boy"	
-"The Blind Girl"	Jun 1 p4 cl
	1841
-"Lessons of Nature"	Oct 9 p4 cl

POETRY (Political)

	1841
-"The Spirit Voice" by C.L.R.	Aug 7 p2 c4
-"We Come! Stil We Come" by R.H.	Aug 21 p2 c4

POETRY (Religious)

	1837
-"The Child's Evening Hymn"	Aug 12 p4 cl
-"The Stranger and His Friend" by James Montgomery	Oct 21 p4 cl
-"The Comparisons"	Oct 21 p4 cl
	1840
-"The Christian Flag" by Spencer Wallace Cone	Sep 19 p4 cl
	1841
-"Sabbath Meditations" by Mrs. L.H. Sigourney	Oct 2 p4 cl
-"Mother, Will You Pray"	Oct 9 p4 cl
-"Land A-Head" by Reverend George Bryan	Nov 13 p4 cl

-"Rose to the Dead" by Mrs. Sigourney	Nov 20 p4 c1
-"God's Acre" by Henry W. Longfellow	Dec 25 p4 c1
POLITICAL ASSOCIATION	
-See Association for the Political Elevation and Improvement of People of Color	
POLITICAL IMPROVEMENT ASSOCIATION (Notice)	
	<u>1838</u>
-Meeting	Sep 29 p3 c4 Oct 6 p3 c4 Oct 20 p3 c4
	<u>1839</u>
	Mar 9,16 p3 c4 Jul 27 p3 c4 Oct 12, 19 p3 c4
POLITICS	
-See Abolition (United States) (Political Action vs. Moral Suasion); Democratic Party; Liberty Party; Voting Rights (Free Blacks); Whig Party	
POMPEY, CAPTAIN EDWARD J. (Nantucket, Massachusetts)	
	<u>1837</u>
-Listed as Master of the New Bedford brig owned by free blacks	Mar 11 p4 c2
-Appointed agent for the <u>Colored American</u>	Jul 15 p3 c4
PONTOU, PAUL (and Osborn and Dixon) (Advertisement)	
	<u>1841</u>
-Land for sale	May 22, 29 p3 c4
POPULATION STATISTICS (British Colonies)	
	<u>1838</u>
-Population figures given for British colonies (White, Slave, Free Colored)	Sep 22 p2 c1
POPULATION STATISTICS (United States)	
	<u>1837</u>
-Black and white (Long Island, New York)	Mar 18 p3 c2

-Blacks (New York City) Mar 25 p3 c3
-Blacks and whites (All slave states) Mar 25 p3 c4
-Black and white (Rhode Island) Apr 1 p3 c3
-Black and white (New Jersey) Apr 8 p3 c3
-Black and white (Pennsylvania) May 20 p3 c1
-Black (Utica, New York) Sep 16 p3 c1
-Black (Providence, Rhode Island) Sep 23 p2 c4
-Black (Syracuse, New York) Sep 30 p3 c2

1838

-Free blacks, (Northern and Southern states) May 11 p1 c1

1839

-Black (New Haven, Connecticut) Jun 29 p2 c1
-Black (Cincinnati, Ohio) Oct 5 p2 c5
Nov 2 p2 c5

-Black (Ohio) Nov 2 p2 c5

1840

-Black and white (New York City) Nov 21 p3 c3
-Black and white (Newark, New Jersey) Nov 21 p3 c3

1841

-Black and white (all states) Feb 13 p4 c2
Jul 3 p3 c2
Oct 9 p4 c4
Oct 16 p3 c2

PORTER, COMMODORE (American Minister to Turkey)

1838

-Arrives in Boston for visit before returning to Turkey Aug 4 p3 c4

PORTER, ROBERT

1838

-Eulogized by the <u>Colored American</u> Sep 29 p2 c4

POTTER, ANTHONY (Swanzey, Massachusetts) (Swansea) (Notice)

1841

-Information on Anthony Potter sought Mar 20,27 p3 c4

POTTS, REVEREND DOCTOR (Notice)

1840

-Will preach in the Second Presbyterian Church of Color Nov 7 p3 c3
Nov 14 p3 c4

POWELL, EDWARD (and Catharine Crummell) (Notice)

1840

-Information sought by a relative — Oct 17 p3 c3-Nov 7 p3 c4

POWELL, WILLIAM P. (Advertisement)

1837

-Elected to committee to study slavery in Washington, D.C. — Nov 18 p3 c3

1840

-Boarding house for seamen — Mar 21 p3 c3-Oct 3 p4 c4

-Partnership with George A. Bodee — Jun 6 p3 c4-Oct 3 p4 c4

1841

-Partnership dissolved and new one consummated — Jul 10 p3 c4-Sep 18 p3 c4

-See also George A. Bodee

POYER, AARON L.

1837

-Praised for closing shop on Sunday in observance of Sabbath — Dec 9 p2 c4

PRATT, WILLIAM WYLLS (Notice)

1840

-Free passage for emigrants to Jamaica — Nov 7 p3 c4-Dec 26 p3 c4

PRAY, MR.

1837

-Speaks at Temperance Jubilee — Apr 1 p3 c1

PRAYER FOR THE SLAVE (Notice)

1837

-Monthly concert — Jul 29 p3 c4

PREJUDICE

-See Racism

PRESBYTERIAN CHURCH (New York City) (Notice)

1837

-Public meeting to express sympathy — Dec 16 p3 c4

1838

-Anniversary fair — May 3 p3 c4

	1840
-Sermon by Reverend Dr. Samuel H. Cox	Mar 14 p3 c3
-Fair by ladies	Apr 25 p3 c3-May 9 p3 c4
-Reopening after being closed for repairs	Oct 3 p3 c3
-Anniversary of the Female Education Society	Oct 17 p3 c4
PRESBYTERIAN CHURCH (Newark, New Jersey) (Notice)	
	1839
-Fair	Feb 16 p3 c4
	1840
	Jul 25 p3 c4
PRESBYTERY OF CHILLICOTHE(Ohio)	
	1837
-Opposes slavery	May 13 p4 c3
PRESBYTERY (Cincinnati)	
	1837
-Refuses to admit slave owners	Apr 29 p2 c1
PRESBYTERY (Genesee, New York)	
	1837
-Sees slavery a sin	Apr 22 p4 c3
PRESBYTERY OF MONTROSE (Pennsylvania)	
	1837
-Passes resolutions against slavery and colonization	May 13 p4 c2
PRESBYTERY OF NIAGARA (New York)	
	1837
-Opposes slavery	May 13 p4 c3
PRESBYTERY OF PORTAGE (New York)	
	1837
-Opposes slavery	May 13 p4 c3
PRICES (Wholesale) (New York City)	
	1839
-Listed	Jan 12 p3 c4 Jan 19 p3 c4 Jan 26 p3 c4 Feb 2 p3 c4 Feb 23 p3 c4 Mar 2 p3 c4 Mar 9 p3 c4 Mar 16 p3 c4

	1840
-Listed	Mar 7 p3 c4 Mar 14 p3 c4 Mar 21 p3 c4 Mar 28 p3 c4 Apr 25 p3 c4 May 9 p3 c4 May 16 p3 c4
	1841
-Listed	Feb 13 p4 c4 Feb 20 p4 c4
PRINCETON WHIG -See Racism (United States)	
PRINTING AND BOOK BINDING (Advertisement)	
	1838
-161 Duane Street	Jun 2 p3 c4- Dec 29 p4 c3
	1839
	Jul 20 p3 c4 Aug 17 p4 c3- Nov 23 p4 c3
PROTESTANT EPISCOPAL FREE CHURCH (notice)	
	1838
-Services	Oct 27 p3 c4 Nov 3 p3 c4
	1839
-Charity sermon	Feb 2 p3 c4
PROTESTANT METHODIST MEETING HOUSE (Notice)	
	1840
-Raising money to build a church and school in Rochester, New York	Jun 6 p3 c4
PROUDFIT, REVEREND DR.	
	1837
-Secretary of the New York Colonization Society praises the abilities of blacks	Mar 25 p2 c4
PROVIDENCE ANTI-SLAVERY SOCIETY	
	1837
-Passes resolution criticizing ministers who do not condemn slavery	Jun 3 p2 c2

PUBLIC DISCUSSIONS (Notice)

1837

-On non-resistance — Dec 2 p3 c4

1841

-On women's rights — Mar 13 p3 c4

-Against threats of Maryland Colonization Convention — Jun 19 p3 c4

PUBLIC SCHOOL SOCIETY

1837

-Members to receive a copy of the Colored American — Mar 25 p3 c2

PUBLIC SCHOOLS (Notice)

1837

-Notice — Sep 2 p3 c4

1838

-Public education of colored children — Dec 15 p3 c3-Dec 29 p4 c4

1840

-Exhibit at public school #1; female department — May 9 p3 c4

1841

-Public exhibit of colored pupils of Brooklyn — Aug 7 p3 c3

PURVIS, ROBERT

1837

-Secretary of the American Reform Society Convention (Philadelphia) — Aug 19 p3 c1

-Criticized for his actions at the convention — Aug 26 p2 c1

-Lawyer for Basil Dorsey, accused fugitive slave — Sep 2 p4 c2

Q

QUARTERLY METHODIST CONFERENCE (Lowell, Massachusetts)

1837

- -Adopts resolutions against slavery and the internal slave trade — Jun 10 p1 c3

QUINCY, EDMUND

1838

- -Praised for anti-slavery lecture — Jun 9 p1 c4

QUONN, MARK (Advertisement)

1837

- -"Marine Pavilion" for boarders — May 27 p3 c4-Dec 30 p4 c4

1838

Jan 13-27 p4 c3
Jun 30 p4 c4-Dec 29 p4 c4

R

RACE (Separation)
-See Separation of the Races

RACISM (Alabama)

1839

- -Alabama law would imprison black crewmen of ships until ship departs — Jun 1 p4 c4

1841

- -Mulatto thrown out of church in Alabama — Apr 3 p2 c1
- -Law authorizes arrest of any free black found along a bay or wharf — Dec 25 p2 c1

RACISM (Churches)

1837

- -Accuses Christian churches and ministers of prejudice and racism — Mar 11 p2 c4; Mar 18 p2 c2; Mar 25 pp2,3 c1,3

-Stresses need for reform of prejudiced attitudes within the church — Apr 1 p2 c3
-Churches making heathens of thousands — Apr 8 p2 c3
-Stresses sinfulness of color prejudice in the church — Oct 7 p2 c1
-Evidence of the spirit of slavery and caste in American Christian churches — Oct 28 p2 c4
-Cites lack of prejudice in two New York churches — Nov 4 p3 c3 let.
-Christian ministers accused of apathy and prejudice toward slaves — Nov 4 p4 c3
-J. W. Duffin describes episode of prejudiced treatment in Presbyterian lecture room — Dec 9 p2 c2
-Discrimination in white congregations criticized — Dec 23 p3 c2

1838

-Quaker condemns prejudice in white churches — Feb 17 p3 c2
-Episcopal seminary refuses to admit black student, Alexander Crummell — Sep 7 p1 c1

1839

-Black girl's entry into Sabbath School causes riot — Sep 7 p4 c2
-Mr. Crummell receives sympathetic resolutions from students at Oneida Institute — Sep 28 p3 c2

1840

-Segregation in churches and seating with few black ministers — Mar 21 p1 c1
-Man excluded from the Methodist church — Oct 24 p2 c1
-See also Negro Pew; Racism (Alabama)

RACISM (Europe)

1837

-Mr. Goodell comments on lack of Racism in Europe — Mar 11 p1 c1
-No color prejudice in England and France — Sep 22 p3 c2

1840

-Charles Lenox Remond experienced no racism in England — Oct 3 p3 c1

	1841
-Lack of racial prejudice in France reported	Jun 12 p3 c1

RACISM (India)

	1837
-Mr. Goodell comments on lack of racism in India	Mar 11 p1 c2

RACISM (Kentucky)

	1841
-Blacks persecuted in Kentucky	Oct 16 p2 c4

RACISM (Maine)

	1837
-Notes color prejudice among white abolitionists	Mar 25 p4 c2

RACISM (Massachusetts)

	1841
-Blacks forcibly ejected from railroad cars	Oct 16 p3 c1 let.
-Frederick Douglass forcibly removed from a railroad car	Oct 30 p1 c2 let.

RACISM (New York City)

	1837
-Blacks denied licenses as carmen or porters	Sep 16 p2 c1

RACISM (Rhode Island)

	1841
-Rhode Island Suffrage Convention disfranchises blacks	Oct 30 p3 c1 ed.

RACISM (United States)

	1837
-Racism defined	Mar 4 p3 c4 ed.
-Mr. Goodell accuses the American Colonization Society of racism	Mar 11 p1 c1
-Accuses Christian churches of being strongholds of color prejudice	Mar 11 p2 c4
-Notes color prejudice in New Bedford shipping industry	Mar 11 p4 c2
-Caste seen as the problem, not racism (from the New York _Evangelist_)	Mar 25 p4 c1
-Notes color prejudice among white Maine abolitionists	Mar 25 p4 c2
-Strongest where there are the most blacks	Apr 8 p3 c3

-Most important subject before the American people	Jun 3 p2 c2
-Needless travel a waste for blacks who face racism on coaches	Jun 10 p2 c3
-Black refused entry onto omnibus in New York (from New York Times)	Jun 10 p3 cl
-Colored American seen too strong in its criticism of racist attitudes	Aug 5 p2 cl let.
-Blacks think those lighter-skinned are better	Aug 19 p2 c3
-Educated people refuse to sit next to a black	Sep 2 p3 cl
-Praises abolitionists for role in reducing prejudice	Sep 9 p2 cl
-Northerners called upon to present good example to Southerners by purging themselves of prejudice	Nov 4 pl c4
-Inconsistent behavior of white Americans toward colored race pointed out	Nov 4 p3 cl
-Color prejudice in the United States compared with Hindu caste system	Nov 11 pl c4
-Reverend Theodore Wright addresses New York Anti-Slavery Society on color prejudice	Nov 11 p3 cl
-Conduct of many northerners toward blacks viewed as inconsistent with criticism of southern slaveholders	Dec 23 p2 c3
	1838
-American ship captain accused of racial prejudice toward black passenger	Feb 17 p2 c2 let.
-Lack of educational opportunities for black children blamed on color prejudice	Mar 3 p3 c2
-United States viewed as a cradle of racism	Mar 15 p2 cl
-American Colonization Society linked with racist views	Apr 19 p2 c3 let.
-Denial that abolitionists increase racism	Jun 2 p2 c3 ed.
-Definition of different prejudices	Jun 2 p2 c4 let.
-Color prejudice the major cause of conflict over freedom and slavery	Jun 9 p3 c3 ed.

-Anecdote relates prejudicial treatment aboard an excursion boat	Sep 8 p2 c3 let.
-Color prejudice exists extensively in the North even though slavery doesn't	Sep 15 pl c4
-Those of mixed blood are often the worst persecutors of colored people	Sep 15 p3 c3
-Facts regarding pro-slavery colleges and seminaries	Oct 13 pl cl
-Discrimination in canal packet boat travel related	Oct 13 p2 c2 let.
-Anecdote emphasizes apparent color prejudices of some blacks	Oct 20 p2 cl let.
-Apparent color prejudice of some blacks seen a result of job necessity	Oct 20 p2 c2 ed.
-Denial that blacks are a degraded race	Oct 27 p3 cl ed.
-Colonizationists feel that blacks are physically inferior	Dec 22 p2 cl
-Causes death of a woman	Dec 22 p2 c2
	1839
-Criticizes racism of citizens who fulfill all other obligations to society	Jan 12 p4 cl let.
-Racism described as absurd and unjust	Jan 12 p2 c4
-Not racism which holds blacks back but their economic condition	Feb 16 p2 c3 let.
-Labor and talent can overcome prejudice	Mar 9 p2 cl ed.
-Racism is not the only cause of blacks' condition	May 11 p2 c2
-Color prejudice compared to insanity and disease	Jul 13 pl c2
-Racism makes it harder for blacks to get an education	Aug 3 p2 c2
-Racism of Princeton Whig criticized	Sep 14 p3 c2
	1840
-Not a part of human nature; stronger in the North	Mar 7 pl cl
-Blacks are subjected to abuse	Mar 21 pl cl
-On the contradictions inherent in color prejudice	Sep 5 pl cl
-The most common prejudice is against color	Sep 26 p2 c2

-Charles Remond experienced a terrible time on the ship to England — Oct 3 p2 c4
-Prejudice in train travel — Oct 24 p2 c2

1841

-Mistreatment of blacks on New England railroad noted and decried — May 1 p1 c3 let.
-Blacks persecuted in Kentucky — Oct 16 p2 c4

RACISM (West Indies)

1837

-Notes lack of color prejudice on St. Thomas Island — Mar 11 p4 c1
-Notes lessening of color prejudice in St. Kitts — Apr 1 p1 c2

1838

-Lack of color prejudice in Haiti noted — Mar 22 p1 c2 let.

RACISM
-See also Blacks (Legal Discrimination)

RAILROADS

1840

-Element of monopoly seen, but North-South roads are helpful to escaping slaves — Sep 26 p2 c2

1841

-People protest against the track south of 14th Street; ask for its removal — Mar 6 p2 c2
-Mistreatment of blacks by eastern railroad conductors reported and decried — May 1 p1 c3 let.
-Massachusetts railroads abuse black passengers — Jun 19 p2 c4; Sep 4 p3 c1
-New York and Harlem Railroad criticized for racial prejudice — Sep 25 p2 c2 let.
-See also Douglass, Frederick; Jinnings, Thomas L.

RAND, DENNIS

1838

-Dies — Aug 4 p3 c4

RANDOLF, JOHN (Virginia)

1837

-Will published — Jul 29 p3 c3

RANTOUS, WILSON (Jamaica, New York)	
	1837
-Elected vice-president of the Jamaica Benevolent Society	May 27 p2 c4
RAWLINGS, MR. (Rollings) (Advertisement)	
	1837
-Board without lodging for three or four gentlemen	Nov 11 p3 c4- Dec 30 p4 c4
	1838
	Jan 13 p4 c3- Feb 17 p4 c3 Apr 12, 19 p4 c3
RAY, REVEREND CHARLES B.	
	1837
-Wife's death eulogized by Samuel Cornish	Mar 4 p3 c2
-Listed as general agent for the Colored American	Apr 1 p3 c1
-Sends $40.00 to the paper	Apr 15 p3 c4
-Sends $66.75 to the paper	Apr 22 p3 c4
-Sends $34.50 to the paper	Jun 17 p3 c4
-To go out as traveling agent in New England	Jun 24 p3 c1
-Writes of his travels in New England	Jul 15 p3 c3
-Will go to upstate New York to raise money and encourage petitions to legislature about black voting rights; also for Colored American Subscriptions	Aug 12 p3 c3 Aug 19 p3 c3
-Refused tea on boat unless he has it in the kitchen; describes travels in New York State	Sep 2 p1 c3
-Cites discrimination against him	Sep 9 p1 c2
-Describes stay in Syracuse, New York	Sep 30 p3 c2
-Describes stay in Geneva, New York	Oct 14 p3 c3
-Describes colored communities in Buffalo and Lockport, New York; raises $60.00 in donations for the Colored American	Nov 4 p2 c2

-Criticizes blacks moving to Canada; tells them to go to the Wisconsin Territory	Nov 18 p2 c3 let.
-Comes back from trip with few subscribers	Nov 25 p2 c3
-Urges attendance at meeting to support Colored American	Dec 16 p3 c4
-Recounts successes of Colored American during first year of publication	Dec 23 p2 c4
	1838
-Receives equal privileges on steamboat trip to Boston	Jun 16 p1 c1 let.
-Describes citizens of Boston as industrious and intelligent but prejudiced	Jul 7 p2 c4
-Describes New England towns and black communities	Jul 28 p2 c4 let.
-Describes tour through western New York; treatment while traveling; praises Gerrit Smith; discusses unity among blacks; abolition movement in Waterville, New York	Sep 1 p2 c3 let. Sep 15 p2 c3 let. Sep 22 p2 c2 let. Sep 29 p4 c1,2 let.
-Describes annual meeting of New York State Anti-Slavery Society	Oct 6 p2 c2 let.
-Describes continued journey through New York	Oct 20 p2 c3 let.
-Praised for sermons on color prejudice; achievements lauded	Oct 27 p2 c2 ed.
-Describes Niagara Falls; visits in Western New York; favors use of term "colored"	Nov 3 pp2,3 c2,3 let.
-Describes black congregations and communities in Troy and Albany, New York	Dec 15 p2 c3 let.
	1839
-Criticizes colonization	Jan 12 p2 c3 let.
-Description and comments on journey through New Jersey	Jul 20 p3 c1 let.
-Describes trip from Philadelphia to Westchester, Pennsylvania	Jul 27 p3 c5 let.
-Describes Pennsylvania towns	Aug 31 p2 c5 let.
-Describes feeling when he first sees a slave	Sep 28 p2 c5 let.
-Describes Columbus, Ohio and other towns	Oct 19 p2 c4,5 let.

1840

-Praised for his anti-slavery work by an Englishman — Apr 4 p3 c1 let.
-Editor and proprietor of the Colored American — Apr 25 p2 c4

1841

-Plans to lecture on dietetic reform before Philomathean Society noted — Apr 10 p3 c4
-Plans trip West — Jun 26 p2 c3
-Describes trip to western New York and Auburn Convention — Jul 3 p2 c3 let.
Jul 17 p2 c2 let.
-Endorses planned New York State franchise convention — Jul 24 p2 c2 let.
-Addresses Buffalo blacks on Troy Convention and Maryland Colonization Convention — Jul 31 p1 c3
-Continues description of New York trip — Aug 7 p2 c1 let.
-Notes return home from trip — Aug 7 p2 c2
See also Voting Rights (Free Blacks) (New York)

RAY, MRS. HENRIETTA D.

1837

-Death eulogized by Reverend Samuel Cornish — Mar 4 p3 c2

RAYMOND, J.T.

1837

-Elected president of the Roger Williams Anti-Slavery Society (New York) — Apr 15 p3 c3

1838

-Becomes agent for the Colored American — Feb 17 p3 c4

READ, TIMOTHY (New Haven, Connecticut) (Notice)

1841

-Opens a select (private) English school — Sep 18 p3 c3

READING ROOM (Notice)

1838

-Opened by Philip Bell — Jul 28 p3 c4
Aug 4 p3 c4

1839

Jan 19 p4 c4-
Mar 16 p4 c4

REASON, CHARLES

	1837
-Appointed vice-president of the Colored Young Men of New York City	Sep 2 p1 c1
-Listed as one of two secretaries of the Colored Citizens of New York	Oct 28 p1 c3
	1838
-Appointed recording secretary of the Political Association	Jun 16 p2 c4
-Secretary at public meeting of the Political Association	Jul 14 p3 c2
	1840
-Listed as secretary of the Phoenixonian Literary Society	Jul 4 p1 c1 let.
	1841
-Attacks Thomas VanRenssalear's conduct and statements	Jul 10 p2 c2 let.
-See also VanRenssalaer,Thomas	

REASON, PATRICK H. (Advertisement)

	1838
-Historical, portrait, and landscape engraver; draughtsman; lithographer; offers instruction	Apr 12 p3 c4- Apr 19 pp3,4 c3,4 May 3 pp3,4 c3,4 Jun 2 p4 c4
-Appointed to the executive committee of the Political Association	Jun 16 p2 c3
-Advertisements continued	Jul 14 p2 c2,4- Dec 29 p4 c3,4
	1839
	Jan 12 p2 c3

RECREATION

	1840
-Summer outings to the country encouraged	Jul 4 p2 c3

REESE, DR. DAVID (Advertisement)

	1838
-Publishes <u>Humbugs in New York</u>	Mar 15 p3 c3
-His pro-slavery book attacked (<u>An Appeal to the Reason and Religion of American Christians, Against the American Anti-Slavery Society</u>)	Apr 5 p3 c3
-Pamphlet ("An Anecdote for a Poisonous Combination")	Apr 19 p4 c2

	May 3 p4 c3
	Jun 2-16 p4 c4
REFECTORY TO LET (Advertisement)	
	1838
-Rental notice	Feb 17 p3 c4
REFORM	
-See American Moral Reform Society; Moral Reform	
RELIGION (General)	
	1837
-Stresses need for religious faith	Apr 1 p2 c4
-Stresses need to adopt Christianity in youth	Apr 8 p4 c2
-Questions whether blacks can belong to white churches	Apr 15 p3 c2 let.
-Stresses religious faith as the most important quality in a woman	Oct 7 p1 c4
-Massachusetts Anti-Slavery Society calls upon Christian ministers to uphold the cause of human freedom	Oct 7 p3 c3
-Criticizes materialism; lack of spirituality	Nov 4 p2 c3 let.
-Biblical passages support the pro-slavery viewpoint	Nov 4 p4 c1
-True religion the means of universal enfranchisement	Dec 16 p2 c2
	1838
-Lack of spiritual preparation for death deplored	Mar 15 p4 c2
-Spirit of devil behind persecution	Apr 12 p3 c1 ed.
-True religion transcends the grave	Apr 19 p4 c1
-Questions regarding family religious devotion	Jul 7 p4 c2
-Importance of studying the Scriptures	Jul 21 p1 c2
-Description of missionary work in Jamaica	Jul 21 p1 c3
-Prayer and faith are mighty weapons against slavery	Jul 28 p3 c1 ed.
-Religious feeling guided English Parliament toward emancipation in the West Indies	Jul 28 p3 c1
-Immensity of God's creation	Aug 11 p1 c4
-Emancipation grows out of the Gospel	Aug 11 p3 c1

-Anecdote stresses despair of an infidel's death	Sep 8 p1 c2
-Anecdote relates conversion of a Jew	Sep 8 p1 c3
-Christians awakening to their anti-slavery duty	Oct 6 p2 c1 ed.
-Ancient and modern Christianity contrasted	Oct 13 p2 c4
-How a true gentleman behaves in church	Oct 13 p4 c4
-Dialogue between Moses and Pharoah about release of Hebrew slaves	Oct 20 p1 c2
-God requires purity of principle and practice	Oct 27 p4 c2
-Christian faith leads to concern for others	Dec 8 p2 c3
-Anecdote describes piety of a ship's crew	Dec 8 p2 c3
-Christians must not put off religion until it is too late	Dec 8 p2 c3 ed.
-Anecdote illustrates the golden rule	Dec 8 p2 c4
-Christianity sustains the slave during his trials	Dec 8 p4 c2
-Separation from slaveholding congregations feared necessary	Dec 15 p1 c3 ed.
-Consequences of faithlessness noted	Dec 15 p1 c4
	1839
-Story of an ex-slave's religious experience	Jan 19 p4 c1 Jan 26 p1 c4
-Importance of religion to those in public political life	Jan 19 p4 c2
-Faith surmounts all difficulties	Mar 9 p1 c4
-On the value and significance of churches	Mar 9 p1 c4
-The only true knowledge is that of Christ	Mar 9 p1 c4
-Religious essay on the nature of heaven	Mar 9 p4 c3
-Anecdote stresses need for faith in times of tribulation	Mar 16 p4 c2
-Only Christianity is able to sustain blacks against persecution	Jun 1 p3 c1 ed.
-Thomas Scott's exposition of the Bible misused by southern ministers (from the Emancipator)	Jun 8 p1 c4

-Not important whether Abraham had slaves or Jesus left slavery existing in the church	Jun 8 p3 c1
-*Colored American* explains why it dwells on the impurities of the church	Jun 8 p3 c2
-On the spiritual nature of man	Jul 13 p1 c5
-Religion in the south ministers to purposes of slavery	Jul 20 p1 c5
-Description of Jesus Christ	Aug 3 p1 c5 ed.
-No excuse for not going to church	Dec 7 p3 c5
	1840
-One must obey God rather than man	Apr 4 p1 c4
-Faith is rewarded	Apr 11 p3 c2
-On the value of public worship	May 16 p1 c3
-Anedcote on the power of religion	May 23 p4 c2
-On the loneliness of a Christian death	May 30 p4 c1
-The preaching of the Gospel brings civilization to heathens	Aug 29 p4 c2
-Anecdote on the necessity of salvation	Oct 31 p4 c1
-Holiness is necessary to salvation	Nov 7 p1 c4
-Description of Puritans in the Age of Milton	Nov 7 p4 c2
-Advice on how to meet God	Nov 7 p4 c3
-On the quality of God's mercy	Nov 14 p1 c2
-On the advance of Protestantism in France	Nov 14 p4 c1
-Prerequisites of the genuine convert	Dec 5 p4 c2
-The Devil's ten commandments	Dec 5 p4 c4
-Story illustrating the Second Commandment	Dec 26 p4 c1
	1841
-Those who die in Christ are not lost	Apr 3 p4 c1
-Christ's gift of love	Apr 3 p4 c2
-Story of a religious soldier	Jun 26 p4 c1
-Anecdote on the truth of Christianity	Oct 9 p1 c4
-See also Churches (Black); Churches (Christian); Churches (Congregational); Churches (Presbyterian); Religion (Methodism); Sabbatarianism	

RELIGION (Episcopalian)

1841

-Examples of church papers contenancing slavery — Sep 18 p1 c3

RELIGION (Judaism)

1841

-World distribution of Jewish communities discussed — Sep 11 p4 c4

RELIGION (Methodism)

1837

-Description of Methodist principles and history of schism between white and colored congregations — Oct 14 p2 c1
-Lists four types of Methodist commitments among colored Methodists — Oct 14 p2 c3
-Lists Methodist's black congregations and membership statistics — Oct 14 p2 c3
-White Methodist ministers criticized for stand on slavery — Dec 16 p2 c1

1838

-Methodist Church sins in accepting slavery; convention needed to consider separation movement — Dec 15 p1 c2

RELIGION (West Indies)

1837

-Describes effects of emancipation upon religious observance — Apr 1 p1 c1

1840

-Public worship increasing since emancipation — Apr 11 p3 c3

REMOND, CHARLES LENOX (Providence, Rhode Island)

1837

-Listed as agent for the Colored American — Mar 4 p4 c4
-Gives speech at Rhode Island Anti-Slavery Society — Nov 25 p2 c4

1840

-Appointed delegate to London Anti-Slavery Convention — May 30 p3 c1
-Speech at convention — Aug 8 p1 c1

-Describes his impressions of the conference — Oct 3 p2 c4 let.
-Stresses advances of abolition cause and praises abolitionists — Nov 7 p1 c1 let.
-Signs abstinence pledge in Edinburgh — Nov 7 p1 c2 let.
-Speaks on slavery at public meeting in Scotland — Nov 7 p1 c2
-Anti-slavery address in Perth, England — Dec 5 p1 c4

<u>1841</u>

-Extract of his speech to the British and Foreign Anti-Slavery Society — Jul 10 p1 c1
-See also Racism (Europe); Racism (United States); Thompson, George

RENSHAW, CHARLES STEWART

<u>1840</u>

-Testifies to the industry and general contentment of black Jamaicans — May 23 p1 c1 let.
-Outlines reasons why emigration to Jamaica would be disastrous — Jul 18 p1 c3 let.
-Educates Jamaicans on American slavery — Nov 7 p2 c3

RENSSELAER COUNTY CONVENTION

<u>1841</u>

-Held by blacks; resolved to circulate petitions for suffrage — Nov 20 p1 c4

RHODE ISLAND SUFFRAGE CONVENTION

<u>1841</u>

-Disfranchises blacks — Oct 30 p3 c1 ed.

RICE, E.A. (Lowell, Massachusetts)

<u>1838</u>

-Listed as agent for the <u>Colored</u> <u>American</u> — Aug 18 p4 c3

RICE, THOMAS D.

<u>1837</u>

-Criticized for ridiculing black people in stage performances — Dec 9 p2 c4

RICE, WILLIAM

<u>1837</u>

-Cited for kindness and generosity toward victims of boating mishap — Oct 14 p4 c2

RICH, WILLIAM (Troy, New York)

1837

-Listed as agent for the Colored American — Mar 4 p4 c4
-Sends in list of thirteen subscribers — Apr 8 p2 c4
-Director of the Union Society of Albany — Apr 15 p1 c3
-Listed as vice-president of the Mental and Moral Improvement Society of Troy, New York — Oct 14 p3 c4

RIGHTS OF COLORED MEN TO SUFFRAGE, CITIZENSHIP, ETC.

1838

-Book published — Mar 3 p3 c3
-Described and recommended — Mar 22 p2 c2 ed.
-Extracts — Apr 5 p3 c1
-Praised — Apr 19 p2 c3 ed.

RIOTS
-See Mob Violence

RISING STATES, THE

1837

-Black-owned vessel described — Mar 11 p4 c2
-Black owned and manned vessel out of New Bedford made whaling voyage — Jul 22 p2 c4
-See also Cuffee, William; Hambleton, William; Johnson, Richard; Pompey, Captain Edward J.

RITNER, JOSEPH

1838

-Governor of Pennsylvania praised for offering reward for rioters — Jun 9 p2 c4 ed.

ROACH, DAVID (Pottsville, Pennsylvania)

1838

-Listed as agent for the Colored American — Jan 13 p4 c4

ROBERTS, GEORGE (Philadelphia, Pennsylvania)

1838

-Marries Ann Whopper — Jun 9 p3 c4

ROBERTS, JOHN B.

1837

-Director of the American Moral Reform Society calls a meeting — Aug 5 p3 c3

ROBERTSON, JOHN

1837

-Elected treasurer of the Mutual Relief Society of New York — Sep 9 p2 c4

ROBINSON, MR. AND MRS. (Boston)

1838

-Tried for kidnapping a black girl from Alabama slavery; convicted — Jan 13 p2 c1

ROBINSON, E. (Advertisement)

1837

-Tailoring — Jun 17 p3 c4; Jul 1 p4 c3-Jul 29 p4 c3

-Opposed to slavery — Jul 22 p3 c4-Sep 23 p4 c4

ROCHESTER COLORED TOTAL ABSTINENCE ASSOCIATION (Notice)

1840

-Pledges received — Dec 4 p3 c3

ROCKWELL, SIDNEY W. (Hartford, Connecticut)

1837

-Listed as agent for the Colored American — Apr 1 p3 c1

ROGERS, MR. (Advertisement)

1837

-Reopens writing school — Sep 30 p3 c4-Dec 16 p4 c4

1841

-Vocal lessons — Jul 17 p3 c3-Sep 4 p3 c4

ROGER WILLIAMS ANTI-SLAVERY SOCIETY (New York)

1837

-Holds meeting — Apr 15 p3 c3

-Public meeting — Jun 10, 17 p3 c4

-Holds public meeting — Oct 7 p3 c4

-Notes plans for public meeting — Oct 14 p4 c3

-Dissolved and reformed as the Zion Baptist Anti-Slavery Society — Dec 9 p3 c4

-See also Horner, J.M.; Octon, L.; Zion Baptist Anti-Slavery Society

ROGERS, NATHANIEL PEABODY

	1840
-Appointed a delegate to the London Anti-Slavery Convention	May 30 p3 c1

ROOT, GENERAL

	1837
-Speaks against slavery at 1821 New York Constitutional Convention	Mar 11 p2 c2

ROSCOE

	1839
-Character sketch by Lord Brougham	Jul 27 p1 c3

ROSE, DOCTOR ROBERT H.

	1838
-His Silver Lake Colony fails	Aug 18 p2 c1

ROTCH, WILLIAM

	1837
-President of the Anti-Slave Society of New Bedford (Massachusetts)	Jul 22 p2 c4

ROUSSEAU, JEAN JACQUES

	1841
-Examined as a moral reformer	Apr 17 p4 c3

ROZELLE (Roselle), DAVID (New Haven, Connecticut)

	1837
-Listed as agent for the <u>Colored American</u>	May 13 p4 c4
-Sends in $4.00 to the paper	Jun 17 p3 c4

RUGGLES, DAVID (Advertisements and Notices)

	1837
-Advertising for a male teacher and a boy	Sep 23 p3 c4-Oct 7 p4 c3
	1838
-Tribute of respect to him	Sep 29 p3 c4
-Has lad of 16, boy of 8, girl of 11	Oct 20 p3 c4-Dec 8 p4 c4
	1839
-Postpones meeting	Mar 9 p3 c3

RUGGLES, DAVID (General)

	1837
-Notes proposed meeting and program of New York Committee of Vigilance	Mar 11 p3 c4
-Announces meeting to raise money for William Dickson	Jul 15 p2 c4
-Announces third anniversary celebration of British West India emancipation	Jul 15 p3 c3
-Announces celebration by Vigilance Committee of August 1st	Jul 29 p3 c3
-Describes kidnapping of black boy who was taken south	Sep 16 p3 c3 let.
	1838
-Requests financial aid for New York Vigilance Committee	Jul 21 p2 c1 let.
-Becomes editor of The Mirror of Liberty	Jul 21 p3 c4
-Tracks down Thomas Lewis who kidnapped and sold three blacks into slavery	Aug 18 p4 c3
-Describes traveling conditions encountered while searching for Thomas Lewis	Aug 25 p3 c4
-Involved in libel suit	Oct 20 p3 c2
	1839
-Discusses his role in libel suit against the Colored American	Jan 26 p3 c1
-Criticized as a do-nothing	Feb 23 p2 c4 let.
-Says editors of Colored American treated him with envy, hatred, and malice	Feb 23 p3 c1
-Paper says it feels pity for him; has backed him against much criticism for years	Feb 23 p3 c1 ed.
-Demands a public investigation of his conduct	Mar 2 p3 c2
-Proceedings of public meeting at which he accused Colored American editors of being responsible for his persecution	Jul 27 p2 c2 ed.
-Accuses Philip Bell of religious activity	Sep 7 p3 c5
-His investigation committee protests the Colored American calling it a "white-washing committee"	Sep 14 p2 c4

	1840
-Praised by Free blacks of Hartford	Jun 13 p1 c4
-Praised by colored citizens of New York City	Sep 5 p2 c4 let.
-Accuses Colored American of numerous offenses; paper responds	Sep 12 p2 c4 let. Sep 12 p3 c1 ed.
-See also Cornish, Reverend Samuel; Fugitive Slaves; Mirror of Liberty; New York Vigilance Committee	
RUIZ, DON JOSE (Havana, Cuba)	
	1841
-Accused of fraud in Amistad case	Jan 2 p1 c3 let.
-Accused of deceit by Amistad captive	Mar 27 p2 c1 let.
RUSH, REVEREND CHRISTOPHER	
	1837
-Elected an honorary member of the Mental and Moral Improvement Association (Troy, New York)	Oct 21 p1 c2
RUSHTON, EDWARD	
	1837
-Criticized George Washington for owning slaves	Nov 18 p1 c1
RUSSELL, CAPTAIN JOHN	
	1837
-Accused of attempted ship-board sale of black slaves	Oct 7 p2 c4
-Sues Colored American for libel	Oct 28 p3 c1
RUSSELL, SAMUEL	
	1837
-Speaks against slavery at 1821 New York Constitutional Convention	Mar 11 p2 c2
RUSSIA -See Serfdom	

S

SABBATARIANISM

1837

-Criticizes Pittsburgh Society of Moral Reform for failure to enforce Sabbath observance — Mar 25 p4 c3
-Speech on the observance of the Sabbath — Apr 1 p1 c4
-Praises John Vashon for closing his business on Sundays — Apr 1 p2 c2 let.
-Expresses hope that all black businessmen will follow Sabbath observance — Apr 1 p2 c2
-Evil consequences of Sabbath-breaking stressed — Nov 11 p2 c2
-Hairdresser praised for keeping shop closed on Sunday — Dec 9 p2 c4 let.

1838

-Church attendance urged — Feb 17 p2 c1

1840

-On the delights of the Sabbath — May 30 p2 c1
-On the benefits of observing the Sabbath — Dec 12 p3 c2

1841

-On the fate of Sabbath-breakers — Sep 11 p4 c2
-See also Slavery (St. Thomas)

SABBATH SCHOOLS

1837

-Spiritual strength of deaf and blind girl related to show utility of Sabbath Schools — Oct 28 p3 c3
-Sailor offered as example of Christian charity for donations to Sabbath School — Dec 9 p2 c1
-Need for Sabbath Schools stressed — Apr 15 p2 c2 let.
-Church schools closed to black children — Apr 22 p2 c2

1838

-Praised — Jun 30 p2 c2 let.
-Schools necessary to promote more interest in black unity — Aug 4 p2 c2 let.

	1839
-Description of Sabbath Schools of Sandwich Islands	Mar 16 p1 c3
-On the value of Sabbath Schools for young minds	Jul 20 p3 c2 ed.
-Formation of new Methodist Sabbath School noted	Sep 7 p2 c2 let.
	1840
-On their positive value	Jul 25 p4 c2
	1841
-Parents urged to send children	Jan 30 p1 c1 let.
-Inquiry into their usefulness	Jun 26 p4 c2
-Exhibition praised	Nov 13 p3 c1

SACRED CONCERT (Notice)

	1841
-Concert and Union Oyster Supper in Bethel Church	Feb 20 p3 c3,4
-Reverend Theodore S. Wright's Church	Mar 6 p3 c4

SAFETY

	1839
-Blacks in New York do not lock their doors; Colored American feels they should	Mar 2 p2 c2 ed.

SAILORS

	1838
-Speech describes sailors and their need for sailors' homes	Jan 30 p1 c2
-Anecdotes illustrating the important lessons taught at a sailors' home	Nov 17 p1 c3 ed.
	1839
-Sailors can and should also have families	Jul 13 p4 c3
	1840
-Sailors home opens	Apr 11 p4 c3
-Progress report on Seamen's Saving Bank	May 16 p3 c3
-Libraries for British seamen established	May 16 p3 c3
-Increasing employment of black sailors viewed with approval; seen to make excellent officers and navigators	Dec 5 p2 c3

SAINT MARK'S SCHOOL (JAMAICA, LONG ISLAND, NEW YORK) (Notice)	
	1841
-For colored children	Feb 27 p3 c4
	Mar 20 p3 c4
-Described and praised	Apr 3 p3 c1
-Advertised	Apr 24 p3 c3- May 29 p3 c4
SAINT MATTHEW'S FREE CHURCH (Notice)	
	1839
-Services	Jun 15 p3 c4- Aug 31 p4 c3
	Sep 14 p4 c3
	Oct 5-19 p3 c4
	1840
-Changes location and ministers	Jul 4 p2 c4 let.
SAINT PETER'S CHURCH (Notice)	
	1838
-Acknowledgement of receipt of proceeds	Feb 10 p3 c4
SAINT PHILIP'S CHURCH (Notice)	
	1837
-Reopened	Dec 16 p3 c4
SANDWICH ISLANDS (Hawaii)	
	1838
-Missionary describes effect of Gospel on local populations	May 29 p2 c2
	1839
-Description of Sabbath schools of Sandwich Islands	Mar 16 p1 c3
	1841
-Described	Jan 16 p3 c3
-See also Science	
SCHOOLS (New York City)	
	1837
-Phoenix School forced to close due to lack of funds	Jul 1 p2 c2
-Black teachers receive less pay than whites	Jul 22 p3 c2
-Teachers wanted for Evening School for Colored People	Oct 28 p4 c4
-Female department of Phoenix High School opens	Oct 28 p4 c3
	1838
-Primary School #1 opens; students requested	Dec 15 p3 c3

	1839
-Episcopal School opens in Long Island	Jul 20 p3 c5
-Clarkson Association for the free instruction of colored women opens	Nov 23 p3 c5
	1840
-Young Ladies Domestic Seminary to hold summer courses	Apr 4 p3 c4
-Public schools open for term; attendance urged	Sep 5 p2 c2
-Evening school opens at Colored Second Presbyterian Church	Nov 7 p3 c4
-Description of public schools; attendance urged	Nov 28 p2 c2
-Webster's School for Study of Sacred Music opens	Dec 19 p3 c3
	1841
-Public school exhibition noted and praised	Jun 12 p2 cl let.
-Williamsburgh citizens plan to start school	Jul 3 p2 cl let.
-Public school exhibition noted and praised	Jul 10 p3 cl
-Attendance urged	Aug 21 p2 c3
-Public school exhibition noted	Sep 4 p2 cl

SCHOOLS (Pennsylvania)

	1841
-Male and Female Seminary established in Philadelphia	Apr 3 p3 cl
-Rules, bylaws and prospectus of new Philadelphia seminary	Apr 3 p3 c4
-Morning song of Male and Female Seminary of Philadelphia	Apr 10 p3 c2

SCIENCE

	1839
-Story of invention of gunpowder	Mar 9 pl c3
	1841
-On the phenomenon of dreaming	Jun 26 pl c2
-Hawaiian volcanoes described	Jul 24 p4 c2

SCOTT, H. AND COMPANY (Advertisement)

	1839
-Pickles, preserves, and jellies	Mar 2 p3 c4- Mar 16 p3 c4

May 11 p4 c4-
Sep 14 p4 c5
Oct 5 p4 c5-
Nov 23 p4 c5

1840
Mar 14 p4 c4-
Jun 6 p4 c4

SCOTT, HENRY (Worcester, Massachusetts) (Advertisement)

1839
-Wants a journeyman hairdresser — Mar 9 p3 c4; Mar 16 p4 c4; May 11 p4 c4

SCOTT, HENRY

1839
-Criticizes color prejudice — Jan 12 p1 c4

1840
-Considers slaveholders beneath contempt — Aug 29 p2 c1 let.

SCOTT, JOHN (Lockport, New York)

1838
-Listed as agent for the Colored American — Jan 13 p4 c4

SCOTT, REVEREND ORIN

1837
-Speaks at fourth anniversary meeting of the American Anti-Slavery Society — May 13 p3 c1

SCOTT, THOMAS
-See Religion (General)

SCOTT, SIR WALTER

1838
-Memoranda on his life and work — Jul 14 p2 c3

SCOTT, GENERAL WINFIELD

1841
-Expresses willingness to become a Presidential candidate — Nov 13 p3 c1

SEAMAN, TIMOTHY

1837
-Elected president of the Colored Young Men of New York City — Sep 2 p1 c1

SEAMAN'S SAVINGS BANK
  -See Sailors

SEARS' CHART OF THE WORLD (Advertisement)

	1837
-Charts, globes	Jan 7 p3 c4- Mar 18 p4 c3

SEARS, ROBERT

	1837
-Elected vice-president of the Roger Williams Anti-Slavery Society	Apr 15 p3 c3
-Printer (Advertisement)	Mar 4 p3 c3,4- Dec 30 p4 c4
	1838
	Jan 13 p4 c3- Jan 20 p4 c2
	Feb 17 p4 c2
	Apr 12, 19 p4 c3
	May 3 p4 c3
	Jun 2 pp1,4 c1,4- Dec 29 p1 c1
	1839
	Jan 12 p1 c1- Jan 26 p4 c4

SECOND COLORED PRESBYTERIAN CHURCH (New York) (Notice)

	1840
-Services	Jul 18 p3 c4

SECOND COLORED PRESBYTERIAN CHURCH (Philadelphia) (Notice)

	1837
-Fair	Sep 30 p3 c4

SEDGWICK, MR.

	1837
-Counsel for George Thompson, (alias Ben), an escaped slave	Apr 8 p3 c2
-See also Irving, Judge; Wilkinson, General	

SEGREGATION
  -See Separation of the Races

SELDON, CLARENCE (Troy, New York)

	1837
-Recording secretary of the Union Society of Albany	Apr 1 p2 c1
	Apr 15 p1 c3
-Delivers address on temperance to the Mental and Moral Improvement Association of Troy	Oct 21 p1 c2

SELF IMPROVEMENT
-See Free Blacks (Self-Improvement)

SEMINOLE WAR
-See Giddings, Joshua; War

SENECA INDIAN COUGH SYRUP (Advertisement)

	1837
-For Sale	Dec 16 p3 c4 Dec 30 p4 c2
	1838
	Jan 13 p4 c3- Jan 27 p4 c2 Feb 17 p4 c3 Mar 8-29 p4 c4

SEPARATION OF THE RACES

	1838
-Discusses benefits of separate settlements	Jun 23 p2 c3
-*Colored American* feels separate settlements would be harmful	Jun 23 p2 c4
-Separate schools and churches likely to perpetuate prejudice	Aug 4 p2 c2 ed.
-Questions quest for entry into white churches	Nov 18 p2 c3
	1839
-Blacks should set up their own churches if they are mistreated in white churches	Feb 16 p2 c3 let.
-*Colored American* opposed to separation	May 18 p2 c2 ed.
	1840
-Discussion of when separation should occur	Aug 22 p2 c2

SERFDOM

	1838
-Ways in which Russian serfdom differs from American slavery	Oct 20 p4 c2

SEWARD, WILLIAM H.

	1837
-Lectures at Auburn meeting on Sunday schools in the Mississippi Valley	Mar 25 p4 c1

	<u>1839</u>
-Message praised	Jan 12 p3 c2
-Extracts from Independence Day speech on equality	Jul 20 p2 c5
	<u>1840</u>
-Yearly message to citizens calling for equal political rights	Nov 21 p3 c3
	<u>1841</u>
-Discussion of his message to the state	Jan 16 p2 c3
-Refused to allow extradition of three fugitive slaves	Apr 3 p2 c2
-Praised for protecting rights of colored citizens	Apr 10 p2 c3
-His message to New York Legislature, refusing to surrender fugitives to Virginia	Apr 17 p1 c3
-States his case for refusing to return fugitives	May 15 p1 c1 let.
-Praised by <u>Colored American</u> for his actions	May 15 p2 c4
-Involved in dispute with Georgia governor over fugitive slave	Nov 13 p2 c3

SHAD, ABRAHAM D. (Chester, Pennsylvania)

	<u>1837</u>
-Listed as agent for the <u>Colored American</u>	Mar 4 p4 c4

SHERIDAN, LOUIS

	<u>1838</u>
-Coerced into migrating to Liberia	Aug 4 p4 c1 let.
-Describes bleak prospects of Liberia colony	Dec 8 p1 c3 let.
-Letter concerning Liberian colonization favorably reviewed	Dec 8 p2 c1 ed.
	<u>1839</u>
-Proof of authorship of anti-colonization letter requested	Jan 19 p2 c3 let.
-Letter from Liberia confirmed by Samuel Cornish	Jan 19 p2 c3 ed.

SHIELDS, FRANCES MARIA (Notice)

	<u>1837</u>
-Girl, age 12, lost	May 20,27 p3 c4

SHIELDS, P.

1837

- -Listed as agent for the <u>Colored American</u> — Mar 11 p4 c4

SHIPPING INDUSTRY

1838

- -Most passenger steamers try to charge the highest prices; an exception is the steamer <u>John W. Richmond</u> — Dec 29 p1 c4 let.

1840

- -Number of arrivals at ports of Boston, New York, and Philadelphia — Mar 14 p3 c2

SIDNEY, THOMAS S.

1837

- -Testifies to confidence in and admiration of Dr. James McCune Smith at meeting of Colored Citizens of New York — Oct 28 p2 c2

1838

- -Denies encouraging resort to physical violence to achieve political enfranchisement — Apr 12 p2 c2 let.
- -Criticized for advocating physical means of obtaining enfranchisement — Apr 12 p2 c2 ed.
- -Appointed Corresponding Secretary of the Political Association — Jun 16 p2 c3
- -Criticized for irresponsible and dangerous views — Sep 8 p3 c1 ed.

1840

- -Honored posthumously by the Phoenixonian Literary Society — Jul 4 p1 c1 let.

SILK CULTURE

1839

- -Description of — Mar 16 p4 c1; May 11 p4 c2
- -Directions for planting silk trees — May 18 p4 c1
- -Considered a profitable business — Jun 1 p2 c1 ed.
- -Directions for sowing seed and raising mulberry trees — Jun 1 p4 c1
- -Description of — Jun 8 p4 c1-Jun 29 p4 c1
- -Diseases of the silk worm — Jul 13 p4 c1

-The reeling of silk — Jul 20 p4 cl
-Encouraged as a profit-making business — Jul 27 p3 cl ed.

SILVER LAKE

1838

-Attempt at black community fails due to poor planning; not black settlers' fault — Aug 18 p2 cl let.
-See also Rose, Dr. Robert H.

SIMMONS, MRS. (Ohio)

1839

-Murders husband — Jun 1 p3 c2

SIMONS, PETER PAUL

1837

-Delivers controversial address on women — Dec 30 p2 cl

SIMSON, S. (Advertisement)

1838

-Ladies hair dressing — Jun 2 p3 c4- Jul 7 p4 c4

SIPKINS, HENRY

1838

-Appointed vice-president of the Political Association — Jun 16 p2 c3
-Death eulogized — Oct 6 p3 c2 ed.; Nov 17 pl cl ed.

SISTER CECILIA'S SOCIETY (Notice)

1837

-Monthly meeting — Apr 8 p3 c4

SKIPWORTH, WILLIAM P.

1838

-Special agent for the Colored American from Zion's Methodist Connection — Jun 23 p4 c4
-Former agent of the Colored American is untrustworthy — Sep 29 p3 cl

SLADE, WILLIAM (Vermont)

1838

-Thanks Massachusetts Anti-Slavery Society for praise of his conduct in Congress — Jul 21 p3 c3 let.

1839

-Sends $2.00 to the Colored American — Feb 16 p3 c2
-Introduced a resolution in the House of Representatives inquiring about mistreatment of slaves — Feb 16 p3 c3

SLANDER

1838

-Causes discussed Nov 10 p1 c3

SLAVE OWNERS

1841

-Hypocritical in their dedication to libery Jun 12 p1 c4

SLAVE REVOLTS

1839

-Revolt in South America described Oct 5 p1 c2

1841

-Insurrection in Trinidad rumored Apr 10 p2 c4
-Attempted revolt in Louisiana reported crushed Aug 7 p2 c2
-See also Amistad

SLAVE TRADE (District of Columbia)

1837

-Supported by Congress Aug 26 p1 c1
-Vice-President Johnson admits power of Congress to abolish Aug 26 p1 c4 ed.

SLAVE TRADE (Domestic)

1837

-250,000 slaves sent to lower south in 1836 (from New York Evangelist) Apr 15 p4 c1

1838

-Massachusetts legislature passes resolution against the domestic slave trade May 3 p2 c4

1839

-Kidnapping and attempted sale of young boys reported Oct 19 p1 c2

1840

-Kidnapped free black regains freedom Jul 18 p2 c3
-Free black unjustly enslaved in New Orleans Aug 29 p2 c1 let.
-Two men accused of kidnapping free blacks Dec 12 p3 c2
-Transactions in Ohio noted and condemned Dec 26 p3 c1 let.

1841

-Trial for abduction and attempted sale of free black girl described Jan 2 p3 c1

-Small boy kidnapped into slavery	Jan 16 p2 cl let.
-Clay and Webster declare Congress has the power to legislate against it	Mar 27 p2 c4
-Slave auction in a church reported	Apr 3 p2 c2
-Warning against kidnappers issued	May 1 p2 c4
-Report of kidnappings of free blacks in New York City	Jun 12 pl c3
-Case of exceptionally high price paid for a slave	Nov 13 pl c4

SLAVE TRADE (International)

	1837
-Portugal abolishes slave trade (December 1836)	Apr 1 p3 c3
	1838
-British cruisers capture three slavers off Montevideo	Aug 4 p3 c4
	1839
-United States seen making enormous profits from the African slave trade	Jun 1 p2 c5
-Three slave ships captured by British	Jun 15 p3 c4
-Speech of Joseph Sturge at Anti-Slavery meeting in London	Jun 29 pl c3
-Discussion of the ease with which American slavers operate	Jul 13 pl cl
-Possible fate of captured slave ships discussed	Jul 27 pl c4
-Failure of government to suppress slave trade noted	Aug 3 pl c2
-Spanish slave trade goes unpunished	Oct 5 pl c3
-Slaver captured	Oct 12 pl c5
-American slaver captured	Oct 12 p4 c2
-The state of the Brazilian slave trade	Oct 19 pl cl
-American slavers listed	Oct 19 p3 c5
-Slaves forced to eat fellow slaves on slave ship	Nov 2 pl c4
-350,000 transported per year	Nov 2 pl c5
-United States schooner will enforce laws against slave trade	Nov 2 p3 c3
-British vessel captures two slave ships	Nov 16 pl c5
-United States consul in Havana accused of aiding trade	Nov 16 p2 c3

-Baltimore District Attorney wants information on slaves allegedly entering that port	Nov 16 p3 c5
-New York men (three) arrested as slave traders	Nov 23 p3 c2
	1840
-Portuguese slaver taken by the English	Mar 7 p3 c2
-Captured slaver described in detail (diagram)	Apr 4 p2 cl let.
-Slaver captured off the African coast	Apr 11 p3 c3
-Report of kidnapping and sale of free blacks	May 16 p3 cl
-Spanish slaver captured off the African coast	May 16 p3 c3
-Two slavers condemned in the United States court	May 23 p3 c3
-Court decision on slave ship captured by the British	Aug 22 p3 c3
-Englishman convicted for his activities	Sep 26 p2 c3
-Slaves from wrecked slaver freed by British authorities	Nov 28 p3 c3
-President VanBuren's message concerning its suppression	Dec 26 p4 c3
	1841
-Statistics on its extent	Jan 16 pl c3
-Ended in Danish West Indies	Jan 23 p4 cl let.
-American slaver condemned by Britain	Jan 30 p2 c4
-Description of attacks on slave trade along the African coast by the British	Mar 27 p4 cl
-Three slavers captured by British	Apr 10 p2 c4
-Twelve slavers of various countries captured by the British	May 1 p2 c4
-Total number of slavers captured from 1837 to 1840	Jun 12 p3 c3
-John Tyler's statement on the slave trade criticized	Jun 19 pl cl
-Inhabitants of Cuba demand its suppression	Jul 24 p2 c2
-Eleven slavers captured	Jul 24 p3 cl
-May soon be abolished in Cuba	Aug 7 p4 c4
-Statistics on the African slave trade	Dec 4 pl c2

SLAVERY (Africa)

	1840
-Considered against God's will by Egyptian Moslems	Nov 14 p2 c4
	1841
-Outlawed in Tunisia	Jun 26 p2 c1

SLAVERY (Alabama)

	1839
-Example of slave laws	Aug 3 p4 c2

SLAVERY (Cuba)

	1840
-Bad conditions described	Apr 8 p3 c3
	1841
-Rumors of pending emancipation reported	Mar 27 p3 c1
-Britain demands suppression of slave trade there	Sep 18 p3 c3

SLAVERY (Danish West Indies)

	1841
-Description and prospects for emancipation noted	Jan 23 p4 c1 let.

SLAVERY (Delaware)

	1837
-Laws and condition of slaves discussed by William Yates	Aug 19 p1 c1 let.

SLAVERY (General)

	1837
-Defines slavery	Mar 4 p3 c1
-President VanBuren presents views on slavery in inaugural address; criticized for his views on slavery	Mar 11 p2 c3
-Describes abominations of slavery	Apr 1 p2 c4
-Dead runaway used as an example to other slaves (from Pittsburgh Gazette)	Apr 1 p4 c3
-Contrasted with principles in the Declaration of Independence	Jul 8 p3 c2 ed.
-Comparison between Mosaic and American slavery	Jul 29 p4 c3
-Slavery worse than factory work in the North	Aug 5 p2 c3 let.
-Essential principles tied to irrationality of man and destruction of property	Aug 12 p3 c2 ed.
-Example of a master who frees his elderly slaves so as not to care for them	Aug 19 p2 c2

-Describes a southern slave caravan in transit; also deplorable conditions of southern slave quarters	Sep 9 p4 c3
-Slavery must be destroyed	Oct 21 p1 c4 ed.
-Relates criticism of slavery by Mississippi planter	Nov 4 p2 c3 let.
	<u>1838</u>
-Testimonials to the inhumanity of slavery	Feb 17 p2 c1
-American Republic the most guilty nation in regard to slavery	Feb 17 p2 c3
-True meaning of natural equality and the way in which slavery violates it	Mar 3 p3 c3
-British sympathiser encourages continued anti-slavery agitation in the United States	Mar 15 p4 c1 let.
-Bodies of dead slaves can be used for anatomical study (<u>Southern Watchman</u>)	Mar 29 p1 c2
-Sin of slavery must be publicly exposed	Apr 12 p2 c4
-Slavery sustained by mistreatment of blacks in the North	Apr 19 p2 c2
-Slaveholders must answer to God	Apr 19 p2 c4 ed.
-Slavery a national sin in America	Apr 19 p2 c4
-A triumph of the weak over the strong	May 3 p4 c1
-Immediate emancipation is the only way for slaveholders to rid themselves of sin	May 3 p4 c2
-Anecdote relates cruel separation of husband and wife	Jun 7 p3 c3
-Man criminally charged with having brought slaves illegally into the United States	Jul 7 p3 c4
-Why slavery is a moral evil	Jul 7 p4 c2 let.
-Slavery produces an aristocracy of the skin	Jul 14 p3 c1 ed.
-Ironic anecdote regarding arguments favoring slavery	Jul 14 p3 c3
-America does not live up to its founding ideals	Jul 21 p2 c2
-Slave owners concerned about increasing their slaves through breeding	Aug 11 p4 c2

-Anecdote relates the sale of slaves by a Presbyterian minister	Sep 1 p3 c3 let.
-Treatment of captured runaways described	Sep 29 p1 c3
-Treatment of slaves at religious services described	Sep 29 p2 c1
-Feelings about slavery in the United States (from <u>Edinburgh Review</u>)	Sep 29 p2 c3
-Anecdote refutes the myth of the happy slave	Oct 13 p1 c4
-Dialogue between Moses and Pharoah about the release of the Hebrew slaves	Oct 20 p1 c2
-Anecdote deploring the separation of a slave family	Nov 3 p1 c4
-In the United States, people do not focus on slavery and its evils in the South	Nov 17 p3 c2
-Christianity sustains the slave in his misfortune	Dec 8 p4 c2
-Congressman Atherton (New Hampshire) introduces pro-slavery resolutions; denounced as a traitor by the <u>Colored American</u>	Dec 22 p3 c2
	<u>1839</u>
-View that Abraham was not a slave holder and that Moses did not authorize slavery	Feb 2 p1 c1,3
-View that slave owners spend between $11 and $15 on an average field hand per year; that slavery cuts down demand for Northern manufactures; that blacks will stay in the South if freed; that slavery is dangerous to political liberty	May 11 p1 c1
-Slaveholders seen to be creating pro-slavery religious institutions	Jun 1 p2 c3 ed.
-Analogy to Rome shows that a republic with slavery is a contradiction in terms	Jun 1 p4 c3 ed.
-A house burned; slaves charged with arson	Jun 15 p3 c1
-Curse of the American nation and the church	Jun 22 p3 c2
-Responsible for the Fall of Rome	Aug 17 p1 c1
-Responsible for the slow progress of blacks	Aug 24 p1 c1

- -Description of the murder of a slave by his owner — Sep 14 p1 c1
- -Slavery nearing its end — Sep 14 p2 c1
- -Slave butchered by his master — Sep 14 p3 c4

<u>1840</u>

- -Traveler relates the horror of slavery — Mar 7 p1 c4 let.
- -Case of white slavery reported — Apr 11 p3 c3
- -Sppeech of an ex-slaveholder — May 2 p1 c1
- -Free white woman spent forty years in slavery — Jun 20 p1 c2

<u>1841</u>

- -Report of London Convention on free labor — Jan 23 p1 c1
- -Description of the plight of a slave family — Mar 20 p1 c3
- -Appellation "peculiar institution" discussed — Apr 3 p2 c3
- -Hinders the moral elevation of blacks — Apr 17 p2 c4
- -Story of a slave turning against his master — Apr 24 p3 c2
- -A slave woman's sermon — May 1 p4 c2
- -Some blacks accused of being pro-slavery — May 29 p2 c2
- -Statistics on slaves in America — Jun 12 p1 c2
- -Fruits of slavery are evil — Jun 26 p2 c3
- -Seen unconstitutional — Aug 28 p1 c3
- -Report of a slave murdered by being burned — Aug 28 p1 c4
- -Compared with the devastation of British Corn laws — Aug 28 p3 c1
- -Irish call for an end to American slavery — Oct 2 p1 c4 let.
- -Southern slaves worse off then Northern free blacks — Nov 13 p1 c2 let.
- -See also Society of Friends; United States Congress

SLAVERY (Iowa)

<u>1839</u>

- -Supreme Court of the territory rules slavery is contrary to the laws of the territory — Aug 3 p3 c4

SLAVERY (Kentucky)

<u>1841</u>

- -Legislature votes down a bill that would strengthen slavery — Mar 6 p3 c1
- -Leading newspapers call for abolition — Mar 27 p2 c4
- -State Legislature debates abolition measure — Apr 17 p2 c3

SLAVERY (Louisiana)

	1839
-Conditions in New Orleans described as terrible (Union Herald)	Jun 8 p1 c3

SLAVERY (Maryland)

	1837
-Describes abominations of slavery in Maryland	Apr 1 p2 c4
	1838
-Incidents of a journey through Maryland related	Mar 3 p1 c2 let.
	1841
-Convention of slaveholders meets	Oct 9 p3 c2

SLAVERY (Massachusetts)

	1840
-First slave described	Mar 14 p1 c4

SLAVERY (Mississippi)

	1841
-Conditions of slaves described	Mar 13 p4 c1
-Mississippi slave case decided in favor of slave-holders	Apr 10 p3 c1

SLAVERY (New York)

	1837
-Speeches at the 1821 Constitutional Convention opposing the continuance of slavery	Mar 11 p2 c2
-Cites revised state statutes regarding slavery	Apr 1 p2 c1
-Young boy kidnapped and sent south; no New York City judge would stop it	Sep 16 p3 c3

SLAVERY (Ohio)

	1840
-Sometimes tolerated in spite of state law	Dec 26 p3 c1 let.

SLAVERY (Pennsylvania)

	1837
-Description of fugitive slave trial in Philadelphia	Oct 7 p4 c2
	1838
-Pennsylvania can be abol-itionized like Massachusetts	May 3 p3 c1

SLAVERY (Saint Thomas)

	<u>1837</u>
-Slaves forced to work on the Sabbath	Mar 25 p1 c1

SLAVERY (South Carolina)

	<u>1840</u>
-Better treatment reported	May 9 p2 c3
	<u>1841</u>
-Bill restrictive of usage of slaves in industry rejected by the state legislature	May 1 p1 c4

SLAVERY (Texas)

	<u>1841</u>
-Sale of slaves prohibited by law	Apr 10 p2 c4

SLAVERY (Turkey)

	<u>1838</u>
-Mild compared to the United States	Jun 9 p1 c3

SLAVERY (Virginia)

	<u>1837</u>
-Reproaches Virginia for oppressive slave laws	Mar 11 p4 c2
	<u>1840</u>
-Governor offers reward for apprehension of fugitives	Nov 28 p2 c3

SLAVERY (Washington, D.C.)

	<u>1837</u>
-Grimke sisters reply to Clarkson criticizing slavery in the District of Columbia	Aug 26 p1 c1
-VanBuren criticized for saying he would veto a bill that would abolish slavery in the district	Aug 26 p1 c4
	<u>1841</u>
-Abolition memorial of citizens of Washington, D.C. to Congress	Jan 9 p2 c2

<u>SLAVERY AS IT IS</u> (Advertisement)

	<u>1839</u>
-New publication for sale	Jun 15 p3 c4- Nov 23 p4 c4

SLAVES

1837
-Seen to be kind Mar 25 p1 c1

1839
-Story of a faithful and virtuous slave Aug 3 p1 c1
-Twenty settle in Mercer County, Ohio Aug 3 p3 c4
-Advancement of an ex-slave described Aug 17 p1 c4
-Progress of ex-slaves in Ohio described Nov 9 p1 c4

1840
-Slave frees himself and family by honest labor and genius May 9 p2 c4 let.
-Georgia pastor frees himself and his family Jul 4 p2 c3
-See also Fugitive Slaves

SLEE, SAMUEL (or Peter B. Hayes) (Notice)

1839
-School teacher wanted for Poughkeepsie (New York) colored school Mar 16 p3 c4

SLEIGH, DOCTOR

1838
-Book criticized for opposing abolitionism Jun 16 p2 c4 ed.

SMITH, ASA B. (Farmington, New York)

1837
-Listed as agent for the _Colored American_ Jun 10 p3 c3

SMITH, CHARLES

1841
-Marries Eliza Cabill Oct 9 p3 c3

SMITH, GERRIT

1837
-Praises the _Colored American_ as a powerful means of elevating blacks Mar 18 p3 c1 let.

1838
-Says Lovejoy's death should unify and enlarge the abolition movement Jan 13 p1 c4 let.
-Praised by Charles B. Ray Sep 29 p4 c1

-Praised by a visitor to his household	Nov 3 p2 c3
-Suggests chartering ships to bring back dissatisfied Liberian colonists	Dec 15 p3 c1 let.
	1839
-Criticizes the Colored American for encouraging support for pro-slavery politicians	Oct 19 p3 c3 let.
-Accused of unjust statements by the Colored American	Oct 19 p3 c3 ed.
-Criticizes Samuel Cornish for his stand on political abolition	Nov 9 p3 c1
	1840
-Nominated for Governor of New York by the Liberty Party	Aug 22 p2 c4
	1841
-Tried to silence the Colored American because of a disagreement with Philip Bell	May 22 p1 c1 let.
SMITH, DOCTOR (Advertisement)	
	1837
-Drugs and medicines; soda water; whitewashers	Nov 11 p3 c4- Dec 16 p4 c3
	1838 Feb 17 p4 c2
	1839 May 11 p4 c3- Jul 27 p4 c3,4 Aug 17 p4 c3,4- Nov 23 p4 c5
	1840 Mar 14 p4 c4- Jun 6 p4 c4
SMITH, JAMES MC CUNE, M.D., M.A. (Advertisement and Notice)	
	1837
-Lectures; medical consultations; Shaker's herbs; bleeding, cupping, and leeching	Sep 16 p3 c4 Sep 23 p3 c3 Nov 11 p3 c4- Dec 30 p4 c3,4

	1838
	Jan 13 p4 c3,4-
	Apr 19 p4 c3
	May 3 p4 c2,3
	Jun 2 p4 c3,4-
	Dec 29 p4 c3,4
	1839
	Jan 12 p2 c4-
	Mar 16 p4 c4
	May 11 p4 c3-
	Nov 23 p4 c4
	1840
	Mar 14, 21 p3 c4
	1841
	Feb 13, 20 p3 c4
SMITH, DOCTOR JAMES McCUNE	
	1837
-Return from five-year educational sojourn in Scotland noted	Sep 9 p3 c1
-His farewell dinner in Glasgow, Scotland described	Sep 9 p4 c1
-Smith praised (Commercial Advertiser)	Sep 30 p2 c4 ed.
-Lectures against phrenology	Oct 14 p3 c3
-Honored at meeting of Mental and Moral Improvement Society (Troy, New York)	Oct 14 p3 c3 let.
-Addresses meeting of Colored Citizens of New York	Oct 28 p2 c1
-Career and education described by Ransom Wake	Oct 28 p1 c3
-Addresses anniversary meeting of Philomathean Society	Nov 4 p3 c1
-Journal describes sea voyage to Europe	Nov 11 p2 c4 Dec 16 p2 c4
-Named to aid editorial department of the Colored American	Nov 11 p3 c2
-Lectures on importance of classical and mathematical studies	Dec 16 p3 c3
-Invited to visit and lecture in Philadelphia	Dec 23 p2 c1 ed.
-Elected an honorary member of the Philadelphia Library Committee	Dec 23 p2 c1
	1838
-Extracts from journal describe abolitionist meeting	Apr 19 p3 c2

-Praises French and British abolitionists in speech to American Colonization Society	Jun 9 p4 cl ed.
-Extracts from journal describe stay in England	Jul 21 p3 c2
-Will be Assistant Editor of the <u>Colored</u> <u>American</u>	Dec 22 p3 c4
	<u>1839</u>
-Addresses anti-colonization meeting; denounces the American Colonization Society	Jan 19 pl cl
-Extracts from his travel journal	Mar 16 p2 cl
-Resigns as editor of the <u>Colored</u> <u>American</u>	Jun 22 p2 c4
	<u>1840</u>
-Objects to black convention in New York	Aug 15 p2 c4
	<u>1841</u>
-Plans to speak on circulation of the blood to Phoenixonian Society noted	Apr 24 p3 c4
-His lecture on the Haitian Revolution	Aug 7 pl c3 Aug 28 pl cl Sep 18 pl cl
-See also Glasgow Emancipation Society; Philadelphia Library Committee; Sidney, Thomas S.	
SMITH, SIR LIONEL (Governor-in-Chief, British West Indies)	
	<u>1838</u>
-Proclaims full emancipation for West Indian slaves	Aug 11 p2 c4
	<u>1839</u>
-Conduct as governor of Jamaica praised	Nov 23 p2 c3
-Colored Citizens of New York express their respect and gratitude to him for his administration of Jamaica	Nov 23 p2 c3 let.
-Expresses compassion for abolition cause in America	Nov 23 p2 c4 let.
SMITH, MORTIMER J.	
	<u>1838</u>
-Listed as agent for the <u>Colored</u> <u>American</u>	Jun 30 p3 c3

SMITH, SERENA (Notice)	
	1840
-Information sought about missing eight-year-old girl	Jul 18 p3 c3
SOCIETE DES AMIS REUNIS (Notice)	
	1837
-Monthly meeting	Sep 30 p3 c4
-Extra meeting	Oct 14 p3 c4
-Monthly meeting	Nov. 4 p3 c4.
-Meeting adjourned	Nov 18 p3 c4
-New officers elected	Dec 23 p3 c4
	1838
-Meeting	Mar 3 p3 c4
	Mar 29 p3 c4
	May 3 p3 c4
	Jun 30 p3 c4
	Aug 4 p3 c4
	Sep 1 p3 c4
	Sep 29 p3 c4
	Nov 3 p3 c4
	Dec 1 p3 c4
	Dec 15 p3 c3
	Dec 29 p3 c4
	1840
	May 30 p3 c4
	Aug 29 p2 c1
	Oct 31 p3 c3
	1841
	Jan 30 p3 c4
	Oct 2 p3 c3
-See also Guignon, Peter; Myers, Francis; Videl, Theodore C.B.	
SOCIETY FOR THE RELIEF OF WORTHY, AGED, AND INDIGENT COLORED PERSONS	
	1841
-Constitution and first annual report	Jan 23 p1 c1
SOCIETY OF FRIENDS	
	1837
-Criticizes slavery and calls for its end	Jul 15 p4 c1
	1838
-Provides funds for the poor	Dec 1 p2 c1

SOCIETY OF ENQUIRY (Oneida, New York)

1837

-Sends $1.50 to the <u>Colored American</u> — Apr 22 p3 c4

SOUTH CAROLINA

1839

-Governor Butler recommends amelioration of laws on slave trials — Jan 12 p3 c2

SOUTHARD, NATHANIEL (Boston)

1837

-Publishes <u>Anti-Slavery Almanack</u> — Nov 4 p3 c2

<u>SOUTHERN WATCHMAN</u>
-See Slavery (General)

SPALDING, REVEREND

1837

-Describes Columbia River Country — Oct 21 p4 cl let.

SPENCER, JOHN C.

1841

-Appointed Secretary of War — Oct 9 p3 c2

SPILLET, JOHN (Advertisement)

1839

-Wants 100 women and girls to pick wool — Jan 19 p3 c4; Feb 9 p4 c4-Feb 23 p3 c4

STANFORD, E. (Salina, New York)

1838

-Listed as agent for the <u>Colored American</u> — Sep 29 p3 c4

STANTON, HENRY B.

1838

-Speech discussed and praised, but disagrees that politics is the answer to the slavery problem — Dec 22 p3 c3

1839

-Delivers speech at American Anti-Slavery Society meeting concerning the power of the free states to abolish slavery in the United States — May 18 pl cl ed.

STATE CONVENTION OF THE COLORED FREEMEN OF PENNSYLVANIA (Pittsburgh) (Notice)

1841

-Convention to meet — Jul 31 p3 c2- Aug 21 p3 c2,3

STATIONARY (Sic)

1838

-For sale at Colored American office (161 Duane Street) (Advertisement) — Jun 16 p4 c4- Dec 29 p4 c3

STEAMBOATS (General)

1839

-Will open up world — Feb 16 p3 c4
-Statistics on accidents — Mar 16 p1 c4

STEVENS, REVEREND

1837

-Speaks at Temperance Jubilee — Apr 1 p3 c1

STEVENS, THADDEUS

1838

-Suggests that public works contractors should provide for education of children of their employees — Sep 22 p4 c2

STEWARD, AUSTIN (Rochester, New York)

1837

-Speaks at fourth anniversary meeting of the American Anti-Slavery Society — May 13 p3 c1

1838

-Listed as an agent for the Colored American — Jul 13 p4 c4

1839

-Anti-slavery speeches praised — Jul 13 p1 c4
Jul 20 p4 c2

1840

-Remarks as President at the Albany Convention — Dec 19 p1 c3

1841

-Remarks as President at the Troy Convention — Sep 11 p1 c1

STEWARD, JOHN B.

1839

-Denounces colonization at New York anti-colonization meeting — Jan 19 p2 c1

STEWARDS' AND COOKS' MARINE BENEFIT SOCIETY

1840

-Holds third anniversary meeting — May 2 p2 c1

STIVES, WILLIAM

1839

-Dies; his life showed the effects of racism on a patriot — Sep 14 p3 c2

STONE, COLONEL

1837

-His unprincipled political doctrine called heresy" — Oct 28 p2 c3

STORY, REVEREND ASA (Hulburton, Orleans County, New York)

1837

-Appointed agent for the Colored American — Aug 19 p3 c2

STOWE, REVEREND

1837

-Speaks at Temperance Jubilee — Apr 1 p3 c1

STRONG, JAMES W.

1838

-Dies after being run down by a horseman — Aug 4 p3 c4

STRUTER, SAMUEL

1837

-Director of the Union Society of Albany — Apr 15 p2 c1

STURGE, JOSEPH

1840

-Participates at London Anti-Slavery Convention — Jul 25 p2 c1; Aug 1 p1 c4

1841

-Arrival in New York City noted — Apr 10 p3 c1

-Poor reception in New York City — Jul 17 p3 c1

STYKE, FRANCIS

1837

-Elected president of the Cranberry Moral Reform Society — Aug 12 p4 c1

SUFFRAGE (Black)
-See Voting Rights (Free Blacks)

SUPERIOR, THE (Advertisement)

1840

-Steamboat excursion planned — Aug 22 p3 c3

SYRIA

1838

-Lectures on Syria — Feb 17 p1 c1

T

TACON, GOVERNOR (Havana, Cuba)

1837

-Accused by the Colored American of the barbarous murder of George Davison — Oct 28 p3 c1

TALLMADGE, MR.

1839

-Commits suicide — May 18 p3 c5

TALMADGE, GENERAL

1837

-Speaks against slavery at the 1821 New York Constitutional Convention — Mar 11 p2 c2

TAPPAN, ARTHUR

1837

-Praises the Colored American as an important aid to the cause of abolition and advancement of colored Americans — Mar 11 p3 c2; Mar 18 p3 c1

TAPPAN, LEWIS

1837

-Praises the Colored American as an important auxiliary to the cause of abolition and advancement of colored Americans — Mar 11 p3 c2; Mar 18 p3 c1

-Member of the Committee of Arrangements for the fourth anniversary of the American Anti-Slavery Society — Apr 8 p3 c2

-Leads Sabbath School — Apr 15 p2 c2

-Learned from Samuel Cornish — May 13 p2 c2
-Spoke at annual meeting of the United Anti-Slavery Society — Aug 5 p3 c4

1838

-Lists objections against the Colonization Society and introduces a critical assessment of it by a Liberian colonist — Dec 8 p1 c1 let.

1839

-His case reversed by the General Assembly; his church privileges restored — Jun 8 p2 c3
-Appeals for donations to the *Amistad* defense fund — Oct 19 p4 c3

1840

-Speaks on the *Amistad* case to the American Anti-Slavery Society — May 23 p2 c2

1841

-Offers $10.00 to aid the *Colored American* — Jan 30 p3 c2 let.
-Attempts to raise money for the *Colored American* — Apr 3 p3 c2

TAPPAN, LEWIS (and S.W. BENEDICT) (Advertisement)

1841

-Sale of Anti-Slavery Books — May 1,8 p3 c4

TAPPAN FEMALE BENEVOLENT SOCIETY

1840

-First annual fund-raising fair to be held — Dec 26 p3 c3

TARTOLA

1837

-Has population of 500 whites and 7,500 blacks; colony of free Blacks rescued from slave ships — Mar 25 p1 c3

TAXPAYERS (Black)

1837

-Prints table of taxpayers in Long Island and Richmond County (New York) — Mar 18 p3 c2

TAYLOR, BENJAMIN F. (Virginia)

1837

-Writes address to Virginians portraying the evils of slavery — May 27 p1 c3

TAYLOR, J. (Brooklyn, Long Island, New York) (Advertisement)

1840

-Hosiery, lace, assorted goods — Dec 26 p3 c4

1841
Jan 2 p3 c4
Feb 6-20 p3 c4
Apr 3 p3 c4-
 Jul 24 p3 c4
Aug 21 p3 c4

TEACHER (Advertisement)

1840

-Desires job of principal or assistant in New York City area — Apr 11 p3 c4-
 May 23 p3 c4

TEACHER (Colored School) (Advertisement)

1841

-Wanted for Trenton, New Jersey — Mar 6 p3 c4
Mar 20 p4 c4

-Wanted for Brooklyn Public School — Aug 7 p3 c3
Aug 14 p3 c4

TEACHERS (Black)

1837

-View that blacks need black teachers — Jun 24 p3 c1

TEMPERANCE (Africa)

1839

-Liquor outlawed in parts of Africa — Mar 2 p3 c3

TEMPERANCE (Connecticut)

1838

-Temperance Society of Colored Americans to meet (Hartford) — Mar 22 p3 c4
Apr 12, 19 p4 c3
May 3 p4 c3

-Temperance Society of Colored Americans to meet (New Haven) — Jul 28 p3 c4
Aug 11 p4 c3-
 Sep 22 p4 c4

-Temperance Society proceedings and resolutions — Oct 13 p3 c2

1839

-Temperance Society meeting proceedings discussed Jun 29 p3 c2
-Temperance Society officers and annual report Nov 9 p2 c3

1840

-Colored American apologizes for overlooking notice of Total Abstinence Society Mar 28 p2 c4
-Temperance Society of Colored Americans promises full support to the Colored American Apr 11 p3 c1
-Temperance Society holds semi-annual meeting Apr 18 p2 c1
-Temperance Society will hold meeting and discuss black conventions Aug 15 p2 c2
-State Temperance and Moral Reform Society meeting planned and held Aug 29 p3 c4
Sep 19 p2 c1

1841

-State Temperance and Moral Reform Society to hold sixth anniversary meeting Aug 21 p3 c1
-State temperance convention states principles; meeting deferred Sep 25 p2 c4
-See also Foster, Henry

TEMPERANCE (Great Britain)

1840

-London temperance societies demonstrate by parading Aug 29 p3 c1

1841

-Statistics of societies in the British Isles Jul 31 p4 c4
-Progress of movement in Ireland evaluated Aug 28 p4 c1

TEMPERANCE (United States)

1837

-Women urged to work for the temperance cause Mar 18 p4 c1
-Pittsburgh Moral Reform Society praised for temperance work Mar 25 p4 c3
-Daniel Vandevere's temperance speech noted Apr 1 p1 c4
-Female Temperance Society formed in Troy, New York Apr 1 p2 c1

-Celebration of Temperance Jubilee noted	Apr 1 p2 c4
-Good health results from temperance	Apr 29 p1 c2
-Societies being formed all over the United States	Apr 29 p1 c3
-Hotel is bought out and now sells no liquor	Jul 29 p3 c3
-Mayor of New York City urged to abolish grog shops	Sep 30 p2 c3 let.
	1838
-Those not for it are against it	Jul 14 p2 c3
-Satire ridicules drinking	Aug 11 p1 c2
-Use of alcohol is the road to ruin	Sep 15 p2 c4
-Abstinence is necessary to purity and virtue	Sep 15 p4 c2
-Intemperance must be exterminated	Sep 15 p4 c3
-More societies needed to fight intemperance	Oct 6 p4 c3
-Evil fate of gambler and drunkard described	Nov 3 p2 c4
-Many miseries of blacks traced to grog shops	Nov 3 p2 c4
	1839
-Abstinence urged for blacks	Feb 23 p2 c2 let. Mar 2 p2 c3
-Intoxication destroys family happiness	Mar 16 p1 c3
-Survey of its progress	Jul 13 p2 c3 let.
-Wine, ale and cider must be put aside	Jul 20 p2 c3
-Its progress surveyed	Jul 20 p2 c4
-Liquor unnecessary for happiness	Jul 27 p2 c2
-A drunkard's death described	Jul 27 p2 c3
-Anecdote about a non-temperate clergyman	Jul 27 p2 c3
-Intemperance linked with crime	Jul 27 p2 c3
-Suicide by a drunkard described	Jul 27 p2 c4
-Liquor is the enemy of happiness	Aug 3 p2 c4
-Liquor is an enemy to religion; destroys marital bliss	Aug 31 p2 c3
-Intemperance destroys man physically and mentally	Aug 31 p2 c4

-Drinking leads to a father's death	Sep 14 p1 c5
-A beggar uses money for drink	Sep 14 p1 c5
-Pennsylvania is fifty years behind New England	Sep 28 p2 c4 let.
	<u>1840</u>
-Liquor kills	Mar 28 p3 c1
-Drunkards become neglectful parents	Apr 11 p3 c2
-Temperance is the principal test of morality	Apr 25 p3 c1
-Anecdote describes gradual dissipation through alcohol	Sep 5 p2 c1
-A temperance appeal	Sep 5 p4 c1
-Total abstinence recommended	Oct 17 p2 c1
-Total abstinence is the only cure for intemperance	Nov 14 p2 c2 let.
-On the true uses of the vine	Nov 28 p4 c2
	<u>1841</u>
-On the evils of grog shops	Feb 6 p2 c4
-Temperance is very popular in Washington, D.C.	Feb 6 p3 c1 let.
-Not for Christians only	Feb 20 p2 c2
-Formation of new total abstinence societies noted	Feb 27 p2 c1 let.
-Liquor in any form is bad; total abstinence is required	Mar 6 p2 c3
-Temperance reform in Baltimore shows success	Apr 24 p3 c1
-Meeting of total abstinence society	May 8 p1 c2
-Total abstinence is the only answer	May 15 p4 c2
-Reasons for total abstinence	May 15 p4 c3
-Drunkenness resembles covetousness	Jun 19 p4 c1
-Anecdote stresses evil effects of drinking on family life	Jun 26 p3 c3
-Brooklyn (New York) blacks organize Temperance Society	Jul 24 p1 c4
-Third National Temperance Convention held in Saratoga (New York); proceedings reported	Aug 21 p4 c1
-Lecture on total abstinence	Sep 25 p1 c1 let.
-Temperance Society formed by blacks of Northampton, Massachusetts	Oct 9 p3 c2
-New York State Temperance Society holds annual meeting	Nov 13 p2 c2

-See also Bowers, John C.; Colored People's State Temperance Society (Connecticut); Female Temperance Society (Troy, New York); Hague, Mr.; Harmony Temperance Association (Westchester, Pennsylvania); Harris, Andrew; Larned, Mr.; New England Colored Temperance Society (Boston); New York State Temperance Society; Pittsburgh Temperance Society; Pray, Mr.; Temperance (Connecticut); Temperance and Moral Reform Society (Wilmington, Delaware); Washington Temperance Societies

TEMPERANCE AND MORAL REFORM SOCIETY (Wilmington, Delaware)

1841

-Addressed by C.C. Burleigh on temperance and morality — May 1 p3 cl let.

TEMPLETON, JOHN N. (Pittsburgh, Pennsylvania)

1837

-Elected secretary of the Pittsburgh Moral Reform Society — May 13 pl c4
-Elected secretary of a meeting to discuss the Pennsylvania Constitutional Convention which proposed the disenfranchisement of blacks — Jul 1 p2 cl

TERMILL, FRANCIS (Chester, New York)

1837

-Sends $3.00 to the Colored American — Apr 29 p3 c4

TEXAS

1837

-Speech on admission to the Union by Representative Phillips of the Mississippi Legislature — Sep 23 pl cl
-Petitions presented in Congress in opposition — Oct 21 p3 c3 let.

1838

-View that some in the South do not want Texas admitted — Jan 20 p2 c4

-New York legislature debates Texas's admission — Apr 19 p1 c1

-Agreement with England to help abolish the slave trade, yet takes part in it — Nov 18 p3 c3

1839

-Involvement in the slave trade stirs controversy — Jun 15 p2 c4

1841

-May be invaded by Mexico — Jan 30 p2 c4

THEATRE

1837

-Condemns theater-going as an evil activity — Oct 28 p1 c1 let.

-Plays and actors who ridicule blacks are criticized — Dec 9 p2 c4

1838

-Criticized as a source of licentiousness — Aug 4 p1 c2 ed.

1840

-Dangers listed — Mar 14 p4 c3

-Very expensive — Mar 21 p4 c2

1841

-Its sinfulness demonstrated — Feb 20 p4 c3

-Closing due to lack of patronage; a good sign — Mar 6 p2 c4

-Criticized as a temple of obscenity — Jun 5 p1 c4

THOMAS, G.W. (Advertisement)

1839

-Panorama of the ancient and modern world — Jul 13 p3 c4- Sep 14 p4 c3

THOMAS, MARIA

1840

-Marries Henry Harris — Sep 19 p3 c4

THOMAS, MRS. RACHEL

1838

-Listed as the first Directress of the Female Assistant Society of New York — Mar 15 p3 c1

THOME, REVEREND JAMES

1837

-Notes arrival on Saint Thomas from the United States — Mar 18 p1 c2
-Spoke at annual meeting of the United Anti-Slavery Society — Aug 5 p3 c1

1838

-Co-authors Emancipation in the West Indies — Mar 22 p3 c2
-Description of missionary work in Kingston, Jamaica — Jul 21 p1 c3

THOMPSON, EDWIN (Lynn, Massachusetts)

1838

-Listed as an agent for the Colored American — Jun 30 p3 c3

THOMPSON, GEORGE (England)

1840

-Participates at London Anti-Slavery Convention — Aug 1 p1 c3
-Anti-slavery work praised by Charles Remond — Nov 7 p1 c1 let.

THOMPSON, GEORGE (Alias Ben)

1837

-Alleged fugitive slave tried before Judge Irving — Apr 8 p3 c1
-See also Sedgwick, Mr.; Wilkinson, General

THOMPSON, RICHARD (Albany, New York)

1837

-A director of the Union Society of Albany — Apr 15 p1 c3

THOMPSON, RICHARD JR. (Advertisement)

1839

-Colored American house (boarders) — Aug 31 p3 c4- Nov 23 p4 c4

1840

Mar 14 p3 c4- Mar 28 p4 c4

THOMPSON, WILLIAM (Notice)	
	1837
-Mistaken identity involving a theft	Jan 28 p3 c4 Feb 4 p3 c4
THUEY, ALEXANDER (Troy, New York)	
	1837
-Vice-president of the Union of Colored People (Troy, New York)	Apr 1 p2 c1
-Member of the Union Society of Albany	Apr 15 p1 c3
-Treasurer of the Mental and Moral Reform Society (Troy, New York)	Oct 14 p3 c4
TILMAN, LEVIN (Camden, New Jersey) (Advertisement)	
	1841
-Country house for sale	Apr 3,10 p3 c4
TILTON, DANIEL (Chilmark)	
	1839
-Commits suicide by drowning	May 18 p3 c5
TOBACCO	
	1837
-Attests to offensiveness of tobacco users and encourages laws against it	Oct 28 p3 c1 let.
<u>THE TOCSIN OF LIBERTY</u> (Albany, New York)	
	1841
-Organ of Liberty Party commences publication	Oct 30 p3 c3
TOMPKINS, MISS FANNY (Advertisement)	
	1840
-Private seminary	Nov 13 p3 c4
	1841
	Sep 18 p3 c3 Oct 2-16 p3 c4
TORTOLA -See West Indies (General)	

TOWNE AND PERKINS (Advertisement)

-Free labor goods — 1839: Jun 15 p3 c4- Nov 23 p4 c5; 1840: Mar 14 p4 c4- Nov 28 p3 c4; Dec 19 p3 c4; 1841: Sep 18 p3 c4- Dec 4 p3 c4; Dec 25 p3 c4

TOWNSEND, REVEREND J.B. (Notice)

-To deliver an address — 1838: Mar 29 p3 c4

TRAVEL

-In olden times — 1840: Sep 12 p4 c1

TREADWELL, S.B.
-See American Liberties and American Slavery

TRINDALL, GEORGE

-Elected treasurer of the Cranberry Moral Reform Society — 1837: Aug 12 p4 c1

TRINIDAD (Advertisement)

-Colored emigrants wanted — 1840: Mar 7-21 p3 c4; Apr 11 p3 c4; May 30 p3 c4- Jul 4 p3 c4

-See also Burnley, William H.; Colonization (General); Emigration (West Indies); Free Blacks (Trinidad); Garrison, William Lloyd; Hunt, Reverend

TROY AND MICHIGAN SIX-DAY LINE (Erie Canal) (Advertisement)

-Canal boat run — 1839: May 11 p4 c4- Nov 23 p4 c5; 1840: Mar 14 p4 c4

TROY CONVENTION (Black)

	1841
-Call issued and committeemen listed	Jul 17 p3 c2
-Endorsed	Jul 24 p2 c2 let.
-Approved by Buffalo blacks	Jul 31 p1 c3
-Call issued and committeemen listed	Jul 31 p3 c2
-Delegates urged to bring wives	Aug 7 p2 c2
-Approved by New York City blacks	Aug 7 p2 c3
-Call issued	Aug 7 p3 c3
-Discussed	Aug 14 p2 c1
-New York City delegation listed	Aug 14 p2 c4
-Supported by Utica, Newburgh, Peekskill, and Syracuse blacks	Aug 14 p3 c1
-Call issued	Aug 14 p3 c3
-Flushing , Long Island elects delegate	Aug 21 p2 c1
-New York City appoints additional delegates	Aug 21 p2 c3
-Delegates from Williamsburg and Hudson listed	Aug 21 p2 c3
-Delegates from Albany appointed	Aug 21 p2 c4
-Call issued	Aug 21 p3 c3
-Appealed to for funds by the <u>Colored American</u>	Aug 28 p2 c2
-Advice on its deliberations	Aug 28 p2 c2
-Delegates listed	Aug 28 p2 c3
-Williamsburg blacks endorse it and elect delegates	Aug 28 p3 c1
-Description of meetings	Sep 4 p2 c3
-Votes financial aid for the <u>Colored American</u>	Sep 4 p2 c4
-Proceedings	Sep 11 p1 c1
-Address to the electors of New York State requesting the franchise	Sep 11 p2 c2
-Address to black citizens of New York State	Sep 11 p2 c4
-Roll of delegates	Sep 11 p3 c1
-Proceedings approved by New York City blacks	Sep 11 p3 c3
-Its "Dollar Plan" to aid the <u>Colored American</u>	Sep 18 p3 c1
-New York City meetings approve its proceedings	Sep 25 p3 c2

TUNISIA

	1841
-Bey of Tunis outlaws slavery	Jun 26 p2 c1

TURKEY

1838

-Turkish musselman has more consistant faith than a Christian — Oct 6 p3 c2

TURNER, REVEREND HENRY C. (Philadelphia)

1837

-Listed as an agent for the Colored American — Jun 3 p3 c4
-Sends $5.00 to the paper — Jul 29 p2 c4

TURPIN, WILLIAM

1837

-Left $8,000 for the education and benefit of colored people; money given to the Female Orphans Society; Colored American protests — Dec 30 p2 c2

TYLER, JOHN

1841

-Becomes President and is accused of slaveholding — Apr 17 p2 c3
-Presidential message on the slave trade criticized — Jun 19 p1 c1

TYSON, WILLIAM A.

1838

-Elected president of the Political Association — Jun 16 p2 c3
Sep 8 p3 c3

U

UNCLES, MR.

1838

-Escapes after arrest for jewel robbery — Aug 4 p3 c4

UNDERWOOD, REVEREND DANIEL

1837

-Vice-president of the Mental and Moral Improvement Society of Troy (New York) — Oct 14 p3 c4

UNION COFFEE HOUSE (Buffalo, New York) (Advertisement)

1838

-Cafe — Jan 13 p4 c4-
May 3 p4 c2
Jun 2 p4 c3

UNION OF COLORED PEOPLE (Troy, New York)
-See Vandevere, Reverend Daniel; Thuey, Alexander

UNION EVANGELICAL MISSIONARY SOCIETY (Hartford, Connecticut)

1840
-Meeting — Dec 25 p3 c4

UNION HALL (Notice)

1841
-Taken for use as a public hall — Oct 2 p3 c3

<u>UNION HERALD</u>
-See Slavery (Louisiana)

UNION METHODIST CHURCH

1841
-Consecrated — Jan 23 p3 c2

UNION METHODIST CONNECTION (Wilmington, Delaware)

1837
-Black church organization — May 20 p2 c2

<u>UNION MISSIONARY HERALD</u>

1841
-Monthly periodical commences publication — Oct 16 p2 c2

UNION PRAYER MEETING (Notice)

1837
-Notice of meeting — Jul 29 p3 c4-Nov 11 p4 c4

UNION SOCIETY OF ALBANY
-See Thuey, Alexander; Union Society of Albany, Troy and Vicinity for the Improvement of Colored People in Morals, Education, and the Mechanic Arts

UNION SOCIETY OF ALBANY, TROY AND VICINITY FOR THE IMPROVEMENT OF COLORED PEOPLE IN MORALS, EDUCATION, AND THE MECHANIC ARTS

1837
-Regular monthly meeting — Jan 28 p3 c4; Mar 11 p3 c3
-Extra meeting — Feb 4 p3 c4
-Holds meeting and drafts a constitution — Apr 15 p1 c3

	1838
-To hold extra meeting	Jun 9 p3 c4
-See also Douge, Michael; Fubbard, James; Harris, Andrew; Johnson, John H.; Seldon, Clarence; Streeter, Samuel; Thompson, Richard; Thuey, Alexander; Vandevere, Reverend Daniel; Wandell, John; Way, Frisly; Williams, James; Wright, R.P.G.	
UNION SUNDAY SCHOOL (Notice)	
	1838
-School open	Dec 29 p3 c4
	1839
	Jan 12 p2 c4
	Jan 19 p4 c4
UNITED ANTI-SLAVERY SOCIETY	
	1837
-Meeting	Apr 15,22 p3 c4
	Apr 29 p3 c2
-First anniversary meeting	Jul 15 p3 c4- Jul 29 p3 c4
-Meeting a success; petitions signed	Aug 5 p3 c1
-See also Wright, Reverend Theodore S.; Zuille, John J.	
UNITED DAUGHTERS OF CONFERENCE (Methodists)	
	1837
-Hold first anniversary meeting	Dec 9 p3 c4
UNITED FEMALE ASSISTANT BENEFIT SOCIETY (Notice)	
	1837
-Exhibition	Feb 18 p3 c4
-See also Female Assistant Society	
UNITED STATES CONGRESS	
	1837
-Northern members urged to rebuke southern colleagues	Apr 1 p3 c2
-Blamed for support of slave trade in Washington, D.C.	Aug 26 p1 c1
-Congress's power to abolish slavery in Washington, D.C. recognized by Vice-President Johnson	Aug 26 p1 c4 ed.
-Should not act on Texas admission during special session	Sep 2 p3 c2

1838

-Congress passes resolution denying slaves the right of petition — Jan 20 p3 c4
-Receives petitions against admitting Texas to the Union — Jan 20 p3 c4
-New Hampshire Congressman Atherton introduces pro-slavery resolutions; denounced as a traitor by the Colored American — Dec 22 p3 c2 ed.

1839

-Vermont resolutions presented to the Senate requesting abolition of slavery and opposing annexation of Texas — Jan 19 p3 c2
-Memorial presented to House requesting recognition of Haiti and abolition of slavery by the citizens of Maryland and Virginia — Jan 19 p3 c2
-Memorial presented to House requesting that all Congressmen be certified pure Anglo-Saxon — Jan 19 p3 c2
-Extracts of Senator Morris' anti-slavery speech — Mar 16 p1 c2

1841

-Congressional Chaplains appraised — Jan 9 p2 c1 let.
-Description of Senate debate on public lands and abolition petitions — Jan 16 p2 c4 let.
-House engaged in debate over contested election; Senate discusses pre-emption bill — Jan 23 p2 c4 let.
-Description of Congressional debate on slavery — Feb 27 p1 c4 let.
-Count of Presidential and Vice-Presidential ballots — Feb 27 p1 c4 let.
-Details of appropriations bill revealed in the House of Representatives — Feb 27 p3 c1 let.
-Will receive representatives for free colored populations in New York, Pennsylvania, Maryland and Virginia — Jun 12 p2 c3
-Veto to Bank Bill received in the Senate — Aug 21 p3 c1
-Report on its deliberations on abolition — Aug 28 p2 c4
-Criticized for confirming appointments of slaveholders — Sep 4 p3 c1

UNITED STATES GOVERNMENT

1837

-Seen to be in the hands of demagogues — Jun 17 p2 c2
-North should not be bound by the idea of "union" — May 6 p3 c2

1838

-Postmaster General opposed removal of postage requirements from newspapers — Jun 16 p3 c2

1839

-Seen more representative of majority than European governments — Jun 15 p1 c5

1841

-Constitutional provision providing for Presidential succession explained — Apr 17 p3 c3

UNITED STATES (Public Lands)

1841

-Description of Senate debate on pre-emption bill — Jan 16 p2 c4 let.
-Blacks excluded from pre-empting public lands — Jan 23 p2 c3
-Senate discusses pre-emption bill — Jan 23 p2 c4 let.
-Pre-emption bill debated in the Senate — Jan 30 p3 c1 let.
-Exclusively white privilege struck from pre-emption bill — Feb 13 p2 c4

UNITED STATES SUPREME COURT

1838

-Denial of decision regarding black suffrage — May 3 p3 c1 ed.

1840

-*Amistad* case pending appeal there — May 23 p3 c1
-Final adjudication of *Amistad* case before it — Dec 19 p2 c3

1841

-John Quincy Adams to plead *Amistad* case before it — Jan 16 p2 c4 let.
-Hears case involving Mississippi slave laws — Feb 27 p1 c3 let.
-Begins to hear *Amistad* case — Feb 27 p3 c1 let.
-Mississippi slave case decided in favor of slaveholder — Apr 10 p3 c1
-See also *Amistad, The*

V

VALENTINE, RICHARD (Cranberry, New Jersey)

	<u>1837</u>
-Elected corresponding secretary of the Cranberry Moral Reform Society	Aug 12 p4 c1
	<u>1838</u>
-Listed as agent for the <u>Colored American</u>	Dec 15 p3 c3

VAN BUREN, MARTIN

	<u>1837</u>
-Presents views on slavery and abolition in inaugural address	Mar 11 p2 c3
-Criticized for views on slavery and abolition	Mar 11 p2 c3
-Criticized for vow to veto bill that would abolish slavery in the District of Columbia	Aug 26 p1 c4
-Promises to keep Americans out of the Canadian situation; praised by the <u>Colored American</u>	Jul 13 p3 c2
	<u>1838</u>
-<u>Colored American</u> will support him over Clay	Mar 29 p3 c2
-Blamed for blacks' loss of suffrage in Pennsylvania (New York <u>American</u>)	Apr 5 p3 c2
-Criticized for not recognizing the Haitian government	Nov 3 p2 c1 ed.
-Criticized for silence on abolition and colonization	Dec 15 p3 c2 ed.
-Samuel Cornish offers his services to the President	Dec 5 p3 c2 let.
	<u>1839</u>
-Accused of a political sell-out to slaveholders	Jul 13 p1 c5
	<u>1840</u>
-Considered unworthy of the votes of American abolitionists	May 23 p2 c2
-Seen partial to slavery	Sep 12 p1 c2
-His memoranda concerning the <u>Amistad</u> case	Nov 28 p1 c4 let.

-Accused of serving the interests of the slave-holding class — Dec 12 p1 c4 let.
-Extracts from his message concerning Indian wars and the suppression of the slave trade — Dec 26 p4 c3
-See also Amistad, The; Haiti

VANDEVERE, REVEREND DANIEL (Troy, New York)

1837

-Director of the Union Society of Albany addresses the fourth anniversary celebration of the Female Benevolent Society of Troy — Apr 1 p1 c3
-Listed as president of the Union of Colored People of Troy — Apr 1 p1 c4
-Speaks on temperance — Apr 1 p1 c4
-Attends the first meeting of the Union Society of Albany — Apr 15 p1 c3

VANLERE, MOSES F.

1837

-Addresses Mental and Moral Improvement Association of Troy, New York — Aug 21 p1 c2

VAN RENSSELAER, GENERAL STEPHAN

1839

-Dies and is eulogized — Feb 9 p1 c1
-Poem in his memory — Feb 23 p2 c4

VAN RENSSALAER, THOMAS

1837

-Listed as president of the People of Color; organization passes resolution praising the Colored American — Mar 18 p3 c1
-Meeting of the United Anti-Slavery Society is chaired by him — Apr 29 p3 c2
-Story of escape from slavery and successful career related — Oct 28 p4 c1
-Advertises petition requesting franchise for blacks in New York Legislature — Dec 9 p3 c3
-Recounts proceedings of meeting to sympathize with Elijah Lovejoy's widow — Dec 23 p3 c1

	1838
-Discussion (with William Johnson)	Dec 22 p3 c3
	1839
-Denounces colonization at New York anti-colonization meeting	Jan 19 p1 c4
-Temperance eating house (Advertisement)	Mar 2 p3 c4 Mar 16 p4 c4 May 11, 18 p4 c4 Jun 1, 15 p4 c3
	1840
-Listed as president of Jamaica Convention	May 9 p3 c2
-Public meeting concerning the franchise for blacks	Oct 17 p3 c4
-Urges colored men not support an abolitionist third party	Oct 31 p3 c1 let.
	1841
-Says blacks are pro-slavery; criticized by the Colored American	May 29 p2 c2 Jun 5 p2 c4
-Defends himself against charges of misconduct	Jun 26 p2 c4 let.
-Attacked by Charles Reason	Jul 10 p2 c2 let.
-Refuses to reply to Charles Reason's accusations	Jul 17 p3 c2 let.
-Urges public expression of gratitude for new anti-slavery law in New York	Aug 28 p2 c1 let.
VAN VECHTEN, ABRAHAM	
	1837
-Speaks against restriction of black franchise at 1821 New York Constitutional Convention	Mar 4 p1 c3
	1838
-Testimonial against restriction of black voting rights	Mar 22 p2 c2
VARIAN, ISAAC	
	1839
-Sworn in as mayor	May 18 p3 c5

VASHON, JOHN B. (Pittsburgh, Pennsylvania)

1837

- -Listed as agent for the Colored American — Mar 4 p4 c4
- -Praised for closing his business on the Sabbath — Apr 1 p2 c2 let.
- -Praises the Colored American — Apr 15 p3 c1 let.
- -Sends $20.00 to the paper — Apr 15 p3 c4
- -Sends $5.00 to the paper — Apr 29 p3 c4
- -Elected treasurer of the Pittsburgh Moral Reform Society — May 13 p1 c4
- -Elected black representative to the Pennsylvania Convention which proposes disenfranchisement of blacks — Jul 1 p2 c1
- -Sends $10.00 to the Colored American — Nov 18 p3 c1 let.

1838

- -Criticizes the American Colonization Society; rejects the Colored Man's Journal — Mar 15 p3 c3 let.

1840

- -Urges support for the Colored American — Mar 7 p2 c1 let.
- -Praises the press as a citadel of freedom — Apr 4 p3 c1 let.
- -See also Voting Rights (Free Blacks)

VERMONT

1837

- -Praised for upholding the spirit of liberty — Dec 9 p3 c4

1838

- -Takes precedence as an abolitionist state — Mar 15 p4 c1 let.

1841

- -Report on gubernatorial election — Sep 18 p3 c1

VIDEL, THEODORE C.B.

1837

- -Elected president of the Societes des Amis Reunis — Dec 23 p3 c4

VIEWS OF THE HOLY LAND (Advertisement)

1840
-Pictorial illustrations — Oct 3,31 p3 c4; Dec 5, 19, 26 p3 c4

1841
-Pictorial illustrations — Jan 2, 23 p3 c4; Feb 6 p3 c4; Mar 6 p4 cl-4; Apr 17 p3 c4
-Second volume — Jun 12 p3 c4

VIRGIN ISLANDS
-See Thome, Reverend James; West Indies (Virgin Islands)

VIRGINIA

1838
-Legislature abolishes branding as a punishment — Jun 16 p3 cl

VIRGINIA CONVENTION FOR THE ABOLITION OF SLAVERY (1828)

1837
-Holds annual meeting and drafts resolutions — May 27 pl c3
-See also Wright, Thomas

VOGELSANG, PETER

1838
-Urges constant but moderate agitation for enfranchisement — Mar 15 pl c3
-Address on the subject of the franchise for blacks — Jul 14 pl cl

1839
-Denounces the Colonization Society at New York anti-slavery meeting — Jan 19 p2 cl
-See also Association for the Political Elevation and Improvement of People of Color; Voting Rights (Free Blacks) (General)

VOTING RIGHTS (Free Blacks - General)

1837
-Prints table of voters in Long Island and Richmond County, New York — Mar 18 p3 c2
-Calls on blacks to vote — Apr 29 p3 c3

-Many blacks who have the right do not vote, but should	Jul 15 p3 cl
	Aug 19 p2 c4
-Meeting called	Sep 23 p3 c4
-Blacks deserve voting rights only when qualified	Sep 30 p2 c4
-Meeting	Nov 25 p3 c4
	1838
-Memorials sent to the Legislature	Feb 3-17 p3 c4
-Civil agitation is the only means of attaining political enfranchisement	Mar 3 p3 c4
-Address by Peter Vogelsang urges constant but moderate agitation for enfranchisement	Mar 15 pl c3
-Philip Bell upholds civil agitation for enfranchisement	Mar 15 pl c3
-Restrictions upon voting rights of black men immoral and unconstitutional	Mar 22 p2 cl ed.
-Testimonials to unconstitutionality of suffrage restrictions	Mar 22 p2 cl
-View of John Vashon and Lewis Woodson tha many Philadelphia blacks voted before being disenfranchised	Apr 5 p3 c2 let.
-Resort to physical force to obtain enfranchisement discouraged	Apr 12 p2 c2 ed.
-Acquisition of property urged as a means of gaining the franchise	Apr 12 p3 cl ed.
-Speech endorses citizenship of free blacks	Apr 19 p2 c3
-Opposition to the Supreme Court decision regarding black franchise	May 3 p3 cl ed.
-Vogelsang's address on the subject of the black franchise	Jul 14 pl cl
-Public meeting	Aug 25 p3 c3
-Modest but firm demands to vote are urged	Nov 3 p3 c2 ed.
	1839
-Fear and apprehension of political action must be overcome	Aug 3 pl c4 ed.
-Disenfranchisement dehumanizes blacks	Oct 12 p2 cl

	1840
-Denied because of racism	Mar 7 p1 c1
-Only political power can stop legal discriminations	May 9 p2 c1 let.
-Public meeting of colored voters	Oct 17 p3 c4
-Blacks urged to insist on voting rights	Dec 5 p2 c1
-Public meeting of colored voters	Dec 19 p3 c3
	1841
-Brooklyn mass meeting; petition drive plans	Jan 2 p3 c3 Jan 9 p3 c4
-Many opposed to slavery will not support voting rights for free blacks	Jul 3 p1 c4
-Great public meeting to extend the franchise	Jul 31 p3 c3
-Series of public meetings and conventions	Sep 18,25 p3 c4 Oct 2-16 p3 c3
-See also Van Vechten, Abraham; Vogelsang, Peter	

VOTING RIGHTS (Free Blacks-Connecticut)

	1838
-State House of Representatives refuses to remove restrictions	Jun 16 p4 c2
	1841
-Petition for elective franchise sent to state legislature	Jun 12 p2 c4

VOTING RIGHTS (Free Blacks-Massachusetts)

	1841
-Urged to exercise the franchise in upcoming elections	Oct 30 p3 c2 ed.

VOTING RIGHTS (Free Blacks - Michigan)

	1841
-Public meeting held; well attended	Mar 20 p2 c4

VOTING RIGHTS (Free Blacks-New Jersey)

	1841
-Colored citizens of Newark meet to sign franchise petition	Feb 6 p1 c4

VOTING RIGHTS (Free Blacks-New York)

	1837
-Speeches opposing restriction of black franchise by 1821 State Constitution	Mar 4 p1 c2
-Calls for dropping franchise restrictions in New York	Mar 4 p2 c4 ed.
-Free blacks petition New York Legislature for voting rights	Mar 11 p3 c2
-People urged to petition the legislature about voting rights	Jul 15 p3 c1
-Calls for petition to legislators	Jul 22 p3 c3
-Blacks pass resolutions to petition the state legislature for the suffrage	Aug 12 p2 c4
-Philip Bell goes to upstate New York to arouse young blacks to petition for voting rights for blacks	Aug 19 p3 c3
-Public meeting says petitions to the legislature are a way to gain voting rights	Aug 19 p3 c4
-Charles Ray and Philip Bell try to build up petition drive; deserve support	Sep 23 p3 c1
-Petition organized to request franchise for blacks from New York Legislature	Dec 9 p3 c3 let.
-Young free blacks urged to gather enfranchisement petitions and money	Dec 16 p3 c1
-Petition to New York Legislature requests repeal of property qualification for black voters	Dec 16 p3 c3
-Names of petition committees printed by wards	Dec 30 p3 c3
	1838
-Petition committees meet	Jan 20 p3 c4
-Describes history of black suffrage in New York	Jan 27 p3 c3 let.
-Public meeting promises unceasing agitation for restoration of the franchise	Mar 15 p3 c4
-Black freeholders urged to vote in the coming election	Nov 3 p3 c2
-Meeting of colored freeholders declare property qualifications oppressive and unjust	Nov 3 p3 c3
-Purchase of real estate urged as a means of gaining the vote	Dec 15 p2 c1 ed.

1839

-Colored American praised for urging accumulation of property to attain the franchise	Jan 19 p3 c2 let.
-Colored American calls for a continuation of the petition campaign and a $100 rent qualification for voting	Feb 23 p2 cl
-Responsibility to gain the franchise rests with blacks themselves	Jul 27 p2 cl ed.

1840

-Those who are eligible urged to register	Sep 19 p3 cl
-Petition campaign urged to demand rights	Oct 17 p3 cl
-New York City citizens plan to petition for the franchise	Nov 14 p3 c2 Nov 21 p3 cl
-Citizens urged to circulate petitions for the franchise	Nov 28 p2 c4
-Text of petition to state legislature requesting the franchise	Dec 5 pl cl
-Restrictions on blacks deplored	Dec 5 p2 c3
-New York City citizens plan to raise funds to publish the franchise petition	Dec 5 p3 c2
-Mass meeting to support franchise petition planned	Dec 5 p3 c4
-Proceedings of New York City mass meeting to petition for the franchise	Dec 12 p2 cl
-New York citizens urged to sign petitions for the franchise	Dec 12 p2 c3
-New York colored citizens plea for political equality	Dec 19 pl cl
-Long Island citizens meet to secure the franchise	Dec 26 p3 cl

1841

-Mass meeting held to gain signatures for franchise petition	Jan 2 p2 c2
-Mass meeting held to secure taxation proportionate to representation	Jan 2 p3 cl
-Mass meetings held in Brooklyn and Long Island to secure the franchise	Jan 2 p3 c3 Jan 2 p3 c3
-Mass meeting in Buffalo to gain signatures for the franchise petition	Jan 9 p3 c2

-Blacks urged to sign franchise petitions	Jan 16 p2 cl let.
-Mass meeting held at Newtown to support the franchise petition	Jan 16 p3 c2
-Blacks urged to send franchise petitions to the New York Legislature	Jan 23 p3 cl
-Mass meeting in Brooklyn supports the franchise petition	Jan 23 p3 c3
-Citizens of Hudson meet to sign the franchise petition	Feb 6 pl c3
-Report of the New York Legislature's reception of the franchise petitions	Feb 13 pl c3 let.
-Bill before the Legislature to grant the franchise to all men over 21 years of age	Mar 20 p3 cl
-Bill to grant the franchise still pending in the legislature	Mar 27 p2 c3
-Universal suffrage bill urged by the Albany Evening Journal	Mar 27 p3 c2
-Suffrage petitions rejected by the New York Legislature	Apr 24 p2 c4
-House refuses to consider the black voting rights amendment	May 8 p2 c4
-Troy Convention's address to New York electors requesting the franchise	Sep 11 p2 c2
-Address of Troy Convention to New York blacks on the subject of the franchise	Sep 11 p2 c4
-Black citizens called upon to act for the suffrage	Sep 18 p3 c3
-Citizens of New York to meet to consider the franchise question	Nov 20 p2 cl

VOTING RIGHTS (Free Blacks-Ohio)

	1837
-Blacks petitioning for the franchise	Jul 22 p2 cl

VOTING RIGHTS (Free Blacks-Pennsylvania)

	1837
-Constitutional Convention trying to disfranchisement blacks	Jun 10 p3 c4
-Measure fails; blacks retain the vote	Jul 22 p2 c2
-Disfranchisement effort may prove successful	Dec 16 p3 cl let.

	<u>1838</u>
-Constitutional Convention inserts "white" into voting qualifications	Jan 27 p2 c3
-View that Colonization Society involved in taking away black suffrage	Jan 27 p3 c2
-Action of the Constitutional Convention violates the preamble of the 1780 Constitution	Feb 3 p2 c2
-Blacks in Pennsylvania write appeal to state's citizens; <u>Colored American</u> suggests they carry it around personally	Mar 29 p2 c1
-Article blames Martin Van Buren for the blacks' loss of suffrage in Pennsylvania (New York <u>American</u>)	Apr 5 p3 c2
-Minutes of public meeting in Pittsburgh; plans to oppose disfranchisement	Apr 12 p3 c2 let.
-Appeal to citizens of Pennsylvania regarding disfranchisement	May 3 p1 c1
-<u>Colored American</u> endorses the appeal	May 3 p3 c1 ed.
-Appeal continued	Jun 2 p1 c1
	<u>1841</u>
-Colored citizens of Philadelphia meet to petition for political enfranchisement	Jan 30 p3 c2
-Public meetings held in Pittsburgh and Philadelphia; some call for state convention of blacks	Mar 6 p1 c4 let.
-State convention urged	Mar 13 p2 c1 let.

VOTING RIGHTS (Free Blacks-Rhode Island)

	<u>1841</u>
-Blacks petition legislature for suffrage rights and are refused	Mar 27 p2 c2
-Rhode Island Suffrage Convention opposes black suffrage	Oct 30 p3 c1 ed.

W

WAKE, RANSOM

	1837
-President of the Colored Citizens of New York	Oct 28 p1 c3
-Describes education and career of Dr. James McCune Smith	Oct 28 p1 c3
	1838
-Plans lecture on oratorical delivery to the Philomathean Society	Mar 3 p3 c4
-Appointed vice-president of the Political Association	Jun 16 p2 c3

WALKER, GILBERT

	1841
-Marries Sarah Phillips	Oct 9 p3 c3

WANDELL, JOHN (Schenectady, New York)

	1837
-Vice-president of the Union Society	Apr 15 p1 c3

WAR

	1837
-William Whipper asserts the benefits of non-aggression as opposed to offensive aggression	Sep 9 p1 c2
	1839
-On the unholiness of wars	Mar 16 p3 c3
	1840
-Southern states will prevent boundary war with Britain	May 9 p1 c3
-Money used for war could be better spent	Jul 4 p4 c1
-Martin Van Buren's message regarding Indian Wars	Dec 26 p4 c3
	1841
-War viewed as likely between America and England	Jan 23 p3 c2 let.
-Opium War in China described	Jan 23 p4 c3
-Imminent between Spain and Portugal	Jan 30 p2 c4
-Black people urged to support America in any war with England	Feb 6 p2 c1 let.
-New on China's Opium War	Feb 6 p3 c3
-Colored Americans should remain neutral in American wars	Feb 13 p1 c4 let.

-Joshua Giddings' congressional speech against the Seminole War	Mar 27 p1 c3
-Skirmish with Indians in Florida reported	Mar 27 p2 c4
-Giddings' speech (continued)	Apr 3 p1 c2
	Apr 10 p1 c1
	Apr 17 p1 c1
	Apr 24 p1 c1
-Seminole War considered ended	Aug 14 p3 c2

WARD, SAMUEL RINGGOLD (Newark, New Jersey)

	1837
-Listed as agent for the <u>Colored American</u>	Mar 4 p4 c4
-Sends $5.00 to the paper	Apr 22 p3 c4
	1838
-Secretary of the Colored Citizens of Newark (New Jersey)	Jul 21 p3 c3
	1841
-Ordained and installed as pastor of the South Butler Congregational Church	Oct 9 p3 c1

WARD, S.R. (or W.F. Gardner) (Bellville, New Jersey) (Advertisement)

	1839
-House for rent	Jun 29 p3 c4- Jul 27 p4 c3 Aug 24 p4 c3

WASHINGTON, D.C. (General)

	1840
-Description of conditions there and in Congress	Dec 19 p3 c1 let.
-Inhabitants petition Congress for limited emancipation	Dec 19 p3 c1 let.
	1841
-Visit to capital described	Jul 31 p1 c4 let.

WASHINGTON, A. (Trenton, New Jersey)

	1838
-Listed as agent for the <u>Colored American</u>	Jan 13 p4 c4
	1839
-Offers financial and moral support to the <u>Colored American</u>	Mar 16 p3 c2 let.
	1840
-Describes communities of Trenton and Princeton	Dec 12 p1 c1 let.

	1841
-Description continued	Jan 2 p2 c2 let.
-Urges missionary efforts in Africa	Jul 31 p1 c1 let.

WASHINGTON, BURDETT

	1838
-Praised for perseverance in freeing his family from bondage	Jul 14 p2 c2

WASHINGTON, GEORGE

	1837
-Edward Rushton criticizes Washington for holding slaves	Nov 18 p1 c1
	1839
-Washington's generosity discussed	Jun 15 p3 c2
-One of his slaves is still alive	Sep 14 p3 c4
	1841
-Obedient as a son	Oct 9 p4 c1

WASHINGTON TEMPERANCE SOCIETIES

	1841
-Praised for successful efforts	Dec 4 p2 c2 ed.

WATERS, REVEREND EDWARD

	1837
-Elected an honorary member of the Mental and Moral Improvement Association (Troy, New York)	Oct 21 p1 c2

WATKINS, REVEREND WILLIAM

	1837
-Elected an honorary member of the Mental and Moral Improvement Association (Troy, New YOrk)	Oct 21 p1 c2
	1838
-Answers the American Moral Reform Socity; criticisms of exclusively black organ-izations	Sep 15 p2 c1 let.

WATTLES, AUGUSTUS

	1837
-Lists twenty colored schools successfully operating in Ohio	Oct 14 p1 c4
-Notes teachers wanted for Ohio schools	Oct 14 p2 c1

-Describes energy and prosperity of colored settlers in Indiana — Oct 28 p4 c2

1838

-Wisdom of his agricultural settlement plan questioned — Feb 17 p3 c3
-Success of black farmers described — Dec 15 p2 c2 let.

1839

-Teaches school with 26 black and 4 white students — Mar 2 p3 c1

WAY, FRISLY (Lansingburgh, New York)

1837

-Director of the Union Society of Albany — Apr 15 p1 c3

WAYNE COUNTY ANTI-SLAVE SOCIETY (Pennsylvania)

1838

-Society of one hundred members; described as somewhat pro-colonization — Mar 29 p2 c1

WEATHER

1841

-Methods for protection from lightning — Oct 9 p4 c2
-Storm causes extensive damage in the east — Oct 16 p3 c1

WEBB, COLONEL

1841

-Concessions made to blacks; distrusted — Nov 20 p2 c3

WEBSTER, DANIEL

1839

-His work as a lawyer paid for by the people of Massachusetts — Feb 16 p3 c3
-Travels to England; praised — Aug 24 p1 c3
-Speech to the National Agricultural Society of England — Aug 31 p1 c4
-In Scotland — Sep 14 p3 c2

1840

-Praised — Dec 26 p2 c4 let.

1841

-Senate speech praised — Feb 6 p3 c1 let.

WEBSTER, WILLIAM C. (Advertisement and Notice)

1840
-School for sacred music — Dec 12 p3 c3-Dec 26 p3 c4

1841
-Juvenile concert by students — Jan 2, 9 p3 c4

WEEKLY REPORT OF INTERMENTS (Notice)

1840
-Burial list — Mar 28 p3 c4
Apr 11 p3 c3

WELCH, JOHN ROBINSON (Notice)

1837
-Lost in New York (February 23, 1837) — Mar 11 p3 c4

WELD, THEODORE DWIGHT

1839
-Extracts from The Bible Against Slavery — Feb 2 p3 c2
-American Slavery As It Is praised — Jun 22 p2 c5

WELDEN, HENNETTA

1840
-Marries John Isaacs — Sep 19 p3 c4

WELLS AND GOMOTT (Manufacturers) (Advertisement)

1837
-Soft soap — Apr 29 p3 c4-Jun 24 p4 c3

WESLEY, JOHN

1837
-Praised for preaching methods and opposition to slavery — Oct 14 p2 c1

WESLEYAN ANTI-SLAVERY SOCIETY

1841
-Formed by the Indiana Methodist Convention — Jan 16 p1 c4

WEST, THE

1839
-Opportunities open to blacks discussed — Feb 9 p2 c3 let.
-Condition of education discussed — Jun 15 p2 c2 let.
-Moving there does not eliminate prejudice — Oct 5 p2 c5 let.

WEST INDIAN

1838

-Recent establishment as a new Jamaican black newspaper noted — Mar 3 p3 c2

WEST INDIES (General)

1837

-Joseph Kimball denies the validity of criticism of newly liberated West Indies blacks — Nov 4 p1 c1

1838

-Elections enlarge liberal voting bloc — Jan 27 p2 c4
-General condition of black status discussed — Jun 23 p4 c2
-Success of emancipation threatened more by white planters than by blacks — Jul 14 p1 c4
-American blacks should rejoice in West Indian emancipation — Jul 21 p4 c3 ed.
-Lacks a colonization movement — Jul 28 p1 c2
-Civil condition of freed apprentices described — Jul 28 p4 c1
-West Indian emancipation a moral example and will start a world revolution against slavery — Jul 28 p4 c1 let.
-Emancipation has proved both safe and right — Jul 28 p4 c2 let.
-Lack of enthusiasm among Americans for emancipation attacked — Aug 11 p2 c3
-Emancipation Proclamation — Aug 11 p2 c4
-Difficulties of black Americans emigrating to the West Indies — Aug 11 p3 c1
-Emancipation working well — Sep 8 p3 c2 ed.
-State of currency and laborers — Oct 20 p3 c1

1839

-Good conditions brought on by abolition — Feb 9 p3 c2
-Pro-slavery men in the West Indies trying to grind down emancipated subjects — Jun 8 p2 c1
-Public confidence and wealth has increased since emancipation — Jul 27 p3 c1 ed.
-Reports of adverse conditions refuted — Sep 7 p2 c4
-Production has not fallen off after emancipation — Oct 5 p1 c5

-News received of great progress	Oct 12 p3 c2 ed.
-Effects of emancipation	Nov 16 p2 c5
-Journey through various islands described	Nov 23 pl cl
	1840
-Results of emancipation praised	Apr 18 p4 c2 let.
-Description of favorable conditions on smaller islands	Jul 25 pl cl
	1841
-Blacks will be taught military tactics	Mar 6 p3 cl

WEST INDIES (Antigua)

	1837
-Behavior of blacks there proves they are not a blood-thirsty race	Apr 8 pl c2
-Abolition of slavery caused increase in religion	Apr 29 p4 c2
-Abolition of slavery caused increase in peace, security, commerce and education	May 6 pl cl
	1838
-Description of conditions of blacks since emancipation	Apr 12 pl cl

WEST INDIES (Barbadoes)

	1838
-Proclamation terminates apprenticeship	Sep 1 p4 cl
	1839
-Description of a successful plantation	Dec 7 pl cl

WEST INDIES (Cuba)

	1840
-Has beautiful birds and flowers, but no Sabbath schools	Dec 5 p3 c3
	1841
-Inhabitants demand suppression of the slave trade	Jul 24 p2 c2

WEST INDIES (Jamaica)

	1838
-Bill for total emancipation passes Colonial Assembly; apprenticeship system ended	Jul 7 p3 c4
-Description of missionary work in Kingston	Jul 21 pl c3

1839

- -Marquis of Sligo praised by blacks for his role in emancipation — Jun 29 p1 c1
- -Slavery there was cruel — Sep 14 p1 c4

1840

- -Testimonial to the industry and general contentment of the working population — May 23 p1 c1 let.
- -Arguments opposing emigration there — Jul 18 p1 c3 let.
- -On the treatment of several newly freed Africans there — Jul 18 p2 c2
- -May suffer severe crop failure — Jul 25 p2 c1
- -Sets example for the behavior of free blacks — Aug 1 p2 c4
- -Many citizens subscribe to the <u>Colored American</u> — Aug 1 p3 c3 let.
- -Situation there for peasantry getting worse — Sep 12 p1 c1 let.
- -Queen of England praises efforts of blacks — Sep 26 p2 c3
- -Island quiet, but had a bad drought — Oct 24 p2 c2
- -Generally improved conditions for laborers noted — Nov 7 p2 c3

1841

- -Government cautioned to respect the rights of freedmen — Feb 13 p2 c3
- -Living conditions described — Mar 6 p1 c3
- -British and Foreign Anti-Slavery Society against immigration at present — Mar 20 p3 c2
- -Drought continues; planters need more laborers — Apr 24 p2 c4
- -Good crops expected, conditions generally good — Jun 19 p3 c1
- -Prosperity noted — Jun 26 p3 c2
- -See also Kimball, Joseph; Renshaw, Charles Stewart; Thome, Reverend James

WEST INDIES (Martinique)

1841

- -Emancipation of slaves appears probable — Jun 12 p2 c4

WEST INDIES (Montserrat)

1837

- -Describes unsettled and restless conditions on the Island — Apr 1 p1 c2

1838

-Termination of apprenticeship system announced — Apr 19 p3 c3
-Emancipation as of August 1st — Aug 4 p3 c2

WEST INDIES (Nassau, Bahamas)

1839

-By-laws of King's College — Dec 7 p1 c3
-Description of curriculum at King's College — Dec 7 p1 c5

WEST INDIES (Nevis)

1837

-Describes physical appearance — Apr 1 p1 c2

1838

-Emancipation as of August 1st — Aug 4 p3 c2

WEST INDIES (Saint Bartholomew)

1841

-Emancipation of slaves probable — Jun 12 p2 c4

WEST INDIES (Saint Kitts)

1837

-Cites increased educational opportunities as a practical result of emancipation — Apr 1 p1 c1
-Describes effects of emancipation upon religious observance — Apr 1 p1 c1

WEST INDIES (Tortola)

1838

-Emancipation as of August 1st — Aug 4 p3 c2

WEST INDIES (Trinidad)

1838

-Revolt among black populace — Mar 22 p3 c4

1839

-Island described and immigration discussed — Aug 31 p1 c4
-Inquiry into advantages of emigration there — Aug 31 p3 c4 ed.
-Employment possibilities discussed — Aug 31 p3 c4 let.
-Encourages black immigration from the United States — Oct 5 p1 c1
-Excitement over Trinidad criticized — Oct 5 p3 c3 ed.
-Its disadvantages for immigration noted — Oct 19 p2 c3 let.
-Committee appointed to examine its resources and condition of recent emigrants — Nov 23 p3 c1

1840

-Report on conditions there — Mar 7 p3 c3
-Emigrants encouraged by government proclamation; workers needed — Mar 7 p3 c4
-Emigrants will probably not be better off than in the United States — Mar 14 p2 c2
-Some could benefit by immigration; 100 waiting to emigrate from Baltimore — Mar 14 p2 c4
-Poor conditions for emigrant laborers described — Apr 11 p2 c2 let.
-Exploitative methods of white planters described; emigration discouraged — Apr 11 p2 c3
-Bad conditions; blacks should not emigrate there — Apr 18 p2 c4
-Immigrants from the United States meet in Trinidad and urge others not to come — Apr 18 p3 c1
-<u>Colored American</u> opposes emigration — May 2 p2 c3 ed.
-Testimonial to good conditions of American immigrants — May 9 p2 c4 let.
-Refutation of positive reports on Trinidad — May 9 p3 c1
-Denial of bad working conditions — May 16 p2 c3 let.
-Abandonment of emigration plans urged — May 16 p2 c4
-Debate on immigration — Jul 11 p2 c3
-Information on conditions sought — Oct 31 p2 c3

1841

-Poor conditions of black population described — Jan 16 p3 c1
-Poor conditions for emigrants described — Feb 6 p2 c3
-See also Hunt, Reverend Thomas; Wright, Reverend Theodore S.

WEST INDIES (Virgin Islands)

1838

-Emancipation as of August 1st — Aug 4 p3 c2

1839

-Abolition of slavery cheaper for owners; population decreasing because of few females and small number of marriages — Nov 9 p1 c3

1840

-Emancipation seen near — Sep 26 p2 c4
-See also Thome, Reverend James

WEST INDIES
-See also Emancipation (West Indies)

<u>WESTERN CHRISTIAN ADVOCATE</u> (Cincinnati, Ohio)

1841

-Editor criticized for failure to take abolitionist stand — Jun 19 p2 c4

<u>WESTERN RESERVE CABINET AND FAMILY VISITER</u> (Ravenna, Ohio) (Advertisement)

1841

-Family newspaper desires subscribers — Mar 13 p3 c4

WHIG PARTY

1837

-Wins election in New York; requested to aid in enfranchising blacks — Nov 18 p2 c3 ed.
-Praised as the party of freedom — Dec 2 p4 cl

1840

-Its support of emancipation and enfranchisement doubted — Dec 12 pl c4 let.

1841

-Accused of hypocrisy in equal rights issue — Apr 17 p2 c2

WHIPPER, WILLIAM (Columbia, Pennsylvania)

1837

-Listed as agent for the <u>Colored American</u> — Mar 4 p4 c4
-Praises paper for criticizing blacks as well as whites — Jul 17 p2 c2 let.
-Secretary of the American Moral Reform Society's Convention — Aug 19 p3 cl
-Criticized for his actions at the convention — Aug 26 p2 cl
-Speaks on peace at the convention — Aug 26 p3 cl
-Asserts benefits of non-resistance over offensive aggression — Sep 9 pl c2
-Protests the <u>Colored American</u>'s denunciation of the American Moral Reform Society — Sep 9 p2 c2 let.
-Benefits of non-resistance — Sep 16 pl c3
-Answers Frederick Hinton's criticism of the Moral Reform convention — Sep 16 p2 c3

-Benefits of non-resistance	Sep 23 p1 c2 Sep 30 p4 c1
	1838
-Whipper wants to continue discussion of disagreements with the Colored American	Feb 3 p3 c2
-Whipper discusses the American Moral Reform Society	Feb 10 p2 c3 let.
-Asserts central propositions of the American Moral Reform Society	Mar 3 p2 c2 let.
-Replies to Colored American	Mar 29 p2 c3 let.
	1840
-Denies complexional differences in the composition of the American Moral Reform Society	Jul 18 p2 c4 let.
	1841
-Criticizes the Albany Convention for separationism	Jan 30 p1 c4 let.
-His criticisms of the Albany Convention rebutted	Jan 30 p2 c2
-Urges that complexional differences be thrown off everywhere	Feb 6 p1 c3 let.
-Criticized for his condemnation of the Albany Convention	Feb 13 p2 c1 let.
-Criticizes Albany Convention for excluding whites	Feb 20 p1 c3 let.
-His criticisms and accusations of separatism refuted	Feb 20 p2 c1 let.
-Criticizes the Colored American	Mar 6 p1 c1
-His criticism answered	Mar 13 p1 c3 ed.
WHITE, EZRA	
	1839
-Pleads not guilty to murder charge	May 18 p3 c5
WHITE, GEORGE H. (Advertisement)	
	1838
-Dental surgeon	Jun 2 p3 c4- Dec 29 p4 c3
-Partner with Joshua Bishop	Dec 15 p3 c3
	1839
	Jan 12 p2 c4- Mar 16 p4 c4 May 11 p4 c4- Nov 23 p4 c4
-Partnership dissolved	Jun 1 p3 c4
	1840
	Mar 21 p4 c3- Nov 28 p4 c4

See also Joshua Bishop

WHITE, HENRY KIRKE

	1839
-Death eulogized	Mar 9 p1 c3 ed.

WHITE, JAMES B. (Portland, Maine)

	1841
-Dies	Oct 30 p3 c4

WHITE, JACOB C.

	1837
-Vice-president of the American Moral Reform Society convention	Aug 19 p3 c1
-Listed as secretary of the Philadelphia Committee	Dec 9 p3 c2

WHITE, SAMUEL (Jamaica, New York)

	1837
-Elected treasurer of the Jamaica Benevolent Society	May 27 p2 c4

WHITTIER, JOHN GREENLEAF

	1839
-Compelled by ill-health to relinquish the editorship of the Pennsylvania Freeman	Jul 20 p3 c2
-Talk with slaveowner described	Sep 7 p4 c2

WHOPPER, ANN (Philadelphia, Pennsylvania)

	1838
-Marries George Roberts	Jun 9 p3 c4

WILBERFORCE COLONY (Upper Canada)

	1837
-Colony criticized by Board of Managers of Babtist Missionary group of Upper Canada	Jul 15 p3 c3
	1839
-Colony not prosperous because of Israel Lewis	Feb 16 p1 c1
-Board of Managers repudiates Israel Lewis as agent and fund raiser	Jul 13 p3 c2 let.

WILBERFORCE, WILLIAM

	1837
-Extract from Benjamin Hughes' eulogy on the character of Wilberforce	May 13 p1 c1 May 20 p1 c1 May 27 p1 c1

	1839
-Character sketch by Lord Brougham	Jul 13 p1 c4
	1841
-Extract from one of his letters	May 1 p4 c4
-Praised as an "ultra" abolitionist	Aug 21 p1 c2
WILES, FRANCIS (Advertisement)	
	1837
-Moving to different boarding house	Apr 22 p3 c4- Jun 24 p4 c4 Sep 16 p3 c4- Dec 16 p4 c3
	1838
	Jan 13 p4 c3- May 3 p4 c2 Jun 2 p4 c3- Sep 1 p4 c3 Oct 20 p3 c4- Dec 29 p4 c4
	1839
	Jan 12 p2 c3- Mar 16 p4 c4 May 11 p4 c3- Jun 29 p4 c4
-New boarding house	Jul 20 p4 c4 Aug 17, 31 p4 c4
	1840
	May 2 p3 c3- Aug 1 p4 c4 Sep 5 p3 c4- Dec 26 p4 c4
	1841
	Jan 9 p3 c4 Jan 16 p4 c4
WILKINSON, GENERAL (North Hampton County, Virginia)	
	1837
-Sheriff claims ownership of alleged fugitive slave, George Thompson (alias Ben)	Apr 8 p3 c2
WILKINSON, SAMUEL	
	1838
-Colonization plan criticized	Jun 16 p3 c4 ed.

WILLIAMS, A. (Salem, Massachusetts)

1838

-Listed as agent for the Colored American — Jun 30 p3 c3

WILLIAMS, ISRAEL

1837

-John Berry attests to his guilt as thief — Oct 14 p3 c1

WILLIAMS, JAMES

1837

-Member of the Union Society of Albany — Apr 15 p1 c3

WILLIAMS, JAMES J. (London Grove, Pennsylvania)

1838

-Listed as agent for the Colored American — Sep 29 p3 c4

WILLIAMS, MARGARET (Troy, New York) (Advertisement)

1841

-Boarding — Jul 24 p3 c3- Sep 18 p3 c4

WILLIAMS, P. (and W.H. Francis) (Saratoga Springs, New York) (Advertisement)

1840

-New proprietors for Mrs. Budd's Boarding House — May 16 p3 c3- Sep 12 p3 c4

WILLIAMS, MRS. PEGGY (East Troy, New York) (Advertisement)

1840

-Boarding house (recommended by W. P. Johnson) — Jun 13 p3 c4- Nov 7 p3 c4

WILLIAMS, REVEREND PETER

1837

-Safe arrival from London noted — Mar 11 p3 c4

-Praises the Colored American — Apr 1 p3 c4

-Could not book passage on an American ship — Apr 22 p2 c3

-Elected honorary member of the Troy (New York) Mental and Moral Improvement Association — Oct 21 p1 c2

	1840
-Death and plans to vote anti-slavery ticket noted	Oct 31 p2 c4
-His funeral eulogy	Nov 7 p1 c3
-Honored by the New York Philomathean Society	Nov 14 p3 c2
	1841
-His likeness offered for sale	Sep 4 p3 c2
-See also Worcester, Noah	

WILLIAMS, R.G.

	1837
-Praises the Colored American as an important auxiliary to the cause of abolition and the advancement of colored Americans	Mar 11 p3 c2 Mar 18 p3 c1
	1838
-His changing position in the American Anti-Slavery Society noted	Mar 3 p3 c2

WILLIAMSON, LEWIS

	1841
-Tells story of his family being kidnapped and sold into slavery	Nov 13 p1 c3

WILSON AND RAY (Advertisement)

	1837
-Union Victualing House (Restaurant)	May 6 p3 c4- Jun 24 p4 c4

WILSON, GEORGE (Advertisement)

	1837
-Rooms to let	May 27 p3 c4- Jul 29 p4 c3

WILSON, HIRAM

	1837
-Inquires about self-sufficiency and responsibility of free blacks in Canada	Mar 4 p4 c1
	1839
-Support requested for his Canadian mission	Jun 1 p2 c2 ed.

	1841
-Criticized for establishing separate schools and churches in Canada for fugitive slaves	Feb 6 p2 c2
-His work in his Canada Mission analyzed	Apr 3 p2 c3
WILSON, WILLIAM J. (Advertisement)	
	1837
-Boot and shoemaker	Jan 14 p3 c4- Jul 22 p4 c3 Aug 19 pl c4 Sep 16 p3 c4- Dec 30 p4 c4
	1838
	Jan 13 p4 c3
WISCONSIN TERRITORY	
	1837
-Charles B. Ray notes emigration opportunities for blacks; land available	Nov 18 p2 c4 let.
	1839
-Proposed as an area of colonization by free blacks	Aug 31 p3 c3 let.
	1841
-Described as a land of opportunity for blacks	Apr 17 p2 c4
WOMEN (Black)	
	1837
-Their place in the home	Mar 18 p4 cl
-Called on to work against drinking and gambling	Mar 18 p4 cl
-Urged to be neat, simple, and ladylike	Jun 10 p2 cl
-Discouraged from too much exposure or ornamentation	Jun 24 p4 cl
-Strong Christian faith an important wifely quality	Oct 7 pl c4
-Economy necessary to the female character	Nov 11 p4 c2
	1838
-Advice on governing a family; submission to the husband counselled	Sep 8 p4 c2
-Mothers must instruct daughters on how to sustain misfortune	Jul 14 p2 c4
-Modesty and reserve stressed	Sep 15 p4 c2
-Importance of a mother's moral influence and responsibility	Oct 6 pl c3
-Proper upbringing for the eldest daughter	Oct 6 p4 c2

-Their duty to encourage public education stressed	Oct 13 p4 c1
-List of rules for wives	Nov 3 p4 c2
-Urged to take an active part in the black community	Nov 17 p2 c1 ed.
-Advantages of early rising for wives	Dec 8 p2 c4
	1839
-Proper behavior toward physicians described	Mar 16 p2 c2
-Warned to stay in their place (the home)	May 18 p3 c1 ed.
-Lecture on female character described	Nov 23 p1 c4 let.
-Suggestions for spare-time activities	Nov 23 p2 c5 let.
-Lack of schools deplored	Nov 23 p3 c1
	1841
-African women till the soil successfully	Jan 30 p4 c3
-Urged to sign petitions against prejudice	Nov 13 p2 c2

WOMEN (General)

	1838
-Have the power to inspire virtuous behavior	Mar 3 p4 c2
	1839
-Roles and jobs changing	May 11 p2 c5
-Their perversenss	Jul 27 p4 c2
-Responsible for building character in their children	Aug 3 p2 c4
-Develop within the domestic circle alone	Aug 17 p1 c4
-List of characteristics: beauty, softness, mercy	Sep 14 p1 c5
	1840
-Hints to young ladies on deportment	Nov 14 p4 c4
-On the growth of female influence	Nov 21 p4 c1
-On the mental virtues of Hebrew women	Nov 28 p4 c4
	1841
-Prerequisites of a good wife	Jan 23 p4 c3
-Advice on economy and order in domestic expenditures	Apr 3 p4 c2
-How to grow old gracefully	Apr 3 p4 c3
-Example of a good mother	Aug 21 p1 c3
-Mission of women foreshadowed in the cradle	Sep 25 p1 c2

WOMEN (White)

1837

-Requested to aid in breaking down racial barriers in female seminaries — Oct 7 p4 c2

1841

-Keeping black female slaves a cause of divorce among white couples — Jan 30 p2 c4
-Siberian women are used as slaves — Jan 30 p4 c4

WOMEN
-See also Family Life

WOMEN'S RIGHTS

1838

-John Quincy Adams defends a woman's involvement in political activity — Jul 28 p1 c1

WOMEN'S SOCIETIES
-See Boston Female Anti-Slavery Society; Daughters of Abyssinia; Female Assistant Society; Female Baptist Association; Female Benevolent Society; Female Branch of Zion; Female Dorcas Society; Female Education Society; Female Mite Society; Female Sinking Fund Society; Female Society for Colored Orphans; Female Temperance Society; Female Trading Association Female Wesleyan Anti-Slavery Society; New York Colored Female Vigilance Committee; United Female Assistant Benefit Society

WOOD, AARON

1838

-Marries Mrs. Florinda Brown — Aug 4 p3 c4

WOOD MECHANICS (Advertisement)

1839

-Two boys desire woodworking trade — Sep 14 p4 c3- Oct 19 p4 c4

WOOD, S.L. (and J.B. Brown)
(Advertisement)

1840

- -Confectionary and fruit store; family supplies — Jul 4 p3 c3-Oct 17 p4 c4

WOODSON, GEORGE (Jackson, Ohio)

1837

- -Listed as agent for the Colored American — Sep 30 p3 c4
- -Obtains subscribers to the Colored American — Oct 14 p3 c1
- -Donates $3.00 to the paper — Dec 23 p3 c3

WOODSON, LEWIS (Pittsburgh, Pennsylvania)

1837

- -Elected corresponding secretary of the Pittsburgh Moral Reform Society — May 13 p1 c4
- -Elected as a black representative to the Pennsylvania Constitutional Convention which proposes the disenfranchisement of blacks — Jul 1 p2 c1
- -Encourages black support for the Colored American — Jul 8 p2 c2 let.
- -Travelling agent and black groups seen as a source of funds for the Colored American — Jul 22 p3 c1 let.
- -Cited as a contributor to the Colored American — Sep 9 p4 c4

1838

- -Pledges support to the Colored American — Mar 15 p3 c3 let.

1839

- -Says the American Anti-Slavery Society does not have to pay his way to their convention — Nov 9 p3 c3 let.
- -Calls for aid for the Colored American — Nov 16 p2 c3

1841

- -Says missionary work in Africa is a Christian duty — Jul 10 p1 c4 let.
- -Encourages African missions in speeches — Aug 7 p1 c2 let.
- -Reports on the Pennsylvania Convention — Sep 18 p1 c4 let.
- -See also Voting Rights (Free Blacks)

WORCESTER, NOAH

1837

-Criticizes treatment of the Reverend Peter Williams (Boston Register and Observer) Apr 22 p2 c3

WRIGHT, ELIZUR JR. (Boston)

1837

-Praises the Colored American as important auxiliary to cause of abolition and advancement of colored Americans Mar 11 p3 c2
Mar 18 p3 c1

1839

-Will edit the Massachusetts Abolitionist May 11 p3 c3

WRIGHT, FANNY

1839

-Masculine assumptions criticized May 18 p3 c1 ed.

WRIGHT, R.P.G. (Schenectady, New York)

1837

-Director of the Union Society of Albany Apr 15 p1 c3

WRIGHT, REVEREND THEODORE S.

1837

-Praises the Colored American Apr 1 p3 c4
-Speaks at the annual meeting of the United Anti-Slavery Society Aug 5 p3 c1
-Caricatures of Wright cited Sep 9 p1 c2 let.
-Addresses the New York Anti-Slavery Society on color prejudice Nov 11 p3 c1
-Awarded $1,000 for services to the American Anti-Slavery Society Dec 16 p2 c3

1838

-Extract from speech on problems of blacks Jan 20 p2 c2
-Addresses audience at examinations of New York Colored Free Schools Apr 19 p2 c4
-Describes trip to New York Anti-Slavery Society's annual meeting Oct 6 p2 c1 let.

	<u>1839</u>
-Denounces colonization schemes as heresy at New York Anti-Colonization meeting	Jan 19 p1 c3
-Wife dies and is eulogized	May 11 p3 c2
	<u>1840</u>
-Benefit fair to be held for his church	May 9 p2 c4
-Publishes anti-colonization pamphlet	May 9 p3 c2
	<u>1841</u>
-Acknowledges Reverend Amos Beman's donation to free Reverend Thomas Hunt from Trinidad	Jan 2 p3 c3
-Plans lecture on reform before the Philomathean Society	Feb 13 p3 c4
-Fair to be held to benefit his church	Apr 17 p3 c3
-See also New York Anti-Slavery Society	

WRIGHT, THOMAS (Virginia)

	<u>1837</u>
-Attends annual Virginia convention for the abolition of slavery	May 27 p1 c3
-Addresses New York Anti-Slavery Society convention upon the acceptance of its annual report	Oct 14 p1 c1

WYOMING VALLEY

	<u>1839</u>
-Description and history	Nov 2 p1 c1

Y

YATES, WILLIAM (Albany, New York)

	<u>1837</u>
-Sends $4.50 to the <u>Colored American</u>	Apr 22 p3 c4
-Praises the meeting of the Philadelphia Association for the Mental and Moral Improvement of People of Color	Jun 24 p2 c3 let.
-Praises Joshua Leavitt	Jun 24 p2 c3 let.
-Discusses slave laws and condition of slaves and free blacks in Delaware	Aug 12 p1 c1 let. Aug 19 p1 c1 let.

-Preparing a book: <u>The Legal Disabilities of Colored Citizens in New York</u>	Sep 30 p3 c1
	<u>1838</u>
-Portions of his book printed	Jan 13 p2 c2
-Gives talk on the legal disabilities of colored people	Jan 13 p3 c2
-Discusses the Pennsylvania Constitutional Convention which limited voting to white males	Jan 27 p2 c3
-Published a book: <u>The Rights Of Colored Men</u>	Mar 3 p3 c3
-Book described and recommended	Mar 22 p2 c2 ed.
-Extracts from book printed	Apr 5 p3 c1
-Book praised	Apr 19 p2 c3 ed.

YOUNG, JOHN (Notice)

	<u>1837</u>
-Information sought by his father	Feb 4 p3 c4

YOUNG LADIES' DOMESTIC SEMINARY (Clinton, New York) (Advertisement)

	<u>1840</u>
-Summer term	Apr 11 p3 c4-May 23 p3 c4

YOUNG MEN'S ANTI-SLAVERY SOCIETY

	<u>1837</u>
-Holds anniversary meeting	May 13 p3 c1
-Forms committee to determine how many blacks in New York City had once been slaves	Jul 15 p2 c4
	<u>1838</u>
-Issues call for city-wide Anti-Slavery Convention	Dec 29 p3 c3

YOUNG MEN'S LITERARY AND MORAL REFORM SOCIETY (Pittsburgh, Pennsylvania)

	<u>1837</u>
-Holds first meeting; adopts a constitution	Sep 2 p1 c2

YOUNG MEN'S PHILADELPHIA LITERARY ASSOCIATION
-See Douglass, Reverend William; Young Men's Union Literary Association

YOUNG MEN'S STANDING CORRESPONDENCE COMMITTEE (Notice)

1837

-Meeting — Dec 2 p4 c4

YOUNG MEN'S UNION LITERARY ASSOCIATION (Philadelphia)

1839

-Holds meeting and elects officers; part of constitution printed — Feb 2 p3 c3
-Passes resolutions eulogizing Reverend William Douglass — Oct 5 p3 c3

YOUNG MEN'S WILBERFORCE DEBATING SOCIETY

1837

-Holds meeting and adopts resolutions attacking murder of Elijah Lovejoy — Dec 23 p4 c2

YOUNG WOMAN (Advertisement)

1840

-Wanted by a small family to do cooking and housework — Mar 14, 21 p3 c4

<u>YOUTH'S CABINET</u>

1837

-A newspaper for children — Nov 4 p3 c2
-Aims and structure described; reviewed by the press — Nov 11 p4 c3
-Advertised — Nov 18 p4 c4-Dec 16 p4 c3

1838

Jan 13 p4 c3

1839

-Advertisement with testimonials — May 11,18 p3 c5
--Plea to parents about its value — Nov 23 p3 c4

1840

-Advertised — Mar 21 p2 c4
Dec 26 p3 c3

1841

-1840 volume praised and recommended — Jan 2 p2 c4
-Advertised — Jan 9 p3 c4
-See also Children's Department <u>Colored American</u>

Z

ZION BABTIST ANTI-SLAVERY SOCIETY	
	1837
-Preamble and constitution	Dec 23 p4 cl
-See also Roger Williams Anti-Slavery Society	
ZION BAPTIST CHURCH (Notice)	
	1839
-Change of address	May 11, 18 p3 c4 Jun 1 p3 c4
	1840
-Fair	Oct 10, 17 p3 c4
-Ladies engaged in fair thanking friends of ministry for donation	Nov 13 p3 c3
-Activities described; congregation praised	Dec 5 p2 c2
	1841
-Praised by the <u>Colored American</u>	Jan 2 p2 c4
-Fair	Sep 11 p3 c3- Oct 30 p3 c4
<u>ZION'S HERALD</u>	
	1841
-Editor criticized for plagiarism	Apr 3 p3 cl
ZION'S METHODIST CONNEXION	
	1837
-Will hold conference	May 20 p2 c2
	1840
-Annual conference to be held on the subject of moral improvement	May 30 p2 c2
-Holds meeting	Sep 19 p2 c3
	1841
-Will hold annual conference	May 15 p2 c4
<u>ZION'S WATCHMAN</u>	
-See Children's Department (<u>Colored American</u>)	
<u>ZION'S WESLEYAN</u>	
	1841
-Newspaper commences publication	Oct 30 p3 c3

ZUILLE, JOHN J.

	1837
-Secretary of the United Anti-Slavery Society	Apr 29 p3 c2
-Appointed Secretary of the Colored Young Men of New York City	Sep 2 p1 c1
-One of four vice-presidents of the "Colored Citizens of New York"	Oct 28 p1 c3
	1838
-Appointed to the executive committee of the Political Association	Jun 16 p2 c3
-Declares disfranchisement degrading to blacks	Jul 14 p3 c2